C. VAN EATON

W9-ATO-813

THE IRWIN SERIES IN ECONOMICS

CONSULTING EDITOR

LLOYD G. REYNOLDS
YALE UNIVERSITY

BOOKS IN THE IRWIN SERIES IN ECONOMICS

DEVELOPMENT OF
ECONOMIC ANALYSIS

by

I. H. RIMA

Associate Professor of Economics
Temple University

1967
RICHARD D. IRWIN, INC.
Homewood, Illinois

© RICHARD D. IRWIN, INC., 1967

ALL RIGHTS RESERVED. THIS BOOK OR ANY PART
THEREOF MAY NOT BE REPRODUCED WITHOUT
THE WRITTEN PERMISSION OF THE PUBLISHER.

First printing, March, 1967

Library of Congress Catalog Card No. 66–28629

PRINTED IN THE UNITED STATES OF AMERICA

TO THE DIAMONDS OF OUR ACRES

IN MEMORY OF MAX HAHNE

PREFACE

Current interest in the teaching of economic theory suggests the usefulness of a book examining its historical evolution. The present volume, therefore, traces the development of the analytical tools and concepts which comprise the body of economic theory. This objective has been served to some extent by books in the history of economic thought as well as by one or two historically oriented books in contemporary economic theory. But neither of these approaches focuses its whole attention on the way in which efforts to explain economic phenomena resulted in the forging of analytical tools and concepts which were subsequently refined, and sometimes rediscovered or discarded, by later thinkers.

The historical evolution of the concepts and analytical tools of economics can hardly be divorced from the environment within which they developed or the specific problems by which they were inspired. Nor can they be separated from the individuals and "schools" with whom they are associated or from the attitudes and preconceptions which they reflect. It is for this reason that a strictly topical approach to the development of economic analysis has been avoided. To single out only one aspect of the theoretical work of an individual or school, is to lose sight of the fact that ideas seldom exist as independent entities but usually are an integral part of a broader body of thought.

The approach of this book is, therefore, chronological. Economic concepts and analytical tools are examined within the time sequence in which they developed, with due recognition of the events and problems of the period and the country in which they evolved as well as the individual thinkers who conceived or refined them. The content of the present volume, therefore, necessarily overlaps, to a degree, that of a book in the history of economic thought. This is particularly the case when its concern is with contributions made before the marginal revolution, when writers on economic subjects were more often moral philosophers and political economists, and pure theory had not yet come into its own. But it selects only individuals and schools whose works have a predominantly theoretical content, and notes only in passing those aspects of their work that are not contributions to economic theory.

The problem of selecting which contributions to include and which to omit becomes more difficult as one approaches the present. After the selections have been made, there is the even more formidable problem of determining the detail with which to review their substance and appraise their significance. One can summarize the legacy from the past with far more assurance than one can select for review those aspects of contemporary theory that seem likely to withstand the test of time. Fully aware that the chapter of today may be the footnote of tomorrow, I have presented, in a historical setting, what appear to be the essentials of modern micro- and macroeconomic theory.

This book is intended primarily for students whose background in economic theory does not go far beyond that presented in a one-year introductory course. Many, perhaps most, students do not learn or retain enough economic theory from a one-year course to enable them to abstract from original readings (or a description of their content) the theoretical principles they contain. There is no choice, therefore, from the standpoint of pedagogy but to teach the requisite theory along with the history of its development. The more advanced student can pass over familiar concepts rather quickly to those which are new, though he will presumably gain new insight into analytical tools and principles which he already knows by studying them within their historical frame of reference. Collateral readings, like those suggested at the end of each chapter, are a particularly useful supplement to the content of this volume for more sophisticated readers and those who wish to focus more broadly and examine the emergence of theoretical concepts and tools as part of the development of economic thought. It is also hoped that those teaching intermediate economic theory, who wish to give their students a historical orientation to the concepts and tools they are studying, will find this book a worthwhile supplement. It is perhaps unnecessary to add that a book will serve best when used for the specific purpose for which it was written—in this case, the history of economic theory taught at the intermediate level.

The manuscript for this book has been used in mimeographed form at Temple University for the past several years and has undergone extensive revision as a result of that experience. I owe a special debt to the many undergraduate and beginning graduate students who responded to my invitation to write a critique. I am also grateful to several colleagues for their comments and suggestions on various parts of the manuscript. Jack Gelfand, of the State University of New York at Albany, was kind enough to read a substantial part of the manuscript. The chapters on contemporary economic theory, especially, benefited from his expertise in this area. Donald McCleod and Nathaniel Jackendoff, both of Temple University, read chapter fourteen, "Contribution to the Theory of Capital, Interest and the Price Level," and suggested improvements. The critique offered by John P. Henderson of Michigan State University was also useful in preparing the final revision of this manuscript, as was that of Robert Campbell of the University of Oregon. Louis Harms, Marian Meinkoth and Karl Niebyl of Temple University also read portions of the manuscript and I appreciate their comments. Finally, my thanks are due to Lloyd Reynolds, who in his capacity as consulting editor of the Irwin Series in Economics was generous in giving of his time and experience whenever I had need of them. Needless to say, responsibility for the final product is mine alone.

I also wish to express my thanks to the Duplicating Department of Temple University and to Miss Bernadette Fleming for her assistance with the typing of the manuscript.

Philadelphia   I. H. RIMA
January, 1967

TABLE OF CONTENTS

Chapter 1   THE ORIGINS OF ANALYTICAL ECONOMICS

While man's speculation about his material environment can be traced to ancient times, the development of analytical economics is of relatively recent origin. Indeed, the emergence of economics as a separate field of inquiry prior to the late Renaissance was a distinct impossibility. Everything militated against it: the nature and limited scope of economic activity, the dominance of the state and church, the force of custom, and the religious and philosophical beliefs which shaped prevailing attitudes toward human activity for the acquisition of wealth. Economic activity for the satisfaction of wants has of course taken place in every age of human history. And since man is a thinking animal, it is reasonable to infer that he has always directed some thought to explaining the material aspects of his life. Speculation on economic matters is therefore undoubtedly as old as human society itself. Analytical or theoretical economics, however, has a much more recent history. Not until the eighteenth century did the content of man's speculation about economic phenomena begin to emerge as economic analysis rather than as economic thought.

Analytical economics as it exists today is distinguished by its methodology and its objective. Generally speaking, its method is deductive; its starting point is a premise or group of premises from which a conclusion is logically deduced. The chain of reasoning thus constructed is necessarily tautological in that the conclusion is inherent in the premises and follows from them. It is not, however, the objective of economic theory to produce mere tautologies; its ultimate objective is to arrive at theorems or propositions about the economic aspects of man's life which have a predictive value. It seeks to establish, with the aid of appropriate tools and concepts, propositions which explain those empirically observable phenomena which arise directly or indirectly when human and material resources are employed to produce want-satisfying goods and services and there is no central decision-making authority. Ideally, the hypotheses which it seeks to establish will also be useful with respect to forecasting probable future trends of economic significance.

By contrast, economics in its preanalytic stages did not exist as a separate subject matter, nor were there analytical tools with which thinkers probed into economic matters. Thus, there are no tracts or discourses we

1

can study to learn about man's earliest speculations concerning his material environment. The economic ideas of the ancients are largely unsystematic and must be extracted from the writings of the priests, lawgivers, and philosophers. While some of these ideas have survived into modern times, though usually in altered form, the content of ancient economic thought is little more than a series of unrelated observations and moral pronouncements on production, consumption, and exchange embedded in writings devoted primarily to religion, ethics, politics, or law. Examination of the reasons why inquiry into economic matters was such a minor aspect of intellectual speculation prior to the eighteenth century is a useful point of departure for an appreciation of the historical development of economic analysis. There is much that can be learned about the positive aspects of analytical economics by inquiring into the impediments which confronted its early emergence as a discipline.

BARRIERS TO ECONOMIC INQUIRY

Attitudes toward Want Satisfaction

Economics did not emerge as a separate field of inquiry until the satisfaction of man's material needs became a desirable goal of human activity. The thousands of years during which the pursuit of wealth was disdainfully regarded could scarcely have produced a systematic body of principles dedicated to explaining acquisition. Indeed, those ancient civilizations which had the least materialistic philosophies are, as might be expected, precisely those in which there exists the most notable paucity of economic ideas.

A negative attitude toward wealth among the ancient peoples is perhaps most clearly in evidence in the thinking of the Hindus and Chinese, although it is typical of oriental thought in general. Oriental philosophy regards happiness as being attained by decreasing material wants. It accepts poverty with fatalistic passivity and views wealth with relative indifference. The material renunciation of oriental philosophy and its denial of the worth of man as an individual make it inconsistent with both economic progress and the development of economic thought.

The ancient Hebrews, while considerably less ascetic than the Chinese and Hindus, also believed that happiness could be achieved without wealth and that the pursuit of riches would lead to sin. The lives of these people were circumscribed by the rules of conduct set forth in the commands of Moses and the prophets. These minutely regulated every phase of human existence, guiding men in their relationships with one another as well as in their personal lives to enable them ultimately to earn everlasting life. The rules were detailed and complex, and understandably embraced also the economic aspects of life. For example, lending upon usury to fellow Hebrews was strictly forbidden with respect not only to money but also to goods. The term "usury" refers here not to an excessive interest rate, which is its present-day meaning, but to any interest charge. Since loans were made primarily for charitable reasons, the Old Testament proscription against the taking of usury introduced a moral standard into economic behavior. There are many other directives of an economic nature in the Old Testament such as the rules concerning the restitution of property, the remission of debt, and the production and harvesting of agricultural output. Many of these rules commemorate events of religious significance such as the seventh day in the story of the creation. These are typical of the economic aspects of the Mosaic law and are of interest to us because they demonstrate that a separate science of wealth is incompatible with adherence to a religious and philosophical code which completely dictates economic behavior.

Even so highly developed a culture as Greece did not produce a separate body of economic thought. This is not, however, because the Greeks were disdainful of material goods. On the contrary, Plato and Aristotle believed that a minimum amount of wealth is essential to the good life. According to Aristotle, the household (*oikos*) exists for the purpose of satisfying men's natural wants. Its activities properly include the production and storage of necessary and useful commodities and their acquisition by exchange for purposes of consumption. It is retail trade, which is exchange for the purpose of making money, that is unnatural, as are all chrematistic activities engaged in for the acquisition of wealth. The most unnatural chrematistic activity in which man can engage is usury. Money, said Aristotle, is intended to function as a medium of exchange and nothing else. It cannot beget money, and its use to make money is a perversion of its proper function.

Aristotle's discussion of the barrenness of money and his condemnation of usury are perhaps the best known and most influential of his economic ideas. Their importance in this discussion and of the distinction which he made between economics (*oikonomik*) and chrematistics (*chrematistik*) is to emphasize and underline the fact that he regarded only those activities that contribute to the attainment of the good life as natural and proper. Economic activities are natural and proper, but they are means to an end, not an end in themselves. The distinction between what is "proper" and "improper," "natural" and "unnatural" is not merely factual; it is moral. Within this framework, economic inquiry could only emerge as applied ethics.

The dominance of Scholasticism during the Middle Ages presented a similar barrier to economic inquiry. The revival of trade, industry, and town life during the twelfth and thirteenth centuries was associated with numerous practices that were in conflict with Christian teaching. Thus, Saint Thomas Aquinas turned his attention in his *Summa Theologica* to such questions as: Is it lawful to sell a thing for more than it is worth?

What are the obligations of buyers and sellers with regard to transactions? Is it a sin to take usury for money lent? In answering these and other questions that arose as a result of expanding commercial activities, Aquinas examined the civil law in the light of Christian teaching and the then recently rediscovered Aristotelian principles of logic. For example, in regard to selling a thing for more than it is worth, Aquinas observed that while such an act is lawful, since human law is unable to forbid everything that is contrary to virture, according to divine law it is unlawful. The individual who has received more than he ought must therefore compensate the person who has suffered a loss. Similarly, while it is not unlawful to sell an article which has a defect, Aquinas reasoned that if a seller is aware of a fault in the thing he is selling, he is guilty of a fraudulent sale and is bound to compensate the buyer for the loss incurred. In short, trade is proper only if equivalents are exchanged. Citing Aristotle, Aquinas maintained that exchange is commendable only if it supplies a natural need. Thus "the exchange of money for money, or any commodity for money, not on account of the necessities of life, but for profit," is improper, for the acquisition of money must not be an end in itself. As long as this view prevailed, economics could not emerge as an autonomous discipline, but existed only as applied Christian ethics.

Dominance of the State

Although Plato and Aristotle differed on numerous points, they both believed that the purpose of man's existence is to live a good life and that this can be achieved only within the city-state (*polis*). To a Greek, the city-state was not merely a legal structure; it was a way of life. Every aspect of daily existence was intimately connected with it. The individual derived his importance from his relation to the state; he was viewed as a citizen who depends on the state and who can contribute to its welfare. But it is the state that is omnipotent. Thus the attention of Greek thinkers was primarily absorbed by political theory, though the theory of the city-state embraced much more than politics in the narrow sense. It was at one and the same time ethics, sociology, and economics as well as political science.

The absorption of Greek thinkers with the origin and functioning of the ideal state and the subordination of the individual to the state necessarily limited the development of the kind of economic thought that emerged. Witness, for example, the contribution of the Greek Xenophon (c. 440–355 B.C.). His work *On the Means of Improving the Revenue of the State of Athens* begins with a description of the natural advantages of Athens as a commercial center attractive to foreigners. Foreigners were regarded as desirable because they were subject to the tax levied on aliens and were therefore a lucrative source of revenue. In similar vein, merchants and shipowners were regarded as superior citizens because they brought wealth to the city. Thus, Xenophon recommended various measures to the state to encourage merchant activity in Athens. He also urged enhanced production of silver and expressed the view that this metal would never lose its value.

These recommendations are noteworthy from our point of view because they reflect the preoccupation with the importance of the state that predominated at that time. While emphasis on the state as an instrument to achieve socially optimal results is not, of course, incompatible with the emergence of what has come to be called social economics, it does preclude the emergence of economics as a body of theory which seeks to explain how socially optimal results can be achieved in the absence of a central authority directing the allocation of resources.

Nature Philosophy

To Plato and Aristotle, man's happiness can be achieved only within the city-state. Thus the search for the good life was at one and the same time the search for the ideal state. But after the disintegration of the Greek city-states and the emergence of the empires of Alexander and later Rome, the conception of man as inseparable from the self-sufficient city-state was supplanted by new schools of thought in which the search for the good life was no longer interwoven with the search for the good state. Thus began the divorce of politics from ethics and an appreciation of man as an individual being rather than a social being who is a dependent part of the whole.

Stoicism was the most influential of these post-Aristotelian schools, and it was through Stoicism that Greek philosophy was introduced into the western world. Stoicism, a philosophy first conceived by Zeno (340–265 B.C.), received its most profound expression in the *Meditations* of the Roman Emperor Marcus Aurelius (A.D. 121–80). According to the Stoics, the universe is systematic and rational, being governed by the all-prevading law of nature. The wise man lives according to nature; his reason guides his conduct so that his actions conform to the dictates of natural necessity. The greatest virtue is acquiescence to natural law through reason. "Be satisfied with your business and learn to love what you were bred to do, and as to the remainder of your life, be entirely resigned, and let the gods do their pleasure with your body and soul." This is the essence of the Stoic philosophy. The belief that happiness is achieved by conforming to the inevitable law of nature suggests a kind of fatalism similar to that characteristic of oriental philosophy, and is not conductive to improvements in the production or distribution of wealth.

The Mode of Resource Allocation

Regardless of the simplicity or complexity of the arrangements and techniques used, the essence of economic activity is the utilization of human and material resources to satisfy wants. It is an inescapable fact that resources are scarce in comparison with the numerous alternative uses to which they can be put. The impossibility of satisfying all wants necessarily poses a twofold problem: first, which wants shall have priority; and secondly, how these wants will be satisfied. On an individual basis, these problems are relatively simple. The individual knows perfectly well what his preferences for goods, services, and leisure are and, if he is free to do so, will use his money income or labor to acquire them in an order which corresponds to his preference scale. Needless to say, this does not imply that individual preference scales are rational, "good," or unchanging, but rather that within the limitation of his own resources the individual will have to choose among his wants and will naturally direct first attention to those that are, perhaps permanently, perhaps momentarily, most important to him. He assesses their relative importance, and the priority he sets up determines how he will allocate his personal resources.

The adaptation of means to ends is considerably more complicated with reference to society as a whole. For while the problem of choice remains, there is no way in which the wants of its various individual members can be made commensurate. Nevertheless, every society must establish some priority among the material desires of its citizens, for the scarcity of resources universally imposes the necessity of choice. The common characteristic of all societies prior to the eighteenth century is that decisions as to which wants would receive priority, and therefore what the allocation of resources would be, were dictated by central authority and reinforced by custom. Since the relative urgency of different wants cannot be compared, any choice by a central authority among them must necessarily have been arbitrary. How well a particular group or individual fared relative to others depended on his status in the social hierarchy, and this reflected the importance attached to his function by society. Soldiers, scholars, priests, artisans, farmers, and tradesmen have performed their functions from time immemorial, but different societies have accorded them varying degrees of status.

In the feudal society of the Middle Ages, for example, the most exalted position was occupied by the lord of the manor, who owned the land and everything on it. He was pledged to protect the lives of the serfs and freemen of his domain. They, in turn, had the obligation to produce food and other products, and to serve in the lord's army. Everyone had a rigidly regulated place in society and a function to perform which custom perpetuated from generation to generation. Each manor constituted a self-sufficient economic, social, and political unit with a distinctly rural character. The nature of production, distribution, and consumption was determined by the orders of the lord and the force of tradition.

In other early societies the source of authority and the criteria according to which wants were given priority differed. But there was an essential similarity; the prime mover of economic activity was compounded of custom and command, and was a reflection of the prevailing philosophical or theological standard for social and moral well-being. Greek, Roman, and medieval thinkers alike concentrated on the problem of organizing the *oikos,* the city-state, the latifundium, or the manor under the direction of the father of the family, the lord, or the king of the realm to promote the welfare of the members of the community. Economic decision making was outside the scope of individual action; and individual acquisition, especially in the form of usury, was strongly censured. Within this framework, there was no soil for the development of economics as it is conceived of in the modern sense. Why resources were allocated as they were required no special explanation. It was a matter of law or tradition. While there was much for the thinker to speculate about, it was in the realm of ethics, theology, and politics, not economics. Not until the evolution of the market system of allocating resources did economics emerge as a separate field of inquiry.

The essence of the market system is the freedom of the factors of production to seek out the most profitable opportunities of employment. Clearly, this mode of allocating resources could not assert itself until the propriety of individual gain became sanctioned by society. Nor could it assert itself until human and material resources came into existence as "agents of production." Land, labor, and capital have of course always existed in a physical sense. But they did not become agents of production until they or their services became available for sale. Prior to the fourteenth century, land was hardly ever sold, and there was certainly no such thing as a real estate market. Indeed, since land was the primary source of wealth and the base of the medieval social structure, every effort was made to insure that holdings would be preserved through such customs as primogeniture and entail. The church was, of course, the largest single landholder. The entire structure of society was to experience profound changes before land was to become commercialized.

Similarly, there was no such thing as a labor market until the human being became emancipated from servitude, whether in the form of slavery, serfdom, or apprenticeship to a guildmaster. Not until he was free to sell his services in a competitive market would there be such a thing as labor in an economic sense. Nor did capital exist in the modern sense of the term. Though tools and equipment existed and funds accumulated even in simple economies, there was no incentive to use them for pioneering new and more efficient techniques of production. In fact, during the Middle Ages the guilds strictly regulated the method and quantity of production.

STIMULI TO ECONOMIC INQUIRY

The Renaissance

The dawning of the Renaissance unleashed the forces that were ultimately to provide the climate for the development of economics as a separate discipline. Historians are not in complete agreement as to the exact time span during which the many and complex forces that were to destroy feudal economic, political, social, and religious life were at work. Usually, the beginning of the Renaissance is placed at the time of the fall of Constantinople in 1453, though many of the events of the eleventh and twelfth centuries heralded the changes that reached fuller development in later centuries. Similarly, the end of the seventeenth century is generally conceived to mark the end of the Renaissance, though many medieval ideas and influences continued into the eighteenth century. The precise dating of this momentous time in human history is, however, considerably less important than the recognition of the tremendous, though gradual, change that took place in every aspect of human life. From an economic and social point of view, it was a period during which commerce revived, new forms of wealth emerged, and a town life dominated by an entirely new social class came into existence. Politically, it was a period which witnessed the growth of powerful national states; and intellectually, it was a time of skepticism, increasing secularization, and a corresponding decline in the authority of the church of Rome.

Since the Crusades preceded the fall of Constantinople, examination of the forces that were to shatter the whole pattern of medieval life may conveniently begin here. Although these expeditions were undertaken as an expression of religious fervor, they ultimately had a far greater economic than religious significance. New and exotic commodities brought back to the fairs of Europe prepared the way for commercial relations on an international scale. During the twelfth century the fairs of Champagne and elsewhere in Europe were the meeting place for merchants from all over Christendom. The revival of commerce promoted the city life which had declined with the breakup of the Roman Empire. Since the townsfolk did not produce their own food, the peasant enjoyed an ever-growing market. Their purchases not only induced him to expand production, but enabled him to amass money with which he could purchase concessions from the lord. By the end of the Middle Ages, therefore, the money economy of the towns, as well as a degree of personal freedom, had spread to the rural area. The development of a money economy carried with it a revision in the concept of wealth. Prior to the period in which money served on a large scale, wealth consisted of land, buildings, animals, jewels—in short, of things that had physical substance. With the introduction of money, the concept of wealth became separated from the use values of physical things and centered upon money itself. With the advent of the commercial revolution, the association of money and wealth became complete.

The Enlightenment

The Renaissance also manifested itself in a wholly new intellectual climate, sometimes referred to as the Enlightenment, which was to stimulate the birth not only of modern philosophy and the Protestant Reformation, but also modern science. Essentially, these developments have a common origin, which is the thesis that human reason, as distinct from divine revelation, is sufficient to discover truth. This thesis destroyed the nexus between faith and reason, and thus between theology and philosophy. This nexus was forged during the Middle Ages, largely through the efforts of Saint Thomas Aquinas. To Aquinas, knowledge was the product not only of reason (philosophy), but also of revelation (theology). All branches of learning (logic, ethics, politics, and economics) were welded together into one great whole through theology.

The reconciliation which he achieved between philosophy and theology was, however, far from permanent and was challenged even from within the church itself. The consequence of the ensuing divorce between reason and faith was a secularism and a religious skepticism which was to characterize intellectual activity from the fifteenth through the seventeenth centuries. In essence, this intellectual revolution asserted the primacy of the individual man capable of reason and possessed of an individual will. These principals became fundamental to the spiritual revolution which is the Protestant Reformation, for Martin Luther's attack against the misuse of indulgences, the worship of images and relics, and other practices which he regarded as pagan is an expression of his emphasis on the individual and of the power of the human mind to discover truth. While Luther's interpretation of Christian teachings was not particularly sympathetic to industry and trade, the reform movements of John Calvin, John Knox, and the Puritans were much more so. Indeed, they adopted such strongly favorable attitudes toward acquisition by useful labor and the judicious and prudent use of wealth that their views have been described as the "Protestant ethic," which launched and encouraged the development of capitalism in northern Europe. At least, this is the thesis which was advanced by Max Weber, the German sociologist and economist, in *The Protestant Ethic and the Spirit of Capitalism*. This hypothesis does, of course, not necessarily tell the whole story, for the fact that northern Europe and England are geographically well located for trade and have a climate and resources conducive to industry is undoubtedly also a factor in their industrial development. But it is a certainty that the adherents of Protestantism were decidedly commercial-minded and possessed of personal attributes which encouraged business activity, and that in this sense the Reformation contributed toward capitalist development and therefore economic thought. Their greater preoccupation with the material aspects of life resulted in attitudes toward work and the acquisition of wealth which were significantly different from those which prevailed when the primary purpose of life on earth was preparation for the life herafter. Acquisition, no longer regarded as a sin, became a virtue; the merchant, no longer regarded as un-Christian because of his activities for profit, grew in stature and came to be regarded as a pillar of the church and the community.

The new intellectualism brought with it not only a quest for new knowledge, but also new techniques for its acquisition and new bases for its evaluation. This was the intellectual revolution in which revelation yielded its place to science. It was to foster rapid progress in botany, anatomy, physics, astronomy, and mathematics and to lead ultimately to the systematic study of social phenomena as well. Once it was recognized that the physical universe obeys certain laws that can be discovered by experimentation and observation, it was only a question of time before it was asked whether the same principles might not also be applied to the social universe to yield laws governing social phenomena.

New Political Concepts

Further stimulus to economic inquiry was to come from changing political developments and ideas. The Reformation was a major source of such political developments. Europe became torn by religious dissension as Protestants and Catholics fought for supremacy. The principal beneficiary of this struggle was absolute monarchy. As monarchy replaced feudal relationships, so taxation superseded personal service as a means of supporting the state. The appearance of the state and the necessarily associated issue of the best way of enhancing its revenue mark the beginning of modern political economy. This was the era of mercantilism, during which economic decision making was not yet liberated from the state and economics was still in its preanalytic phase. Subsequently, economics was divorced from politics and thus constituted, at last, a separate field of inquiry.

The divorce of economics from politics required the development of the concepts of the natural order and the natural law. These concepts became the vehicle for the political and economic liberalism of Adam Smith and the Physiocrats in the eighteenth century. Both derive from the Stoic philosophy, which eventually passed, through the writings of Cicero, into Roman legal conceptions. According to Roman jurists, natural law is not only universal and immutable, but is also the foundation of the state, since it existed prior to the founding of any state. Thus the state is "an assemblage of men associated in consent to law." This is different from the Greek view of the state as the outgrowth of natural necessity. Roman thinkers thus contributed two ideas which were to affect profoundly future political and economic thought: first, the idea of universal law; and secondly, the idea of the state being based on mutual consent. These two ideas provided the foundation for the conception of individual rights, without which modern capitalism would not have evolved. While Roman thinkers contributed little as far as the development of economic thought is concerned, it is Roman law, with its emphasis on private property and freedom of contract, which constitutes the basis for the legal doctrines and institutions of capitalism.

These were given new expression during the seventeenth century and reflect one aspect of the new Weltanschauung, or conception of the world, which emerged during the Renaissance and Reformation.

The Renaissance and the Reformation gave birth to the idea of the "masterless man," the autonomous individual created in the image of God and therefore inherently good, but individually responsible for his own salvation. The idea of man as possessing an individual will and therefore the powers to think and do things gave the man of the Renaissance an estimate of his own worth and importance in the scheme of things that would have been inconceivable for the man of the Middle Ages. Thus, he challenged the uncompromising authority of the monarch who claimed to rule by divine right, for such authority was in conflict with the whole conception of an autonomous individual subject only to his own conscience and the dictates of "right reason." This is the seventeenth-century conception of natural law that was propounded by the Dutchman Hugo Grotius.

Grotius' secularized version of natural law was especially significant in regard to defining the natural rights that reason demonstrates as belonging to individuals by virtue of their humanity. These are the inalienable rights which cannot be abrogated by law and which John Locke later formulated as the "right to life, liberty and property." The rising commercial classes were quick to embrace this philosophy, for it reflected their own growing aspirations. As a result of their enhanced economic status during the period of mercantilism, they eventually challenged privileges based on birth and social position. They thought of the rights of individuals to own property and the fruits of their own labor; to speak, to write, to assemble, and to worship as they chose; to have the right to fair trial and freedom from arbitrary imprisonment and cruel or unusual punishment. Thus the same burgher class which supported the absolutism of the Tudors during the sixteenth century later led the Glorious Revolution which culminated in establishing the supremacy of Parliament. This protest against the unlimited power of the sovereign marks the first victory of liberalism over absolutism, a victory which was later echoed in the American Revolution for independence from Britain in 1776 and the French Revolution of 1789.

The growth of political freedom was paralleled by greater economic freedom, which gave rise to new economic problems and phenomena requiring explanation. As will become clear in Chapter 2, some headway was made during the period of mercantilism in the development of economic concepts and tools of analysis. But the subject of inquiry during this period was political economy rather than economic analysis. Purely economic analysis did not emerge until the Physiocrats concerned themselves with the economic conditions which prevailed in France during the 1750's. Their writings mark the emergence of economics as a separate subject matter with analytical tools and concepts appropriate to its purpose.

THE CONDITIONING OF ECONOMIC THEORIES

The economic theories of the past, as well as those which are contemporary, are the product of numerous influences and factors affecting one another. Actual economic phenomena have unquestionably directed inquiry in every age. It has not been uncommon, therefore, for historians of economic thought to advance the hypothesis that the emergence of particular theories is explicable in terms of the historical events that preceded or coincided with their germination.[1] Writers who offer this explanation of causality see the development of economic thought primarily as an attempt to understand and rationalize experience.

The Weltanschuung, or philosophical outlook, of a particular period or writer has most assuredly also been a factor which has influenced the kind of economic thought which developed. It affects not only the selection of phenomena about which to speculate, but also the character of the speculation which results. Some historians of economic thought have therefore sought an explanation for the germination of particular economic ideas in the minds of particular individuals in terms of the philosophical and psychological foundations which appear to underlie them.[2]

Most economic theories also have political connotations. That is, they either have been conceived within the framework of a particular political setting or have been used to support policies whose implementation requires particular political institutions. This relationship has led at least one writer to advance the hypothesis that particular theories evolved in order to lend support to policies and programs which seemed politically and socially appropriate at particular times in history.[3]

Each of these hypotheses offers its own particular insight into the development of economic thought. And yet, each leaves something to be desired. The historical relativists, for example, have usually been overly simple in their interpretation of historical events and have tended to deemphasize those which did not lend support to particular theories. Nor have they been able to demonstrate the processes by which events and ideas have interacted and shaped one another through time.

Explanations of the development of particular economic doctrines in

---

[1] See, for example, W. Stark, *The History of Economics in Its Relation to Social Development* (London: K. Paul, Trench, Truber and Co., Ltd., 1945; and Eric Roll, *A History of Economic Thought* (3d ed.; New York: Prentice-Hall, Inc., 1956).

[2] A classic example of a writer who has explained economic doctrine in terms of its philosophical foundations is James Bonar, *Philosophy and Political Economy* (2d ed.; London: George Allen and Unwin, Ltd., 1909). Walter A. Weisskopf has given a psychological interpretation of the development of economic thought; see *The Psychology of Economics,* The University of Chicago Press, Chicago, Illinois, 1955.

[3] See Leo Rogin, *The Meaning and Validity of Economic Theory* (New York: Harper & Bros., 1956).

terms of their underlying philosophical and psychological foundations have not been systematic or convincing. In a bygone era, when writers on economic subjects were more often professors of moral philosophy, or at least avid students of philosophy and social ethics, the interrelationship between economics and other disciplines also involving human behavior was much closer than it appears to be at present. Nor has there always been a very clear relationship between economic theory and the formulation of policy. Especially since the end of the nineteenth century have we witnessed the emergence of analytical concepts which bear no clear relationship to the institutional setting or prevailing philosophical or psychological doctrines. This would appear to indicate that it is possible for economic ideas to germinate quite independently of events and social and political ends. Furthermore, many a concept of a bygone era has survived the reference frame within which it was originally conceived. These are the essential truths which possess a validity independent of the philosophical and political beliefs of their authors and which have become incorporated in the body of principles accepted by succeeding generations. Other concepts have not stood this test of time and have purely historical interest. All this is not to say that modern economics is completely divorced from a host of preconceptions, philosophical and otherwise, which are reflected in the propositions laid down. It is difficult to avoid one's biases, particularly in a field like economics. Indeed, some modern Catholic economists do not regard it as inappropriate to draw conclusions concerning economic behavior from premises grounded on Christian ethics. Similarly, at least some adherents of the modern welfare school have a noticeable ethical bias. However, in general, economic analysis is moving in the direction of propositions which have no ethical content. The resulting body of thought is sometimes called "scientific" or "positive" economics as opposed to "normative" economics, whose propositions are in the field of economic ethics.

In the chapters which follow, we shall examine the unfolding of economic theories and their related concepts and analytical tools from the period of mercantilism to the present. Each contribution will be presented, insofar as possible, in the philosophical framework within which it was originally conceived and associated with the particular events, the period in history, and the individual or school to which it relates. This is done because it seems unlikely that one can achieve a very profound insight into the theories of the past without a lively appreciation of the spirit, philosophy, and events of the times in which they were conceived. Association is not, however, explanation. Our objective is not to explain why economic thought emerged as it did. Rather, we seek to examine the development of the concepts and tools of analysis which have been fashioned over time to explain economic phenomena. Our approach, therefore, is historical as well as analytical. A sense of history is essential to the comprehension and appreciation of the theories of the past. But their real significance lies in their survival as part of the present body of economic principles.

SUGGESTIONS FOR FURTHER READING

MARGENAU, HENRY. "What Is a Theory" in *The Structure of Economic Science* (edited by S. R. KRUPP). Englewood Cliffs, N.J.: Prentice-Hall, Inc., 1966.

NABERS, LAWRENCE. "The Positive and Genetic Approaches" in *The Structure of Economic Science* (edited by S. R. KRUPP). Englewood Cliffs, N.J.: Prentice-Hall, Inc., 1966.

POLANYI, KARL, *et al.* *Trade and Markets in Early Empires*. Glencoe, Ill.: Free Press, 1957. Especially chapter v.

ROBBINS, LIONEL. *Nature and Significance of Economic Science*. London: Macmillan Company Ltd., 1933.

TAWNEY, R. H. *Religion and the Rise of Capitalism*. New York: Penquin Books, 1947.

WEBER, MAX. *Protestant Ethic and the Spirit of Capitalism*. Trans. TALCOTT PARSONS. New York: Scribner, 1948.

GENERAL REFERENCES

History of Economic Analysis, the magnum opus of the late Professor Joseph A. Schumpeter is the most comprehensive and sophisticated treatise available. There are also numerous textbooks on the history of economic thought which can serve as useful collateral reading either because they include contributions of a less theoretical nature than those which are the focus of this book or because they provide interpretations and examine the impact of economic ideas in a way which is precluded by the scope of this inquiry. Two books on contemporary economic analysis are also included in the list which follows because of their historical orientation; each is marked with an asterisk.

BELL, JOHN F. *A History of Economic Thought.* New York: Ronald Press Co., 1953.

*BLAUG, MARK. *Economic Theory in Retrospect.* Homewood, Ill.: Richard D. Irwin, Inc., 1962.

BONAR, JAMES. *Philosophy and Political Economy.* 2d ed. London: George Allen and Unwin, Ltd., 1909.

*FELLNER, WILLIAM. *The Emergence and Content of Modern Economic Analysis.* New York: McGraw-Hill Book Co., Inc., 1960.

FERGUSON, JOHN M. *Landmarks of Economic Thought.* 2d ed. New York: Longmans, Green & Co., Inc., 1950.

GIDE, CHARLES, and RIST, CHARLES. *A History of Economic Doctrine.* Translated by R. RICHARDS. 7th ed. Boston: D. C. Heath & Co., 1948.

GRAY, ALEXANDER. *The Development of Economic Doctrine*. New York: Longmans, Green & Co., Inc., 1933.

GRUCHY, ALLAN G. *Modern Economic Thought: The American Contribution*. New York: Prentice-Hall, Inc., 1947.

HANEY, LEWIS H. *History of Economic Thought*. 4th ed. New York: Macmillan Co., 1949.

HEILBRONER, ROBERT. *The Worldly Philosophers*. New York: Simon and Schuster, Inc., 1953.

HEIMANN, EDUARD. *History of Economic Doctrine*. New York: Oxford University Press, 1964.

HOMAN, PAUL T. *Contemporary Economic Thought*. New York: Harper & Bros., 1928.

HUTCHISON, TERRENCE W. *A Review of Economic Doctrines, 1870–1929*. Oxford: Clarendon Press, 1953.

LEKACHMAN, ROBERT. *A History of Economic Ideas*. New York: Harper & Bros., 1959.

LEKACHMAN, ROBERT (ed.). *The Varieties of Economics*, 2 vols. Cleveland: The World Publishing Co., 1962.

ROGIN, LEO. *The Meaning and Validity of Economic Theory*. New York: Harper & Bros., 1956.

ROLL, ERIC. *A History of Economic Thought*. 3d ed. New York: Prentice-Hall, Inc., 1956.

SCHUMPETER, JOSEPH A. *History of Economic Analysis*, New York: Oxford University Press, 1954.

SELIGMAN, BEN. *Main Currents in Modern Economics*. New York: Free Press of Glencoe, Inc., 1962.

TAYLOR, OVERTON H. *A History of Economic Thought*. New York: McGraw-Hill Book Co., Inc., 1960.

WHITTAKER, EDMUND. *Schools and Streams of Economic Thought*. Chicago: Rand McNally & Co., 1960.

ZWEIG, FERDYNAND. *Economic Ideas: A Study in Historical Perspective*. New York: Prentice-Hall, Inc., 1950.

There are also several collections of readings from original sources and essays on economic thought or about the works of specific contributors with which the reader will find it useful to be acquainted.

ABBOTT, LEONARD D. (ed.). *Masterworks of Economics*. Garden City, N.Y.: Doubleday & Co., Inc., 1949.

GHERITITY, JAMES A. (ed.). *Economic Thought; A Historical Anthology*. New York: Random House, 1965.

KEYNES, JOHN MAYNARD. *Essays in Biography*. London: Macmillan & Co., 1933. Rev. ed. London: Rupert Hart-Davis, 1951.

MONROE, ARTHUR E. (ed.). *Early Economic Thought*. Cambridge: Harvard University Press, 1924.

NEWMAN, PHILIP; GAYER, ARTHUR; and SPENCER, MILTON, eds. *Source Readings in Economic Thought*. New York: W. W. Norton & Co., Inc., 1954.

PATTERSON, S. HOWARD, ed. *Readings in the History of Economic Thought*. New York: McGraw-Hill Book Co., Inc., 1932.

SCHUMPETER, JOSEPH A. *Ten Great Economists*. London: Oxford University Press, 1951.

SPENGLER, JOSEPH J., and ALLEN, W. (eds.). *Essays in Economic Thought: Aristotle to Marshall*. Chicago: Rand McNally & Co., 1960.

SPIEGEL, WILLIAM H. (ed.). *The Development of Economic Thought*. New York: John Wiley & Sons, Inc., 1952.

VINER, JACOB. *The Long View and the Short*. Glencoe, Ill.: Free Press, 1958.

WILSON, GEORGE W. (ed.). *Classics of Economic Theory*. Bloomington, Ind.: Indiana University Press, 1964.

References which apply only to particular chapters and suggestions for further reading beyond what is noted under the General References given above will be appended to individual chapters. Most of these direct the reader to areas of controversy and interpretation, to background material and related disciplines, or to areas beyond the scope of this text.

Chapter 2

THE CONTRIBUTIONS OF
THE MERCANTILISTS TO
ECONOMIC ANALYSIS

INTRODUCTION

The Period in History

The origin of some theoretical concepts in economics can be traced to the period of mercantilism. However, mercantilist thinkers were, in the main, practitioners dedicated to improving their own fortunes and those of their nation in the struggle against other states for supremacy. The ultimate test of the strong state was the ability to wage war, make conquests, and hold colonial areas. This presented problems different from those encountered during the Middle Ages. The lord of the manor recruited from his own domain men and materials for warfare. But the modern state came to depend on an army of mercenaries who were in the employ of the sovereign. The modern state needed money: with money the sinews of war could be acquired. The essence of mercantilism was therefore statecraft (*Staatsbildung*), and economic policy became a primary instrument to promote the simultaneous development and growth of the economy and the state.

The revival of trade during the Renaissance and the emergence of a money economy had already cemented the association of money and wealth. While the accumulation of the precious metals of which money consisted was not uncommon in the ancient world nor in the Middle Ages, during the period of mercantilism England as well as the countries of western Europe pursued the acquisition of gold as a matter of national policy. Spain had an advantage over her rivals as the result of her colonizing ventures after the discovery of the New World, for she alone had direct access to gold. The others, largely unsuccessful in their gold-seeking expeditions, had to devise other ways to increase their stocks of the precious metal. Thus, they directed their attention to the formulation of policies designed to promote a favorable balance of payments, the presumption being that if they sold more to foreigners than they bought, the surplus would return to them in gold. They also regulated production, giving special attention to the growth and manufacture of exportable commodities and those which would promote domestic self-sufficiency, and encouraged the growth of population.

Regulations to accomplish these ends were especially stringent in France and reached their zenith under Jean Baptiste Colbert, who was Minister of Finance under Louis XIV from 1661 to 1683. During his administration, every aspect of production was brought under state control, including the relations between masters and workmen in the guilds, and methods and quality standards of manufacturers. Certain manufacturers, such as the famous Gobelin tapestry firm, were "royal manufacturers" owned and operated by the state. Dependence on foreign manufactures was lessened by encouraging craftsmen to immigrate to France, and bounties were granted to encourage shippers and shipbuilders. Colbert's administration also witnessed the expansion of the French colonial empire and the growth of successful trading companies which conducted colonial trade as a monopoly of the crown. He was so thoroughgoing in introducing measures to stamp out remaining feudal elements and secure absolute power for the state that "Colbertism" is virtually synonymous with French mercantilism.

Sources of Mercantilist Thought

A tract entitled *A Brief Treatise on the Causes Which Can Make Gold and Silver Plentiful in Kingdoms Where There Are No Mines,* which was written by an Italian merchant, Antonio Serra, in 1613, is generally regarded as the earliest written exposition of mercantilistic thought. The last systematic presentation of mercantilistic doctrines was Sir James Stewart's *Inquiry into the Principles of Political Economy,* published in 1767. Between these dates, there appeared a large volume of tracts, pamphlets, and articles from which may be extracted ideas and policy recommendations to which the label "mercantilistic" has been given. Examination of this literature, however, reveals such a diversity of ideas and recommendations that to describe them simply as mercantilistic tends to obscure and minimize their differences.

A considerable portion of the English literature of this period came from the merchants, whose role in the economy was such that they in particular came to identify the substance of wealth with money in the form of precious metals. While their funds were used to buy raw materials, tools, and labor, the continuation of enterprise required the restoration of capital funds to their original monetary form through the sale of goods. Since they thought of domestic trade as merely circulating existing stocks of money, it was foreign trade that they especially prized. Here, they looked to the state to facilitate their efforts by controlling the relationship of imports and exports, regulating interest rates and exchange rates, and chartering joint-stock trading companies with monopoly privileges such as the British East India Company and the Merchant Adventures.

Since the accumulation of treasure was a primary aim of the sovereign, and its acquisition depended on the foreign trade balance, there necessarily evolved a unity of interest between the state and the merchants.

Insofar as a heterogeneous group of writers may be said to have a chief spokesman, Thomas Mun (1571–1641) is generally regarded as most representative of the English mercantile interests of his day.[1] That he was also the most influential appears evident from Adam Smith's famous critique of mercantilism in *The Wealth of Nations*. Smith discusses the nature and shortcomings of mercantilism almost exclusively in terms of Mun's *England's Treasure by Forraign Trade,* even though other writers had produced a voluminous number of papers, pamphlets, essays, and tracts and Sir James Stewart's *Inquiry into the Principles of Political Economy* had been published.

Mun was during his lifetime a successful merchant, a director of the East India Company, and a member of the Board of Trade. After the loss of a company vessel carrying a gold shipment, he wrote *A Discourse of Trade from England into the East Indies* (1621) to clear the East India Company of the bullionists' charge that its export of specie was contrary to the best interests of the country. The *Discourse* was so obviously a special interest plea that it is much less impressive than his later work *England's Treasure by Forraign Trade,* which was published posthumously.

Not all businessmen were, however, of one mind. Some were enthusiastic nationalists; others were provincial and favored a continuation of medieval localism; and still others thought in terms that transcended national boundaries. The arguments of such English exponents as Gerard de Malynes, Dudley Diggs, and Thomas Mun, while marking them as spokesmen for the business interests of their day, reflect wide differences in their ideas and policy recommendations. It is understandable that the flow of ideas from merchant-authors, together with those of the philosophers, government officials, and scientists who also turned their attention to economic matters, resulted in a very heterogenous body of literature. It is no easy task, therefore, to set forth mercantilistic doctrines. We can examine the leading ideas on foreign trade, money and interest, and labor and production; and yet, our efforts will not yield a homogeneous body of thought. This is particularly the case when we deal with the more advanced mercantilist writers, such as Sir William Petty, who are forerunners of economic liberalism, even though they dealt with mercantilistic problems. Although the end of the mercantilistic period is generally regarded as coinciding with the appearance of Adam Smith's *Wealth of Nations,* it must be borne in mind that, in England at least, many mercantilistic restrictions had already become obsolete by the middle of the eighteenth century, and that those that remained were regarded with irritation rather than approval.

Compared with their English contemporaries, the people who wrote on economic matters in France, Germany, and Austria were considerably

---

[1] E. A. J. Johnson, *Predecessors of Adam Smith* (New York: Prentice-Hall, Inc., 1937), chap. v, "Mun, the Strategist," p. 77. It is suggested that Mun's book was the model on which *The Wealth of Nations* unconsciously was patterned.

less numerous than in England. Nor were they predominantly merchants or members of the nobility. Another point of difference is that they were even more exclusively concerned with applied economics than were their English counterparts, whose writings, though crude and unsystematic, laid the foundation for numerous concepts from which modern tools of analysis, especially in the area of international trade and monetary theory, were to develop.

ECONOMIC ANALYSIS

The Balance of Trade and the Acquisition of Wealth

The concept of the balance of trade is the most important tool of economic analysis developed by the mercantilist writers. In modern terminology the term "balance of trade" includes only merchandise imports and exports, whereas the "balance of payments" includes, in addition, invisible exports and imports, long term and short term capital and gold. Merchandise and invisible exports, exports of monetary metals and transfers of claims on the domestic economy to the rest of the world are designated as plus items in the balance of payments. Commodity and invisible imports, imports of monetary metals and acquisitions of claims vis a vis the rest of the world set up an outward flow of foreign exchange to other countries and are designated as negative items in the balance of payments.

If a country has a surplus of commodity and invisible imports, this will be balanced by an outward movement of specie, new foreign debts or diminished foreign assets. Conversely, an excess of merchandise and invisible exports will be offset by an inflow of gold or the acquisition of claims on the rest of the world. It is in this sense that the balance of payments, which is nothing more than an accounting statement of a country's foreign transactions, must always be in balance. That bullionist, mercantilist, and cameralist writers did not understand this principle is evident in their argument that a nation should strive for a favorable balance of trade as a matter of national policy. By this, they meant an excess of merchandise and invisible exports relative to imports which would be offset either by a flow of gold or by foreign credits. Since their primary concern was with the acquisition of treasure, they advocated policies that would insure the import of gold to compensate for a surplus in the balance of trade. They thought it highly desirable to maintain a permanently favorable balance of trade, failing to recognize that a continuous inflow of gold would eventually produce a reverse flow of specie. This principle was subsequently developed by David Hume.

Mercantilist writers were also so wedded to the notion that the wealth of the nation consists of its stock of precious metals rather than goods that they failed to perceive the advantages inherent in geographical specialization of production. Relatively few mercantilists showed any awareness of the fact that wealth consists of goods that can be used for consumption or further production. Moreover, they believed that the wealth of one nation could only be augmented at the expense of other nations, since the supply of gold is relatively fixed. The mercantilist conception of wealth, therefore, provides the rationale for their theoretical analysis as well as their policy prescriptions.

Although all writers, regardless of national origin, were essentially in agreement as regards the goal of building a strong state through the accumulation of treasure, some presented cruder theoretical analyses and narrower policy recommendations than others. For example, the English bullionists urged complete prohibition of the export of bullion and the establishment of the Office of Royal Exchanger to regulate foreign exchange transactions. These proposals grew in vehemence after the loss at sea of a vessel of the East India Company, carrying a large shipment of gold. The most heated protest against the privilege of that company came from the pen of Gerard de Malynes.[2] He urged the state to control the exchange dealings of private financiers, whose transactions he believed not only caused bullion to flow out but also raised interest rates by decreasing the amount of bullion in the realm.

Malynes' arguments reflect a strong medievalist view of moral justice. While he recognized that the use of bills of exchange facilitated foreign trade, he argued that only transactions taking place at exchange rates that are *par pro pari,* that is, at rates reflecting the bullion content of the currencies involved, are consistent with the requirements of moral justice. A divergence of exchange rates from parity was viewed as the result of corrupting activities by dealers in exchange which imposed an injustice on one of the parties and also caused bullion movements to take place. He thought that bullion would either flow into a country or be drained away, depending on the direction of the movement of exchange rates above or below par. Only at stable exchange rates would no bullion movement take place. Malynes' proposed remedy was that the Royal Exchanger should handle all foreign exchange transactions, and that such transactions, in being made only at the *par pro pari,* would preserve the treasures in the kingdom.[3] The modern counterpart of Malynes' *par pro pari* is the mint par of exchange, which is today, of course, divorced from moral connotations.

Some mercantilists took exception to the proposal that all bullion exports should be prohibited, maintaining that the outward flow of specie

---

[2] Gerard de Malynes, *A Treatise on the Canker of England's Commonwealth* (London, 1601); *The Maintenance of Free Trade* (London, 1622); *The Center of the Circle of Commerce* (London, 1623).

[3] Another supporter of policies to restrict bullion exports was Edward Misselden, with whom Malynes engaged in arguments regarding trade and exchange regulations. However, in defending his views in *The Center of the Circle of Commerce*, Malynes reversed his position and argued favorably for the export of bullion to purchase goods abroad. See Johnson, *op. cit.,* chap. iv, "Misselden, the Critic."

would actually contribute to the goal of achieving a favorable overall export balance. No one presented this view with greater vigor and clarity than Thomas Mun. His central argument in *England's Treasure by Forraign Trade* was that the export of specie results in purchases of goods which, when reexported at advantageous prices, bring back more specie than had originally been exported. The defense of the special cause of the East India Company is abandoned in this work, and the argument is presented from the viewpoint of the statesman or greatly enlightened businessman who was conscious primarily of the interests of the nation.

Mun begins by distinguishing between natural and artificial riches as a basis for national opulence. A notion of capital which is generally identified with stock or financial capital, though it is sometimes confused with both money and wealth, is subsequently introduced. Drawing an analogy between the kingdom and a private estate which can be impoverished by careless spending or enriched by an orderly conversion of goods into money and money into goods, Mun designates that portion of natural or artificial wealth which is used to yield a surplus as "stock." He argues that the wisest way to employ stock is in foreign trade, for this will increase wealth and treasure if care is taken to achieve a favorable balance. In Mun's own words:

"The ordinary means, therefore, to increase our wealth and treasure is by Forraign Trade wherein we must ever observe this rule; to sell more to strangers yearly than we consume of theirs in value. For suppose that when this Kingdom is plentifully served with Cloth, Lead, Tin, Iron, Fish and other native commodities, we doe yearly export the over-surplus to forraign Countreys to the value of twenty two hundred thousand pounds, by which means we are enabled beyond the Seas to buy and bring in forraign wares for our use and Consumptions, to the value of twenty hundred thousand pounds; By this order duly kept in our trading, we may rest assured that the Kingdom shall be enriched yearly two hundred thousand pounds, which must be brought to us in so much Treasure, because that part of stock which is not returned to us in wares must necessarily be brought home in treasure. . . ."[4]

It is thus that Mun adopts Misselden's notion of the balance of trade and emphasizes that it is the relationship between aggregate imports and exports that is crucial, not the relationship between specific imports and exports. Mun is also well aware of the significance of invisible items of trade as a source of additional foreign credits, for he says: "The value of our exportations may be much advanced when we perform it ourselves in our own Ships, for then we get not only the price of our wares as they are worth here, but also the Merchants gains, the charges of ensurance and

---

[4] "England's Treasure by Forraign Trade," 1664 by Thomas Mun in John R. McCulloch (ed.), *Early English Tracts on Commerce* (Jarrold and Sons, Ltd., Norwich, 1952), pp. 125–26.

freight to carry them beyond the seas. . . ."[5] In order to cultivate a favorable balance, he urges that the country should strive for self-sufficiency to diminish its imports and practice frugality to have more available for export. The consumption of luxuries is to be discouraged, but "if in our rayment we will be prodigal, yet let this be done with our own materials and manufactures, as Cloth, Lace Imbroideries, Cutwork and the like, where the excess of the rich may be the employment of the poor, whose labours notwithstanding of this kind, would be more profitable for the Commonwealth, if they were done to the use of strangers."[6]

The advantages to be derived from trade can be maximized only if judgment is used in pricing. Commodities should be sold at high prices only "so far forth as the high price cause not a less vent in the quantity." Where there is competition from other suppliers or substitutes are readily available, "we must strive to sell as cheap as possible we can, rather than lose the utterance of such wares." These observations concerning the relationship between price and the quantity of a commodity which can be sold reveal Mun's understanding of what in modern terminology is called demand elasticity. Similar awareness of the relationship between price and demand is also evident in his recommendations regarding export and import duties. High export duties, he reasoned, may be harmful, for by "indearing them [English exports] to the strangers use, it hinder their vent." Import duties, on the other hand, should be high enough to discourage consumption of foreign goods in England and low on goods intended for reexport.

The most controversial matter pursued by Mun concerned the export of specie as a means to increase England's treasure. It was in regard to this issue that he came into conflict with the bullionists, who strongly advocated complete prohibition of gold exports. The essence of his argument was that when gold is used in trade to acquire goods which are then available for subsequent reexport at advantageous prices, even more gold will be returned to England than was originally sent out. To keep gold in the kingdom does not multiply wealth; on the contrary, it will raise prices and diminish exports. Money must be used as capital in order that more wealth will ultimately emerge. Outward movements of gold to acquire goods for reexport are analogous to the seedtime and the harvest, says Mun, for "if we only behold the actions of the husbandman in the seed-time when he casteth away much good corn into the ground, we will rather accompt him a mad man than a husbandman: but when we consider his labours in the harvest which is the end of his endeavours, we find the worth and plentiful encrease of his actions."[7]

---

[5] *Ibid.,* p. 129.

[6] *Ibid.*

[7] *Ibid.,* p. 141.

Monetary Analysis

Most mercantilists were aware of the direct relationship between the quantity of money and the level of prices, maintaining that "plenty of money in a Kingdom doth make the native commodities dearer." The earliest theoretical analysis of the relationship between the quantity of money and inflationary price increases was made by the French philosopher Jean Bodin. He attributed the marked price rise experienced by western Europe during the sixteenth century primarily to the inflow of monetary metals from South America, thus emphasizing what is today treated as M in our modern equations of exchange. He also observed that monopolies, through their policies of restricting output, and large demands by consumers for luxury commodities contributed to price increases. Thus, he was not unaware of the significance of what is today designated as T and V in the transactions version of the equation of exchange.

In the now familiar form introduced by Irving Fisher in the 1920's, the equation of exchange states:

$$MV = PT$$

In this equation, M designates the monetary means of payment available for conducting transactions in the economy, V designates the average number of times the units of payment change hands in a given period of time, P stands for the average level of prices, and T for the quantity of goods and services available to be purchased. The equation, as it stands, is nothing more than the truism that the monetary value of the goods and services paid for is equal to the monetary value of the goods and services sold. It becomes analytically useful only within the framework of a hypothesis as to how the elements in the equation behave. Fisher, making certain assumptions with respect to T and V, maintained that there is a direct causal relationship between the quantity of money and the general price level. He argued that, other things being equal, the general price level will vary directly with the quantity of money. This is a conclusion with which mercantilists were in accord, though they lacked the analytical framework that was later developed.

Since few mercantilists favored inflation, it seems contradictory, therefore, for them to favor a continuous accumulation of monetary metals via a favorable balance of trade. But there is an explanation for this seeming contradiction of obectives which may be found in the effect they thought changes in M would have on T rather than on P. That is, they reasoned that increases in the amount of money "quicken trade" instead of producing an inflation of prices and thereby rescued their advocacy of a favorable balance of trade, with its associated inflow of specie, from a seeming contradiction of objectives.

This line of reasoning reflects an awareness that a growing volume of money and credit is essential to continued expansion of the physical volume of trade. Since the embryonic state of the credit system at that time precluded a well-functioning system of note issue (demand deposit creation being a still later phase of banking development) mercantilist emphasis on the desirability of accumulating greater quantities of gold in order to expand the money supply is more comprehensible than it would be if the credit system had been better developed. They reasoned that an inflow of hard money would keep interest rates low, while the downward pressure on prices which would result from an inadequate supply of money would serve to dampen further expansion of economic activity.

While the relationship between the quantity of money, prices, and interest rates was not clearly understood until much later, when a distinction was made between the money rate and the real rate of interest, the mercantilists seemed to sense the necessity of avoiding downward pressure on prices if the expansion of commercial activity is to be facilitated. Though they thought of these relationships in purely monetary terms, real factors, which they did not understand, are involved. That is, falling prices have the effect of raising the real rate of interest, and this impedes economic expansion. It is the value of a loan in terms of the goods and services it represents, rather than money rates as such, which affects the worthwhileness of borrowing. If the price level is falling, the principal value of a loan in real terms is necessarily rising, since the borrower contracts to repay a given number of dollars which will purchase more goods and services at low prices than at higher prices. What the mercantilists failed to understand was that the reason why an increased quantity of money is associated with a lower rate of interest is not simply due to the greater supply of funds thus available for borrowing, but because this is generally associated with an increase in real income. But this is a relationship which the mercantilist monetary theory of interest overlooked. It was not until the writings of David Hume, Anne Robert Jacques Turgot, and Richard Cantillon that real as opposed to monetary theories of interest began to evolve.

John Maynard Keynes, in writing his "Notes on Mercantilism" at the conclusion of *The General Theory of Employment, Interest and Money* in 1936, suggested that the mercantilists anticipated some of his own thinking. He reasoned that their recognition of the stimulating effect of low interest rates on the level of investment is indicative of their awareness that there is a tendency for the propensity to save to be high relative to the inducement to invest and that this factor is responsible for the tendency of the economy to equilibrate at less than full-employment levels. Since modern techniques of monetary management and public investment to stimulate employment were not then at hand, Keynes regarded the mercantilist policy of encouraging inflation through a favorable trade balance as a perfectly rational way of expanding the money supply and thereby lowering interest rates and stimulating investment and employment.

It is not difficult to perceive a Keynesian flavor in mercantilist warnings against holding money idle and in their references to the employment-creating effects of a favorable trade balance.[8] The analogy must, however, not be carried too far; the Keynesian analysis relates only to industrial economics. The type of unemployment experienced by predominantly agrarian economies such as England was before the Industrial Revolution, is very different from the involuntary type associated with insufficient aggregate demand and the resulting underinvestment as it manifests itself in advanced industrial economies. Keynes was guilty of analyzing mercantilist thought within an institutional framework entirely foreign to its historical period.

Mercantilist Views on Production and Related Matters

Preoccupation with the aggrandizement of the state and the acquisition of treasure set the stage for a number of corollary doctrines and policies designed to foster the achievement of these goals. The theory of production is of major importance in this connection, for the creation of the largest possible export surplus necessarily required maximum utilization of the factors of production. To some writers, natural resources were the basis for wealth, while others regarded labor as a more important factor than natural resources. Lewes Roberts, for example, viewed the earth as "the fountaine and mother of all riches," while Petty said that "labor is the father and active principle of wealth as land is the mother." The policy counterpart of both viewpoints is to be found in measures to increase natural resources and the productivity of labor by discouraging idleness and introducing specialization. Even before Smith's celebrated description of the advantages of division of labor in the manufacture of pins, Petty observed that "cloth must be cheaper when one cards, another spins, another weaves, another draws, another dresses, another presses and packs, than when all the operations above were clumsily performed by the same hand."

Mercantilistic writers distinguished between productive and unproductive labor in terms of its contribution to national opulence. Manufacturers and farmers were regarded as productive, though the warmest praise was, understandably, reserved for the merchants. Retailers, clergymen, doctors, lawyers, and entertainers were generally regarded as unproductive; and it was urged that the government hold the number of unproductive

---

[8] This hypothesis is also advanced by W. D. Grampp in his provocative article, "Liberal Elements in English Mercantilism," *Quarterly Journal* of Economics, Vol. LXVI (November, 1952). Grampp takes the position that the main objective of mercantilist policy was to achieve full employment rather than a favorable balance of trade per se.

people to a minimum, in order to direct their labor to some more useful occupation. Mercantilistic ideas on production are part of their legacy from the Scholastics of the medieval period, who viewed God's bounty as the origin of wealth and production as the exploitation of this bounty by labor. Thus, Thomas Hobbes wrote that "plenty God usually either giveth freely, or for labor selleth to mankind."[9] Emphasis on the appropriation of natural or divine bounty by the efforts of man's labor is to be found throughout British economic literature in the period before Adam Smith wrote. Virtually without exception, it was urged that government must increase both the quantity and the utilization of "natural" wealth and labor. Thus, Mun advocated the growing of hemp, flax, cordage, and tobacco on wastelands,[10] and the exploitation of fisheries in the North Sea, which are "our own natural wealth and would cost nothing but labor."[11] Similarly, Roger Coke proposed that idle workers be employed to reclaim wastelands.[12] Willful idleness was not to be tolerated, and there is an abundance of literature setting forth proposals to make England's population as productive as possible. This is the responsibility of government, for if people are idle, "that is for want of being rightly governed."[13]

Still another aspect of mercantilistic emphasis on the importance of labor in production is the encouragement of population growth, not for the sake of mere numbers but to increase the size of the working force. Attention was frequently called to Holland, a very prosperous country which, though it had few resources, was enriched through the industry of its people; and Spain, which was impoverished through its sparse population, though it was rich in colonial mines. Proposals to increase population by encouraging early marriage and immigration are so common to most of the English writers of this period that they cannot be typically associated with the name of any one specifically. It was generally accepted that a large population, by keeping wages close to subsistence levels, would not only reduce the cost of producing goods but would also discourage the idleness that might become associated with higher wage levels.

One of the most interesting bits of mercantilistic reasoning incorporating views on both labor and balance of payments is the argument which appeared in successive issues of the *British Merchant* regarding foreign-paid incomes.[14] Briefly, the line of reasoning pursued was that when goods were exported, foreigners would pay for the wages of the workmen employed in making them, whereas imports would involve like payments to foreigners. The obvious duty of government would therefore be to minimize

---

[9] Thomas Hobbes, *Leviathan* (London, 1691), p. 127.
[10] "England's Treasure by Forraign Trade," in McCulloch, *op. cit.*, p. 127.
[11] *Ibid.*, p. 130.
[12] Roger Coke, *A Discourse of Trade* (London, 1670), pp. 16–17.
[13] Attributed to Malachy Postlethwayt by E. A. J. Johnson, *op. cit.*, p. 287.
[14] See Johnson, *op. cit.*, chap. xv, for a complete description of these views.

foreign imports in order to achieve a favorable balance of foreign-paid income. The most desirable import is bullion, not only because it is wealth but also because it has little labor incorporated in it as compared with the manufactured commodities which England concentrated on exporting.

CONCLUDING REMARKS

During the era of mercantilism, economic behavior began to manifest itself through commercial rather than exclusively household and other noncommercial activities. Accordingly, mercantilist thinkers emphasized the importance of commerce and industry, and the role of the state in promoting economic development and national wealth. The policies that they looked to the state to pursue emphasized the growth of the labor force, by natural increase and the encouragement of immigration, and its employment in productive activities. The possibility of increasing productivity by specialization was appreciated, but the role of innovation in increasing the productivity of labor was still too infrequently observed to receive much attention. The importance of increasing efficiency in the use of land and other natural resources in order to reduce the cost of wage goods was also given considerable attention. All these measures were thought of as contributing to the maintenance of a favorable balance of trade which served to increase the supply of money and precious metals. Money was thus thought of as playing an active role in economic development because it supposedly kept rates low and prevented unfavorable price movements.

The economic analysis which emerged in connection with these recommendations was, by modern standards, crude and unsystematic. The mercantilists were practitioners rather than theorists, and their interest was in economic policy rather than in analysis. Much of their analysis was implicit in their discussions on policy, and even when given explicit formulation, it lacked the rigor that was to become associated with the inquiries of their eighteenth-century followers. Mercantilist thinkers did not, therefore, make many significant contributions to the body of economic theory, but it should not be overlooked that their inquiries did stimulate interest in economics as a science and thus prepared the way for modern analysis. They also promoted an appreciation of the relationship between economic theory and the application of theory to the solution of practical problems and the achievement of objectives. In this sense, they provided a rationale for economic analysis and encouraged its future development by making the "usefulness" of theory apparent to subsequent thinkers, even if they themselves contributed little to pure theory.

SUGGESTIONS FOR FURTHER READING

HECKSCHER, ELI. *Mercantilism*. Translated by MENDEL SHAPIRO. 2d ed. London: George Allen and Unwin, Ltd., 1955.

JOHNSON, E. A. J. *Predecessors of Adam Smith.* New York: Prentice-Hall, Inc., 1937.

KEYNES, JOHN MAYNARD. *The General Theory of Employment, Interest and Money,* chap. xxiii. New York, Harcourt, Brace & Co., 1936.

MUN, THOMAS. "England's Treasure by Forraign Trade," in JOHN R. McCULLOCH (ed.), *Early English Tracts on Commerce* (Norwich: Jarrold and Sons, Ltd., 1952).

SPENGLER, JOSEPH J. "Mercantilism and Physiocratic Growth Theory," Part I, pp. 3–54, in BERT F. HOSELITZ and JOSEPH J. SPENGLER, *et al. Theories of Economic Growth,* Glencoe, Ill.: Free Press of Glencoe Inc., 1960.

VINER, JACOB. *Studies in the Theory of International Trade,* chaps. i–ii. New York: Harper & Bros., 1937.

Chapter 3

ECONOMIC ANALYSIS DURING THE TRANSITION TO CLASSICISM

INTRODUCTION

The Environment and Leading Contributors

A reaction to mercantilistic views began in the second half of the seventeenth century which caused economic thought to enter into a transitional phase. During this phase the businessman was displaced as the chief inquirer into economic questions, and the attitude and methodological approach which later characterized the writings of the classical era slowly began to appear. The newly emerging attitude was one of increasing liberality; people began to believe that greater freedom from governmental restrictions would be advantageous to themselves as well as to the economy. This attitude reflected the gradually evolving idea that the economic system is a self-generating autonomous organism which does not require management from above, but functions best when allowed to regulate itself. A hedonistic philosophy of material gain and enjoyment, as opposed to the medieval view of the virtue of self-denial, was also gaining acceptance. According to this philosophy, prodigality is not immoral but is the life of trade. Economic progress thrives under the stimulus of self-interest and higher levels of personal consumption. Later, seventeenth- and early eighteenth-century writers gave ideological expression to these beliefs in the doctrine of laissez-faire and sought to discover the laws which govern the functioning of self-regulating economic systems.

These liberal trends in economic thinking were particularly evident in England, whose growing middle class included many who were engaged in trade and industry. France and Holland also had some early proponents of liberalism, but Italy and Germany as yet shared little disposition to displace mercantilistic ideas. Thus, it was the English writers in the main who gave currency to more liberal ideas and who prepared the ground for the development of economic theory. Before 1660, economic theory was virtually nonexistent; after 1776, with the publication of Adam Smith's *Wealth of Nations,* economics was firmly launched as a discipline.

At the beginning of the transition period, the individuals best suited by experience and interest to write on economic matters were businessmen like Josiah Child (1630–99) and Nicholas Barbon (1637–98). Child was a merchant who sold supplies to the English navy and eventually became the largest single stockholder in the East India Company.[1] His most famous work is a pamphlet, *Brief Observations,* published in 1668, in which he undertook to prove that England could equal the prosperity of the Dutch if she would follow policies which he believed to be the source of Holland's great wealth. He believed a low rate of interest to be the most important of these and was a strong advocate of a reduction of the legal rate of interest.

Nicholas Barbon was also a businessman, though he earned an M.D. degree from Utrecht in 1661. His earliest business interest was in building, and he had ample opportunity to become prosperous as a result of the destruction of most of the city of London by the Great Fire. He was also astute enough to develop the first workable plan for writing fire insurance and ventured into mortgage banking. He wrote many pamphlets on fire insurance, building, and banking, but his leading work is *Discourse on Trade* (1690).

Though the social benefits of commerce were more appreciated at the time Child and Barbon wrote than they were earlier, merchants were still not highly esteemed. On the contrary, their recommendations were so generally suspect that merchant-authors often preferred to write anonymously or preceded their writings with prefaces which denied that their policy recommendations would benefit them privately.[2] These denials notwithstanding, the fact is that private interests were seldom really subordinated to the public good, and public suspicion of merchant-supported proposals was more frequently justified than not. Their recommendations that the legal rate of interest and the bullion content of silver coins be reduced (the latter was done in 1696) provided reason for suspicion. Though the prosperity of the Dutch was generally thought to be associated with their relatively low interest rate, the fact that low interest rates would also benefit borrowers, such as Child and Barbon were, raised doubts about the honesty of their denials. Nor was the argument that devaluation would make the country richer as convincing as it might have been if it were not apparent that it would also benefit those who had hoarded bullion or old coins whose silver content had not been reduced by clipping. This was an opportunity which Barbon had as a banker, although he pointed out that banks would also profit if coins were fewer and heavier, for "nothing can be

---

[1] A most interesting account of the lives and works of some leading writers of this transitional period in the history of economic doctrine is William Letwin, *The Origins of Scientific Economics* (London: Methuen and Co., Inc., 1963).

[2] Josiah Child's *Discourse about Trade* (1690), an anonymous republication of his earlier *Brief Observations,* is typical of efforts to conceal authorship. The Preface was written by the publisher, who assured the reader that the writer was not a trader and that the manuscript came to him very accidentally.

of greater advantage to banks than scarcity of money when men will be glad to take a bank note for want of it."[3]

The recommendations which men like Barbon and Child made were virtually unsupported by any kind of economic analysis. Typically, they argued for their proposals on the ground that they had worked well previously or because current policies produced unsatisfactory results. Another technique of argumentation was to refute the objections others made against the policies they recommended. But there was no attempt to derive the general principles on which the policies recommended must necessarily rest if they were to work as was claimed. It is plain, therefore, that what was most urgently needed in order that economics make headway as a science was a deductive system which derives its conclusions from a set of premises. The only critique that can then be made is that the premises are false or inappropriate, or that the reasoning is imperfect. Failing this, the conclusions are valid, irrespective of the personal interests of the author, for the conclusions are inherent in the premises. In short, economics required the methodology which René Descartes had already introduced in his *Discourse on Method* to lay a foundation for natural science.

The method followed by Sir Dudley North (1641–91) in his pamphlet, *Discourse upon Trade,* is essentially Cartesian, though it was constructed by a man with relatively no formal education. Though he came from a family which was fairly accomplished academically, North had so little inclination for classical study that he was sent to writing school, where he became skilled in penmanship, arithmetic, and weights and measures. He then was apprenticed to a merchant with the Levant Company. Many of the next twenty years were spent abroad, principally in Turkey, where he accumulated enough from his various trading activities to return to England and a life of ease in his early forties. He had also acquired such vast technical information about every aspect of trade that in 1683 he was appointed Commissioner of Customs and later elected to Parliament.[4] It was during this period that North became increasingly aware that private and public interests frequently diverge and that it is necessary to separate the two when inquiring into economic matters. The method by which he thought this could be accomplished is described in the *Preface to Discourses* (1692) written by his brother Roger North. Here, the extent to which private interests might interfere with objective thinking in economic matters is candidly recognized, and it is asserted that objective thinking in economic matters requires that conclusions be "built on clear and evident truths." It is, in short, necessary to lay down premises that are incontrovertible and to reason from these premises to the conclusions they

---

[3] Nicholas Barbon, *A Discourse concerning Coining the New Money Lighter, in Answer to Mr. Locke's Considerations about Raising the Value of Money* (1696).

[4] Roger North, *Lives* (3 vols.; London: George Bell & Sons, 1826), Vol. II, pp. 132 ff., 153–54, 180–82.

imply. Thus the earliest beginning of deductive analysis in economics is Sir Dudley North's pamphlet, *Discourse upon Trade*. Unfortunately, this pamphlet made little impression and was soon forgotten. As was subsequently often the case in the history of economic thought, its rediscovery came too late to be of more than historical interest.

The writings of Sir William Petty and John Locke mark a turning point in the development of economics because neither was associated in even the remotest way with the business world. Sir William Petty (1623–87) served for a time in the Royal Navy before studying medicine in the Netherlands.[5] He then enjoyed an academic circle for a time but chose to leave it to serve as Physician General to the army in Ireland during the rebellion. Afterwards, he was commissioned to survey the lands which were to be distributed among Oliver Cromwell's soldiers. The experience not only familiarized him with land rents and taxes, but encouraged him to pioneer what he conceived to be an empirical approach to economic inquiry. His *Political Arithmetick* (1690) presented an impressive array of numbers concerning land, cattle, houses, shipping, gold, merchandise, people, etc.; but these were illustrative rather than actual data, so that Petty's technique was essentially that of deductive logic, in which premises and conclusions were given expression in hypothetical numerical terms. Though he liked to think of himself as an empiricist, his work is much more in the nature of a contribution to economic theory. This is particularly true of his *Treatise of Taxes and Contributions,* which predated his work on political arithmetic.

The philosopher John Locke (1632–1704) was another contributor to the literature of the transition period. He received a thoroughly classical education at Christ Church, Oxford, where he also took a medical degree.[6] Like Petty, Locke practiced his profession only on a limited scale. He became personal physician to Lord Ashley, who was Chancellor of the Exchequer, and soon also became his personal secretary and assistant. It was in this way that he was brought into contact with matters of trade, such as the proposal concerning the reduction of the interest rate. He undertook to draft a reply to Child's *Brief Observations* in which he examined, from the standpoint of natural law, the effect a reduction in the rate of interest would have. He also became so well versed in colonial problems that he was appointed in 1673 as Secretary to the Council for Trade and Plantations. He returned to private life two years later and turned his attention to works like the *Treatise of Civil Government* and the *Essay concerning Human Understanding,* which established him as one of the great philosophers of his day. But he also continued to interest himself in economic questions. Monetary problems, in particular, claimed his attention and led

---

[5] Details of Petty's life are readily available in Emil Strauss, *Sir William Petty* (London, Bodley Head, 1954).

[6] Maurice Cranston, *John Locke* (New York: Macmillan Co., 1957).

to his book *Some Considerations of the Consequences of Lowering of Interest and Raising the Value of Money*. This work examined the nature and determination of interest and rent, and the value of land, from the standpoint of natural law. He asserted that the permanence and inexorability of natural laws makes inapporpriate any law which is contrary to the laws of nature. Adherence to this principle led him to the conclusion that natural law, not man-made law, should determine interest rates and the value of coins.

Locke's approach to examining economic questions had profound implications for the development of economics. It suggested that the social universe is governed by a body of laws precisely as is the natural universe. Locke's work, therefore, helped established the pattern of later economic analysis. Whereas seventeenth-century writers typically addressed themselves directly to practical questions and policy proposals, the method of approach subsequently became to discover the principles concerning particular phenomena such as value, price, interest, etc., in order to examine the relevance of these principles to particular problems.

David Hume (1711–76) is also among the transitional thinkers whose economic writings helped to break the influence of mercantilistic principles. Though he was primarily a philosopher, his *Political Discourses* (1752) include numerous essays which contain some significant contributions to theoretical economics, the most significant of which are "Of Money," "Of Interest," "Of Commerce," and "Of the Balance of Trade."[7]

The significance of the contribution made by the Irish-born English financier Richard Cantillon (1680–1734) to economic theory is debatable; if it is judged in terms of the merit of its content, it is probably not overgenerous to regard him as the cofounder, along with Adam Smith, of the classical school. But if we judge instead on the basis of the impact he had in his own time, his role in the history of economic analysis is considerably less significant. His *Essay on the Nature of Commerce in General* was not published until twenty years after his death and then forgotten until it was rediscovered and rescued from virtual oblivion by William Jevons in 1881.[8] The most significant impact of the essay was on the Physiocrats, particularly as regards their emphasis on land as the source of wealth. Victor Riquetti, Marquis de Mirabeau had a copy, and several of the ideas developed in his *L'Ami de Homme* (1760) paralleled those introduced by Cantillon in his essay.

The subject matter of economic inquiry was also undergoing a change. Although the Industrial Revolution was not yet under way, com-

---

[7] The economic writings of Hume are available in Eugene Rotwein, *The Economic Writings of David Hume* (Edinburgh: Nelson, 1955).

[8] This essay was originally written in English and translated into French by Cantillon to make it available to a friend. It was reprinted in 1892 by G. H. Ellis for Harvard University.

mercial capitalism was already evolving into industrial capitalism. Compared with its status in the previous century, manufacturing, as contrasted with agriculture, had grown greatly in importance. New products and modes of production, new forms of enterprise and credit facilities had been developed. These changes were accompanied by the pauperization of numerous farmers, the decay of many agricultural areas, the impoverishment of many handcraftsmen, and considerable technological unemployment. During the heyday of commercial capitalism the central problem was trade and the growth of merchant capital through profitable exchange. With the growth of industry, production rather than exchange became the central problem.

Naturally, not every writer of this period found himself in conflict with every aspect of mercantilistic thinking or policy. On the contrary, all were mercantilists to some degree, though certain aspects of their thinking were closer to the ideas of Adam Smith and the Physiocrats, who wrote during the eighteenth century, than to those of their predecessors. Classification of writers such as Petty, North, Locke, Hume, and Cantillon is therefore somewhat arbitrary. They may be treated either as later or liberal mercantilists, or as forerunners of economic liberalism. While sufficient reason can be advanced for either treatment, the important thing to recognize is the transitional nature of their thought.

CHANGING CONCEPTS DURING THE TRANSITION PERIOD

The Nature of Wealth

The mercantilist concept that gold and silver are the wealth of a nation and that every effort should be made to preserve and augment the supply of precious metals was rapidly becoming outmoded during the transition period. Even some of the merchants were becoming free of the bullion illusion. Nicholas Barbon was among the first to recognize that while gold and silver have characteristics which make them particularly satisfactory for coining, there is no greater advantage to be derived from accumulating them than any other commodity. "If there could be account taken of the balance of trade, I can't see where the advantage of it could be. For the reason that's given for it—that the overplus is paid in bullion and the nation grows so much richer . . . is altogether a mistake. For gold and silver are but commodities, and one sort of commodity is as good as another so be it of the same value."[9]

Dudley North attacked another aspect of the mercantilist view of trade when he disassociated riches from gold and silver. Mercantilists viewed trade as being essentially warfare; one nation gained what the other lost. North asserted, on the contrary, that trade is mutually advantageous,

---

[9] Barbon, *op. cit.*, p. 40.

for no one will accept a smaller value in exchange than he gives up. Moreover, he asserted, it is not trade which enriches men the most, but production, particularly of manufactured goods; "he who is most diligent, and raiseth most Fruits or maketh most of Manufactory, will abound most in what others make or raise; and consequently be free from Want and enjoy most Conveniences, which is truly to be Rich, altho there were no such thing as Gold, Silver or the like amongst them."[10]

David Hume also disputed the mercantilist identification of wealth with money and trade. His essay "Of Money" asserted that money merely represents "the real strength of the community" which is "men and commodities."[11] Though he recognized that an increase in its quantity will raise prices and serve as a temporary stimulus to trade, he mentioned that the happiness of people is not affected by the quantity of money.

Hume also examined the old mercantilist dogma that the prosperity of other countries will undermine domestic employment and industry. His essay "Of the Jealousy of Trade" maintained that international specialization is the basis of prosperity and remarked that "as a British subject, I pray for the flourishing commerce of Germany, Spain, Italy and even France itself." His unique attitude eventually bore fruit in the commercial treaty concluded with France in 1786.

The Quantity Theory

Although the notion that the level of economic activity is related to the supply of money was already common in mercantilist days, John Locke gave the principle, which is now known as the quantity theory of money, a more refined statement than had been given previously. In particular, he pointed out "the necessity of some proportion of money to trade," though he recognized that it is hard to determine what that proportion should be. The quantity of money needed to carry on trade is hard to determine because it depends also on "the quickness of its circulation[;] . . . to make some probable guess we are to consider how much money it is necessary to suppose must rest constantly in each man's hands as requisite to the carrying on of trade." This recognition of the importance of the velocity of circulation was the most sophisticated treatment of the quantity theory which had yet been made. Later writers formulated these ideas on the velocity of circulation and the volume of trade with greater precision, but Locke deserves credit for a greatly improved statement of the quantity theory of money. Unfortunately, however, he was led via his quantity theory of money to advocate the desirability of an export surplus. He thought this would be to England's advantage because it would cause specie

---

[10] Dudley North, "A Discourse concerning the Abatement of Interest," in McCulloch, *op. cit.*, p. 516.

[11] David Hume, "Of Money," *Essays* (London: Longmans, Green & Co., 1912), Vol. I, p. 319.

to flow in and thereby enable her to sell at high prices and buy cheaply in other countries which have low prices because they have less bullion.

David Hume saw the fallacy of Locke's thinking on this matter. He recognized the relationship between the quantity of money, the price level, and international flows of specie. Whereas mercantilists believed that a nation can continuously accumulate gold if it has a favorable balance, Hume pointed out that it is not possible for gold to flow continuously in one direction. A nation which has a favorable balance, and therefore acquires gold, will also experience a rise in its domestic price level. This will cause it to lose its export trade and stimulate imports for domestic use. Specie will therefore always adjust itself to the actual needs of trade. Thus "a government has great reason to preserve with care its people and its manufactures. Its moneys it may safely trust to the course of human affairs."[12] Hume also examined the transformation which takes place as a primitive barter economy develops into a money economy. He noted that exchange economies experience increasing specilization and growth. The power of the state is also enhanced in a money economy, for the sovereign may then "draw money by his taxes from every part of the state, and what he receives goes farther in every purchase and payment."

Cantillon also recognized the relationship between the value of money, trade, and domestic and international prices. Starting with the assumption that new mines are discovered, he traced the spread of inflation through the economic system as a result of the additional purchasing power received by those engaged in mining. These people are able to outbid others whose incomes are fixed, with the result that the additional money will cause generally higher prices as it is absorbed into the economy, unless it is offset by an increase in the volume of trade. Rising prices in any country will quite naturally cause people to expand their purchases from countries in which prices have not yet risen. The home market will therefore become depressed, and gold will leave the country to pay for foreign imports until eventually prices will again be low enough to induce domestic buyers to buy at home rather than abroad. He concluded, therefore, that no country permanently benefits from the discovery of precious metals.

Cantillon also noted that inflationary price increases can result from an increase in the supply of paper money as well as from more metallic money. He thought that price increases resulting from increased paper money are likely to prove disastrous because money, lacking an intrinsic value, is likely to be refused acceptance, thereby touching off a precipitous decline in the price structure. This is precisely what happened in France following John Law's famous experiment with a paper currency. Cantillon refused to endorse that proposal when it was presented to him, predicting that it would have unfortunate results.

---

[12] David Hume, "Of the Balance of Trade," *ibid.*, Vol. I, p. 345.

The Propriety of Interest and Determination of Its Rate

The problem of interest, especially as regards the establishment of a legal rate, generated a large volume of literature throughout the period. The earliest of these contributions, like Josiah Child's, contained virtually no theory. Child was quite simply in favor of reducing the legal rate of interest in order to duplicate the advantages enjoyed by Dutch traders. He asserted it would make the country richer but offered no explanation why he thought it would have this effect.

Petty's views on interest were also relatively unsophisticated but do offer a theoretical explanation which relates the interest rate to the rent which land can earn. He thought that if a lender can demand repayment of a loan at any time, he is not entitled to interest. But if money is lent for a fixed period of time, the lender is entitled to "a compensation for this inconvenience which he admits against himself." Then, anticipating the Physiocratic analysis of a century later, he maintained that if the security of a loan is undoubted, the rate of interest is equivalent to the "Rent of so much Land as the money lent will buy"[13] He also suggested that if the security of a loan is in doubt, "a kind of ensurance must be interwoven with the simple natural interest."[14] These observations led him to conclude that it is useless to try to fix interest rates by law.

Nicholas Barbon, who was also opposed to fixing interest rates by law, had a more sophisticated view of the relationship between interest and rent. Land is "natural stock" and earns rent. Capital is "wrought stock"; its return is therefore like the return to land. "Interest is commonly reckoned for money, because the money borrowed at interest is to be repaid in money. But this is a mistake, for the interest is paid for stock; the money borrowed is laid out to buy goods or pay for them before bought. No man takes up money at interest to lay it by him and lose the interest of it."[15]

The "wrought stock" to which Barbon was referring is processed goods which merchants sell as opposed to the unprocessed goods farmers sell exactly as nature produces them. The farmer hires land for which he pays rent in order to acquire the natural stock, while the merchant acquires processed goods, or "wrought stock," in order to sell it. Dudley North had much the same idea when he talked of the "stock lord" who receives a return called interest for permitting others to use the property he has accumulated in the form of money.

Perhaps if Barbon's and North's inquiries had not been associated so specifically with the activities of the merchant, they would have formulated more clearly the principle of interest as the net yield of capital. That is, they

---

[13] Charles H. Hull, *Economic Writings of Sir William Petty,* 1899, reprinted by A. M. Kelley, New York, 1963–4, Vol. I, p. 48.

[14] *Ibid.*

[15] Barbon, *op. cit.,* p. 31.

did not conceive of stock as a separate and distinct factor of production which is entitled to a functional reward. Later, in the nineteenth century, "wrought stock" was plainly identified as a separate factor of production, distinct from labor and land, and entitled to a return equivalent to its net yield. But this is a much more advanced notion than either Barbon or North had of stock and its return.

Just as the seventeenth-century concept of stock related generally to money rather than real capital goods, so the explanation of interest was as a monetary rather than a real phenomenon. Thus, Locke wrote: "That which most sensibly raises the rate of interest of money is when money is little in proportion to the trade of the country."[16] North similarly applied price analysis to the explanation of interest rates. "That as more Buyers than Sellers raiseth the price of a Commodity, so more Borrowers than Lenders, will raise Interest."[17] David Hume also argued that the rate of interest depends on the demand and supply of borrowers and lenders. If there is "a great demand for borrowing but little riches to supply that demand," the rate of interest will be high. Viewing profits as interdependent with interest, he asserts that it is not the quantity of gold and silver that causes the interest rate to be high, but the volume of industry and commerce. The commercial classes, especially, contribute to a reduction of the interest rate, for their frugality and rivalry for gain reduces not only profit but interest.

Rent and the Value of Land

Though the problem of interest was frequently approached from the standpoint of the rent of land, the problem of rent was also dealt with in connection with the value of land itself. How much, asked Petty, would rent-yielding land be worth? He was apparently unaware that the value of land is related to the rate of interest. Thus, instead of capitalizing the return in terms of the rate of interest, he suggested that the purchase price that will be paid for land depends on the number of years a prospective purchaser and his immediate descendants are likely to enjoy the yield. In the *Treatise of Taxes,* he estimates that three generations of males may be expected to live concurrently for twenty-one years, and that the value of land is therefore equal to that number of times its annual rent.

John Locke, however, was aware of the relationship between the price of land and the interest rate. He reasoned that the value of land depends on the income that can be derived from it, and that the value of land and its income bear the same relationship to each other as the principal of a loan bears to the interest it earns. The value of land is established by capitalizing its rental income in terms of the interest rate. Thus, given a certain rental

---

[16] From Locke's early manuscript on interest in Letwin, *op. cit.,* App. V, p. 278.

[17] North, "A Discourse concerning the Abatement of Interest," in McCulloch, *op. cit.,* p. 522.

income, the value of land will be raised if the interest rate in terms of which it is capitalized is lowered.

The Value of Commodities

The problem of the value of commodities was also beginning to be of concern to the thinkers of the transition period, although it was not yet a distinct topic of inquiry for most. Petty's value theory must, for example, be extracted from his inquiry into the "mysterious nature" of rent. Rent, he maintained, is the agricultural surplus which remains after the seed and the farmer's subsistence are deducted from the proceeds of his harvest. This view of rent as a differential surplus, which is price-determined rather than price-determining, anticipates by some 150 years the theory of rent which, during the classical era, was to become associated with David Ricardo. Petty thought that the value of an agricultural worker's product in excess of his own subsistence may be considered as rent. Since the value of a laborer was regarded as the cost of his subsistence, the monetary value of his product would be equal to the amount of gold that could be produced in the same labor time as the worker's food. Thus, if equivalent amounts of labor time are involved in producing different commodities, they would tend to have equal values in exchange for one another. Labor time, therefore, became the common denominator of all values for Petty. He thus foreshadowed the labor theory of value which subsequently was associated with Adam Smith, David Ricardo, and Karl Marx.

Although Petty considered labor more important than land in creating value, he also struggled with the problem of attributing some part of value to land. He maintained that all things should be measured by "two natural denominations, which is Land and Labor," and regarded the establishment of a natural par between these two elements as a major problem of political economy. This would imply that rent is price-determining and that land and labor are joint determinants of value. Petty struggled with this difficulty time and again, but he was unable to resolve it.

Cantillon arrived at essentially the same explanation of value as Petty. He attributed value to the amount of labor and land required in production; the cost of labor and materials drawn from land were seen as determining the "intrinsic value" of commodities. The latter would, he thought, never vary. But the market price will fluctuate above or below the intrinsic value, depending on the state of demand and supply. By demonstrating how increasing or decreasing demand will raise or lower the price of a commodity and thereby encourage or discourage production, Cantillon advanced an explanation of the nature and functioning of the price system as the automatic mechanism through which an otherwise unregulated economy regulates itself. This view of the self-regulatory nature of a price-directed economy was later to become the core of the classical and neoclassical systems of economics. Thus, Cantillon may be considered as an early classicist or, at least, as a forerunner of classical economic thinking.

CONCLUDING REMARKS

The period of the transition, which began about the middle of the seventeenth century and lasted roughly until *The Wealth of Nations,* is usually regarded as the "dark age" which preceded the Renaissance of the classical era. The general impression is that little of interest happened during this transition period with respect to economics. Viewed in this light, the ideas in Smith's great classic appear to have sprung, full-blown, from one mind. This conception of the intellectual climate of the transition period is, however, quite inaccurate, for it was in fact an era which was animated by many inquiring minds. While economics had not yet become established as a separate discipline, perhaps because there was so much theological and political controversy and such great interest in the natural sciences, the ground from which the classical tradition subsequently germinated was being prepared. It was necessary for mercantilistic ideas of long standing to be sloughed away before the newer, more liberal ideas could take hold. It was necessary for a new conception of the economic order to be established, namely, the conception that the economic order is essentially a self-regulating organism. Medieval attitudes toward the propriety of acquisition and consumption also needed to be replaced by a hedonistic psychology which regarded material self-interest as being not only proper but essential to prosperity. All these changes in attitudes and values were taking place during the transition period. Without them, Smith's work could not have commanded the reception it got. From this point of view, the philosophic and attitudinal changes of the period are even more significant than are the actual theoretical developments, though the latter are by no means insignificant. The distinction between money and wealth, and the explanation of the international specie flow mechanism especially, are principles which rank with those discovered by classical writers; and some of the inquiries into the determination of the interest rate which were made during the transition are more advanced than many which followed.

SUGGESTIONS FOR FURTHER READING

CHALK, A. F. "Natural Law and the Rise of Economic Individualism in England," *Journal of Political Economy,* Vol. LIX, No. 4, August, 1951, pp. 332–47.

HORSEFIELD, J. KEITH. *British Monetary Experiments, 1650–1760.* Cambridge: Harvard University Press, 1960. Especially Part II.

JOHNSON, E. A. J. *Predecessors of Adam Smith.* New York: Prentice-Hall, Inc., 1937.

LETWIN, WILLIAM.   *The Origins of Scientific Economics*. London: Methuen & Co., Ltd., 1963.

NORTH, DUDLEY.   "Discourses on Trade" (1691), in JOHN R. McCULLOCH (ed.), *Early English Tracts on Commerce* (Norwich: Jarrold and Sons, Ltd., 1952).

ROBERTSON, H. M.   *Aspects of the Rise of Economic Individualism*. Cambridge: England, The University Press, 1933.

SEWALL, H. R.   "The Theory of Value before Adam Smith," *Publications of the American Economic Association*, Series III, ii, No. 3 (1901).

VICKERS, DOUGLAS.   *Studies in the Theory of Money, 1690–1776*. Philadelphia: Chilton Co., 1959.

Chapter 4

THE CONTRIBUTIONS OF

THE PHYSIOCRATS TO

ECONOMIC ANALYSIS

INTRODUCTION

Origins and Philosophy of Physiocracy

The reaction against the doctrines and restrictive practices of mercantilism was, if anything, more violent in France than in England. France had prospered little from the industry-stimulating measures introduced by Jean Baptiste Colbert, since the French economy, unlike the English, was basically agrarian. Added to this, the wealth of the country was drained by unsuccessful colonial wars and extravagant expenditures at court, both of which required high taxes to support them. The difficulty of assessing personal income and the exemption of the clergy and nobility from taxation caused the burden to fall almost exclusively on the commoner landowner and the peasant. This impoverished the rural classes to such an extent that demands for reform became increasingly insistent until, at last, they culminated in the French Revolution. But prior to this great explosion, the Physiocrats presented an eloquent plea for "revolution from above."

Some of the observations and recommendations which were made by the Physiocrats were anticipated in the writings of Pierre Boisguilbert (1646–1714) and Sébastien de Vauban (1633–1707). Both of these writers were reacting to the adverse conditions which prevailed in France during the period following the reign of Louis XIV. Understandably they put their greatest emphasis on tax reforms and the abolition of export duties on grain. Boisguilbert, foreshadowing the Physiocrats, regarded land as the primary source of wealth and criticized the mercantilist emphasis on precious metals. He viewed wealth as consisting of the supply of necessary and convenient things required by man to satisfy his diverse wants. The primary requisite for the creation of wealth he maintained, is the elimination of man-made obstructions to natural harmony, such as tax abuses, customs duties, monopolistic guild practices, court extravagances, and large public debts. Vauban made tax reform his particular concern and proposed that a single poll tax replace all other direct taxes. Unfortunately, the reforms proposed by Boisguilbert and Vauban brought them dishonor rather than praise. The absolute monarchy of the *ancien régime* tolerated little criticism. Their writings were suppressed; but their ideas nevertheless survived, and many were incorporated in reform efforts which came later with the Physiocrats. Pleas for reform and even programs for reform, such as the *Project for the Royal Tithe* which Vauban offered in 1707, were apparently inadequate by themselves. What was needed, in addition, was a philosophy and a systematic analysis which would provide a rationale for reform by explaining the source of the ills which plagued the French economy. The Physiocrats, or "Economists," as they preferred to call themselves, were to supply these needs.

An abundance of materials had been stored up by the middle of the eighteenth century out of which a new discipline, to be known as economics, would soon emerge. Though Greek philosophy was its ultimate source, its beginnings were more precisely to be found in the emergence of modern science during the post-Renaissance period. The investigations and researches which culminated in the Newtonian system indirectly stimulated the rise of social science. The recognition that physical events obey certain laws made it reasonable to inquire whether there also are laws governing human events, and whether ways of improving the social environment might be prescribed on the basis of these principles. The Physiocrats scrutinized social processes with a view to discovering causation and a principle of regularity, just as Sir Isaac Newton and other physical scientists had done before them with respect to natural phenomena, and as John Locke had attempted to do with the social phenomena he examined.

The Physiocratic system is primarily associated with François Quesnay, physician to Madame de Pompadour and later Louis XV, who, partly as a result of his early experiences with farming and partly as a result of his belief in the primacy of nature, interested himself in the plight of the French peasantry and its relationship to the ills of France. Quesnay directed his inquiries toward explaining the nature and creation of wealth, and the relationship which the mode of its circulation bears to the well-being of the economy. The inference was plain hat something definite might be done to prevent the progressive diminution of the country's wealth which had been taking place during the long and ill-fated reign of the Bourbon kings. The idea of reform was, of course, not new. What made the Physiocratic program unique was, first, that it was articulated with a theoretical system which purported to explain the creation, circulation, and reproduction of the nation's wealth; and secondly, that it was predicated on the continuance of monarchy and the existing class structure.

The term "Physiocracy," which was first used by Dupont de Nemours, means "the rule of nature." Quesnay accepted the idea that a divine providence has ordained the existence of a universal and inherently perfect natural order. Conformity to the laws of the natural order will insure maximum happiness, whereas infringement of the fixed laws of nature will call forth correspondingly disastrous consequences. Man, as a rational creature created by a benevolent Providence, will tend to conform in all his activities to a design above himself. This philosophy suggests that it is both unnecessary and undesirable for governments to regulate. Legislation which conforms to nature is superfluous, and that which is in conflict with nature is certain to be defeated because, in the long run, the law of nature is supreme. This is the basis for the famous maxim, *Laissez faire, laissez passer,* which was to figure so importantly in the subsequent development of economic theory. With it, the Physiocrats unavoidably invited comparison between France as it was under the absolute rule of a divine right monarchy and the France that might have been under a system of perfect liberty.

So great was the discrepancy between the *ancien régime* and the ideal that it would appear that the Physiocratic philosophy and doctrines heralded the Revolution, although it was not their intent to alter the social status quo. On the contrary, the Physiocrats were enthusiastic supporters of the monarchy and nobility. To them, the rule of nature meant not lawlessness, but rather the absence of unnecessary legislation. The function of the sovereign is merely to give expression to the divine wisdom that already rules the universe, and in so doing, he should be an absolute despot. Contrary to the popular notion that the task of governing is extremely complicated, the Physiocrats maintained that in practice, there would be relatively little for kings to do, for every reasonable person would obey the rule of nature if only he were acquainted with it.[1] Every enlightened individual would recognize that the king is merely the instrument through which the laws of nature are carried out. The Physiocrats thus held the principle of political liberty in utter contempt, because elected representatives cannot always link personal and group interests for the entire nation. Only the hereditary monarch, permanent and without self-interest, can harmonize the interests of all. It should be obvious, therefore, that the Physiocrats were not proponents of democratic self-government. Nor was theirs a plea for benevolent despotism. They wanted merely an enlightened despot, who, recognizing that the only road to happiness is to acquiesce to the rule of nature, would bring about a revolution from above.

ECONOMIC ANALYSIS

Methodology

The work of Quesnay and his disciples marks the beginning of economics as a discipline. Using the process of abstraction, they were the first to

---

[1] An oft-repeated anecdote associated with this contention concerns the visit of Mercier de la Rivière to Catherine the Great of Russia to advise her concerning the new constitution. He is purported to have told her that the wisest policy she could follow was simply to let things alone to take their own course, for nature would rule, to which advice she responded by wishing him a prompt goodbye.

seek out the existence of general laws according to which economic phenomena behave. By closing the gap between free will and natural law that had so long divided theology and science, they laid the groundwork for the systematic study of social phenomena on an empirical level. Philosophers such as Descartes, Hobbes, and Hume had already abandoned acceptance of supersensual sources of knowledge, holding instead that knowledge is achieved postnatally and that the facts thus perceived constitute the whole of human wisdom. The Physiocrats dealt with facts, the facts of a society sick with abuses and already on the verge of revolution; and from these observations they constructed their theory of an ideally functioning economy which would tend automatically to achieve optimum results but for the disturbances injected by human beings uneducated in the ways of the natural order. While the predetermined providentialism which made their economic laws inexorable in their operation is quite different from the "necessity" attaching to generalizations known to us today as economic laws, they nevertheless laid additional groundwork for Adam Smith and all those after him who used the deductive method. They also constitute the first group of thinkers whose ideas were, in general, so acceptable to all that most individual identities, with the exception of Quesnay, are lost in that of the group as a whole, so that they are the first thinkers to constitute a "school of thought."

Concepts

We are indebted to the Physiocrats for an analysis of production and wealth which, although imperfect, is greatly in advance of mercantilist views. In mercantilist thinking, it will be remembered, wealth consisted of treasure, and it was believed that only trade could make a nation prosperous. The Physiocrats maintained that wealth consists of goods which are produced with the aid of nature in industries such as farming, fishing, and mining. This line of thought is in advance of the mercantilist idea, even though the restriction of wealth to the output of the primary industries is unduly narrow.

Their belief that only land is the source of wealth led them to think that only the labor engaged in primary occupations, farming in particular, is productive. They conceived of the economy as being comprised of three classes: the "proprietor class," the "cultivator class," and the "sterile class." The nature of each of these classes and its role in the economy are to be understood and appraised in relationship to the creation of what the Physiocrats called the *produit net,* or net product. A class is productive only if it is capable of producing a net product, that is, an output of greater value than its own subsistence requirements. The cultivator class, whose members are primarily tenant farmers renting land from the proprietors, are uniquely able to do this. They and others who work with the land, such as miners, fishermen, and the like, were thought to be the only ones capable of producing a net product because they alone have the advantage of the assistance of nature. Nature, as it were, labors alongside those engaged in primary pursuits. Its bounty manifests itself in a net product which is a true surplus in excess of the subsistence requirements of the labor involved. The sterile class, on the other hand, which includes all those not belonging to the other two classes, produces no such surplus. Finished products produced by artisans, for example, have a value in excess of the raw materials they embody, which is equivalent only to the labor expended in the transformation process. There is therefore no surplus associated with their efforts, and this is the reason why they are termed sterile or unproductive. While only the cultivators and others engaged in primary occupations are members of the productive class, it must be emphasized that it is the land rather than their labor which is the source of the surplus.

The status of the proprietors in Quesnay's social classification is not a matter of common agreement, nor was Quesnay himself consistent in his earlier and later writings. In his earlier expositions, he regards the proprietors as being sterile because they are not directly engaged in raw material production. This suggests that he thought of their rental incomes as being unearned. Later, he took the position that landowners are at least partly productive because they maintained the permanent improvements made on land and also performed the necessary functions of government. Mercier de la Rivière and Abbé Baudeau, two of Quesnay's more ardent followers, both took the position that the landlords are productive because they, or their forebears, bore the original cost of clearing and draining the land, and that these efforts gave them a claim to its fruits which took precedence over those of the present cultivators. In any event, the Physiocrats reasoned that in order to preserve the flow of the net product to the landlord, the cultivators, like the artisans, are entitled only to subsistence.[2]

The Physiocrats regarded the activity of artisans as considerably more acceptable than that of those engaged in trade and finance, for those so engaged do add value to the raw materials they fabricate. The incomes they receive are therefore earned and tend to equal the values they create, and they have legitimate values to exchange against agricultural commodities. Their presence in the economy is necessary to maintian a *bon prix* for farm commodities. Needless to say, however, manufacturing is desirable only if it does not diminish the agricultural market or inhibit the growth of agricultural capital.

---

[2] To classify artisans, domestic servants, merchants, financiers, and anyone else who is not a cultivator as "sterile" is obviously an unfortunate and inconsistent choice of terms, for it does not distinguish between those who are, within the framework of Physiocratic thinking, capable of producing their own subsistence and those who are not. Quesnay himself was not completely consistent, for in an unpublished article, "Hommes," he said that domestic servants may be indirectly productive if they free some of the energies of the agricultural classes. See Henry Higgs, *The Physiocrats* (New York: Macmillan Co., 1897), p. 127.

Since the primary industries, agriculture in particular, are the source of the net product upon which the prosperity of the nation rests, agriculture would be encouraged above all in an ideally functioning economy. This would require that the number of persons engaged in trade and finance be kept to an absolute minimum. The Physiocrats viewed their activities with disdain because they thought them incapable of producing any new values whatever. They were thought of as being merely engaged in exchanging values. Some middlemen were of course regarded as necessary to the functioning of the economy; but, maintained Quesnay, retailers are present in far greater numbers than is required for the distribution of goods. Moreover, the large merchant capitalists are engaged in *trafic* which is frequently speculative and directed toward a favorable balance of trade, thereby helping artificially to channel resources into industry, to the consequent detriment of agriculture. The incomes they receive are parasite incomes which can only represent a deduction from the net product. Since they themselves produce no values, and the farmers and artisans receive no more than their subsistence, it is certain that they are supported out of the net product. This injury to the economy is compounded by the waste of much of their income on luxury commodities which are subsidized by the state or imported from abroad.

The "Tableau Economique"

The Physiocrats regarded their description of the creation and circulation of wealth among the three classes to be their primary contribution to the science of economics. Inspired by William Harvey's discovery of the circulation of blood in the human body, Quesnay constructed a table which, by means of zigzag lines crossing over from one column to another, as in Figure 4–1, is intended to demonstrate the interdependence of economic classes which nourish and sustain one another by means of their expenditures.

The *Tableau Economique* is the first attempt to demonstrate the nature and achievement of equilibrium from a macroeconomic point of view. It depicts an economy which is assumed to be closed and stationary; that is, foreign trade is absent, and savings are equal to the replacement needs of capital. It is also assumed that there is private property in land, the owners receiving rent from the cultivators who supply their own capital and employ whatever wage labor they require. The analysis is limited to the agricultural sector of the economy; and the net product, which is the focal point of the analysis, is explicitly the output of the agricultural sector. No attention is directed to the sterile sector of the economy nor to individual enterprises or financial organizations, and all exchanges are interclass exchanges rather than interindividual exchanges. In short, the *Tableau* is designed to explain the manner in which the net product is created and circulated among the three classes of society and ultimately reproduced the following year.

Quesnay's table consists of three columns which are headed "Expenditures Relative to Agriculture," "Expenditures from Revenue," and "Sterile Éxpenditures Relative to Industry." That the circulation of both goods and money is involved is not entirely clear from the *Tableau,* though it is implicit in the analysis. It is, however, stated by Baudeau and implied in Quesnay's discussions that at the end of the harvest the farmers have the money stock of the nation as well as the economy's entire net product. The size of the net product reflects the capital investment (*advances annuelles*) made in agriculture during the year. Such investments are assumed by Quesnay to produce a net product of 100 percent over and above the expenses of production, which are taken to include the farmer's profit. Thus, if 2,000 livres are invested, there will be a net product of 2,000 livres available to be paid to the landlords as rent. Payment of these rents, shown by dotted horizontal lines moving from the first column to the second, initiates the circular flow of money and goods during the ensuing year.[3] Landlords' expenditures out of the incomes they receive are assumed to be directed in equal proportions toward the purchase of agricultural products and products produced by the artisans and other members of the so-called "sterile class." Lines moving outward from the center column to the left and to the right illustrate the expenditure streams by which purchasing power is circulated from the proprietor class to the other two classes of society in return for the products they produce. By expending its revenue of 2,000 livres equally upon agricultural and nonagricultural products, the proprietor class has caused both the productive and the sterile classes to receive 1,000 livres, out of which they purchase their subsistence needs, raw materials, capital requirements, services of various kinds, etc.

Since the result of expenditures made on primary products, as represented by the flow of purchasing power to the column on the left, is quite different from that associated with the expenditures on manufactured products or services, these two expenditure streams must be examined separately. All expenditures directed toward production on the land, whether in agriculture, mining, fishing, or forestry, will yield a net product which Quesnay assumes throughout to be 100 percent. Thus a net product of 1,000 livres is again created and is paid as rent to the landlords, as shown by dotted horizontal lines moving from the first column to the second. This is the amount over and above the farmer's expenditures, including replacement of his capital and his profit. Actually, the income of the farmer in Quesnay's *Tableau* is really equivalent to a wage of management and interest and capital rather than profit. Profit, in its modern-day

---

[3] The livre is a former French money of account originally equal to a pound of silver. It was gradually reduced in value and replaced by the franc.

conception, is thought of as a reward for the entrepreneurial function of risk bearing. The concept of the entrepreneur and a distinct income share rewarding his function was to be introduced subsequently by Jean Baptiste Say.

Assuming once more that landlord revenues, which now amount to 1,000 livres, are equally divided between purchases from the productive class and the sterile class, 500 livres will again be spent on products of the land. This investment will again yield a net product of 100 percent, or an

FIGURE 4–1

THE "TABLEAU ECONOMIQUE"*

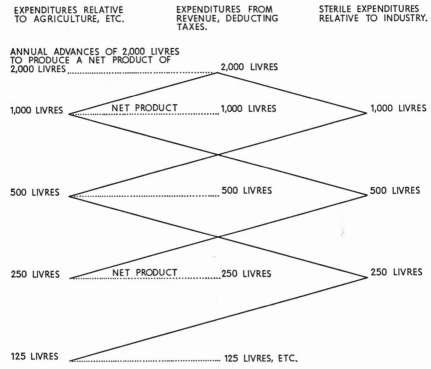

EXPENDITURES RELATIVE TO AGRICULTURE, ETC.

EXPENDITURES FROM REVENUE, DEDUCTING TAXES.

STERILE EXPENDITURES RELATIVE TO INDUSTRY.

ANNUAL ADVANCES OF 2,000 LIVRES TO PRODUCE A NET PRODUCT OF
2,000 LIVRES .... 2,000 LIVRES

1,000 LIVRES   NET PRODUCT .... 1,000 LIVRES   1,000 LIVRES

500 LIVRES   500 LIVRES   500 LIVRES

250 LIVRES   NET PRODUCT .... 250 LIVRES   250 LIVRES

125 LIVRES .... 125 LIVRES, ETC.

* From a presentation by Marquis de Mirabeau in "Elements de la Philosophie Rurale."

additional 500 livres, which will flow to the landlords as rent. Each subsequent expenditure for the products of the productive sector will reproduce itself in the same way. It would, however, complicate the table unnecessarily to follow the expenditure of successive rental payments. The *Tableau* shown in Figure 4–1, therefore, traces only the circulation of the first 2,000 livres.

Unlike expenditures made on primary products, landlord purchases from the sterile class are incapable of facilitating the creation of a net product. Returning to the assumption that landlords expend their revenue of 2,000 livres equally on the products from the other two classes, the sterile class is now also in receipt of 1,000 livres. This amount is shown on the right side of the table and represents all expenditures in the economy except those associated with the extractive industries. It includes such items as interest payments, transportation costs, purchases of foreign goods and services, payments to domestics, and lodgings, as well as payments for manufactured goods. Again assuming an equal division of expenditures, one half, or 500 livres, is spent on the products of the extractive industries, and the other on the products and services of the other members of the sterile class. Thus, one half of their revenues, as indicated by the diagonal lines moving to the left-hand side of the table, are used "productively" and will result in a net product, and the other half is consumed "unproductively" and is therefore not conveyed to the left side of the table. All expenditures made by the landlords and artisans on products produced by the extractive industries facilitate new investment in these fields and thus assist in the creation of a net product. Conversely, if the consumption of goods and services provided by the sterile classes increases, it will be at the expense of agricultural products and therefore will precipitate a decline in annual advances and annual reproduction. Excessive expenditure by the sterile classes or by others on their products was seen as inimical to the well-being of the entire economy because it destroyed the pattern of expenditures which the Physiocrats regarded as essential to the prosperity of the nation.

They were concerned also about the rate of savings and, unlike most thinkers who were to follow them, did not consider savings in the economy to be desirable, regardless of their source or the use to which they are put. They saw money as more than the "wheel of circulation" Smith thought it to be. They were concerned with hoards and the impact which these would have on the *bon prix* of agricultural products and, therefore, the net product. The manner of living pursued by the landlords, especially the king, as the largest landholder, and members of the sterile class therefore determine not only the kind of economic activity conducted in the nation, but also the level of national wealth. The moral of this observation is obvious and is the basis for most of the reform measures proposed by the Physiocrats.

The Physiocrats, their followers, and admirers considered that this demonstration of the circular flow of money and goods had great significance. Typical of the esteem in which it was held was the observation of Mirabeau that there have been three great inventions since the world began. The first is writing, the second is money, and the third is the economic table.[4]

---

[4] Higgs, *op. cit.*, p. 57.

PROPOSALS FOR REFORM

Tax Reform

The real meaning of the *Tableau* emerges when its pure theory is articulated with Physiocratic proposals for reform.[5] The essence of the theory which the *Tableau* intends to support and demonstrate is that only nature can produce a net product and that an ideal economy would maintain only those activities and practices which would not encroach upon its creation. France, under the Louises, was far from this ideal. It suffered a variety of tax abuses, trade impediments on a national as well as an international level, an unnecessarily large merchant class, an unsound agricultural organization, monopolized industrial enterprises, and an ever-expanding public debt associated with unsuccessful colonial wars and lavish court expenditures.

Proposals for tax reform had long been a central issue in France. In a predominantly agricultural country, it is obvious that the bulk of governmental revenues had to be derived from the land, especially in view of the difficulty of taxing less tangible forms of wealth. Tradition, however, exempted the clerical and lay nobility from the *taille*, as the land tax was known, thus shifting the bulk of the taxes to the third estate. The burden imposed thereby on the poor, miserable peasant became intolerable; but what is more, the revenues collected fell so short of the needs of government that large-scale public loans from professional speculators and financiers were necessary. Many of these individuals further enriched themselves through the privilege of tax farming as well as farming out trading rights in certain commodities. Much of the fortune they accumulated tended to be drained into speculation at home or abroad, or hoarded. In either case the Physiocrats believed these practices lessened the demand for agricultural commodities and contributed to the impoverishment of agriculture. However, these moneyed interests became so essential to the sovereign that it was virtually impossible for men such as Richelieu, Colbert and Turgot to introduce economy measures in the court.

The Physiocrats proposed not only that hereditary land tax exemptions be eliminated, but also that the entire complex conglomeration of taxes currently levied be replaced by one single tax, the *impôt unique,* to which all landholders would be subject according to their respective shares of the net product. Needless to say, this proposal met violent opposition not only because of the financial burden it would have imposed on those previously free from taxes, but also because it would have deprived them of a cherished symbol of class status.

The logic of the Physiocratic proposal was quite clear and simple.

---

[5] An interesting interpretation of Physiocracy is given by Norman J. Ware, "The Physiocrats: A Study in Economic Rationalization," *American Economic Review,* Vol. XXI, No. 4 (December, 1931).

Only land was capable of yielding a net product, or surplus, in excess of the subsistence requirements of those who labored on it. The supply price of laborers' services tended to be no more than the value they added to the product; and consequently, they were regarded as being incapable of bearing taxes. Any taxes levied on them, reasoned the Physiocrats, came to rest ultimately on the only possible source of payment, namely, the net product. We encounter here, in embryonic form, our modern theory of tax shifting, according to which taxes can under certain circumstances be shifted forward to the purchasers of the product by being added to the price they pay, or shifted backward to the factors of production if it is possible to reduce the payments made to them. The Physiocrats thought of tax shifting not in this, the modern sense, but rather associated it with the reduction of the net product that would take place if taxes were imposed on the members of the cultivator or sterile classes. They reasoned that if taxes were levied on the farm laborers, it would necessarily reduce their ability to finance the next crop, thereby reducing the net product that would become available after the next harvest. In this way, the proprietor class would come to bear the burden of the tax. In like manner, if the tax were imposed on the sterile class, it would reduce their purchases from the cultivators, which would diminish the net product. Thus the Physiocrats reasoned that it would be sounder and more economical to levy a tax on the net product in the first instance. It was suggested that this *impôt unique* would not need to absorb more than one third of the net product. They expected that if expenditures were curbed and the productivity of agriculture was increased, a levy of this size would be adequate to meet the revenue needs of the state.

The Reorganization of Agriculture

The improvement of agricultural productivity was regarded as fundamental to the successful functioning of the single-tax system, and this the Physiocrats proposed to accomplish by reorganizing agriculture on a more capitalistic basis. French agriculture was typically conducted on a small scale, each individual tenant farmer cultivating a small acreage with a minimum investment. Only by the introduction of *grande culture* in the place of the present *petite culture* could agricultural productivity be enhanced, and thereby the net product be substantially increased. From the standpoint of the social and economic structure, this would of course mean that the relatively large number of small peasant farmers would be superseded by relatively few capitalistic farmers, who would be able to introduce the more progressive methods of production that are practical only when conducted on a larger scale. From the standpoint of its impact on productivity, the Physiocratic proposal for agricultural reorganization undoubtedly makes sound sense, but it should also be obvious that a measure which promised to convert a major portion of the land-hungry peasantry into wage labor was not likely to gain popular support.

Trade

It has already been noted that the Physiocrats regarded the activities of traders as unproductive, because they thought that trade merely involved the exchange of equal values. Such activities were therefore thought to be incapable of producing new wealth. This was considered to be the case whether the exchange took place on a domestic level or internationally. The variance between this line of reasoning and that of the mercantilists should be immediately obvious. The latter held that trade is the only way to increase the wealth of a nation and that every effort should be made to secure a favorable balance. Under Colbert, trade in France was strictly regulated with precisely this end in view. Clearly, the Physiocrats were to find themselves in opposition to both the mercantilist and Colbertist points of view, for both of these were directed toward achieving a favorable balance of trade. In terms of Physiocratic thinking, the latter was not merely incapable of creating any new wealth, but actually tended to diminish wealth by reducing the demand for agricultural products.

How, then, can we explain the Physiocratic support of free trade? Is it not inconsistent with their position that commerce is unproductive? Present-day supporters of free trade, after all, do so on the ground that it will enhance the wealth of the participating countries, not by increasing their gold holdings, but by securing them a greater quantity and better quality of goods and services than they could enjoy on the basis of their domestic production alone. But this is not the line of reasoning pursued by the Physiocrats, although theirs is the first free-trade position of note, and they are generally regarded as the first supporters of international laissez-faire. This is not to say that they were greatly enthusiastic about free trade as we think of it today. Rather, they were opposed to the kind of restrictive measures that, at their time, typically impeded the movement of goods, domestically as well as internationally. The export of corn was prohibited, while imports were permitted, and precisely the reverse set of regulations was applied to manufactured products. This they considered incompatible with the natural order.

CRITICISMS OF PHYSIOCRATIC VIEWS

Say and the Law of Markets

Physiocratic denial that money is always promptly restored to the income stream called forth the criticism of Jean Baptiste Say (1767–1832). Say had considerable business experience before he was appointed to a chair of political economy at the Conservatoire des Arts et Metiers and later the College de France. Like the Physiocrats Say recognized that interruptions to the circular flow are injurious to the economy, but he denied that prosperity required a pattern of consumption in which a large fraction of total expenditures is for raw produce. In the first edition of his *Traité* (1803), Say presented the thesis, later known as the law of markets, that production and not consumption underlies prosperity. He reasoned that production automatically generates the purchasing power required for consumption. The surplus of each producer exchanges against that of others, with money serving as a medium of exchange, and the aggregate value of the goods demanded to be bought is exactly equivalent to the value of those given in exchange for them.[6] It is possible for too much of one product to be produced, on occasion, to clear the market at a satisfactory price; but it is impossible to produce too much of all products, since the aggregate demand for products is identical with the aggregate supply which has been produced.

Say used his law of markets to criticize those who, like the Physiocrats, argued that "parsimony" results in underconsumption and overproduction, and that unproductive consumption is better than frugality. He argued, on the contrary, that consumption is an effect of production and that it is necessary to curb unnecessary unproductive consumption because saving is necessary to facilitate capital formation. The sixth edition of his *Traité* specifically emphasized the importance of frugality to the progress of opulence.[7] While this view coincided substantially with that of Adam Smith, whose work Say undertook to interpret for French readers, the entire question of the relationship between saving, investment, and prosperity was shortly to become a very controversial issue.

Adam Smith and the Productivity Concept

Though Smith had great admiration for many aspects of Physiocratic thinking, he correctly considered their concept of wealth as originating only in the agricultural sector to be unduly restrictive. He thought that they erred greatly in representing artisans, manufacturers, and merchants as altogether unproductive.

> We should not call a marriage barren or unproductive, though it produced only a son and a daughter to replace the father and the mother, and though it does not increase the number of human species, but only continued it as it was before. . . . A marriage which affords three children is certainly more productive than a marriage which affords only two, so the labour of farmers and country labourers is certainly more productive than that of merchants, artificers and manufacturers. The superior produce of one class, however, does not render the other barren or unproductive.[8]

---

[6] Jean Baptiste Say, *Traité* (1st ed., 1803), pp. 175–77.

[7] Say, *Traité* (6th ed., 1827), pp. 112–22.

[8] Adam Smith, *An Inquiry into the Nature and Causes of the Wealth of Nations,* Ernest Rhys edition (London: Everyman's Library, 1910), Vol. II, pp. 168–69.

These criticisms, while interesting and constructive, indicate that Smith himself made an untenable distinction between productive and unproductive labor. Actually, the idea that only agricultural labor is productive is somewhat difficult to comprehend, even within the confines of Physiocratic thinking, since the Physiocrats maintain that it is really nature that is the source of the net product rather than labor. For how can they justify the receipt of the net product by landowners if they themselves are not productive? Are they not mere parasites enjoying fruits they did not bring forth? The high respect in which the landowners were held certainly gives no evidence of this point of view. To them, the existence of private property was a part of the natural order, and landed proprietors existed by the will of God. In short, the right of private property is regarded as a divine institution from which the prior claim to the net product by the landlords is derived. This line of reasoning seems metaphysical to the modern reader but it has been suggested by the authors of a work which is now a classic that recognition of the fact that the Physiocrats knew no organization of society other than a feudalistic one may have persuaded them of the necessity of landed property in much the same way that Aristotle defended slavery.[9]

CONCLUDING REMARKS

The Physiocrats concerned themselves with both the level of economic activity and the allocation of resources. The crucial factor, in their view, insofar as the level of economic activity is concerned, is that the continuity of the circular flow be maintained by means of an appropriate pattern of consumption. It is not consumption as such which is required, they thought, but the kind of consumption that will cause a sufficient portion of national income to be spent on a raw produce.

Money was regarded as being essentially a medium of exchange which facilitated the transfer of goods and services among the three classes. Thus the *Tableau* emphasized the real as opposed to the pecuniary nature of exchange and the importance of expenditures in maintaining the circular flow. Their emphasis on the interdependence of production and consumption was probably the inspiration of Say's law, though Say emphasized the primacy of production as opposed to consumption, thereby disputing not only the importance of agricultural as opposed to other kinds of production but also the importance of avoiding hoarding.

Physiocratic doctrines did not attract many followers in England, though there were aspects of their thinking that Smith admired. Their views on parsimony, in particular, were not shared. It was, on the contrary, the view of Adam Smith and Jean Baptiste Say which was to predominate in

---

[9] Charles Gide and Charles Rist, *A History of Economic Doctrines* (7th. ed.), translated by R. Richards, Boston. D. C. Heath and Co. 1948, p. 41.

England. Indeed, Say's law had such a formidable influence that it served, for all practical purposes, to eliminate from theoretical speculation the question of the level of economic activity and focused attention almost entirely on the question of resource allocation and pricing. Not until the period of the 1930's was there again substantial interest in the level of economic activity and inquiry into the impact of hoarding. It is interesting to note in this connection that as crude as the Physiocratic concept of hoarding was, it is surprisingly suggestive of the Keynesian treatment, in which hoarding is related to reductions in effective demand. Theirs was a more realistic approach than that of their contemporaries and later liberal followers, who assumed that all savings are always productively invested.

We are also indebted to the Physiocrats for their demonstration of the appearance of a surplus, a phenomenon which was to occupy the attentions subsequently not only of Adam Smith and David Ricardo, but also of Karl Marx. Clearly, in the history of production, man must pass beyond the stage of bare subsistence before a surplus of any kind is a possibility. Since the earliest and simplest civilizations are fundamentally agrarian, the first appearance of a surplus is likely to be in the agricultural sector. Such an economy is not likely to be an exchange economy, but rather one in which the use values created are directly appropriated.

Although the exchanges described in the *Tableau* are expressed in terms of money, it is the circulation of the use values in which the Physiocrats are interested. Thus the problem of determining exchange value, which was to loom so importantly in the later development of economic thought, was virtually ignored by the Physiocrats. Furthermore, there was no appreciation of the subjective elements that affected the determination of value and price. The prices for which goods sold in the market were implicitly cost-of-production prices which are a summation of the subsistence costs of those who participate in making goods available for sale. Turgot, whose thinking along these lines was considerably more advanced than that of his contemporaries, appreciated that there were many factors an individual would take into consideration in valuing a good. But it remained for Étienne de Condillac to present a more thorough consideration of value. He wrote: "Value is not an attribute of matter, but represents our sense of its usefulness, and this utility is relative to our need. It grows or diminishes according as our need expands or contracts."[10] Furthermore, he realized that scarcity, which makes want satisfaction more difficult, and abundance, which makes it less difficult, cause exchange values to be greater or less, depending upon the quantities available relative to the demand for them. Thus, he establishes not merely the psychological basis of value, but also anticipates what in the later French, English, and Austrian analysis became known as final or marginal utility, that is, the additional

---

[10] Étienne de Condillac, *Le Commerce et le gouvernement* (1776), p. 15.

satisfaction associated with the last unit of a good acquired. But it was to take approximately a hundred years before a similar approach found its way into English political economy.[11]

Although we cannot accept the Physiocrats' notion that the gross product of an economy consists only of agricultural goods nor their concept of productive labor, this does not alter the originality or usefulness of their demonstration of the production and circulation of output and income for the economy as a whole. They demonstrated conclusively that the economic process consists of a flow of goods and a flow of money income. Our modern concepts of gross national product and gross national income are based on the recognition of the fact that the total income earned in a given period of time is exactly equivalent to the value of the total product produced. Similarly, our concept of net national product is arrived at by making appropriate deductions from the gross national product. Only depreciation is deducted in the modern scheme of national income and product accounting, whereas Quesnay, deducting also the subsistence requirement (i.e., wages) of the cultivators, conceived of the net product as representing only the surplus available to the landlord as rent. However, the Physiocrats, no less than present-day national product estimators, had a concept designed to arrive at the net results of the economy's performance for a given period of time. It is perhaps unnecessary to add that they did not make quantitative estimates of the sort that are today compiled by the United States Department of Commerce.

SUGGESTIONS FOR FURTHER READING

BLOOMFIELD, A. I. "Foreign Trade Doctrines of the Physiocrats," *American Economic Review,* Vol. XXVIII, No. 4 (December, 1938).

GIDE, CHARLES, and RIST, CHARLES. *A History of Economic Doctrines,* chap. i. Translated by R. RICHARDS. 7th ed. Boston: D. C. Heath & Co., 1948.

HIGGS, HENRY. *The Physiocrats.* New York: Macmillan Co., 1897.

SPENGLER, JOSEPH J. "The Physiocrats and Say's Law of Markets," *Journal of Political Economy,* Vol. LIII (September–December, 1945). Reprinted in JOSEPH J. SPENGLER and W. ALLEN, editors, *Essays in Economic Thought: Aristotle to Marshall.* Chicago: Rand McNally & Co., 1960.

WARE, NORMAN J. "The Physiocrats: A Study in Economic Rationalization," *American Economic Review,* Vol. XXI, No. 4 (December, 1931).

---

[11] William Jevons' book *The Theory of Political Economy* was first published in 1871. See Chap. 12 below.

Chapter 5

THE CONTRIBUTION OF ADAM SMITH TO ECONOMIC ANALYSIS

INTRODUCTION

Life and Times (1723–90)

The year 1776 marks a fateful year for economics. The deposition of Turgot as Minister of Finance brought a virtual conclusion to the influence of the Physiocrats; and the publication, in the same year, of Smith's *Wealth of Nations* introduced a set of principles that became the cornerstone of what was to become the classical tradition. The efforts of Petty, Stewart, North, Cantillon, Hume, and the Physiocrats were only stepping stones to the preparation of the work which, in scope and content, was to become the point of departure for all who followed, whether in the classical tradition or in opposition to it.

Like most great works, *The Wealth of Nations* is the product of the man and the times. With respect to the times, it may be observed that during the last quarter of the eighteenth century the English business scene was already dominated by the capitalist enterpriser who hired wage labor and frequently did business using the corporate form of organization. Agriculture was still the most important industry, and the rural classes were still well off; but the technical strides being made, particularly in the textile and metalworking industries, were soon to call forth the Industrial Revolution. England had passed through its most extreme period of protectionism, and its foreign trade was making great forward progress as the huge trading companies of bygone decades gradually lost their privileges. Nevertheless, the restraints were still numerous and onerous, especially with the colonies, and the psychological moment to revolt had now come. *The Wealth of Nations* is, first and foremost, an attack against the principles and practices of mercantilism. It is not, as is sometimes erroneously contended, a plea for extending industrialization and advancing the interests of businessmen. On the contrary, Smith directs some of his most pungent criticisms against manufacturers and traders, reserving his sympathies for the workingman and his warmest plaudits for agriculture. It must also be remembered that the Industrial Revolution was still in its most embryonic stages. True, the spinning jenny and the water frame had already been invented, and James

59

Watt had patented his steam engine in 1769; but their widespread practical application was still a thing of the future. In short, the England of Smith's day was primarily commercial and agricultural rather than industrial. But it was not to take many more decades before the Industrial Revolution was to emerge.

It was also a time of changing social and political relationships. Ideas of political liberalism had come to the forefront in England even before the French Revolution sounded the call of freedom elsewhere in Europe. Within this framework, economic theory also was acquiring new concepts and broadening its scope. Cantillion's *Essay on the Nature of Commerce in General* and Stewart's *Inquiry into the Principles of Political Economy* represented a serious effort in the direction of systematic study of the operation of the economy. Petty had successfully stated the problem of value which was to become the focal point of classical theory. There were also advances in respect to understanding the nature of money and the determination of interest, and the importance and advantages of free trade. But despite the brilliance of some of these pioneering efforts, economic investigation was still far from systematic. It is the great achievement of Smith and those who followed him in the classical tradition that they brought order into a field of inquiry that was still largely haphazard and unsystematic.

What was there about Smith that made his efforts more fruitful than those of his several able contemporaries whose intellectual curiosity led them to explore along many of the same paths as he? It has often been suggested that there was nothing really unusual about Adam Smith the boy or the man. He himself is said to have remarked: "I am a beau in nothing but my books." He lived a rather uneventful life with his widowed mother, devoting himself largely to academic pursuits, although he also served as Commissioner of Customs in Edinburgh from 1778 until his death in 1790. Except for his sojourn in France as tutor to the young Duke of Buccleuch, which position brought him a lifetime pension, he traveled little. Even so, his natural talents, coupled with his educational experiences at Glasgow College and later at Balliol College, Oxford; his contacts with such associates as Francis Hutcheson, who was his teacher at Glasgow, David Hume, his friend of a lifetime, and many of the Physiocrats whom he met during his travels in France; as well as the opportunity for firsthand observation in the expanding commercial metropolis of Glasgow, enabled him to produce the great creative work which is *The Wealth of Nations*.

THE WEALTH OF NATIONS

Philosophical and Psychological Background

Smith dwelt at length on the ethical values of life before turning his attention to subjects which today constitute the major concern of economic inquiry. This is not to say that *The Wealth of Nations* was a by-product of his broader interests, but rather that it represented a capstone to his career as a philosopher. At the University of Glasgow, he lectured on the whole field of moral philosophy after the manner of his teacher, Francis Hutcheson, who classified his subject into four branches: natural theology, ethics, jurisprudence, and political economy.

The concern of moral philosophy, said Smith, is human happiness and well-being. Of this, the ancient moral philosophers were well aware, for they sought to examine "the happiness and perfection of a man, considered not only as an individual but as a member of a family, of a state, and of a great society of mankind. . . ."[1] This view was sharply different from that which had flourished during the Middle Ages, when it was believed that happiness is inconsistent with virtue and that the only true virtue is self-denial. Although the material progress of the modern world rendered the medieval view of morality increasingly indefensible, it nevertheless persisted into the eighteenth century. It was much in evidence, for example, in an essay entitled *The Fable of the Bees, or Private Vices and Publick Benefits,* written by Dr. Bernard de Mandeville. De Mandeville's thesis was that man's vices, specifically the quest for luxuries and material gain, generate wealth. His implication was that if the virtue of self-denial were practiced, material progress would come to a standstill.[2]

The *Fable* attracted wide attention; most of De Mandeville's contemporaries considered it worthy of a reply. Smith regarded his system of moral philosophy as "wholly pernicious," for it "seems to take away altogether the distinction between vice and virtue."[3] Smith himself saw the desire for worldy gain in an entirely different light. He viewed the pursuit of riches as merely one aspect of every individual's desire to better himself. This desire, says Smith, is with us from the womb to the grave and operates in every sphere of our lives. "It is not from the benevolence of the butcher, the brewer, or the baker that we expect our dinner, but from their regard to their own interest. We address ourselves not to their humanity, but to their self love, and we talk to them not of our necessity, but of their advantages."[4] Self-interest is thus seen as manifesting itself in every aspect of man's behavior and activity. In the economic sphere, it prompts the division of labor and the accumulation of capital, thus enhancing productivity. In the field of justice, it operated, Smith believed, to promote a high degree of efficiency in the English courts which tried to hear as many cases as

---

[1] Adam Smith, *An Inquiry into the Nature and Causes of the Wealth of Nations,* Vol. II, p. 255. This and the following references to this work are to the edition of Ernest Rhys (London: Everyman's Library, 1910).

[2] From the Preface.

[3] Adam Smith, *The Theory of Moral Sentiments,* p. 451. This and subsequent references to this work are to the edition published by George Bell & Sons, Ltd., 1911.

[4] Smith, *The Wealth of Nations,* Vol. I, p. 13.

possible because they functioned on the basis of the fees they collected from parties who came before them.[5] It was precisely the absence of the principle of self-interest that Smith found so deplorable with regard to English universities. His years at Oxford convinced him of the adverse affect on the quality of instruction where professors are paid without due regard for their efforts. By contrast, the teachers of ancient Greece, who were compensated on the basis of the number of students they attracted, were much more efficient, in Smith's opinion, than the majority of those he encountered at Oxford. Self-interest, then, is the motive which naturally drives men, and impediments to its operation generally have an adverse effect. Moreover, this is precisely the motive which *ought* to prevail, for, says Smith, "I have never known much good done by those who affected to trade for the public good."[6]

To some Smithian scholars, the emphasis on self-love and self-interest which we encounter in *The Wealth of Nations* appears to be somewhat at odds with the principle of sympathy advanced in his *Theory of Moral Sentiments*. That volume begins with the observation: "How selfish soever man may be supposed, there are evidently some principles in his nature which interest him in the fortune of others and render their happiness necessary to him though he derives nothing from it except the pleasure of seeing it." It is, says Smith, imagination which prompts even the mean individual to sacrifice his own interests at times to the greater interests of others, for only his own imagination enables him to have a conception of anyone else's sensations. Individual morality is thus seen as being shaped through introspective psychology. "If, upon placing ourselves in his situation, we thoroughly enter into all the passions and motives which influence it, we approve of it, by sympathy with the approbation of this supposed equitable judge. If otherwise, we enter into his disapprobation and condemn it."[7]

Our own experience thus underlies the growth of moral sentiments. If man grew up in isolation without communication, it would be impossible for him to conceive of any of these sentiments, but "bring him into society and he is immediately provided with the mirror that he wanted before."[8] We see the world through our own senses; and because we desire, above all, the sympathy and approbation of our fellowmen, it is necessary for each of us to regard his happiness not in that degree in which it appears to himself but in that degree in which it appears to mankind in general. Thus the desire of the individual for the approval of society, as well as the censure of his own conscience, tends to keep him doing right. The individual and

---

[5] *Ibid.*, Vol. II, p. 208.
[6] *Ibid.*, Vol. I, p. 400.
[7] Smith, *The Theory of Moral Sentiments*, p. 162.
[8] *Ibid.*

society move naturally toward the same end, and mankind will prosper in proportion as the individual is permitted freedom to choose his own way. Conscience and sympathy will always deter undesirable conduct in the economic sphere as well as in every other. Thus, belief in the morality of sympathy and the influence of social experience leads Smith ultimately to faith in the role of liberty in the functioning of the natural order.

The theory of the social origin of moral judgments and standards is fundamental to the doctrine of the harmony of individual and national interests which pervades *The Wealth of Nations*. All of the economic interests the individual pursues are largely acquired in the course of his social experience. The individual, as a product of the society in which he lives, is of necessity concerned with social approbation. It appears reasonable, therefore, to interpret the doctrine of sympathy as developed in *The Theory of Moral Sentiments* as the conceptual antecedent of the doctrine of the natural order set forth in *The Wealth of Nations*.[9]

The philosophy on which Smith's economic principles are based is nowhere specifically mentioned in *The Wealth of Nations*. Yet, it pervades his entire work to an even greater extent than the philosophy of naturalism colored the writings of the Physiocrats. Above all, Smith was dedicated to "the simple system of natural liberty." Standing at the center of his system is the individual who follows his own interests while promoting the welfare of society as a whole, for such is the nature of the natural order. The Physiocrats also equated the existence of the natural order with the ideal society, but with a difference. For the Physiocrats, the natural order was to be discovered through the intellect and brought to fruition through enlightened despotism. For Smith, the existence of the natural order is a fact. It exists in spite of human interferences.

A variety of beneficent economic institutions are spontaneously generated within the framework of the natural order. Among them are the division of labor, the development of money, the growth of savings and the investment of capital, the development of foreign trade, and the adjustment of supply and demand to each other. These and other institutions of the spontaneous order spring into existence as a result of man's self-interested behavior and operate for the benefit of society as a whole.

Smith's psychology must likewise be culled out of his literary efforts, as it is not specifically set forth in either of his major writings. He does, however, appear to follow David Hartley, John Locke, and his good friend David Hume in regarding sensation as the source of ideas and knowledge.

---

[9] See Glenn R. Morrow, "Moralist and Philosopher" in J. M. Clark *et al.* (eds.), *Adam Smith, 1776–1920* (Chicago: University of Chicago Press, 1928), for an interesting essay on the relationship between *The Theory of Moral Sentiments* and *The Wealth of Nations*. Jacob Viner has explored the same issue, taking the point of view that there are divergences between *The Theory of Moral Sentiments* and *The Wealth of Nations* which are impossible to reconcile. His essay, "Adam Smith and Laissez Faire," is included in the same volume.

Plan and Scope

The Wealth of Nations is divided into an Introduction, which sets forth the plan of the author, five books, and an Appendix. The first book is "Of the Causes of Improvement in the Productive Powers of Labour, and of the Order According to Which Its Produce Is Naturally Distributed among the Different Ranks of the People." Book II is "Of the Nature, Accumulation and Employment of Stock," and Book III is "Of the Different Progress of Opulence in Different Nations." These three books are primarily a presentation of economic principles. Book IV, entitled "Of Systems of Political Economy," and Book V, "Of the Revenue of the Sovereign or Commonwealth," take Smith into the area of political economy.

Even today *The Wealth of Nations* is an interesting book to read. Its author knew how to intersperse facts with illustrations and persuasive reasoning. The result is neither repetitous or complicated in its logic, but rather, remarkably straightforward and simple, with a genuine feeling for his fellow man unmistakably in evidence.

Smith is the first of the great eclectics who wove into a harmonious whole the more important ideas of predecessors and contemporaries alike. The influence of Hutcheson and Hume is particularly in evidence; he also owed much to the Physiocrats, especially Turgot and Quesnay and such liberal mercantilists as North, Petty, Child and Tucker. Other important ideas germinated from his disagreement with De Mandeville. It is worth noting that *The Wealth of Nations* contains remarkably few references to the writings of other authors and that Smith was perhaps less scholarly in this regard than he might have been. However, he knew precisely what to extract from other works and how to use it to make his final product in every way unique and peculiarly his own, though many individual ideas and even illustrations are not original with him.

THE THEORY OF PRODUCTION

The Nature and Sources of Wealth

"The annual labour of every nation is the fund which originally supplies it with all the necessities and conveniences of life which it annually consumes, and which consists always either in the immediate produce of the labourer, or in what is purchased with that produce from other nations."[10] This is the statement with which Adam Smith began his inquiry into the nature and causes of the wealth of nations. The primary difference between his conception of the nature and source of wealth and that of the Physiocrats is thus immediately brought into focus. Not nature but human effort

---

[10] Smith, *The Wealth of Nations,* Vol. I, Introduction, p. 1.

makes commodities available. It is also evident that Smith considered a nation to be well off in accordance with its supply of "necessaries and conveniences" in relation to the number of its inhabitants. Goods, not gold, thus constituted the wealth of a nation. This becomes abundantly clear in Book IV, which deals at length with mercantilism, but is also implied at the very outset of his inquiry.

Though it served to distinguish his position from that of the Physiocrats, his initial emphasis on labor also laid the groundwork for future misunderstanding. He was subsequently interpreted as taking the position that labor and labor alone is the source of wealth, though he nowhere excluded stock and land as productive factors. The terminology "factors of production" is not to be found in Smith's work; but, as will be seen later, his treatment of income shares as functional rewards suggested that he thought of labor, stock, and land as separate factors of production which are entitled to receive their separate shares of the annual product in the form of wages, profit, and rent. His emphasis on labor was not intended to deny the importance of either capital stock or land but rather to call attention to labor, as opposed to the forces of nature, as the prime mover of production. Without the cooperative efforts of labor, neither land nor capital would be able to bring forth anything.

The Division of Labor

Having emphasized the importance of labor in production, Smith proceeds in Book I to inquire how the productive powers of labor may be enhanced. Drawing on the trade of the pinmaker for illustrative purposes, Smith tells us that labor is most effective in production when division of labor is practiced.[11] He calculates that division of labor makes it possible for ten workers to produce 48,000 pins per day, so that each worker produces the equivalent of 4,800. Without division of labor, a worker might not even make one pin in a day, and certainly not 20. He was greatly impressed with this enhancement of the productivity of labor, and his description has become a classic, though he was certainly not the first to describe either the process or its effects. It might also be noted that his example illustrates that the English economy had not yet entered upon an industrial revolution.

He observes that division of labor enhances the dexterity of each worker, saves time by making it unnecessary to shift from one type of work to another, and also stimulates the invention of laborsaving devices. The result is a great increase in the quantity of work that a given number of people can perform. It is to the division of labor that Smith attributes the relatively high standards of living that prevailed during his day for even the lowest ranks of people and concludes "that the accomodation of an Euro-

---

[11] *Ibid.,* Vol. I, p. 7.

pean prince does not always so much exceed that of an industrious and frugal peasant as the accomodation of the latter exceeds that of many an African King, the absolute master of the lives and liberties of ten thousand naked savages."[12]

Division of labor comes into existence spontaneously without the necessity of human wisdom, planning, or intervention; it is the consequence of the "propensity to truck, barter, and exchange one thing for another."[13] This inclination to trade is found only in man and is but one expression of his self-interested behavior. Only by exchanging his surplus with others can he acquire all the goods he has need of; and in order to serve his own interests, he appeals to the self-interest of his fellowmen. "As it is by treaty, by barter and by purchase that we obtain from one another the greater part of those mutual good offices which we stand in need of, so it is this same trucking disposition which originally gives occasion to the division of labour."[14]

Manufacturing generally lends itself better to division of labor than agriculture, and although the richest countries generally excel their neighbors in agriculture as well as manufacturing, their superiority is usually greater in manufacturing.[15] Everywhere, the practicality of engaging in division of labor is limited by the size of the market to be served.[16] Thus, Smith anticipates later discussions concerning the limits of what is today known as increasing returns to scale. He also observes that regions of relatively sparse population afford little opportunity to carry on division of labor, whereas well-populated areas and those made easily accessible by good water and land transportation will be more likely to enjoy its advantages.

Productive and Unproductive Labor

Both the mercantilists and the Physiocrats employed the notion of productive and unproductive labor. For the former, the criterion of productivity was the degree to which the effort contributed to securing a favorable balance of trade, while the latter believed that only workers engaged in the extractive industries were productive, in that they were assisted by nature, which alone is capable of creating a surplus. Unfortunately, Smith also thought in terms of productive and unproductive labor, and created considerable confusion with his distinction not only as regards the discussion itself, but also as regards its compatibility with other parts of his theory.

In the third chapter of Book II, he observes that some labor realizes itself in a vendible commodity and is thus to be considered as "productive,"

---

[12] *Ibid.,* p. 11.

[13] *Ibid.,* p. 12.

[14] *Ibid.,* p. 13.

[15] *Ibid.,* p. 6.

[16] *Ibid.,* p. 15.

while certain other labor is "unproductive" in that it does not "fix or realize itself in any particular subject . . . which endures after that labour is past and for which an equal quantity of labour could afterwards be purchased." The labor of domestic servants, entertainers, professional men, government servants, and others among "the most respectable orders in the society" fall into this class.

The foregoing distinction between productive and unproductive labor is also coupled with two other grounds on which the one type of labor is distinguished from the other. The first is the relationship of labor to the creation of value. Thus, he observes that productive labor "adds to the value of the subject on which it is bestowed." The effort of labor engaged in manufacturing is in this class, while that of menial servants is not. Elsewhere, he observes that productive labor creates a surplus which goes to the owner of stock.

Thus, the labourer of a manufacturer adds, generally, to the value of the materials which he works upon, that of his own maintenance and of his master's profit. . . . Though the manufacturer has his wages advanced to him by his master, he, in reality, costs him no expense, the value of those wages being generally restored, together with a profit, in the improved value of the subject upon which his labourer is bestowed.[17]

The notion of labor as the creator of a surplus is pursued in a somewhat different vein in Book IV, in which Smith writes of the Physiocratic system. Here, he makes the observation that the labor of artisans and traders is not as productive as that of farmers because agricultural workers produce not only their own subsistence and profit on the stock of their employer, but also rent for the landlord. Like the Physiocrats, Smith was persuaded that in agriculture, nature labors alongside man and produces a surplus. His predilection for agriculture is equally apparent in Book II, which is devoted to the accumulation and employment of capital, and in which he insists that capital employed in agriculture is the most productive. "The capital employed in agriculture, therefore, not only puts into motion a greater quantity of productive labour which it employs, it adds a much greater value to the annual produce of the land and labour of the country, to the real wealth and revenue of its inhabitants."[18] It was on these grounds that Smith believed that a nation should give preference to agriculture and pursue other economic activities only as its increasing capital accumulation permits. He regarded manufacturing as the second most productive activity, followed by domestic trade. Foreign trade is the least advantageous field of investment, returning lower profits and more difficult of supervision than capital invested at home.

Smith's distinction between productive and unproductive labor is

---

[17] *Ibid.*, p. 295.
[18] *Ibid.*, p. 325.

untenable and created confusion in at least three areas of economic thinking. First, his exclusion of services as part of the national product and the designation of the work of those who render them as unproductive labor was later recognized as incorrect. Secondly, his identification of revenues in excess of wages in manufacturing enterprises as a "surplus" blurred the difference between profit and interest. This was unfortunate because the latter are functional returns rewarding two distinct activities, namely, the entrepreneurial function of risk bearing and management, and the lender's function of making available funds. It also helped lay a basis for the theory of labor exploitation. The third area of confusion concerns the productive powers of land and its relationship to the appearance of rent. Like the Physiocrats, Smith entertained the idea that there is something unique about the productive powers of land and that labor employed on it furnishes a rent in addition to profit on stock. This created an erroneous idea of the nature of rent and the circumstances under which it arises.

The most meaningful interpretation of Smith's distinction between productive and unproductive labor is in connection with saving and capital accumulation. It is clear from his third chapter in Book II, "On the Accumulation of Capital or of Productive and Unproductive Labor," that he is concerned with the effect of using savings to satisfy the desire for luxuries by those who are prodigal instead of channeling them into uses that will enhance the supply of fixed or circulating capital. He is, in effect, arguing that savings should be used in such a way that they will create a flow of income and new equipment, and that failure to use savings in this manner is an impediment to economic growth. This line of reasoning is somewhat obscured by his observation that "what is annually saved is as regularly consumed as what is annually spent, and in nearly the same time too; but it is consumed by a different set of people."[19] This seems to imply that it matters little whether income is used for consumption or saving because savings flow back into the income stream via investment. Hoarding is implicitly regarded as an exceptional occurrence in this context. While Smith seemed to be aware that people sometimes have a demand for money as a store of value, he believed that money is primarily desired as a medium of exchange. In effect, therefore, he eliminated the store-of-value function of money and did not seriously entertain the idea that hoarding could diminish the flow of income payments in the economy. On the contrary, he pictured the frugal man as contributing to the public welfare because his savings are used to set productive labor into motion and to add to the stock of fixed capital. This view of the relationship of savings and investment anticipates the dictum which subsequently became important in economic analysis as "Say's law."

---

[19] *Ibid.,* p. 302.

THE THEORY OF VALUE AND EXCHANGE

The Origin and Use of Money

Having considered production and the manner in which division of labor enhances man's ability to create goods, Smith turns next to a consideration of exchange value. Specialization facilitates the creation of individual surpluses which enable their owners to command other people's surpluses in exchange for their own. This requires that their relative worth or value be established in the marketplace and poses the problem of explaining what determines the value a commodity has in exchange for other goods or for money. It is to this problem that Smith devotes himself in the fifth chapter of Book I, which deals with the real and nominal prices of commodities. This analysis is preceded, quite logically, by his explanation of the origin and use of money.

The use of money, like the division of labor, is viewed by Smith as a spontaneous development resulting from man's self-interested behavior. The use of money eliminates the inconvenience of barter situations. Thus, Smith tells us that "in order to avoid the inconvenience of such situations, every prudent man in every period of society, after the first establishment of the division of labour must naturally have endeavoured to manage his affairs in such a manner as to have at all times by him, besides the peculiar product of his own industry, a certain quantity of some one commodity or other such as he imagined few people would be likely to refuse in exchange for the produce of their own industry."[20] Many different commodities, he observes, have served this purpose, but the precious metals seem particularly well suited to it. These observations are, of course, commonplace today, and every discussion since has been couched in almost identical terms.

Use Value and Exchange Value

Having disposed of the discussion of the origin of money, Smith proceeds next to his consideration of value. He begins by noting that commodities may have use value or exchange value and that:

Things which have the greatest value in use have frequently little or no value in exchange; and on the contrary, those which have the greatest value in exchange have frequently little or no value in use. Nothing is more useful than water; but it will scarce purchase anything, scarce anything can be had in exchange for it. A diamond, on the contrary, has scarce any value in use; but a very great quantity of other goods may frequently be had in exchange for it.[21]

---

[20] *Ibid.*, p. 20.
[21] *Ibid.*, p. 25.

Such are Smith's introductory remarks concerning the phenomenon of value.

Today's student of economics will probably have little difficulty in discerning several errors in the sentences just quoted. First, a commodity cannot possibly command other commodities in exchange unless it has value in use; only the ability to yield satisfaction to a user would make a commodity worth acquiring by giving up other goods or money. Smith's failure to recognize this rather obvious relationship was most significant for the future development of value theory, for it led to the attempt to explain exchange value without reference to utility. Some one hundred years were to elapse before English political economy specifically took utility into consideration in explaining value.[22]

A further error of Smith's famous opening statement on value is his failure to recognize the significance of the relative scarcity of the commodity at the margin. It is clearly misleading to compare a single diamond to the total supply of water. If he had compared the utility of a single diamond with the utility of a single unit of water, he could not have been misled. The fact that some goods are free illustrates beyond doubt that the utility afforded by a commodity may be quite unrelated to its exchange value. But it was not until it was recognized that it is the ratio of exchange between individual units that should be compared that the paradox of the diamond and the water was resolved. Such a comparison makes it perfectly plain that water commands little or nothing in exchange, while a diamond commands a great deal, because the supply of diamonds is so much smaller in relation to the intensity of the desire for them than is the case with water. It is surprising that Smith was unaware of this relationship, for it was clearly pointed out by John Locke[23] and others.[24] Finally, Smith applied a personal moral standard in deciding that a diamond has no use value. The fact that one does not approve of the consumption of a particular commodity, or that its use may be harmful or even illegal, does not deprive the commodity of its utility. The mere fact that a commodity can command a price is sufficient evidence of its utility.

Labor and Value

Having thus discarded utility, Smith turned his attention next to the role of labor as a determinant of value. It is no simple matter to describe or comprehend his account of the relationship between labor and value, for it is at many points contradictory and confused. He begins by telling us that "the value of any commodity, therefore, to the person who possesses it, and who means not to use or consume it himself, but to exchange it for other

---

[22] See Chap. 12 below.

[23] See his early manuscript on interest in *Letwin, op. cit.,* appendix V, p. 291.

[24] See H. R. Sewall, "The Theory of Value before Adam Smith" *Publications of the American Economic Association* Series III, ii, No. 3, 1901 pp. 66–124.

commodities is equal to the quantity of labour which it entitles him to purchase or command. Labour, therefore, is the real measure of the exchangeable value of all commodities."[25] Elsewhere, he says, "its value to those who possess it, and who want to exchange it for some new production is precisely equal to the quantity of labour which it can entitle them to purchase or command."[26] These statements express what may be referred to as the labor command theory of value, according to which a commodity has a value equivalent to the labor it can command in exchange for itself either directly or indirectly in the form of some other commodity. When used in this sense, labor serves as a measure of value.

Other statements, however, just as clearly put forth the idea that labor is the cause or determinant of value. Thus, says Smith, "the real price of everything, what everything really costs to the man who wants to acquire it, is the toil and trouble of acquiring it."[27]
But he also says:

In that early and rude state of society which precedes both the accumulation of stock and the appropriation of land, the proportion between the quantities of labour necessary for acquiring different objects seems to be the only circumstance which can afford any rule for exchanging them for another. . . . It is natural that what is usually the produce of two days' or two hours' labour, should be worth double of what is usually the produce of one day's or one hour's labour.[28]

These statements put forth a labor cost theory in which labor is the cause or determinant of value rather than simply the measure of value.

Several questions concerning these relationships may now be asked: First, if labor is the measure of value, why are values commonly expressed in money prices? Secondly, can labor not be both the cause and the measure of value—that is, can we not assign a value to a commodity in accordance with the amount of labor it contains and measure its worth in terms of some other commodity or group of commodities containing the same amount of labor? If this is possible, there is no incompatibility between the labor command theory and the labor cost theory. Finally, is it not possible that Smith intended the labor theory of value to apply only in "that early and rude state of society" and considered that the cause of value after the appropriation of land and the accumulation of stock might not be labor alone? The latter two questions are especially pertinent in trying to understand Smith's theory of value.

In regard to the first question, Smith says that once barter ceases, it becomes "natural" to exchange commodities for money rather than other

---

[25] Smith, *The Wealth of Nations,* Vol. I, p. 26.
[26] *Ibid.*
[27] *Ibid.*
[28] *Ibid.,* p. 41.

commodities. Gold and silver are the most satisfactory monetary media, but they vary in value, like all other commodities, depending on the quantity of labor required to mine them. Corn (grain) also can be used to measure value, but it too will vary in value, depending on the quantity of labor required for its production.[29] He concludes, therefore, that labor is the only universal as well as the only accurate measure of value, or the only standard by which we can compare the values of different commodities at different times and places, in spite of the fact that values are commonly expressed in terms of money.[30]

The problem of explaining the determination of exchange value is analytically distinct from the problem of measuring value though Smith himself saw no difficulty in conceiving of labor both as a cause and as a measure of value. He reasoned that commodities will have greater or less exchange value depending on the quantity and quality of the labor they contain. It does not matter, then, whether we speak of the value of the commodity or the value of the labor congealed in it. Thus, Smith tells us in the beginning of the sixth chapter of his first book that in "that early and rude state of society" which antedates private property in land and the accumulation of capital, a commodity has value in accordance with the amount of labor congealed in it, and commodities containing equal amounts of labor will be exchanged equally for one another. Under these circumstances, there is no difficulty concerning the use of labor both as a cause and as a measure of value because factors other than labor do not exist, and all transactions involve equivalents of labor. The labor cost of a commodity is exactly equal to its labor command.

The only problem that Smith conceived to exist in this state had to do with the fact that equivalents of labor time were not automatically equivalents of labor content, since some labor is more difficult, unpleasant, or dangerous, or requires more training, dexterity, or ingenuity. But this does not introduce a major difficulty, for such differences in the quality of labor will be reflected in different rewards. "In the advanced state of society, allowances of this kind, for superior hardship and superior skill, are commonly made in the wages of labourer; and something of the same kind must probably have taken place in its earliest and rudest period."[31] He took it for granted that the market process of wage rate determination will automatically result in a wage commensurate with the labor performed by each worker and that wage differentials will be reflected in commodity values. The subject of wage differentials is thus introduced into the discussion of the value problem. The subject is not pursued further until a later chapter, but it is already apparent that Smith believed that the market sets commodity prices in accordance with the worth of the labor embodied in the

---

[29] *Ibid.*, p. 31.
[30] *Ibid.*, p. 32.
[31] *Ibid.*, p. 42.

commodities. Thus, he concluded that commodities would be exchanged for one another in accordance with their content of labor, the latter being the product of time, hardship, and ingenuity. "If among a nation of hunters, for example, it usually costs twice the labour to kill a beaver which it does to kill a deer, one beaver should naturally exchange for or be worth two deer."[32]

No problems of interpretation are involved with respect to Smith's discussion of the precapitalist era which antedates land ownership and capital accumulation. The only factor of production is labor, and commodities are exchanged for one another in accordance with the labor they contain. Labor is thus both the cause and the measure of value. Moreover, in this state of things the whole product belongs to labor. There is neither landlord nor capitalist with whom it must be shared. Not until land becomes privately owned and the accumulation of capital has taken place does a share of the product go to the owner of stock and the landlord. In this state of things, the whole produce of labour does not always belong to the labourer. He must, in some cases, share it with the owner of the stock which employs him.[33] . . . As soon as the land of any country has all become private property the landlords, like all other men, love to reap where they never sowed, and demand a rent even for its natural produce.[34]

These statements have great significance for Smith's labor theory of value. For if the worker must share the product with the owner of the stock and the landlord, it must be concluded either that labor does not create the whole product in an advanced society and that the shares going to the landlord and the capitalist are just rewards that they have earned, or that the laborer is being deprived of a part of the product that is rightfully his. The first interpretation is tantamount to recanting the labor theory of value, at least as it applies to the advanced state, and the second interpretation introduces a theory of labor exploitation. Which interpretation approximates most closely Smith's position? Our examination of the nature of profit and rent, and their relationship to natural and market price, will help us to decide.

Profit, Rent, and Natural and Market Price

Smith tells us that as soon as stock becomes accumulated, the value of a product resolves itself into two parts: wages and profits. The profits of stock are not to be conceived of as payment for a special kind of labor, namely, the labor of inspection or direction, because they bear no relationship to the disutility of the labor. "They are regulated altogether by the value of the stock employed and are greater or smaller in proportion to

---

[32] *Ibid.*, p. 41.

[33] *Ibid.*, p. 43.

[34] *Ibid.*, p. 44.

the extent of this stock. . . . In the price of commodities, therefore, the profits of stock constitute a component altogether different from the wages of labour and are regulated by quite different principles."[35]

Not only are profits distinct from wages as regards their origin, but what is more, there is no indication that Smith considered the receipt of profits as being anything but justified. He tells us that the owner of stock would have no interest in employing his stock if his revenues did not leave something over and above the cost of materials and wages to reward him for the hazards he assumes.

Profits are not the only additional income share that will be encountered in an advanced society. Rent, too, will make its appearance as soon as the land of a country has become privately owned.

The wood of the forest, the grass of the field and all the natural fruits of the earth, which when land was in common, cost the labourer only the trouble of gathering them, come, even to him to have an additional price fixed upon them. . . . This portion, or what comes to the same thing, the price of this portion, constitutes the rent of land, and in the price of the greater part of commodities makes a third component part.[36]

Smith's attitude toward the receipt of rent by the landlords is less than warm, for he tells us that landlords love to reap where they have never sowed.[37] But they are no different from other men in this respect, and Smith regards the receipt of rent as being quite as "natural" as the receipt of profits.

There exists in every society or neighborhood an average or ordinary rate of wages, profits, and rents which is "natural" with respect to the time and place it prevails. Thus, when a commodity sells for a price which is just high enough to compensate the worker, the landlord, and the owner of stock at the natural rate, the commodity is being sold at its "natural price." It is then being sold for precisely what it is worth.[38] This is not to say that a commodity will always sell for its natural price. From time to time, changes in the relationship between the demand for it and the supply of it will cause the market price to rise above or fall below the natural level. But such a deviation tends to be corrected, for the supply will naturally tend to suit itself to the effective demand, thus causing the market price to rise or fall, as the case may be, until it again equals the natural price. "The natural price, therefore, is, as it were, the central price to which the prices of all commodities are continually gravitating. Different accidents may sometimes keep them suspended a good deal above it, and sometimes force them down even somewhat below it. But whatever may be the obstacles which hinder

---

[35] *Ibid.,* p. 43.
[36] *Ibid.*
[37] *Ibid.,* p. 44.
[38] *Ibid.,* p. 49.

them from settling in this centre of repose and continuance, they are constantly tending towards it."[39] Thus, the long-run natural price is seen by Smith as a long-run equilibrium price which tends always to be reestablished as a result of short-run adjustments of demand and supply.

Smith did not think of demand and supply in the schedule sense in which we think of them in modern analysis, but rather as the willingness of market participants to buy or sell at a particular price rather than at various possible prices. Nevertheless, it is useful for us to think of the restoration of the market price to the level of the natural price as a result of short-run shifts of the supply schedule. Thus, when Smith refers to the supply of a commodity as too small to satisfy the "effectual demand," so that the market price rises above the natural price, he is really thinking in terms of an upward shift in the supply curve. Conversely, when the supply is too large for the effectual demand, market price will sink below natural price because, in modern terminology, the supply curve will shift downward. Only when the quantity brought to market is just sufficient to supply effectual demand and no more will market price be equal to natural price. It is clear, therefore, that Smith conceived of the interaction of demand and supply as determining prices in the short run, under competitive conditions. The long-run price, that is, the natural price, was, however, thought to be independent of demand forces. It was thought to be determined solely by the costs incurred on the supply side of the market. These costs were implicitly assumed to be constant, that is, not affected by the rate of output. More than a century later, Alfred Marshall was to demonstrate that in a constant-cost industry, demand exerts no influence on price but merely determines the level of output. But this is a special case, and Smith erred in neglecting the role of demand in the determination of the long-run equilibrium price. A similar neglect of demand was to become typical until the advent of the marginal revolution toward the end of the nineteenth century.

Smith's awareness of the role of competition in the pricing process becomes clear in his seventh chapter. Here, he notes not only the significance of a large number of sellers, but also the effect of market knowledge and resource mobility in limiting the ability of market participants to influence price. Indeed, the only prerequisite of pure competition which he did not note is product homogeneity. His treatment of monopoly, however, is very cursory. He makes reference to articles that are in fixed supply because they are not reproducible and to the possibility of monopoly prices on account of "secrets of manufacture." He thinks of monopoly price as being "upon every occasion the highest which can be squeezed out of buyers," indicating that he has some appreciation of the role of demand as setting the upper limit to monopoly price.

What is the significance of Smith's explanation of natural price for the

---

[39] *Ibid.,* p. 51.

labor theory of value? Smith nowhere denies the right of the owner of the stock to receive profit or of the landlord to receive rent. On the contrary, he regards the existence of these shares as being "natural" once "that early and rude state of society" (before the advent of privately owned land and accumulated stock) is past. What this implies from the standpoint of the value problem is that the cost of production tends to be the long-run determinant of value. Smith does not, of course, say this. Nowhere is the validity of the labor theory of value specifically limited to a primitive society. The dilemma thus becomes obvious. Does labor create all value, so that the deduction of a share for the landlord and the owner of stock represents exploitation of what rightfully belongs to the worker? It never occurred to Smith to reason along these lines, for his was a beneficent society in which there was no dichotomy of class interests. But the door to a theory of class conflict was opened to those who, like Marx, would argue that the deduction of rent and profit from the total revenue of the sale of a commodity necessarily meant a discrepancy between its labor cost and its labor command.

THE THEORY OF DISTRIBUTION

Wages

Smith's original lectures at Glasgow dealt only with production. The inclusion of four chapters on distribution in Book I of *The Wealth of Nations* conceivably reflects the influence of the Physiocrats or, as suggested by Edwin Cannan, Cantillon's *Essay on the Nature of Commerce in General*. His explanation of the distributive shares as component parts of natural price which tend toward competitive rates under his "obvious and simple system of liberty" is not of major significance as far as the central theme of *The Wealth of Nations* is concerned. But as England became more industrialized and the great conflict between the landed interests and the rising manufacturing class and between the latter and the growing class of wage earners became intensified, his discussion of the distributive shares assumed great social significance.

His discussion of wages suggests virtually every theory of wage rate determination ever devised. He begins by referring once again to the early and rude society which precedes the accumulation of capital and the private ownership of land, and tells us that under those conditions the produce of labor constitutes the natural recompense or wages of labor.[40] In this state, it is unnecessary to share the product with either the owner of stock or the landlord, and labor's share would have increased with all the improvements in its productive powers resulting from the division of labor if this state had continued. This utopian state being no longer in existence, Smith proceeds

---

[40] *Ibid.*, p. 57.

to discuss the various factors that are operative in the determination of wage rates.

The first explanation offered is the bargaining theory. He maintains that "what are the common wages of labour depends everywhere upon the contract usually made between these two parties, whose interests are by no means the same. . . . It is not, however, difficult to forsee which of these two parties must, upon all ordinary occasions have the advantage in the dispute, and force the other into a compliance with their terms."[41]

Although employers generally have the advantage in the wage bargain, even the poorest grade of labor must receive at least enough to maintain himself and his family. Subsistence, Smith believed, set the minimum below which wages could not fall in the long run. Wages may of course rise considerably above this rate if the demand for workmen is great, in precisely the same way a commodity price may rise above its natural level. This demand, says Smith, is governed by the size of the wage fund which employers have available to give employment. This fund is accumulated out of revenues in excess of their own living requirements and the capital requirements of business. "The demand for those who live by wages, therefore, necessarily increases with the increase of the revenue and stock of every country, and cannot possibly increase without it. The increase of revenue and stock is the increase of national wealth. The demand for those who live by wages, therefore, naturally increases with the increase of national wealth, and cannot posibly increase without it."[42]

Thus, Smith relates increasing wages to increasing national wealth. He continues with a discussion of the level of wages in different parts of the world, noting that wages are especially high in North America because of its small population and the rapidity of increase in its national wealth. China, on the other hand, has a very low level of wages because it has long been stationary. Wage rates in Great Britain are not so high as in North America, but they are above subsistence for even the poorest grade of labor. This is evident, says Smith, from the fact that summer wages are always higher than winter wages, although living costs are greater in the wintertime.[43]

In his observation on wage rates in different parts of the world, Smith also notes the relationship between the rewards of labor and the growth of population. He notes that "every species of animals naturally multiply in proportion to the means of their subsistence and no species can ever multiply beyond it."[44] Thus, when wages are high, as they are in North America, the rate of population growth tends to be high, whereas low wage

---

[41] *Ibid.*, pp. 58–59.
[42] *Ibid.*, p. 61.
[43] *Ibid.*, pp. 62–65.
[44] *Ibid.*, p. 71.

rates are associated with a stationary population. This relationship was later to become the subject of a detailed inquiry by Thomas Malthus. Smith, however, did not entertain the attitude of general pessimism that is encountered in Malthus' essay with respect to the growth of population, for while the latter was concerned in the main with the dire consequences of population pressure and the available means of subsistence, Smith noted that high wage rates also increase the "industry of the common people" and thus contribute to the rising standard of living associated with greater division of labor.

Smith believed that the long-run trend of wages would be upward and considered that this was not merely a symptom of an advancing economy but also a cause of progress. For though rising wages are dependent upon increases in stock, they also enhance the productive powers of labor and thereby facilitate the accumulation of capital. Even though population tends to expand to the very limits of subsistence, Smith evidently believed that the incentive to save rather than to be prodigal is so strong that additions to the wage fund coupled with the productivity increases associated with capital accumulation would tend to make the living standard of wageworkers rise. Thus the specter of a stationary state, in which the great mass of people live in misery, did not loom upon Smith's horizon. Not until the day of Malthus and Ricardo was the optimism of Smith to be replaced by an attitude of such general pessimism that economics became known as the "dismal science."

Profits on Stock and Interest

The profits of stock, says Smith, are closely related to the wages of labor, falling when wages rise and increasing when wages decline. Their average level depends on the accumulation of stock. The nature, accumulation, and employment of stock are not discussed until Book II, in which it is explained that it is not until an individual has accumulated financial reserves (stock) in excess of his own subsistence requirements that he will try to use these reserves in a manner which will earn additional income. "His whole stock, therefore, is distinguished into two parts. That part which, he expects, is to afford him revenue is called his capital. The other is that which supplies his immediate consumption. . . ."[45]

Fixed capital consists of machinery, tools, buildings, and improvements on land which "yield a revenue or profit without changing hands," whereas circulating capital creates a revenue only by "circulating or changing masters." It consists of money, the stock of provisions, raw materials, and partly manufactured and completed goods not yet disposed of to their proper consumers. All useful machines and instruments are originally de-

---

[45] *Ibid.,* p. 243.

rived from and must be supported by circulating capital in order to afford a revenue. All capital is the result of savings.

Capitals are increased by parsimony, and diminished by prodigality and misconduct.

Whatever a person saves from his revenue he adds to his capital, and either employs it himself in maintaining an additional number of productive hands, or enables some other person to do so, by lending it to him for an interest, that is, for a share of the profits.[46]

Thus, it is evident that Smith thought of increases in stock as the source of additions to the wage fund. The size of this fund determines the demand for labor; and depending upon the size of the laboring population, it determines whether the average level of wages will rise or fall. Increases in stock are generally associated with falling profits as well as rising wage rates, for mutual competition in the same trade will reduce the rate of return.[47]

The level of profits, says Smith, is so fluctuating that it cannot be ascertained precisely. The most reliable gauge of the level of profits is the level of interest. "It may be laid down as a maxim that whenever a great deal can be made by the use of money, a great deal will commonly be given for the use of it; and that whenever little can be made by it, less will commonly be given for it. . . . The progress of interest, therefore may lead us to form some notion of the progress of profit."[48]

Smith expressed his opposition to the prohibition of interest, maintaining that it increases rather than diminishes the evil of usury, for nobody will lend without such a consideration for the use of his money as is suitable not only to the use that may be made of it but to the difficulty and danger of evading the law.[49] It is clear, therefore, that the term "interest" is used by Smith, and indeed by others before him, as a payment made for the use of borrowed funds. He tells us that there is a minimum rate of interest which must compensate for the risk of lending, and the lowest rate of profit must be enough to compensate the investor after he has made interest payments to the lender. Interest is thus regarded by Smith as part of gross profit, and "net profit" is a rate of return on capital whose level can be inferred from the market rate of interest. The entire income of a businessman who provided all or most of his capital, as was not uncommon when businesses were predominantly organized as proprietorships or partnerships, was simply regarded as profit. Today, of course, the return on equity capital would be labeled as interest rather than profit. But early thinkers on the subject,

---

[46] *Ibid.,* p. 301.
[47] *Ibid.,* p. 78.
[48] *Ibid.,* p. 79.
[49] *Ibid.,* pp. 85–86.

not only Smith but Malthus and Ricardo as well, made no functional distinction between interest and profit. They thought of the profit of the businessman as being essentially a yield on his capital investment. That the businessman performs other functions, such as risk bearing, management, and innovation, and is not necessarily a provider of funds, was still unrecognized or given only passing notice. Their primitive theory of profit was therefore essentially a yield-on-capital explanation of interest.

With regard to the rate of profit, Smith believed that the average would be in the neighborhood of approximately double the rate of interest on well-secured loans.[50] Reasoning that there is competition for the employment of capital, which is largely mobile enough to flow from one part of the economy to another in response to profit opportunities, Smith concluded that the same *rate* of return would tend to prevail in all industries, though the actual *amount* would vary, he believed, with the amount of capital invested. The rate of profit would tend to decline with the progress of accumulation relative to the supply of labor. While the explanation of the decline in the rate of profit was not associated by Smith with the tendency toward diminishing returns as additional quantities of labor and capital are applied to a fixed supply of land, as was later emphasized by Ricardo, his discussion of the trend of income shares in areas abundantly populated and capital-rich, as compared with newer and still underdeveloped economies, anticipates the Ricardian analysis of the effect of progress on income distribution.

Rent

Although some consideration has already been given to rent as a component part of natural price, along with profit and wages, Smith devotes his lengthy closing chapter of Book I to this matter. Here, he virtually abandons his earlier view of rent and makes it a differential return.

Rent, it is to be observed, therefore, enters into the composition of the price of commodities in a different way from wages and profits. High or low wages and profits are the causes of high or low prices; high or low rent is the effect of it. It is because high or low wages and profits must be paid in order to bring a particular commodity to market, that its price is high or low; but it is because its price is high or low, a great deal more, or very little more, or no more, than what is sufficient to pay those wages and profits, that it affords a high rent, or a low rent, or no rent at all.[51]

Land which is used to produce food is the only land which "always and necessarily affords some rent to the landlord."[52] How much this rent will be depends on the fertility and location of the land. The greater the

---

[50] *Ibid.*, p. 87.
[51] *Ibid.*, p. 132.
[52] *Ibid.*, p. 147.

demand for the product, the higher the price which the landlord, as a monopolist, will be able to demand for his product above the minimum necessary to pay wages and profit. This is the essence of the differential surplus theory presented later by Ricardo, and it is perhaps superior to it in some respects because it discusses different conditions under which rent will emerge.

Smith concludes his lengthy chapter on rent with some observations about the long-run trend of the various income shares and the role which their recipients play with respect to the society as a whole. It is his expectation that every improvement in the economy as a whole will raise the real rent of land either directly or indirectly. This is not because of the efforts of the landlords, a class of men whom Smith considered to be naturally indolent, but rather because of the reduction in labor requirements resulting from improvements. However, it was not Smith's intention to single out the landed gentry as the object of his attack. Opposition to the landed interests did not become an issue until industrialization had become sufficiently advanced to make cheap labor, and therefore cheap food, a primary requisite. But a basis for the destruction of the harmony of social interests had clearly been laid, though the eventual conflict was, for the time being, obscured by Smith's philosophy of a beneficent natural order. If anything, Smith's criticism was reserved for traders and manufacturers. They are "an order of men whose interest is never exactly the same with that of the public, who have generally an interest to deceive and even to oppress the public and who accordingly have upon many occasions, both deceived and oppressed it."

THE ARGUMENT FOR ECONOMIC LIBERTY

Economic Progress among Different European Nations

Book III, "Of the Different Progress of Opulence in Different Nations," provides a historical perspective for the devastating attack on infringements against economic liberty which Smith delivers in Book IV. In it, he reviews the development of European industry and agriculture from the time of the decline of the Roman Empire. He notes that in many nations the progress of opulence has been impeded by the pursuit of policies that conflict with what he regards as the natural course of things. If the natural course of development is allowed to assert itself, the capital of every nation will be directed first to agriculture, then to manufacturing and domestic trade, and last of all to foreign commerce.[53] This is the order of capital development which he believed to be most profitable and most conducive to welfare.

Having completed this comparatively brief historical survey, Smith

---

[53] *Ibid.*, p. 340.

proceeds with his examination of different systems of political economy. This is done in Book IV, which is devoted to the commercial and agricultural systems.

The Attack on Mercantilism

The task of exposing the fallacies of the commercial system is begun by examining the policy of seeking a favorable balance of trade to augment the nation's gold supply and wealth. Smith argued that the notion that a nation is rich if it has a great deal of gold, just as a man who has gold is wealthy, is erroneously to identify money with wealth. While the inflow of gold is undoubtedly in the interest of the merchants, for a country that has no mines of its own to gain gold by pursuing a favorable balance of trade is as unnecessary as it is foolish. It is unnecessary because a country can always acquire all the gold it has need of in the same way it acquires any other commodity it does not produce at home, namely, by trade, which will automatically respond to the effective demand for a commodity. "We trust with perfect security that the freedom of trade, without any attention of government, will always supply us with the wine which we have occasion for; and we may trust with equal security that it will always supply us with all the gold and silver which we can afford to purchase or to employ, either in circulating our commodities, or in other uses."[54] The special characteristics of gold and silver are, in fact, such that they are more easily transported than most commodities. But if for any reason it is impossible to satisfy the effective demand for the precious metals, this shortage will cause less inconvenience than would be encountered in regard to virtually any other commodity because a well-regulated paper money could supply the need for a medium of exchange, "not only without any inconveniency, but, in some cases, with some advantages."[55] Nor is it necessary to accumulate treasure in order to carry on foreign wars, for "fleets and armies are maintained, not with gold and silver, but with consumable goods."[56]

Foreign trade is desirable, in Smith's view, when it appears spontaneously in the natural course of a country's economic development. But the acquisition of gold and silver is an insignificant benefit to be derived from it. The primary gain from trade is that it provides a market for a country's surplus products and, by extending the market, facilitates further division of labor. The great gain derived from the discovery of America was not the additional gold it brought to Europe, but the advantage to all trading countries of acquiring commodities cheaper than they could be produced at home. "Whether the advantages which one country has over another be natural or acquired is in this respect of no consequence. As long as the one

---

[54] *Ibid.*, p. 381.

[55] *Ibid.*, p. 383.

[56] *Ibid.*, p. 386.

country has those advantages, and the other wants them, it will always be more advantageous for the latter rather to buy of the former than to make."[57] Thus, there is a natural distribution of products among the different countries of the world which will come into existence automatically if only restrictive measures do not prevent their development. Later on, David Ricardo and John Stuart Mill were to elaborate the basis for territorial specialization in their theory of comparative cost and to point out the advantages accruing to the consumer if there is free trade. Smith was more concerned with the disadvantages of mercantilist restrictions on traders and producers; but unlike the arguments of the early antimercantilists, his were the first such arguments to be made by a personally disinterested individual. The Physiocrats were, of course, also free traders, but their hostility to restrictive measures was an aspect of their program for agricultural reform, and there was no attempt to demonstrate the positive advantages of international trade. Smith, however, undertook to demonstrate that protection is not only useless but may actually be disadvantageous to the economy because it will tend to bring about a different allocation of capital than would occur under conditions of free trade. "No regulation of commerce can increase the quantity of industry in any society beyond what its capital can maintain. It can only divert a part of it into a direction into which it might not otherwise have gone; and it is by no means certain that this artificial direction is likely to be more advantageous to the society than that into which it would have gone of its own accord."[58] There are, in general, only two circumstances in which it is desirable to lay some burden on foreign industry for the encouragement of the domestic; the first is when the industry is necessary to the defense of the country, and the second is when a tax levied on a foreign commodity would merely equal the tax imposed on the domestic commodity. The latter policy "would leave the competition between foreign and domestic industry, after the tax as nearly as possible upon the same footing as before it."

The Agricultural System

Having devoted eight chapters to an analysis and criticism of mercantilism, Smith turns his attention, in the concluding chapter of Book IV, to Physiocracy. During his travels to France, he had personal contact with the authors of that system. While he regarded their argument that agriculture is the sole source of revenue and wealth, and that artificers, manufacturers, and merchants are unproductive, as being incorrect, he nevertheless had warm praise for them.

Though in representing the labour which is employed upon land as the only productive labour, the notions which it inculcates are perhaps too narrow and

---

[57] *Ibid.*, p. 403.
[58] *Ibid.*, p. 398.

confined; yet in representing the wealth of nations as consisting, not in the unconsumable riches of money, but in the consumable goods annually reproduced by the labour of the society, and in representing perfect liberty as the only effective expedient for rendering this annual reproduction the greatest possible, its doctrine seems to be in every respect as just as it is generous and liberal.[59]

He commended them not only for understanding the true nature of the wealth of nations, but also for realizing the essential role of economic freedom in promoting its growth.

CONCLUDING REMARKS

Although *The Wealth of Nations* was, in the main, an attack on the English commercial system, it was also intended as a policy guide—a key to the wealth of nations. Smith believed that the natural trend of economic development is upward and that this trend is most likely to manifest itself within the framework of an "obvious and simple system of liberty." Interpreted in modern terminology, this is a system which embodies the characteristics of perfect competition. Such a system would facilitate the accumulation and direction of capital into those avenues that the Smithian theory of different employments of capital emphasized as being most desirable from the standpoint of maximizing welfare.

The productivity of a given amount of capital is measured by the amount of value it adds to the stock of "necessaries and conveniences." Since capital is comprised of circulating capital in the form of the wages fund, as well as of fixed capital, the allocation of capital implies also the allocation of labor. As has already been noted, some labor is unproductive, and the income thus received does not correspond to value added but is a transfer income. Capital employed in agriculture is most productive, in Smith's view, for it yields not only wages and profit but also a surplus which is paid as rent to the landlord. Manufacturing ranks second in the hierarchy of productive employments, followed by domestic trade and finally foreign trade. The implication is that if businessmen are free to seek out the best opportunities for maximizing gains, the most productive employments will be sought out first. It is also implied that the activities in which the state engages will be minimal because the labor of the sovereign and other governmental servants is "unproductive." The incomes they receive are transfers and do not correspond to value added.

While the treatise that Smith produced expressed a harmony of social interests, it also showed how and why social conflict might arise. His labor theory of value and his theory of surplus laid the foundation for a definite dichotomy of class interests. He expressed his faith in the operation of the "invisible hand" in securing the interests of all members of society, but also

---

[59] *Ibid.*, Vol. II, p. 172.

had second thoughts about the role which different classes played with respect to the society as a whole. Of landowners, he entertained a low opinion indeed; they are frequently not only incapable of understanding the significance of any proposed change in policy but are actually ignorant of their own interests. The recipients of profit are, by training and inclination, best able to understand proposed changes in policy, but they are a class of men who are "interested to deceive and even oppress the public." Thus, elements of disharmony were present in Smith's analysis, but social conditions were not yet ready for them to ripen into actual conflict.

Conflict did not emerge until the mechanization of industry became widespread. Until that time, increases in capital were primarily associated with increases in the wages fund, just as Smith contended, and, therefore, with the improvement in the welfare of the mass of workers. But the subsequent appearance of capital in the form of machinery was to make questionable Smith's doctrine that the accumulation and employment of capital would automatically coincide with the advancing material progress of all classes of society. That the large mass of people would always benefit from the policy of laissez-faire, which Smith applauded so warmly, was also to be challenged.

But these challenges do not diminish in the least brilliance of Smith's insight into the optimizing results of perfect competition. If there is perfect competition, there is no area of conflict between private and social interests. Each individual, independently seeking to maximize what he considers to be his own selfish interest, will nevertheless contribute to the social welfare. This thesis, in addition to counteracting the then prevailing view that every action for private gain is necessarily antisocial, also laid the groundwork for future propositions concerning the optimal characteristics of perfect competition. Precisely why these results would obtain under perfect competition was not clearly understood. But with Smith's analysis of the operation of the invisible hand, a major step was taken in the direction of understanding the significance of perfect competition in optimizing the results of economic activity. Reliance on perfect competition to achieve optimum results was subsequently built into classical as well as neoclassical analysis, though a thorough examination of the requirements of the economic optimum and their relation to perfect competition was delayed until the 1930's, when they were explored by writers on socialism in connection with economic planning to achieve maximum welfare.[60]

SUGGESTIONS FOR FURTHER READING

BITTERMAN, HENRY J. "Adam Smith's Empiricism and the Law of Nature," *Journal of Political Economy,* Vol. XLVIII, Nos. 4, 5 (August–October, 1940).

---

[60] See Chap. 17 below.

CLARK, JOHN M. *et al.* *Adam Smith, 1776–1926.* Chicago: University of Chicago Press, 1928.

GINZBERG, ELI. *The House of Adam Smith.* New York: Columbia University Press, 1934.

ROSENBERG, N. "The Institutional Aspects of the Wealth of Nations," *Journal of Political Economy,* Vol. LXVIII, No. 6 (December, 1960).

SCOTT, W. R. *Adam Smith as a Student and Professor.* Glasgow: Jackson and Co., 1937.

SMITH, ADAM. *The Wealth of Nations.* New York: Modern Library, Inc., 1937. [Originally published 1776].

THE CONTRIBUTION OF THOMAS MALTHUS TO ECONOMIC ANALYSIS

INTRODUCTION

Life and Times (1766–1834)

An anonymous essay which was to become one of the most discussed works of modern times was published in 1798. It bore the title *An Essay on the Principle of Population, as It Affects the Future Improvement of Society with Remarks on the Speculations of Mr. Godwin, M. Condorcet and Other Writers*. It had been written by Thomas Malthus, an ordained minister of the Church of England. Relatively few copies of the original edition circulated, for its subject matter was both unpopular and controversial. But the *Essay* soon became the center of heated discussion, and six editions appeared during the author's lifetime. The original is substantially different from subsequent ones, not only in length, for the author added numerous qualifications and evidence to document his thesis, but also in content.

Malthus was born in 1766 to a distinguished family. His father, a lawyer by profession, was a friend of such men as Rousseau and Hume. He sent his son to be educated in Cambridge; upon graduation, he entered the ministry of the Church of England, and was in charge of a parish at the time his famous essay was written. It was subsequently revised after extensive travel in Germany, France, and the Scandinavian countries. Shortly afterward, in 1805, he was appointed professor of history and political economy at the East India College, where he remained for the rest of his life. It was during these years that he enjoyed a close friendship with David Ricardo and helped found the Political Economy Club in 1821 and the Royal Statistical Society in 1834.

The span of Malthus' lifetime coincided with years that were revolutionary in the industrial as well as in the political world. The Industrial Revolution, still in its embryonic stage when Adam Smith wrote, brought with it not only improved methods of production and transportation, new forms of business organization, and better banking and credit facilities, but also the factory system with its many attendant evils. The ever-growing urban population, whose employment opportunities were reduced by technological progress, presented a troublesome problem. These difficulties were compounded by recurrent economic crises which gave rise to periodic commodity gluts. The problem of overproduction therefore became an issue, as did the whole question of the "effect of machinery." The possibility that French revolutionary ideas might spread into England as a result of difficulties of the working class was the great fear that haunted the wealthy. The practical aim of English politics became to forestall a similar uprising by improving the conditions of the urban working class enough to safeguard the existing social structure. William Pitt's bill of 1798, calling for the extension of relief to large families, is typical of the sort of "safety valve" measures proposed.

The economic burdens of the urban poor became especially acute when the Napoleonic wars ended in 1815. While England was relatively prosperous during this lengthy and expensive struggle, its termination was accompanied by a state of general depression. The problem of widespread unemployment was complicated by continued high food prices, whose relationship to the Corn Laws became a major issue to which Malthus and his contemporary, David Ricardo, were to address themselves. The Corn Laws, which had been in existence since mercantilist times, were intended to stabilize the price of grain through a system of import duties and bounties which became effective in accordance with the domestic supply. In years of good harvest the market price of grain fell, and the duty became effective, whereas in years of poor harvest the market price of grain rose, and the duty was decreased. Under this system, English imports were virtually duty-free from 1795 to 1812 because the continued growth of population caused grain prices to remain high in spite of increased acreage and better cultivation methods.[1] Thus the Corn Laws themselves had little to do with keeping the price of grain high during the Napoleonic wars. However, landlords became especially concerned about their continuation when the return of peacetime conditions and the prospect of large imports threatened to lower crop prices. Manufacturers and merchants, on the other hand, were quick to realize the advantages which free trade would yield them because of the relationship between wage rates and low food prices.

The Nature and Philosophical Basis of Post-Smithian Economics

Post-Smithian economics, of which Malthus was a leading figure, was predominatly pessimistic in its outlook. It addressed itself chiefly to the problem of explaining the distribution of income among the three social classes. In this approach, it reflected problems which were too pressing and widespread to be obscured by belief in a natural order in which harmony is always assured. Thus the thinkers who followed Smith described an economic system whose laws of operation they conceived to be dictated by a

---

[1] Edwin Cannan, *A History of the Theories of Production and Distribution in English Political Economy* (London Staples Press, 1953), pp. 148–52.

supreme but by no means beneficent natural order. Instead of the "invisible hand" operating to promote the good of all, though this is no part of man's intention, emphasis was now placed on the necessity of man's adaptation to the exigencies of nature in order to avoid the unpleasant consequences of his own shortcomings.

Post-Smithian economics also reflects the effect of utilitarian ethics on the thinking of the political economists of the day. Utilitarianism sought, on the one hand, to introduce a principle, analogous to Sir Isaac Newton's in the natural sciences, on which a science of moral and social life could be founded and, on the other, to provide a basis for a reform movement known as philosophical radicalism. This movement was associated primarily with Jeremy Bentham and James Mill, although the ideas on which it is based are drawn principally from David Hume and the French philosopher Claude Adrien Helvétius.[2] Like Hume, Bentham believed that human behavior is the product of sense experience rather than reason. By identifying the pleasant sensations which individuals can be observed to experience with moral goodness, and painful sensations with evil, Bentham made Hume's psychics the foundation for a system of social ethics. The practical application of this ethical system required a "felicific calculus," or quantitative measurement of the pleasures and pains associated with various actions or modes of behavior. Bentham's view was that pleasures and pains differ quanitatively, depending upon their intensity, duration, certainty or uncertainty, propinquity or remoteness, fecundity, and extent, but they do not differ qualitatively. In his system, therefore, there are no pleasures which are superior or inferior and, consequently, none which rank higher or lower from a moral standpoint. Only the individual can judge which actions or experiences give him quantitatively more pleasure and which are, in this sense, better.

Bentham thought it possible to sum up pleasures and set them against pains, conceived of as negative pleasures. "The balance, if it be on the side of pleasure, will give the good tendency of the act upon the whole, with respect to the interests of that individual person; if on the side of pain, the bad tendency of it upon the whole."[3] By assuming that all individuals count equally and that a given action is associated with identical experiences of pleasure or pain for everyone, he extended the felicific calculus to society as a whole. He concluded that conduct should be judged morally according to its effects on the balance of human happiness. But this conclusion necessarily raises the question as to whether the egoisms which motivate human conduct are harmonious with each other, as Smith maintained, or are in conflict with each other. The French philosopher Helvétius took the posi-

---

[2] Elie Halévy, *The Growth of Philosophical Radicalism* (New York: Augustus Kelley, 1949), chap. i.

[3] W. Stark, ed. *Jeremy Bentham's Economic Writings* (London: George Allen and Unwin, Ltd., 1954), Vol. 3, pp. 436–7.

tion that individuals do not spontaneously identify their interests with the general interest. It was his influence which led Bentham to the idea that education and legisation will contribute to the greatest happiness of the greatest number. Education will contribute to the more perfect attainment of the goal of maximum utility by impressing on people more appropriate "associations"; while reform, particularly of the legal system, will penalize unacceptable behavior and provide an incentive for behavior which will promote the social welfare.

Malthus' Political Philosophy

Although Malthus did not write a treatise on political philosophy, his views on the pressing issues of his day indicate that he was largely guided by utilitarian principles. He considered that the goal of politics is the greatest happiness of the greatest number and that the rule for achieving that end is observation, based on experience, of what actually secures the desired end within the particular institutions and interests of England as a nation. A cosmopolitan point of view is conspicuously absent, perhaps as a reaction against Rousseau and Godwin. He was, in some ways, set apart from other utilitarians of his day; specifically, he tended to be conservative, perhaps even reactionary, where others were philosophical radicals. Thus, he defended the traditional English class structure, which most others tended to criticize. Furthermore, he shared neither their anticlerical views nor their optimism for greatly improving the lot of the large mass of humanity.

While Malthus' work does not have a predominantly religious quality, though he was a clergyman in good standing, his utilitarianism has its foundation in his theological views. It is the intention of the Creator to procure what is good for His creatures, and it is this apparent purpose which mankind must fulfill. It is man's reason which must select among the various human impulses in order to carry out the design of the Creator. This design is to be discovered by applying the principle of utility to our actions. It is by examining the consequences of our impulses and subjecting them to the test of utility that we shall gradually acquire the habit of gratifying them only when they will add to the sum of human happiness and thus promote the intention of the Creator. This is the only test by which we can know, independently of the revealed will of God, whether an impulse should be acted upon. It is in this manner that theological postulates behoove us to discipline our impulses to promote not only our own happiness but that of the great majority of our fellowmen as well. The happiness of the whole is the natural outgrowth of the happiness of individuals. It is not institutions and laws, as Godwin maintained, but ourselves who bear the responsibility for human unhappiness. Human happiness is, in fact, he argued, most likely to be attained within existing institutions, specifically the existing form of English constitutional government. His counsel was thus for the preservation of the existing legal, social, and economic status quo. Regardless of the issue, whether the Poor Laws, the Corn Laws, or the problem of maintaining effective demand, he was consistently in favor of preserving the then existing class structure and relying on the principle of utility to improve human society.

THE ESSAY ON POPULATION

Philosophical Background

Malthus' original interest in the population problem was incidental to the much broader question of the reforms proposed by the philosophical radicalists. The spark that kindled the *Essay* was struck as a result of discussions between himself and his father, Daniel Malthus, concerning the arguments of William Godwin, whose new book *The Enquirer* had recently been published. Godwin's earlier *Political Justice* had already proposed a "simple form of society, without government," in which the perfectibility of man will ultimately be realized. This volume, which has been called the first textbook of philosophical radicalism, held that the institutions of the present society, especially as they affect the distribution of wealth, militate against the achievement of perfection and happiness. Reason, argued Godwin, dictates that an equal division of wealth will provide for simple wants and leave ample leisure time for an intellectual and moral improvement which will ultimately establish perfection and happiness on earth.

The French philosopher Marquis de Condorcet had much the same vision, though he relied more on science than morals to produce the ideal society. Like Godwin, he believed in the perfectibility of man, but he emphasized the progress inherent in the cumulative character of knowledge in the arts and sciences, which would produce advances to offset the growth of population. The prospect of overpopulation was viewed as existing only in a future too distant for present contemplation. It was this utopian dream of a golden age of equality and happiness which Malthus' *Essay* was to shatter, for he foresaw the specter of excessive population as a permanent impediment to the improvement of society.

The Postulates

Malthus argued that he required only two postulates to prove the unattainability of the millennium Godwin and Condorcet foresaw: the first, "that food is necessary to the existence of man"; the second, that "the passion between the sexes is necessary, and will remain nearly in its present state."[4] The first postulate is axiomatic; and the second, Malthus argued, Godwin had failed to disprove. He maintained that the instinct for marriage is permanent, though there are admittedly individual exceptions, and that

---

[4] Thomas Malthus, *First Essay on Population* (*1798*), Reprints of Economic Classics (New York: Augustus Kelley, 1965), p. 11.

the operation of the principle of population would make it impossible to attain the millennium. The potential increase of population, when unchecked, is in a geometrical ratio, whereas subsistence can increase only in an arithmetical ratio.

> A slight acquaintance with numbers will shew the immensity of the first power in comparison with the second.
> By that law of our nature which makes food necessary to the life of man, the effects of these two unequal powers must be kept equal.[5]

This implies that there must exist a strong and constantly operating check on population because of the difficulty of obtaining subsistence. This difficulty must necessarily be severely felt by a large proportion of mankind.

Malthus supports his contention that the growth power of population is geometrical only by the experience of the United States, in which population doubled itself in 25 years. This growth potential was then compared with the potential increase of the annual food supply. Our knowledge of the qualities of land, reasons Malthus, indicates that under the most ideal conditions imaginable the increase which can be achieved in 25 years might equal the present produce.

> Let us then take this for our rule, though certainly far beyond the truth; and allow that, by great exertion, the whole produce of the Island might be increased every twenty-five years, by a quantity of subsistence equal to what it at present produces. The most enthusiastic speculator cannot suppose a greater increase than this. In a few centuries it would make every acre of land in the Island like a garden. Yet this ratio of increase is evidently arithmetical.[6]

It is obvious, therefore, that the growth powers of population greatly exceed those of the food supply.

Diminishing Returns

Although Malthus did not explicitly set forth the tendency of diminishing returns on land it is implicitly assumed in his ratios. For while man's subsistence consists of lower forms of animal and vegetable life which, unchecked, also tend to increase in a geometrical ratio, so that it might be presumed that the human population and its food supply would be equally capable of growth, this is the case only when the supply of land is large enough to accommodate the expansion. Because the earth's surface is limited, increasing the food supply necessarily means the application of added productive effort at the margin, where the returns are proportionately less, unless the existing land supply can be made more productive via technological improvements. The problem begins to show itself as soon as a given quantity of land has been brought under cultivation and the animal

---

[5] *Ibid.*, p. 14.
[6] *Ibid.*, p. 22.

and human population have consumed all available food, for then only more effective use of the given supply of land can increase its food-producing potential. This, in Malthus' view, is assuredly more difficult than the increase of living beings by their own act, for he had in mind such increases in the food supply as are made possible by the same methods and techniques as made available the old supplies.

If it is accepted that to raise additional food, in the absence of changes in productive methods, requires more labor per unit of output, while to bring new population into the world is independent of such requirements, the disparity between the growth rate of population and the food supply is readily apparent. This does not imply, as is sometimes suggested, that Malthus believed the geometrical increase is true of man alone, while the arithmetical increase is true of plants and animals. The geometrical increase is characteristic of all things living when furnished with proper nourishment. The power of increase of the lower plants and animals is perhaps even greater than that of man, but their actual increase is quite slow for want of the land supply from which all subsistence, human and otherwise, must be derived. If good land could be gotten in abundance, the increase of food from it would be in a geometrical ratio even greater than that of man. But because good lands are limited in supply and ultimately all under cultivation, increasing the food supply eventually becomes a laborious process which yields increases only at a diminishing rate. Thus, even if one could create an ideal social system, such as Godwin envisioned, in which checks on population would be eliminated or greatly reduced, it would not be long before the pressure of checks would reassert itself, not from any fault of man but because the earths' productiveness does not expand with population.

That there is a tendency toward diminishing returns had, of course, already been noted. Turgot, in particular, had stated the matter quite lucidly.[7] James Anderson, a Scot, who was a prolific writer on economic subjects besides being a farmer, discussed diminishing returns in relationship to rent.[8] But the nineteenth-century English economists appear to have been influenced less by the work of their predecessors than the actual experience of England during the Napoleonic wars. For not only did agricultural prices increase significantly, but large tracts of previously untilled lands were brought under cultivation. It was also recognized that the high price of raw produce, which enables it to yield a high rent, is due to diminishing returns. It would probably have been surprising if the relationship between increasing population and recourse to poor soils had not stimulated inquiry. The observations of Edward West are particularly

---

[7] Anne Robert Jacques Turgot, *Observations sur le Memoire de M. de Saint-Peravy* (1768).

[8] James Anderson, *An Inquiry into the Nature of the Corn Laws with a View to the New Corn Bill Proposed for Scotland* (1777).

pertinent in this connection, for it is he, rather than Mathus or Ricardo, who gave the law of diminishing returns precise formulation, although the latter are more responsible for its prominent place in English political economy.

Checks on Population Growth

From the contradiction between the geometrical ratio of population growth and the arithmetic ratio of the growth of the food supply, Malthus concluded that population increase must necessarily be checked in some manner. In his first edition of the *Essay,* he surmised that such checks would be resolvable into either misery or vice, and that Godwin's hypothesis regarding the ultimate perfectibility of man was therefore rendered untenable. Godwin and Condorcet were wrong, he argued, in attributing all inequality to human institutions. Rather, it is human nature, with its tendency to marry and multiply, which is the most serious obstacle to improvement. No other conclusion is possible if we begin, as Malthus did, by assuming that the desire for food and the desire for marriage are equally urgent and that there is a strong tendency toward diminishing returns from land.

The principle of population thus presented was received as a major contribution to political economy, though it also provoked great protest.[9] Even Godwin acknowledged its value while pointing out that among the more enlightened classes it was not uncommon to postpone marriage to avoid the burden of too great a family and this prudence was precisely the ideal behavior he foresaw as being attainable for the entire population. History has since indicated that this mode of behavior is not beyond man and demonstrated that if Godwin overrated the role of reason, Malthus equally overrated the role of passion.

Malthus eventually saw that he had perhaps placed undue emphasis on vice and misery as checks, and made revisions over the next five years before republication of his *Essay.* In the new edition, he took the position that while man cannot remove the necessity of checks, because there is always a tendency of population to outrun subsistence, he can, with his own self-control, alter their mode of operation. For in addition to the positive checks of misery and vice, there is the preventative check of moral restraint. Moral restraint is interpreted to mean the postponement of marriage until such time as a family can adequately be supported, and the practice of continence outside of marriage. He observed that vice and misery were the primary checks in ancient and primitive societies, whereas moral restraint predominates in modern civilizations. Prudential restraint became the only morally acceptable check to Malthus. Educate the individual, he urged, to postpone marriage until he is capable of supporting a family and to avoid irregular gratification.

---

[9] Kenneth Smith, *The Malthusian Controversy* (London: Routledge and Kegan Paul, 1951), Book II, "The Development of Controversy."

This can best be accomplished, Malthus believed, within the framework of a social system which will encourage people to practice moral restraint. The system which promises the most desirable results in this regard is the existing one of private property, including its characteristics of economic inequality and social class structure, provided it also assures opportunity to those who are ambitious and prudent to rise by their own efforts. The Poor Laws encourage indolence and raise the level only of the weakest members of society, and this is at the expense of the others. If people knew they could not count on parish relief, the ordinary motives of self-interest would force them to help themselves. It was on these grounds that Malthus became an enthusiastic supporter of popular education which would teach enlightened self-interest; at the same time, he opposed the continuation of poor relief.

The Tendency toward Subsistence Wages

One of the main implications deriving from the Malthusian theory of population is that the level of real wages will tend toward subsistence unless the rate of population growth is sufficiently checked by moral restraint. Malthus and his contemporaries thought of the wage rate as depending on the ratio between the labor force and the size of the wage fund. Since it was generally assumed that the wage fund represents a constant proportion of the capital stock, it follows that the continued growth of the population, and thus the labor force, will depress the wage rate to the lowest level compatible with subsistence. This tendency could of course be offset if capital stock, and therefore the wage fund, increases more rapidly than the population. Thus, Malthus associated rising wage rates with a high ratio of capital to labor, whereas falling wage rates were associated with a low ratio of capital to labor. This is a conclusion with which modern economists are in accord, but for a different reason. Modern analysis recognizes that a high ratio of capital to labor affects labor's marginal productivity and consequently its claim to income.

The Tendency for Rents to Rise

Just as the growth of population tended to be associated with a downward pressure on wage rates if there was a wage fund of a given size, so it was also associated with a tendency for rents to rise. Malthus' inquiry into *The Nature and Causes of Rent* addressed itself primarily to the question of whether rent is, as implied by Smith and even the Physiocrats, a monopoly income. This was also the position of David Buchanan, whose argument that rent is the result of a monopoly of land appears to have had a good deal to do with Malthus' inquiry. The inquiry was also associated with the Corn Law controversy. Malthus observed at the outset of his inquiry that this subject "has perhaps a particular claim to our attention at the present moment on account of the discussions which are going on respecting the Corn Laws, and the effects of rent on the price of raw produce and the progress of agricultural improvement." This pamphlet antedated the appearance of Ricardo's *Essay on the Influence of a Low Price of Corn on the Profits of Stock.*

Malthus advanced three reasons for the appearance of rent. He argued, first, that land produces more than enough to maintain its cultivators.[10] This fact alone makes rent "a bountiful gift from providence" rather than the result of monopolistic scarcity. Secondly, he argued, the necessaries of life are uniquely capable of "creating their own demand or of raising up the number of demanders in proportion to the quantity of necessaries produced."[11] It is because population increases with the food supply that its price rises above its cost of production and creates a surplus. Must we not therefore grant, Malthus asks, that its appearance is a clear indication" of a most inestimable quality in the soil, which God has bestowed on man—the quality of being able to maintain more persons than are necessary to work it?"[12] Here, Malthus clearly regards the appearance of rent as being inherent in the progress of society according to the dictates of natural law. The third cause of rent is that the most fertile land is comparatively scarce, and, except in a new country, there is not enough to supply all our wants. When it becomes necessary, because of population growth and diminishing returns, to resort to inferior lands, the products produced thereon will have to be high enough in price to pay their costs of production, and superior lands will then receive rent.

The comparative scarcity of fertile land was viewed in a very different light by Malthus than by his contemporary, David Ricardo. To Malthus, it seemed obvious that not all land can be equally fertile or equally well situated. The superiority of the best land is thus regarded as "a bountiful gift from Providence." This view is expressed in his *Principles of Political Economy* in which he concludes his chapter "Of the Rent of Land" with the statement that "in every point of view, then, in which the subject can be considered, that quality of land which, by the laws of our being, must terminate in rent, appears to be a boon most important to the happiness of mankind; and I am persuaded that its value can only be underrated by those who still labour under some mistake, as to its nature, and its effects on society."[13] Ricardo, on the other hand, was persuaded that rent was due to the niggardliness of nature, which not only caused rents to rise but caused them to absorb a progressively larger proportion of the national product in an insultated economy. It was on these grounds that he advocated the repeal of the Corn Laws in opposition to Malthus.

---

[10] Thomas Malthus, *Principles of Political Economy* (*2d ed., 1836*), Reprints of Economic Classics (New York: Augustus Kelley, 1964), p. 140.

[11] *Ibid.*

[12] *Ibid.,* p. 147.

[13] *Ibid.,* p. 217.

THE PROGRESS OF POPULATION AND WEALTH

The "Effectual" Demand for Labor

In the *Essay,* Malthus was especially concerned to examine the laws which regulate population growth. In the *Principles,* this inquiry was intended to examine the factors which determine increases in subsistence and therefore make possible the growth of population. Subsistence consists of the supplies of food and other necessaries which the worker and his family require for their living. The ultimate limit on the growth of subsistence derives from the supply of land, its fertility, and the state of progress of the arts which govern production. However, while the size of the population is ultimately limited by subsistence, Malthus thought that in many countries the number of inhabitants was actually fewer than could be supported in relative comfort. This led him to inquire what sort of obstacle or impediment existed to prevent the population from advancing to a size compatible with the physical possibility of providing subsistence. He concluded that the chief impediment to progress in the number and well-being of the population is the failure of what he termed "effectual demand" for labor.[14]

While the thesis that the growth of population depends on the effectual demand for labor is implicit in the *Essay,* it is overshadowed by his concern with the relationship between population and the food supply and the checks of vice, misery, and moral restraint. Later, however, he became increasingly concerned with examining the factors which determine what he called the effectual demand for labor. He reasoned that the ability of population to grow depends on the effectual demand for labor.[15]

The effectual demand for labor is reflected in the extent of its employment. Employment regulates the wages of labor, and the latter determine the power of the laborer to acquire food and necessaries for the support of himself and his family. Employment therefore also regulates the size of the family the worker is able to support. The demand for labor is, in turn, "proportioned to the rate of increase in the quantity and value of those funds, whether arising from capital or revenue, which are actually employed in the maintenance of labor."[16] Accumulation is therefore essential to the progress of population and wealth, for it makes it possible to augment the wage fund out of which labor is supported. Effectual demand for labor requires that there be additions to the wage fund. But there must also be a demand for commodities. Without a demand for commodities, the demand

---

[14] *Ibid.,* pp. 231–40.

[15] This aspect of Malthus' work is discussed in an interesting essay by Joseph J. Spengler, "Malthus' Total Population Theory: A Restatement and Reappraisal," *Canadian Journal of Economics and Political Science,* February–May, 1945.

[16] Malthus, *Principles of Political Economy, op. cit.,* p. 234.

for labor will diminish. If income receivers are too thrifty, there is likely to be a depression of wealth and population which is caused by the presence of gluts.[17]

Commodity and Capital Gluts

During the first decade and a half of her war with France, Great Britain enjoyed an era of almost continuous prosperity. The post-Napoleonic war years, however, were interrupted by periods of severe industrial stagnation. Domestic depression was aggravated by failure of revival in foreign trade and by a poor harvest, which raised the price of bread. Moreover, the new Corn Law of 1815 effectively excluded foreign grain. It was this chain of events which led Malthus to maintain that Great Britain was experiencing the effects of an insufficient demand for capital as the result of a decline in the demand for consumer goods.[18] He thought that the English social structure, and consequently the distribution of income, encouraged such a large volume of saving that it produced a glut of commodities as well as capital. Another important reason, he believed, for the fall in the demand for goods and the resulting redundancy of capital was the decrease in governmental military expenditures in the transition from war to peace. The cessation of these expenditures, coupled with the expanded productive capacity made possible by earlier rapid accumulation, resulted in a volume of production which was too great for the revenue that was available to purchase it.

Malthus was by no means the only or perhaps even the first student of economic crisis. Karl Marx, in fact, maintained that Jean Charles Sismondi was responsible for ideas generally attributed to Malthus. While Sismondi's first theoretical work, *La Rechesse Commerciale* (1803) was strongly in the tradition of Adam Smith, his later *Nouveau Principle de l'Economie politique* (1815), written against the background of the crises of the early nineteenth century, questioned the self-equilibrating character of the capitalistic system. It laid particular emphasis upon the ever-increasing productive powers of the modern capitalistic system, and reasoned that the worker, having only the purchasing power of subsistence wages, is unable to purchase all the products the system is capable of producing. Periodic excess and unemployment are the inevitable outcome, which, with the progress of further technological advances, will necessarily become worse because competition among capitalists to employ capital profitably will intensify overproduction. Thus, Sismondi emphasized the atomistic competitive character of production which, in conjunction with the inadequacy of consumer purchasing power, manifests itself in the most striking feature of economic crises: overproduction.

---

[17] *Ibid.,* pp. 314–30.
[18] *Ibid.,* pp. 413–37.

Contemporaries such as Jean Baptiste Say, James Mill, and David Ricardo regarded depressions as inevitable concomitants of economic progress. But they emphatically denied that there could be either a general overproduction of goods or an overaccumulation of capital in the long run. This conclusion derived from their acceptance of Say's law, which maintained that aggregate effective demand is necessarily the equivalent of aggregate supply.[19] Since goods are intended to be exchanged for other goods, every act of production simultaneously creates a market for the whole product produced by making available the monetary means of purchasing it. Specific commodities may at times be produced in greater quantities than the demand for them warrants, but a state of general overproduction, or glut, is impossible. However, even such maladjustments will tend to correct themselves. If the supply of a given commodity is excessive, the losses incurred in its production will soon diminish its supply; while, conversely, if the supply falls short of current demand, the resulting high profits will expand output so that individual demands and supplies tend to be balanced.

Ricardo drew still another conclusion, namely, that an overaccumulation of capital is also an impossibility. Capital, he argued, will never be accumulated in a greater quantity than can be productively employed. Its accumulation depends on the long-run trend of profits, and this is contingent on the productivity of labor and the margin of cultivation. If accumulation proceeds at a greater rate than can assure profitability, the motive for continued accumulation will disappear. Low rates of profit would make "unproductive consumption," by which Ricardo and Malthus meant expenditures not aimed at further production, more attractive. In short, Ricardo took it for granted that low rates of profit would alter the proportions of spending and savings so that less capital would accumulate.

Malthus, on the other hand, maintained that capital accumulation is not automatically limited by a decline in the rate of profits. He observed that "while it is quite certain that an adequate passion for consumption may fully keep up the proper proportion between supply and demand, whatever may be the powers of production, it appears to be quite as certain that an inordinate passion for accumulation must inevitably lead to a supply of commodities beyond what the structure and habits of such a society will permit to be consumed."[20] While he fully agreed that some degree of frugality is necessary and desirable, he held that saving pushed to excess will destroy the motive for production by reducing what might be termed the "effective demand" for commodities. Although he did not specifically

---

[19] Jacob Hollander has maintained that the generalization known as Say's law was, in fact, conceived by James Mill before it was developed by Say. See Hollander's *Introduction to Ricardo's Notes on Malthus* (Baltimore: Johns Hopkins Press, 1928). In any event, Mill evidently taught the principle to Ricardo.

[20] Malthus, *Principles of Political Economy,* p. 325.

define the term "effective demand," he apparently meant the ability and willingness of the community to buy a commodity at a price equivalent to its labor command value, that is, at a price which will enable the producer to cover his costs plus profit at the prevailing rate. He regarded the market price of the commodity, which results from the interaction of supply and demand, as much more important than the natural price. For while he agreed with Ricardo that rising food costs would gradually eliminate profits through their impact on wages, since wages and profits vary inversely, he maintained that a theory which explains short-run variations in profits is necessary to explain the phenomenon of gluts. He maintained that when profits rise, "there will be a tendency to spend a smaller proportion of the gains and to save a greater." This increase in savings results in the employment of more "productive" laborers and thus in a greater quantity of goods available for purchase. But because the number of persons remains the same in the short run, and because it takes time to learn new habits of consumption, the effective demand for consumer goods is not large enough to offset the reduction which results from the savings of capitalists and other wealthy persons. The result is that goods can be sold only at prices lower than the costs of production, so that ultimately the reduction of profits destroys the capacity to save.

Malthus believed that James Mill and David Ricardo committed a serious error in maintaining that accumulation of capital would assure a demand for goods. Their argument, he said, proceeded on the premise of a handicraft economy in which money serves merely to implement the exchange of commodities for one another; whereas, in fact, in a society which is composed of a class of proprietors and a class of laborers, exchange also involves the exchange of capital in the form of the wage fund and labor. Malthus maintained that in dealing with the problem of gluts, Mill as well as Ricardo, in effect, assumed away the capitalistic labor market by conceiving that exchange consisted in the main of the exchange of commodities, which had value in accordance with the labor they embodied. He, on the other hand, equated value with labor command. Thus, within the framework of Malthus' definition of values, Say's law could not hold because the aggregate demand for goods consists of subsistence wages (labor commanded), while aggregate supply consists of this quantity plus profit. The inadequacy of effective demand and gluts is therefore the logical counterpart to his theory of value.

Unproductive Consumption

Malthus reasoned that in a society comprised of proprietors and laborers, the origin and use of most income shares militates against an adequate level of effective demand for commodities. Specifically, wages impinge upon profits, and capitalists are more interested in accumulation than in making large expenditures on consumer goods. Their savings increase productive capacity and therefore aggravate the problem of maintaining effective demand. It is for this reason that Malthus looked to the expenditures of the rentier class and other unproductive consumers to maintain the level of effective demand. Since rent is a differential surplus, its expenditure adds to effective demand without adding to costs of production, whereas other forms of income are costs of production as well as sources of purchasing power.

There are other classes of unproductive consumers—menial servants, statesmen, physicians, judges, lawyers, clergymen, etc. The expenditures of these persons also add to the effective demand for goods and thus offset the deficiency of consumer demand which arises out of the savings process. Malthus maintained that it is absolutely essential for an economy with great powers of production to have a body of unproductive consumers. Unproductive consumption is the safety valve which he viewed as diminishing the undesirable effects of too rapid accumulation. Without it, the economy will experience periods of commodity gluts and capital redundancy.

Progress and the Structure of the Economy

The effectual demand for labor, and therefore the growth potential of population, is also affected by the structure of the economy. Malthus thought that the effective demand for labor is best maintained in an economy in which the balance between the industrial and agricultural sectors is such that the country is always independent of foreign sources of food. Unlike Ricardo, he was in favor of restricting free trade in corn, on the ground that it would contribute to maintaining the effectual demand for labor. His argument is presented in his article *The Grounds of an Opinion on the Policy of Restricting the Importation of Foreign Corn* (1815). In it, he argues that it is desirable for England to encourage domestic production of grain on a scale that would make her independent of foreign supplies, even though it would tend to raise English crop prices. This position is, he tells us, mainly the result of French legislation restricting the export of corn. Since England was greatly dependent on exports from France to supplement her home supply, he argued that a system of free trade would render domestic supplies inadequate in years of scarcity abroad. In view of England's special circumstances, therefore, he argued in favor of protection.

His second reason for advocating a restricted corn trade for England was his observation that increased industrialization tends to be accompanied by more frequent and more severe business fluctations, which particularly burden the lower classes, and that it is therefore desirable in England, which is "the most manufacturing [country] of any ever recorded in history," "that its agriculture should keep pace with its manufactures, even at the expense of retarding in some degree the growth of manufactures."[21] He thus concluded that in England, agricultural protection was in the interest of general abundance and advantageous to the working class by protecting it against adverse price movements originating abroad as well as minimizing the evil effects which would be associated with rapid industrialization.

He observed that while predominately agricultural economies also tend to be poorer than those which are more industrialized, the "premature check" to the progress of the population is due to the remains of the feudal system. While he asserted the primary importance of agriculture in promoting the progress of population and wealth, subsequent editions of his *Principles* became increasingly cognizant that industrialization also contributed to maintaining and enhancing the effectual demand for labor.

CONCLUDING REMARKS

The impact of an individual's work may manifest itself in a variety of ways. First, and perhaps foremost, it may influence subsequent work in terms of method or content in its own discipline. It may also become incorporated in some way into policy measures and so guide the solution of practical problems. Finally, it may inspire new work in other fields of knowledge. Malthus' efforts have the distinction of having borne fruit in all these directions.

There is, first of all, his contribution to the development of pure economic theory. In Malthus' day the principles which subsequently became known as the "laws of classical economics" were only beginning to be forged and he contributed greatly to their development, in terms of both content and methodology. At a time when the emphasis of inquiry was at least as much on practical policy as on the discovery of principles (witness the fact that Malthus was the first of a long line of Cambridge economists to be known by the title Professor of Political Economy) Malthus used the deductive method to establish formal principles. Both the principle of population and the principle of effective demand are propositions he established by means of deductive logic.

In establishing these principles, Malthus pioneered in applying the methods of deductive logic to the complex world of daily events. These events crystallized themselves to Malthus chiefly in the form of worker misery. The poverty suffered by the laboring classes before the Napoleonic wars was afterward compounded by unemployment. Malthus directed his attention to both aspects of the poverty problem. His approach was that of the moral scientist schooled in the a priori method of the Cambridge tradition. To this, he added a wealth of historical and contemporary factual information which guided him in the proper selection and formulation of

---

[21] Malthus, *Observations on the Effects of the Corn Laws* (1814).

the premises from which he ultimately arrived, by means of deductive logic, at his conclusions. His principle of population was offered to explain the determination of the supply of labor and was the basis for the conclusion that the only way of improving the standard of living of the laboring classes was the control of numbers. The principle of effectual demand maintained that the aggregate demand for labor is derived from the aggregate demand for commodities and determines the ability of population to grow. Malthus maintained, on the basis of this principle, that excessive savings are associated with gluts of commodities and capital, and therefore with an inadequate demand for labor.

The importance of Malthus' principle of effective demand has come to be appreciated only in this century. Not until the worldwide depression of the 1930's was the principle of effective demand to be reiterated and extended by John Maynard Keynes. In the long interim the conclusions derived from Say's law were presented with such effectiveness that it was accepted that any economy whose operation is guided by a freely operating price system will tend automatically fully to employ its resources. Thus, Malthus' name has been immortalized forever by his principle of population and is even now remembered only by relatively few for his principle of effective demand.

In the western world the triumphs of technology and the practice of contraception have intervened to counteract the dire implications of Malthus' theory of population growth. But given the premises from which Malthus started, no other conclusion is possible than the one at which he arrived. This is all too evident in areas of the world like Asia, in which the premises on which Malthus rested his conclusions are empirically verifiable.

Though the *Essay* prompted angry protests when it first appeared, its eventual impact on the English Parliament is apparent in the passage of a new Poor Law in 1834 which, in comparison with the earlier legislation, greatly limited aid to the poor, particularly of illegitimate birth. Malthus' principle of population was also significant in causing the first census to be taken in 1801. It also inspired innumerable empirical and theoretical works on demography, besides serving as an inspiration to Charles Darwin in the development of his theory of evolution.[22]

SUGGESTIONS FOR FURTHER READING

BONAR, JAMES. *Malthus and His Work*. London: George Allen and Unwin, Ltd., 1924.

GRAMPP, WILLIAM D. "Malthus on Money Wages and Welfare," *American Economic Review*. Vol. XLVI, No. 5 (December, 1956).

---

[22] *Life and Letters of Charles Darwin,* New York: D. Appleton, 1897, Vol. I, p. 83.

HALÉVY, ELIE. *The Growth of Philosophical Radicalism*. New York: Augustus Kelley, 1949.

MALTHUS, THOMAS. *First Essay on Population* (*1798*). Reprints of Economic Classics. New York: Augustus Kelley, 1965.

———. *Principles of Political Economy* (*2d ed., 1836*). Reprints of Economic Classics. New York: Augustus Kelley, 1964.

SMITH, KENNETH. *The Malthusian Controversy*. London: Routledge and Kegan Paul, 1951.

SPENGLER, J. J. "Malthus' Total Population Theory: A Restatement and Reappraisal," *Canadian Journal of Economics and Political Science* (February–May, 1945). Reprinted in SPENGLER and ALLEN, *op. cit.*

Chapter 7

THE CONTRIBUTION OF DAVID RICARDO TO ECONOMIC ANALYSIS

INTRODUCTION

Life and Times (1772–1823)

The classical tradition achieved the apex of its development with the work of David Ricardo. It is remarkable that a person of his background should have made such a distinguished contribution to economics, since he was destined, as a youth, to a business rather than an academic career. His father, a native of Holland, of the Jewish faith, settled in England and eventually became a member of the Stock Exchange. Young David was already in his father's employ at the age of 14, and it was fully expected that this would be his lifework. Indeed, he amassed a fortune in the exchange at such an early age that he had ample time to devote himself to such studies as took his fancy. This was accomplished largely on his own resources, for his marriage to a Quaker and subsequent conversion to Christianity estranged him from his father.

His first acquaintance with the subject to which he was to contribute so importantly was through Smith's *Wealth of Nations,* which came into his hands in 1799.[1] However, a decade was to elapse before anything bearing Ricardo's authorship was to appear in print. The subject matter of his contributions clearly reflected the transformation England had undergone in the forty-odd years that had elapsed since the appearance of Smith's great work. Population, in spite of emigration, had increased substantially. Though England was still able to feed herself and even exported some grain as late as 1812 and 1813, the price of bread became a major issue. Nor was industrialization to relieve the problem, for manufacturing processes were also dependent on products of the soil. Moreover, the introduction of machinery created new problems quite unlike those which confront a predominantly agricultural nation.

It was the currency question which stimulated Ricardo's initial writing effort. The English monetary system had, like the rest of the economy, undergone substantial change. In Smith's day, money consisted largely of

---

[1] John R. McCulloch (ed.), *The Works of David Ricardo* (London, 1886), pp. xvi–xxxiii, "Life and Writings of Mr. Ricardo."

coin and paper notes, redeemable in gold, issued by the Bank of England and relatively few rural banks. The subsequent growth in the number of rural banks, largely unregulated with respect to their issue of paper currency, led to the assumption of central bank functions by the Bank of England. When, however, that bank was forced, toward the end of the Napoleonic wars, to suspend the redemption of its notes in gold, the value of English currency was no longer related to the value of gold. For Ricardo, the rise in the market price of bullion and the fall of the exchange rate which took place was the stimulus to a careful inquiry. His analysis of these phenomena, intended for his own edification, was shown to the editor of the *Morning Chronicle,* who persuaded him to allow their publication in letter form. The response to his observations was sufficiently great to induce him to enlarge upon his subject in a tract entitled *The High Price of Bullion: A Proof of the Depreciation of Bank Notes.* With its publication, Ricardo became an active participant in the famous bullion controversy, one of the major issues of the day.[2] The issue was the cause of the great depreciation of paper money and the associated rise in prices, an upheaval of such proportions that an investigation was undertaken by the Bullion Committee. Ricardo found the cause of these phenomena in the overissue of paper money.

In 1815, Ricardo published his *Essay on the Influence of a Low Price of Corn on the Profits of Stock,* in which he advanced a strong argument for free trade in grain, in opposition to Malthus. In the following year, he made another contribution to the literature on money and banking with his *Proposals for an Economical and Secure Currency with Observations on the Profits of the Bank of England.* The latter essay concerned itself with the value of money; and in it, Ricardo took the position that it is unnecessary for a currency to have intrinsic worth. Rather, what is essential is that the supply of a paper currency be sufficiently limited to maintain its value on a par with the value of gold. He offered a plan for maintaining the value of paper currency on a par with gold without making it convertible into coin in order to save the expense associated with metallic currency. This plan, which was subsequently adopted by the Bank of England, proposed that bank notes be made convertible into bars of gold bullion of a standard weight and purity instead of making them convertible into gold coin. Although the plan was effective in checking the overissue of notes, it was later decided to continue a mixed currency, even though it was more expensive to maintain than one which consisted exclusively of paper because the pound notes which replaced sovereigns became subject to forgery.[3]

By the time Ricardo published his work on the *Principles of Political*

---

[2] See below, pp. 208–10.

[3] McCulloch, *op. cit.,* pp. xxii–xxiii.

Economy and Taxation in 1817, he had already earned a considerable reputation as a writer on current issues. This interest was ultimately to carry him into the House of Commons. He took his seat in 1819 as a member for Portarlington and exercised considerable influence. His contributions to the literature on current affairs continued. In 1820, he contributed an article to the Supplement of the *Encyclopaedia Britannica* on the "Funding System" and, in 1822, his tract on *Protection to Agriculture,* which, even if he had never written anything else would, in the opinion of his biographer, "have placed him in the first rank of political economists."[4]

Although his style of writing was extremely abstract, there was nothing unrealistic about the issues to which Ricardo addressed himself. Indeed, the problems were many and pressing, and hinged closely on the fact that the country was becoming ever more populous and restrictions on the importation of grain continued to exist. The island had long since experienced diminishing returns on land, and yet the landed interests exerted pressure for an increase in protection at a time when its abolition appeared to be called for. It was largely because of the pressure of diminishing returns that Ricardo found himself unable to share Smith's optimism regarding the future well-being of the large mass of the population. Without free importation of corn, he argued, food could not be cheap. Wages, therefore, would necessarily rise, and this would tend to lower profits and arrest further accumulation. His analysis was thus oriented to the question of economic progress; but unlike Smith, he regarded progress as being closely associated with the trend of the distributive shares. This was an intensely practical issue which necessarily led Ricardo into the policy question of the Corn Laws. It is important to recognize that Ricardo's analysis, particularly as it relates to the trend of the distributive shares, is presented within the context of an "insulated" economy, that is, an economy which does not import agricultural products. As such, it is specifically oriented to the issue of the Corn Laws and the consequences inherent in their continuance.

PRINCIPLES OF POLITICAL ECONOMY AND TAXATION

Introduction

The major part of Ricardo's *Principles* was written in a single year and incorporated many of the ideas which had already been presented in his tracts and pamphlets. It appears to have been undertaken at least partly at the urging of James Mill.[5] The issues to which he addressed himself were pressing, and he could not allow himself a long period for revision and reflection, as did Smith. Partly on this account, and perhaps because of his

---

[4] *Ibid.,* p. xxix.

[5] John Stuart Mill, *Autobiography,* London: 1873, p. 27.

own lack of academic training, his book suffers from a poor arrangement of subject matter and is generally less than polished. His style is abstract in the extreme and seldom relieved by digressions into history or philosophy of the sort we find in Smith's volume. His rigorously deductive method was to set the pattern for much of the subsequent work in the field of political economy. This is not to say that political economy became divorced from philosophy and psychology, but rather that many of the observations which were previously made concerning human behavior and social institutions could now be accepted as postulates upon which subsequent analysis could be based. The high degree of abstraction we encounter in Ricardo's work should not, however, blind us to the fact that he was an intensely practical man with wide experience and knowledge of his contemporary world.

THE THEORY OF EXCHANGE VALUE

The Measurement of Exchange Value

Smith, it will be recalled, regarded labor as the only unvarying measure of value. Ricardo disagreed and maintained that the value of labor is no less variable than that of gold or silver or corn. Its value is determined in precisely the same manner as the exchangeable value of any other commodity. There is no commodity which is truly an invariable measure of value. "Of such a measure it is impossible to be possessed, because there is no commodity which is not itself exposed to the same variations as the things the value of which is to be ascertained; that is, there is none which is not subject to require more or less labour for its production."[6] Ricardo, however, recognizes that his analysis of price will be greatly facilitated by having an invariable measure of value. He suggests, therefore, that the production of gold might be assumed to take place with the aid of a combination of fixed and circulating capital which approximates the average quantity employed in most industries. If this assumption be granted, we may regard money made of gold as an invariable standard of value and thus be able to conclude that changes in the price of any given commodity are the result of changes in the exchange value of that commodity rather than changes in the value of the standard in terms of which it is being measured. Ricardo's analysis of exchange value, therefore, is premised on the assumption that the value of the monetary unit of account, in terms of which values are expressed, does not change. This assumption, which subsequently became fundamental to value analysis, makes money a passive unit of account which facilitates more convenient and efficient exchanges, but in no way alters the final relationships which result. While increases or decreases in

---

[6] David Ricardo, "Principles of Political Economy and Taxation" in *The Works and Correspondence of David Ricardo,* Piero Sraffa and Maurice Dobb (eds.) Cambridge, England: The University Press, 10 volumes, 1951–55 Vol. I p. 43–44. Subsequent references are to this edition of Ricardo's work unless otherwise noted.

the money flow will tend to raise or lower all prices and temporarily alter exchange ratios because some money prices move more rapidly than others, these are short-run disturbances. The explanation of value in exchange relationships quite properly assumes such variations to be absent. Thus, when Ricardo refers to price, it is synonymous with exchange value; and unless he specifically refers to "market price," he means "natural price," or the price in terms of embodied labor.

The Source of Exchange Value

Ricardo began his analysis of exchange value by recalling Smith's distinction between value in use and value in exchange. He asserts that for a commodity to have value in exchange, it is essential that it have utility, although utility is not a measure of that value. Having utility, commodities derive their exchangeable value from their scarcity and from the quantity of labor required to obtain them.[7]

Some commodities derive value from their scarcity alone. Such objects as rare pictures, books, coins, and other art objects which no amount of labor can reproduce are in this class. The implication is that when supply cannot be adjusted, demand will rule in the determination of exchange value. The great bulk of commodities are, however, reproducible and therefore derive their value not from scarcity but from the labor requirements of production.

Commodities have past labor as well as present labor embodied in them. Though Smith talked of that early and rude state of society which preceded the accumulation of capital, there was never a period in history, Ricardo observed, when capital was nonexistent. "Without some weapon neither the beaver nor the deer could be destroyed; and therefore their value would be regulated not solely by the time and labour necessary for their destruction, but also by the time and labour necessary for providing the hunter's capital, the weapon by the aid of which their destruction was effected."[8] Thus, Ricardo appears to identify capital with labor. He was of course conceiving of real capital rather than money capital and included within this category, as did Smith, not only such instruments of production as buildings, machines, tools, and equipment but also circulating capital, which is comprised primarily of the wage fund out of which productive workers are supported. The primary role of capital, with Ricardo as with Smith, therefore, is the employment of labor through advances from the wage fund. The consumer goods workers purchase continue to be part of the real investment of the economy, and the new goods they produce represent the reproduction of this capital in another form. Their sale merely reimburses the wage advances previously made plus profits.

---

[7] *Ibid.*, p. 12.
[8] *Ibid.*, p. 23.

Exchange value, therefore, is proportional not only to the direct labor involved in production, but also that which is "bestowed on the implements, tools, and buildings with which their labor is assisted."[9]

Though Ricardo accepted the principle that the ratio of exchange between goods will reflect their cost of production, including not only the current rate of wages but also the current rate of profits, he has often been regarded as an exponent of the labor theory of value.[10] Actually, he was not particularly concerned with explaining the ratio of exchange between commodities. His primary interest was in explaining alterations in exchange values because such variations affect the distributive shares going to laborers, capitalists, and landlords.[11] Ricardo reasoned that *changes* in the rate at which two commodities are exchanged for one another derive from changes in their relative content of past and present labor. This implies that exchange values are not affected by wage rate differences between workers, or by changes in the level of wages and profits, or by the inclusion of rent in the price of a product. Let us proceed with each of these in turn, bearing in mind that Ricardo's theory of value is a labor theory only in a very special sense.

The Influence of Wage and Profit Levels on Exchange Values

Labor is not homogeneous, and different commodities are certain to be produced with different kinds and qualities of labor as well as different quantities. Qualitative differences between labor of the same duration will be reflected, Ricardo maintained, in the wage rates prevailing in the market. But, he argued, these differences will not affect exchange values. If the labor embodied in one commodity is superior in some way, and therefore more highly paid than that embodied in some other commodity, the effect is precisely the same as if a greater quantity of labor had been used.

Nor did Ricardo think that variations in the level of wages would have any influence on exchange values. A change in the wage level will only affect the level of profits. This results because Ricardo, like Smith before him, conceived of wages and profits as varying inversely with each other. Thus the exchange value of two goods remains the same if their labor content does not change. Only the ratio between wages and profits is changed by an alteration in the level of wages and profit.

While there necessarily will be wage rate differences among different kinds of labor, Ricardo believed that capital is sufficiently mobile and the

[9] *Ibid.,* p. 24.

[10] Consult Oswald St. Clair, *A Key to Ricardo* (New York: Kelley and Millman, Inc., 1957), pp. 26–27 and Mark Blaug, *Ricardian Economics* (New Haven: Yale University Press, 1958), pp. 33–37 for a discussion of this issue.

[11] See John M. Cassels, "A Reinterpretation of Ricardo on Value," *Quarterly Journal of Economics,* Vol. XLIX (May, 1935), pp. 518–32; also "Introduction to Ricardo's Works," written by Sraffa, in Sraffa and Dobb, *op. cit.,* Vol. I, Secs. IV–V.

opportunities for its employment are sufficiently competitive to insure a uniform rate of profit throughout the economy in the long run. The prices of all commodities would thus comprise the same percentage of profit on all the capital invested in their production, so that variations in the level of profits are not a source of variations in exchange value. While this principle is later qualified to take cognizance of different proportions of fixed and circulating capital and capitals of unequal durability, it enabled Ricardo to conclude, after also eliminating rent as a determinant of exchange values, that variations in the relative values of commodities are derived from variations in the quantities of labor required to produce them.

The Influence of Land Rent on Exchange Values

Ricardo's initial examination of the phenomenon of rent in the *Principles* is occasioned by the necessity of inquiring whether "the appropriation of land, and the consequent creation of rent, will cause any variation in the relative value of commodities, independently of the quantity of labour necessary to production."[12] He defines rent as the compensation which is paid to the owner of land for the original and indestructible powers of the soil. Such rent is distinct from the return from capital improvements on land or the presence of valuable commodities such as coal, stone, or timber. The latter give rise to profits rather than rent, and these are regulated by different factors than those which regulate rents.[13]

When a country is first settled and there is rich and fertile land available in abundance relative to the size of the population to be supported, there will be no rent on any part of the land. Land is, in effect, a free good under such circumstances. It is not until the growth of population and the progress of society require land of a second degree of fertility to be brought under cultivation that rent will emerge on land of the first quality. This rent will depend on the difference in the productive powers of the two pieces of land. With each subsequent need to bring less productive land under cultivation, rent will appear on land which previously yielded none and will increase on those lands which already yield rent. Envision the application of a given quantity of labor and capital to lands which, in consequence of their fertility and/or situation may be regarded as the best grade. The output which is produced will have an exchange value which reflects the labor and capital embodied in it. The whole price

---

[12] Ricardo, *Principles of Political Economy and Taxation, op. cit.,* Vol. I, p. 67.

[13] However, Ricardo was not always consistent in his use of the term "rent." For example, he says that the payments to the owners of mines for permission to work them are for the minerals removed and not for the original and indestructible powers of the soil. He also suggests, in a note at the end of his chapter on poor rates, that a portion of the capital used by landlords may be "amalgamated with the land, and [so] tends to increase its productive powers, [that] the remuneration paid to the landlord for its use is strictly of the nature of rent, and is subject to all the laws of rent."

will therefore be absorbed by wages and profit, and the land itself will command no return. If, in consequence of a growing population, it becomes necessary to employ land which is inferior to that first employed, and an equal amount of labor and capital is applied in its cultivation, a smaller output will now be obtained. It costs more to produce the same product on second-grade land. The value in exchange of units of a product so produced is regulated by the same principle which ruled with respect to the output produced on the best grade of land, namely, the labor and capital embodied in its creation. However, there cannot be two rates of exchange for different units of the same product when they are sold in the same purely competitive market. Thus the exchange value of the entire output is regulated by the least favorable production requirements. The exchange value or price of units of a commodity produced under more favorable circumstances is precisely the same as that of units of the same commodity produced under less favorable circumstances. To whom does the difference go, and why? Since only one rate of wages and one rate of profit can prevail, it goes to the owner of superior land in the form of rent. Ricardo therefore concluded that rent is not a cause of the exchangeable value of a product, but the result of it.

Precisely the same result would obtain if additional labor and capital are employed on land already under cultivation instead of bringing in new land. This is the alternative which will be chosen if it will produce a greater product than can be gotten from the cultivation of additional land.

> In such case, capital will be preferably employed on the old land, and will equally create a rent; for rent is always the difference between the produce obtained by the employment of two equal quantities of capital and labour. . . . In this case, as well as in the other, the capital last employed pays no rent.[14]

The payment of rent, however, does not cause an increase in the exchangeable value of raw produce. Exchange value is regulated by the quantity of labor bestowed in production on that land which pays no rent. Thus, says Ricardo, "corn is not high because a rent is paid, but a rent is paid because corn is high, and it has been justly observed that no reduction would take place in the price of corn, although landlords should forego the whole of their rent."[15]

The Ricardian theory of rent lends itself readily to modern terminology and apparatus, for it is in essence a marginal productivity theory.[16]

---

[14] Ricardo, *Principles of Political Economy and Taxation, op. cit.,* Vol. I, pp. 71–72.

[15] *Ibid.,* pp. 74–75.

[16] J. B. Clark and Philip H. Wicksteed were first to appreciate this aspect of Ricardo's theory of rent. See J. B. Clark, "Distribution by a Law of Rent," *Publications of the American Economic Association, Series* 3, IV (1903), pp. 154–65 and P. H. Wicksteed *Co-ordination of the Laws of Distribution* (1894) (London: London School Reprint No. 12, 1932).

Assume a situation in which a product, say wheat, is produced on four grades of land of equal area. Production proceeds with the application of successive equal doses of labor and capital to these fixed quantities of land. The total and marginal outputs yielded are summarized in Table 7–1. That portion of the table relating to total output reflects the tendency toward diminishing returns as additional equal doses of labor and capital are applied to lands A through D, each being progressively less productive than the preceding one. The right-hand portion of the table relates to the additional or marginal output associated with the application of additional doses of labor and capital to each grade of land. Strictly speaking, marginal analysis should involve very small increments, whereas the numbers used here are quite large, but they suffice to illustrate the relationship between the total and the marginal product.

TABLE 7–1

Inputs of Labor and Capital	Total Output of Wheat				Marginal Output of Wheat			
	A	B	C	D	A	B	C	D
0..........	0	0	0	0	...	...	...	...
1..........	400	300	200	100	400	300	200	100
2..........	600	475	300	...	200	175	100	...
3..........	750	575	...	...	150	100	...	...
4..........	850	...	...	...	100	...	...	...

If it is now assumed that each dose of labor and capital costs $100 to employ and that the price of wheat on the market is $1.00, it is obvious that the output potential of land of grade A warrants the application of four doses of labor and capital, whereas land D warrants the application of only one. This is the case because the marginal cost of these inputs is exactly equal to the marginal value product, which is the marginal physical product multiplied by the market price. The market price is equal to the marginal cost of production and, under competitive conditions, is the same to all sellers. On land of grade D the cost of labor and capital absorbs the entire product, whereas lands C, B, and A yield a surplus of $100, $275, and $450, respectively. These amounts go to the landlord as rent; and land of grade D, the marginal land, is no-rent land. This is the extensive margin of cultivation, yielding an output whose value is just equal to the labor and capital cost of producing it.

The same principle is applicable to intramarginal land; thus, it pays to cultivate grades A, B, and C intensively until the value of the marginal product produced is just equal to the marginal cost of producing it. Cultivation will therefore continue until the returns at the intensive margin of cultivation are equal to those at the extensive margin. The variable factor, that is, the labor and capital component, receives the value of the marginal product as its return, while the fixed factor, land in this instance, receives the difference between the total revenue and the portion going to labor and capital. This difference is the surplus Ricardo called rent. It is not part of the cost of production in that its elimination (for example, by a tax levied on it) would not affect the size of the product which a given quantity of labor and capital could produce. Only the costs of labor and capital must be met to assure that the output will be forthcoming. Thus, the price must be high enough to cover the labor and capital cost of using marginal land, or its output will not be forthcoming. But a product price equal to the marginal cost of producing on marginal land leaves a surplus on better than marginal land. It is in this sense that rent is determined by price and will increase with every rise in the labor and capital cost of producing output as the extensive margin of cultivation is extended.

Ricardo's Qualification of the Labor Theory of Value

While Ricardo was at great pains to demonstrate that changes in the rate at which two commodities are exchanged for one another derive from changes in their relative content of past and present labor, and are not affected by the rate of wages or profit, his examination of the effect of different capital structures actually introduced a modification to this principle. He observed that when the ratio of fixed to circulating capital is increased, or capital of greater durability is employed, it has the effect of increasing the length of time which must elapse before the final products can come to market. Capitalists must therefore be compensated for the greater time lapse by greater profits. It follows that goods produced with equal amounts of fixed capital or capital of greater durability cannot sell at the same price as those produced with more circulating capital or less durable capital, even if the same quantity of direct labor is involved. Thus the effect of different capital structures is to qualify the principle that relative values are proportional to the relative quantities of labor used in production.

The significance of this qualification has been a source of controversy and discussion from the outset. Ricardo himself seemed unclear on the matter. On the one hand, he minimized the importance of the modification and maintained that commodities are valuable in proportion to the quantity of labor bestowed on them.[17] On the other, he seemed to sense that the qualification he proposed brought to the forefront the role of capital in the production process and involved the cost of the capital component. The classic case in which he and his contemporaries came to grips with this problem was their effort to explain why wine has a greater value than grape juice, though no additional labor has been applied.[18] Ricardo eventually

---

[17] "Letter to J. B. Say," in the *Works and Correspondence of David Ricardo, op. cit.,* Vol. IX, p. 169.

[18] "Letter to McCulloch," *Ibid.,* p. 330.

concluded that there must be some element other than accumulated labor in capital and that this other element is waiting. Thus, he appeared to be on the very brink not only of adopting a more sophisticated concept of capital, but also of giving up the proposition that exchange values are in proportion to the relative quantities of labor.

To appreciate why Ricardo, in fact, did neither of these things, we need only remind ourselves that with respect to the value problem, he was concerned with explaining changes in exchange values rather than the ratio of exchange between goods at any moment of time. Furthermore, he was concerned with the value problem only insofar as it affected the determination of the distributive shares. Different capital-labor ratios necessarily mean that a change in the level of money wage rates, and therefore the rate of profit, must have an impact on the price structure. Ricardo realized that if the level of wages is rising, it will cause the prices of goods produced with a smaller capital-labor ratio to rise relative to those produced with a greater capital-labor ratio. Industries like agriculture, which operate under diminishing returns, are labor- rather than capital-intensive. The prices of their products will therefore rise relative to that of gold, which, it will be recalled, serves Ricardo as an invariable measure of value by virtue of his assumption that it operates with an average capital-labor ratio. On the other hand, the prices of manufactured goods will fall, for they are produced under capital- rather than labor-intensive conditions. Since Ricardo assumed that wage goods consist of agricultural products, while manufactured products are the luxuries consumed by capitalists and landlords, he was able to conclude that though the long-run trend of the economy's total product is up, the share going to labor in real terms will not increase.

DISTRIBUTION

Rent as a Distributive Share

Ricardo's theoretical analysis was directed primarily to the examination of the problem of distribution. His attention was focused on explaining the determination of rent, wages, and profit, and their probable future trend. "To determine the laws which regulate this distribution is the principal problem in Political Economy; much as the science has been improved by the writings of Turgot, Stewart, Smith, Say, Sismondi, and others, they afford very little satisfactory information respecting the natural course of rent, profit and wages."[19]

While his primary emphasis is on rent, it is the trend of the rate of profit which is most significant for economic progress. For high rents do not cause but rather accompany low profits. The latter, in turn, are the result of

---

[19] David Ricardo, *Principles of Political Economy and Taxation, op. cit.,* Vol. I, Preface.

the high cost of labor, which depends on the cost of producing food at the margin of cultivation. The productivity of labor in the production of nonwage goods is relatively unimportant, in Ricardo's view, to the progress of profit and wealth. The doctrine of land rent is therefore the heart of his whole distribution theory; the explanation of the trend of wages and profits is articulated with the progress of rent.

It has already been seen that Ricardo identified rent as a differential which appears on superior land. Its appearance hinges, first, upon the law of population growth and, second, on the inability of additional applications of labor and capital to presently employed lands to yield anything but decreasing returns. Neither of these principles is, of course, original with Ricardo, but it remained for him to deduce a new theory of rent from them. Although he made some reference to the possibility of improvements in agriculture, he nevertheless believed them to be greatly inferior to those available in the manufacturing industries and thus concluded that the progressive decline in the fertility of land would necessarily be associated with rising food prices and therefore rising rents. The portion of the annual revenue which goes to the landlord will increase in the normal course of economic development because the exchange value of products produced on the land will increase relative to manufacturing commodities.

The tendency for rent to increase is crucial to the future of both wages and profits, and from it derive the generally pessimistic conclusions which are associated with Ricardian analysis. It is also fundamental to the dichotomy of class interests which emerges so clearly in his thinking and which forms the theoretical basis for his position on the Corn Laws and other questions of policy. For while rent seemed a perfectly legitimate form of income to Malthus, who shared the Physiocratic view that it is a bounty of nature, Ricardo viewed it instead as the outcome of the niggardliness of nature. He regards the absence of rent in a new country in which land is still abundant as proof that this contention is valid. Rent emerges as soon as the pressure of population necessitates resort to inferior lands because there is then an increase in the quantity of labor required to produce raw produce on such lands. The interests of landlords are thus antagonistic to those of every other class in society. For while other classes have an interest in the improvement of production techniques in agriculture and free importation of raw produce, the interests of the landed proprietors are best served by a rapid growth of population and a continuation of the Corn Laws.

The hypothesis that land rent is a differential surplus rather than income produced by labor effort had decidedly antisocial implications, not so much to Ricardo as to some of his contemporaries. James Mill, for example, argued in favor of the confiscation of rent. Ricardo admits the possibility of doing this by means of taxation, for a tax on rent would affect rent only; it would fall wholly on landlords and could not be shifted to any class of consumers.[20] Nevertheless, he appears reluctant thus to burden the owners of property.

Wages

Ricardo's explanation of rent is central to his theory of distribution, for it determines the proportions of the income shares received by labor and capital. The wages of labor may be considered first. What effect is the operation of the law of population and the tendency toward diminishing returns, from which Ricardo deduced his law of rent, likely to have on the income that goes to labor? The prospects are far from optimistic. The total amount which is available to be paid out to all who live by wages is the equivalent of the wage fund, that is, that portion of the supply of real capital which consists of consumer goods customarily bought with wages. At any moment of time, therefore, the wage per worker is determined by the size of the wage fund and the number of workers to be paid. The total available in the wage fund cannot be increased except as a result of savings by the capitalist class, and it was implicitly assumed that in the short run, at least, there were unlikely to be any substantial additions. The average real wage per worker in the short run, therefore, is nothing more than the ratio of the wage fund to the labor supply.

It is likely that in the long run, there will be new capital formation and thus additions to the wage fund. But there will also be a continuous growth in population and consequently a persistent tendency for the real wage income to approximate the subsistence level of the worker and his family. This is the essence of Ricardo's statement that "the natural price of labour is that price which will enable the labourers one with another to subsist and perpetuate their race without increase or diminution."[21] In the short run, the real wage can of course rise above this level, but such a rise would encourage larger families, both by encouraging earlier marriages and more births and by enabling more children to survive to maturity. Conversely, if the level of real wages should fall temporarily below the minimum support level, the resulting decline in the birth rate and higher mortality rate would limit population growth and the labor supply, and therefore facilitate the return of the wage rate to its natural level.

The natural level of wages is the rate which reflects and equals the cost of the subsistence requirements of the worker and his family. It is because real wages are constantly tending toward their natural level that even with increases in the supply of capital and the wage fund, and improvements in the state of the arts, Ricardo foresaw little, if any, long-run improvement in the workers' economic status. Agricultural production

---

[20] *Ibid.,* p. 235.
[21] *Ibid.,* p. 93.

lends itself less to scientific improvement than does manufacturing, and advances in the latter do little to make the resort to inferior lands unnecessary. Simultaneously, continuous population growth tends to offset whatever real gains are made.

Money wages will of course tend to rise, for the increasing labor cost of producing raw produce at the margin of cultivation will raise the money price of provisions and therefore the nominal wage the worker must receive in order to support himself and his family. It is even conceivable that a decrease in real wages will be obscured by an increase in money wages—that the worker may be less well off in terms of goods even though his money wages are rising. The only hope for permanent improvement in the workers' lot is therefore to be found in the restriction of numbers. This is precisely in accord with Malthus' observation, but Ricardo had less faith in the check of moral restraint than he did.

Profits

It has already been demonstrated that Ricardo believed that the rate of profit to be secured from different employments of capital would always tend toward equality. But what of the trend of this uniform rate? Ricardo, like Smith, believed that profits and wages always vary inversely with one another. He had already reasoned that the money wage rate would necessarily rise because of the increasing labor cost of producing food at the margin of cultivation. The future trend of profits therefore is necessarily downward. Profit, it will be recalled, was conceived by Ricardo, as well as Smith and Malthus, as consisting of the entire net income received by businessmen who both own and manage and generally provided the capital funds for a business. Part of this net income, namely, the return on capital provided by the businessman himself, would be called interest today. Ricardo, however, was less concerned with presenting a functional explanation of profit than with explaining its future trend in relation to economic progress.

The rate of profit depends on the rate of wages; the worker must at least get his subsistence, and the remainder goes to the capitalists in the form of profit. As long as the rate of profit is high enough to enable capitalists to save and invest, the supply of capital, and therefore the wage fund, will increase. This facilitates the support of an increased labor supply. But with the continued growth of population, necessitating resort to inferior soils, the growth rate of national income will tend to be reduced as the labor cost of producing food and other raw produce increases. The share going to land rent increases, as does the nominal wage rate. Although this serves to reduce profit levels, the worker is no better off in terms of what his money wages will purchase. Ultimately, profits will fall so low as to discourage all further growth of capital and, consequently, population. This cessation of growth ushers in the "stationary state," in which neither capital nor population experiences further growth. In this state the level of wages is barely adequate to support the population as subsistence levels, while rents absorb the bulk of the national income, and profits are at a minimum. Whether this minimum is equivalent to a zero profit Ricardo did not say. He did not address himself to the question as to whether some minimum rate of profit is necessary not merely to continued growth, but simply to stimulate the capitalist into continuing to perform his function within the framework of the stationary state. Ricardo's failure in this regard is an aspect of his neglect of the functional nature of profit. We have no answer from him, therefore, as to whether the profit residuum will eventually disappear altogether, or whether its presence in some minimal amount is essential to the continued existence of the system.

The chief adversaries in the Ricardian system are the capitalists and the wage earners, for while the normal trend of rent is upward, high or low rents do not cause either low profits or high wages. High rents are the result of an inexorable law of production according to which the yields of progressively poorer land cause the total output to increase at a diminishing rate. But the division of the remainder between profits and wages is the result of the distribution process. Increases in either share can only be at the expense of the other; and since rising food costs necessitate a progressive increase in moey wages, profits are ever pressed downward. But the gain of the worker is in money terms only; real wages tend to remain at subsistence levels as growing population pressure forces the cultivation of progressively pooror land.

The Effect of Machinery

In his last revision of the *Principles,* Ricardo introduced a chapter entitled "On Machinery," which examined the effect on the distributive shares of converting circulating capital into fixed capital. This examination was introduced because he felt it necessary to alter his conclusion concerning the effect which the introduction of machinery would have on the various income shares. He had originally concluded that apart from the inconvenience attendant on shifting labor from one employment to another, the introduction of machinery was beneficial to all classes. Landlords, capitalists, and laborers would, under long-run competitive conditions, all enjoy the advantage of buying at a lower price commodities produced with the aid of machinery. However, his reexamination of the problem caused him to alter his view and conclude instead that "the substitution of machinery for human labour is often very injurious to the interests of the class of labourers."

To illustrate the basis for the change in his conclusion, he hypothesizes a situation in which a capitalist employs a capital of £20,000 in carrying on a business in which he is jointly a farmer and a manufacturer. Ricardo supposes that £7,000 of the total capital is allocated to fixed capital such as buildings and implements, while the remaining £13,000 is used as circulating capital in the support of labor. The capital is assumed to yield a profit of 10 percent, or £2,000, so that annual gross revenue amounts to £15,000. Thus the capitalist has £2,000 annually for his own consumption and £13,000 for the maintenance of labor in the subsequent year.

If, in the following year, the capitalist employs half his men in producing food and necessaries as usual, and half in producing a machine, he will as usual pay out £13,000 as wages. However, the composition of his product will be altered, for he will now obtain a machine worth £7,500 and food and necessaries worth £7,500. After deducting £2,000 for his own expenses from the revenue gotten from the sale of the food and necessaries, he will have a circulating capital of only £5,500. Since the wage fund previously amounted to £13,000, the equivalent of £7,500 worth of labor will become redundant as a result of the change in the proportions between fixed and circulating capital. Thus, Ricardo concluded that the introduction of machinery could be harmful to the working class when its introduction is associated with a reduction in the size of the wage fund. This conclusion is subsequently modified by the observation that these undesirable effects need not materialize if machinery is financed out of savings rather than by converting circulating capital into fixed capital.

While Ricardo's analysis focused attention on the problem inherent in the substitution of capital for labor in the short run, it neglects the analysis of long-run factors which might mitigate these short-run effects. The analysis does not, for example, consider the effect of unemployment on wage rates, which, if perfect competition is assumed, must be flexible in a downward direction and therefore lead directly or indirectly to the reabsorption of labor. Secondly, while Ricardo realizes that mechanization will increase productive efficiency in the sense of reducing the labor requirements for production, it also means that under competition the total output of goods will increase, and the prices of these goods will fall. Even though money wages decline in consequence of unemployment in a particular case, the real wages of those who are employed may be no lower, and those of workers elsewhere in the economy will certainly be higher. Thus the real value of the wage fund may be maintained even without additional saving because of the effect of machinery on the production of a larger output. In any event, it is clear that the machinery question should not be examined exclusively, as Ricardo did, from the standpoint of its effect on the income shares, but must be integrated into the examination of commodity and factor values. Failing to do this, the whole discussion leaves the impression of being an afterthought which is superimposed on the original analysis. It does, however, reflect the growing concern with the problem of technological unemployment.

Concluding Remarks on the Wage Fund Doctrine

The preceding discussion of the determination of wages and profits and the way in which they are likely to be affected by the conversion of circulating into fixed capital indicates that the wage fund theory performed a dual role in that it was used, at one and the same time, as a theory of wages and as a theory of capital. As a theory of capital, it conceived of the capitalists of the economy as setting aside a predetermined portion of their revenue for making advances to labor during the course of the production process. Labor therefore subsists on that part of the economy's real capital which consists of the wage goods it consumes. The sale of labor's output merely replenishes the capital stock which was advanced to the laborers, plus the capitalists' profit. As a theory of wages, it conceived of the average wage rate as being determined by the ratio of the wage fund and the population.

The weakness of applying the wage fund doctrine to any but a strictly agricultural economy is that production is a continuous process. Output does not typically become periodically available for sale, as is implicitly assumed in the wage fund model, but flows continuously into inventories at more or less the same rate as inventories are depleted by consumption. The net effect, therefore, is that capital, interpreted as a supply of wage goods, is maintained intact.

Another difficulty of the wage fund doctrine is that it provides no basis for explaining the proportions in which a business will employ labor and capital. These proportions depend both on the relative marginal cost of using labor and capital and on the value of their marginal products. Without the concepts of marginal cost, productivity, and factor substitution it cannot be explained why the proportions between circulating capital and fixed capital are what they are to begin with, or why the proportions change.

Nevertheless, the wage fund doctrine enabled the classicists to reach substantially correct conclusions with respect to the possibility of raising the average wage for a given labor force with a given level of technology. They concluded that the average wage rate can rise *only* if the capital stock rises. Today, we recognize that increasing wage rates do indeed require an increase in capital; however, we explain rising wages not in terms of an increasing wage fund but in terms of the increase in the marginal productivity of labor when it is combined with more capital. But whereas marginal productivity theory provides a basis for understanding the proportions in which the factors will be used in production, the wage fund doctrine does not.

It should, however, be recognized that the wage fund doctrine was fruitful in another direction, namely, in providing a foundation for the theory of capital. The idea that the wage fund is the source of capitalist advances to the worker ultimately led to the idea that capital bridges the time gap between production and consumption, and that there is a necessary cost inherent in shifting resources from producing goods for immediate consumption as opposed to producing goods whose final products become available only after a lapse of time.

INTERNATIONAL TRADE AND FINANCE

Income Shares and the Corn Laws

Ricardo's interest in and contribution to international trade theory is closely related to his analysis of value and distribution. Specifically, great care was lavished on explaining the inverse relationship between wages and profits, and thus the impossibility of increasing profits except by means of a reduction in wages. Any measure that operates to reduce wages, maintained Ricardo, will simultaneously operate to increase profits.

The extension of foreign trade is precisely such a measure. He is therefore critical of the Corn Laws and, in opposition to his contemporary Malthus, advocates the reduction of protection, especially on agricultural commodities. The latter he regards as particularly unsuited to large-scale protection because they are largely wage goods and the benefits of foreign trade are associated with the importation of these commodities rather than those which are consumed by the rich. "Foreign trade, then, though highly beneficial to a country . . . has no tendency to raise the profits of stock, unless the commodities imported be of that description on which the wages of labour are expended."[22] It is thus through the effect of free trade in agricultural products on wage rates and profits that Ricardo articulates his views on the Corn Laws with his analysis of value and distribution. The ever-present tendency toward diminishing returns from land, which puts constant upward pressure on the labor cost of producing food at the margin of cultivation, is seen as raising money wages and consequently the rent of land. Rising money wages, however, do not make the worker better off, for his corn wage remains at subsistence and at the same time depresses the rate of profit, thereby harming not only the capitalist but also impeding the accumulation of capital upon which the advancement of society depends. It was on these grounds that Ricardo urged that a transition toward freer trade be gradually effected. Only by importing a cheaper food supply could England hope to minimize the dire consequences of diminishing returns. A continuance of protection would simply reinforce the inexorable tendency for money wages and rents to rise and for profits to fall.

Protection for manufactured commodities was considered less of an issue, not only in principle but also as concerns policy. This is because Ricardo regards the rise of manufactured commodity prices above their

---

[22] *Ibid.*, p. 133.

natural levels as temporary gains that will be eliminated by the inflow of capital into those undertakings, with a consequent reduction of profits. Only the protection of agricultural commodities can exert a permanent influence on profits, and this in a downward direction, because it affects the real cost of labor's subsistence.

Actually, Ricardo did not contemplate so rash a program as complete elimination of agricultural protection. Rather, he argued that duties on raw produce should be made high enough to offset the relatively greater tax burden of the landowning class.[23]

Comparative Cost

The advantages of free trade had already been taken note of by Adam Smith, who observed that under free trade conditions a nation will specialize in producing the goods for which it is best suited. While this observation is correct enough as far as it goes, it does not embrace all aspects of geographical specialization. What, for example, if a nation is naturally superior in the production of several commodities, or perhaps even in all commodities? Or conversely, what if a nation does not enjoy any natural superiority? What then determines the area of specialization and which goods will tend to be exported or imported under conditions of free trade? Ricardo's doctrine of comparative advantage was formulated with a view to providing guidance on such questions and is a distinct improvement over eighteenth-century antimercantilist writings. The latter arguments for free trade generally expressed the advantage to a country of importing those commodities that could either not be produced at home at all or could only be produced at an absolutely greater cost than they could be produced abroad. Adam Smith, at least, did not elaborate the case for free trade any further than this. Ricardo, however, emphasized comparative rather than absolute differences in cost as the basis for specialization and exchange.

His now classic illustration hypothesizes a situation in which the labor of 120 men in England could produce a quantity of wine which could be produced in Portugal by the labor of 80 men, while a quantity of cloth could be produced in England with the labor of 100 men and in Portugal with the labor of 90 men. Portugal thus produces both wine and cloth at a lower labor cost than does England, but she produces wine at a comparatively cheaper cost than she does cloth. Similarly, England produces cloth at a comparatively lower labor cost than wine. Thus, under free trade conditions, England will specialize in producing cloth and will import wine. That is, the wine-to-cloth ratio in England is 6/5 whereas it is 8/9 in Portugal. England can therefore gain more wine by importing it from Portugal in exchange for cloth than she can by producing wine herself.

---

[23] *Hansard's Parliamentary Debates,* speeches of May 8, 1820; April 3, 1822; April 29, 1822 (N.S., Vols. VI–VII).

Precisely the same thing is true in Portugal with respect to cloth. It requires relatively less labor to produce wine in Portugal than to produce cloth.

Ricardo did not indicate how the ratio at which wine and cloth would be exchanged for each other would be determined, but he assumed that the commodities would be exchanged for one another at a ratio of one unit of cloth to one unit of wine. This is close to being midway between their comparative cost ratios, and the gains of trade are almost equally divided at this ratio.[24] This gain manifests itself in the saving of labor made possible by importation. England is saving the equivalent of 20 labor-hours by importing wine, for it would have cost her 120 labor-hours to acquire wine by producing it at home. Similarly, Portugal, in exchanging one unit of wine for one unit of cloth, will save herself 10 labor-hours by importing cloth instead of relying on domestic production. Both countries will therefore gain from specialization and exchange because England can obtain more wine per labor-hour by importing it than by producing it herself; conversely, Portugal can obtain more cloth per labor-hour by importing it than by producing it herself. The movement of commodities will therefore be advantageous to both countries.

Precisely how the gains from trade will be divided between the participants is not made clear by Ricardo, but the implicit assumption that one unit of wine will be exchanged for one unit of cloth suggests that the terms of trade must lie between 6/5 and 8/9, which is approximately a ratio of one to one. It is not clear how he arrived at this ratio. James Mill and J. R. McCulloch, however, also stated that the benefits from trade would generally tend to be equally divided.[25] Subsequently, it was pointed out that the terms of trade are determined by reciprocal demand, that is, by the relative strength of the demand by the two countries for each others' products. Robert Torrens appears to have been the earliest exponent of this idea, but it was John Stuart Mill who developed this notion in a manner which gained it general acceptance among economists. Discussion of the concept of reciprocal demand will therefore be postponed to the chapter on Mill which follows.

The Ricardian illustration of comparative cost involves a number of implicit assumptions. These assumptions are that trade takes place in two commodities only, and only between two countries; that there are free competition, adequate time for long-run adjustments, and constant labor costs; and that the supply prices of the two commodities are proportional to the labor costs of production, and that the latter also reflect the real or psychic costs of production to labor. Credit for formulating the doctrine of comparative cost is sometimes claimed for Torrens, and he was indeed the

---

[24] The ratio exactly midway between the comparative cost ratio is one cloth to 47/48 wine.

[25] John R. McCulloch, *Principles of Political Economy* (4th ed., 1849), p. 147.

first to use the term "comparative cost."[26] But it appears that the doctrine was not integrated with other aspects of Torrens' thinking and that major credit for the doctrine and its general acceptance is due to Ricardo.

The International Financial Mechanism

David Hume had already put forward the hypothesis that under a metallic currency system the amount of metal in each geographical area is self-regulating. Ricardo elaborated on this idea, maintaining that the distribution of precious metals among trading countries will be such that transactions among them will tend to constitute a barter relationship. That is, the balance of payments will have a tendency to be in equilibrium without the necessity of using gold or silver to settle differences.[27] Should this distribution not exist, forces will come into play which will tend to restore equilibrium and bring about a distribution of precious metals which is compatible with it. The operation of these forces involves the international application of the quantity theory of money. Thus, if there is disequilibrium in the balance of payments between two countries, the one with the favorable balance will experience an increase in its exchange rate, while the one with the unfavorable balance will experience a decrease in its exchange rate.

Ricardo maintained that the invariable cause of an unfavorable balance of trade, and therefore of international gold flows, is the relative "redundancy" of currency.[28] The issue of redundancy was central to the bullionist controversy in which Ricardo was an active participant. The events leading up to this controversy may be reviewed briefly.[29] Largely because of the demands for advances made on it by the government starting with the outbreak of the war with France in 1793, the Bank of England found it necessary to suspend specie payments of its notes beginning early in 1797. This suspension initially induced an inward flow of bullion, which eased the strain on the bank and produced a general resurgence of confidence. Subsequently, however, toward the end of 1799, and more particularly from 1809 to the end of the war, the sterling exchange rate fell, and bullion was quoted at a substantial premium over paper. This would of course not have occurred over such a prolonged period of time on a fully convertible international gold or bimetallic standard. Prior to the suspension of specie payments, England was *de jure* on a bimetallic standard, though the undervaluation of silver at the mint kept her *de facto* on a gold

---

[26] Lionel Robbins, *Robert Torrens and the Evolution of Classical Economics* (New York: St. Martin's Press, 1958), pp. 21–24.

[27] Ricardo, *Principles of Political Economy and Taxation, op. cit.,* Vol. I, p. 137.

[28] *Ibid.,* Vol. VI, pp. 25–26.

[29] N. S. Silberling, "Financial and Monetary Policy of Great Britain during the Napoleonic Wars," *Quarterly Journal of Economics,* Vol. XXXVIII (Feb. 1924, con't May 1924).

standard. Gold coin, however, could not legally be melted down, nor could gold bullion be exported.[30] Metallic money was supplemented by Bank of England notes, which circulated largely in the London area, bills of exchange drawn on local banks, and, to a limited extent, bank deposits subject to check.

On a metallic standard, convertibility into either gold or silver of all claims circulating as part of the monetary stock would have prevented more than temporary divergence from par. The situation was such, however, that the sterling exchange was at a marked and prolonged discount, while bullion commanded a premium over paper. At the same time, English prices rose substantially relative to those prevailing abroad. The cause of these relationships constituted the central theoretical issue of the bullion controversy. The issue was whether or not the paper pound was depreciated. The bullionists, with whom Ricardo aligned himself, took the position that it was. The most impressive rebuttal to his views was made by a Mr. Bonsanquet, a merchant who presented his opinions in his *Practical Observations*. Ricardo subsequently published his *Reply to Mr. Bonsanquet's Practical Observations on the Report of the Bullion Committee,* which is generally regarded as one of the most brilliant essays ever written on a controversial issue in the field of economics. This essay set forth the view that the premium of bullion over paper currency, the relative rise in English prices over those abroad, and the fall of the sterling exchange below par are prima facie evidence of depreciation. He attributed this depreciation to the fact that the quantity of currency was greater than that which it would have been possible to maintain if the principle of convertibility had been adhered to.

The Report of the Bullion Committee called attention to the continued high premium on gold and low foreign exchanges as evidence of the existence of excess currency, and advocated resumption of cash payments at the old par to be undertaken within two years. Ricardo found himself in complete accord with this proposal. He urged that the Bank of England gradually diminish the volume of notes in circulation until the price of gold and silver returned to their mint par. Until this is done, he maintained, the foreign exchange will be unfavorable to England, and gold will continue to be exported, while domestic prices will continue high and currency values continue depreciated.

---

[30] There were no dealings in gold coin at a premium over paper, for this would lead to suspicion of intent to violate the law against melting down coins. Full-weight coins, however, tended to pass out of circulation, disappearing into hoards either for export on government account or for illegal export. Ricardo observed that repeal of the law against melting and export would cause gold coin to have the same premium as bullion over paper money. Conversely, if the law against melting and export were strictly enforced, exportable bullion would command a premium over both gold coin and paper money. (See Jacob Viner, *Studies in the Theory of International Trade* [New York: Harper & Bros., 1937], p. 137.)

If the Bank directors had kept the amount of their notes within reasonable bounds; if they had acted up to the principle which they have avowed to have been that which regulated their issues when they were obliged to pay their notes in specie, namely, to limit their notes to that amount which should prevent the excess of the market above the Mint price of gold, we should not have been now exposed to all the evils of a depreciated, and perpetually varying currency.[31]

Thus, Ricardo concluded that if the price of bullion rises above its mint price by more than the cost of shipping it abroad, this is conclusive proof of overissue or redundancy.[32] Such redundancy, as has already been noted above, was regarded by Ricardo as the "invariable" cause of disequilibrium in the balance of trade. However, he recognized that redundancy can also be produced by "a diminution of goods or by an actual increased quantity of money (or, which is the same thing, by an increased economy in the use of it) in one country; or by an increased quantity of goods or by a diminished amount of money in another."[33] In other words, redundancy can be caused either by forces operating on the supply of goods or by the supply of money.

CONCLUDING REMARKS

Ricardo's primary theoretical concern was the division of the nation's product among the three main social classes in the form of wages, profit, and rent. In his view, the probable long-run tendency of these shares is governed by the cost of producing labor's subsistence. Since he implicitly assumed a given level of agricultural technology as well as a constantly growing population, the tendency toward diminishing returns forced a resort to progressively inferior lands and, consequently, rising food costs. Thus, he regarded freedom to import food products from countries which have a comparative advantage in terms of labor cost as the most effective way of alleviating the upward pressure on food costs which underlies the determination of the income shares in the long run.

It is because Ricardo's main concern was the problem of distribution that he addressed himself primarily to explaining changes in exchange values over time. The price of a good would, he thought, reflect its cost of production, including not only the current rate of wages but also the current

---

[31] Ricardo, D. "The High Price of Bullion" in J. R. McCulloch ed. *The Works of David Ricardo, op. cit.,* p. 287.

[32] In order to prevent disturbances to the balance of payments arising from excess issue, the bullionists recommended that the note issue be made convertible. The adherents of the currency school, however, contended that convertibility alone is an inadequate safeguard and that what is required is the regulation of note issue in such manner as to correspond to the fluctuations that would have taken place if the currency were purely metallic.

[33] Letter to Malthus, *Works and Correspondence of David Ricardo, op. cit.,* Sraffa and Dobb eds., Vol. VI, pp. 25–26.

rate of profits. Ricardo's value theory can therefore be interpreted as a labor theory only in a very special sense. And even this adherence to the labor theory is limited by his recognition that the relative values of commodities are not governed exclusively by the quantities of labor embodied in them, but depend also on the proportions between fixed and circulating capital and on the durability of capital, because these affect the length of time which elapses before commodities can come to market.

While Ricardo conceived of different capital structures as influencing the time flow of labor-created values to market, as will be seen in the next chapter, Nassau Senior had a far better understanding of the nature of capital and its role in the production process, and a broader concept of the cost of production emerged from his analysis. It will also be seen that while John Stuart Mill's restatement of the theory of value was intended to be essentially Ricardian in nature, what he actually produced is quite un-Ricardian. The labor theory of value did not, therefore, survive among those whom we may collectively refer to as the orthodox economists. Rather, it was perpetuated, though with a difference, among the economic heretics, chief among them Karl Marx.

The cost of capital is not the only cost element Ricardo neglected to treat; rent is another such element. Rent in the Ricardian sense applies only to land as a whole because there is no necessary supply price which must be met in order to call forth the supply of land in the aggregate. But once it is recognized that there are competing uses for land and that land can be shifted from one alternative to another, it follows that it will tend to be used in that alternative in which it is most productive and that it will command a scarcity payment in that alternative, which is just as much a cost factor, and hence a price determinant, as the necessary costs of labor and capital. This type of payment is now known, quite appropriately, as the "transfer price" of the agent. From the point of view of the individual firm hiring a factor, transfer prices are part of the production cost, even though they are a surplus from the point of view of the entire industry or the economy as a whole, in the sense that their elimination would not affect the supply of that factor. Only if the services of a factor, say land, are limited to a single alternative is the entire reward considered to be rent from both an individual and a social point of view because its transfer price is then equal to zero. When such rewards accrue to factors other than land, they are known as quasi-rents. Such rents are unlikely, however, to exist in the long run because no agent is completely nonreproducible or incapable of alternative uses.

Modern economists have little inclination for a special theory to explain the rent of land. They recognize, in the first place, that land, far from being a free gift of nature, requires the outlay of developmental and maintenance costs, and that there are few, if any, resources available for use without such costs. In this sense, land is not very different from capital goods or even reproducible human labor, even though its supply is less elastic than that of other factors. Furthermore, it is unrealistic to think of land as being used only to produce a particular agricultural product. This is the sense in which Ricardo thought of it. He conceived of land beyond the extensive margin of agricultural use as being left in idleness, whereas a given area of land is likely to have several alternative uses to which it can be put. It will command a scarcity payment in any of these alternatives and will actually be employed in that alternative in which it is most productive. The transfer price associated with this employment is necessarily a cost to the hiring firm and will therefore be price-determining rather than price-determined.

While the explanation of value generally accepted in Ricardo's day was a cost-of-production theory, there were some who pointed out that utility could not be neglected. Samuel Bailey, in particular, pointed out that the relative nature of value implies that utility is a cause of value and not just a prerequisite, as Ricardo maintained.[34] It is plain from his observation that Ricardo's dictum that reproducible commodities derive their value from the quantity of labor required to make them, rather than scarcity, is untenable. Reproducible goods may be less scarce relative to the demand for them than those which exist permanently in fixed supply, but they are scarce nonetheless. Thus, demand and utility, as well as cost of production and supply, determine exchange values, whether the commodities being exchanged are reproducible or not. However, those who criticized Ricardo for neglecting the demand side of the price problem were unable to show how demand affects price. Jean Baptiste Say, for example, while he emphasized that exchange value is dependent on utility, failed to recognize the relationship between utility and supply. Consequently, he was unable to explain why water, for all its utility, does not command a price. Nassau Senior, although he too emphasized utility as a cause of value, also failed to perceive this relationship. The net result was that criticisms of Ricardo's theory of value on the ground of its failure to recognize the role of utility more specifically came to naught until the marginal revolution of the 1870's.

With respect to its long-term significance, Ricardo's demonstration of the construction and use of rigorous deductive analysis is no doubt a primary contribution. It was he who perfected the technique of abstraction; and this, rather than his substantive conclusions, is the basis for his long-term influence on economic analysis. His doctrine of comparative cost remains, of course, as a substantive contribution to modern principles. The differential theory of rent is significant primarily as a forerunner of the marginal productivity theory of distribution rather than as the basis for

------

[34] Samuel Bailey, *A Critical Dissertation on the Nature of Measures and Causes of Values; Chiefly in Reference to the Writings of Mr. Ricardo and His Followers* (1825).

explaining distributive shares among the different classes of society. The problem of distribution is handled very differently by neoclassical economists; and even though Alfred Marshall was to revitalize Ricardo's cost-of-production theory of value, he did so with major additions and alterations as will be seen in chapter XV.

SUGGESTIONS FOR FURTHER READING

BLAUG, MARK. *Ricardian Economics.* New Haven: Yale University Press, 1958.

CASSELS, JOHN M. "A Reinterpretation of Ricardo on Value," *Quarterly Journal of Economics,* Vol. XLIX (May, 1935). Reprinted in JOSEPH J. SPENGLER and W. ALLEN (eds.), *Essays in Economic Thought: Aristotle to Marshall.* Chicago: Rand McNally & Co., 1960.

MEEK, R. L. "Decline of Ricardian Economics in England," *Economica,* Vol. XVII, No. 65, Feb. 1950.

ROBBINS, LIONEL. *Robert Torrens and the Evolution of Classical Economics.* New York: St. Martin's Press, 1958.

ST. CLAIR, OSWALD. *A Key to Ricardo.* New York: Kelley and Millman, Inc., 1957.

SRAFFA, PIERO, "Introduction to Ricardo's Works" in SRAFFA and DOBB (eds.). *The Works and Correspondence of David Ricardo.* 10 vols. Cambridge, England: The University Press, 1951–55.

STIGLER, GEORGE. "Ricardo and the 93% Labor Theory of Value," *American Economic Review,* Vol. XLVIII, No. 3 (June, 1958).

Chapter 8

THE CONTRIBUTIONS OF
Chapter NASSAU SENIOR AND
8 JOHN STUART MILL TO
ECONOMIC ANALYSIS

INTRODUCTION

While the contributions of Nassau Senior (1790–1864) and John Stuart Mill (1806–73) to economic theory have not secured them a leading place in its history, it would be a serious omission to neglect their work. Mill was undoubtedly a thinker of greater stature and influence than Senior, though Senior's contributions have generally been less appreciated than they deserve.[1]

As the son of James Mill, John Stuart Mill was reared in an intellectual environment consciously designed by his father to train him to carry on the tradition of both Bentham and Ricardo. Mill's *Autobiography* (1861) relates his first introduction to the study of economics at the age of 13 under his father's careful supervision via Ricardo's *Principles of Political Economy and Taxation*. This was followed by an equally intensive study of Adam Smith. Mill subsequently spent a year in France, partly at the home of Jean Baptiste Say, and upon his return to England was assigned the task of preparing marginal notes for his father's *Elements of Political Economy* (1821). He was only 19 when he began contributing articles on economics to the *Westminster Review*. In addition, he had also carefully examined utilitarian philosophy and became a member of the circle of philosophic radicals. He was not yet 20 when he edited the five volumes of Bentham's *Rationale of Evidence*.

It was not long afterward, however, that Mill experienced a severe mental crisis which he described in his *Autobiography* as a "conviction of sin," the sin being his acceptance of utilitarianism. Actually, he never rejected utilitarianism in its entirety, though he became sharply critical of certain features of Bentham's system. Specifically, he rejected the view that human behavior was entirely governed by self-interest, as Bentham implied, and even ventured to suggest that the reason why Bentham attached little importance to sympathy and benevolence as influencing conduct was be-

---

[1] See E. R. A. Seligman, "Some Neglected British Economists," *Economic Journal,* Vol. XIII, 1903, pp. 335–63; pp. 511–35; reprinted in his *Essays in Economics* New York: Macmillan (1925).

cause he himself was devoid of these characteristics.[2] He also maintained that there are qualitative differences among pleasures and that the estimation of pleasure does not depend on quantity alone. But these criticisms seem to constitute, in the final analysis, a revision or qualification of Benthamism rather than a rejection, for Mill continued to think that the morality of behavior is to be judged in terms of its effect on happiness.

Mill attempted to fill the void created by his dissatisfaction with utilitarianism by reaching out for new ideas to the writings of the English Romanticists, such as Samuel Taylor Coleridge and Thomas Carlyle, and the philospher Auguste Comte. He was also greatly interested in the views of the utopian socialists. The ideas he derived from these sources created an intellectual dilemma for Mill, for he tried to reconcile them with the earlier and deeply ingrained influences of Benthamism and Ricardianism. Consequently, Mill's standard approach to almost every subject was to begin with a preliminary statement of received doctrine which he subsequently proceeded to qualify and revise until much of the original principle was swept away. While these qualifications stemmed largely from his deep sense of humanitarianism and social purpose, they nevertheless created conflicts which he was unable to resolve. He was, for example, a great champion of individual liberty; the eloquence of his defense of freedom on the basis of its own moral worth made his essay *On Liberty* (1859) a classic in the English language. He was also a great social reformer. But his political theory provided no criterion for judging the circumstances in which a society is justified in placing a limitation on personal freedom. Rather, the case which he made for social legislation is derived from his humanitarian ideals.[3]

His treatment of economics presents a similar problem of consistency. He started with Ricardian principles, but was so much impressed with Comte's objective of creating a complete science of society that he came to view political economy as a study of people, institutions, and customs and not just as the formulation of laws governing production, exchange, and distribution. Thus the aim of his *Principles of Political Economy* was to provide not only an exposition of Ricardian theory but, more important, to examine the social and political milieu within which Ricardian generalizations work themselves out. Since Mill conceived of these environmental factors as exerting their main influence on the distribution of wealth, the logic of his distinction between pure economics and applied economics was to provide a foundation for a broad program of reform designed to alter the institutions which affect this distribution. This approach enabled Mill to be

---

[2] "Bentham," reprinted in John Stuart Mill, *Dissertations and Discussions* (3d ed., 1875), Vol. I, p. 353.

[3] George Sabine, *A History of Political Theory* (rev. ed.; New York: Henry Holt & Co., Inc., 1950), pp. 705–15.

sympathetic with the dreams of the utopian socialists to establish cooperative communities while he was also the last great exponent of classicism.

Compared with Mill, the details of Nassau Senior's life present a
rather colorless picture. He was the son of a vicar, was educated at Oxford,
and was admitted to the bar in 1819. He became a member of the Political
Economy Club in 1823 and in 1825 became first Drummond Professor of
Political Economy at Oxford. He held the post for five years and was
appointed for a second time in 1847. During the interim, he was professor
of political economy at King's College in London, though he resigned under
pressure when he advocated the confiscation of some of the revenues of the
Established Church of Ireland for the benefit of Roman Catholics. He also
was a member of the commission for administering the Poor Laws and
wrote a large number of pamphlets and letters on the Poor Laws and the
Factory Acts. The first edition of his *Outline of the Science of Political
Economy* was published in 1836 and incorporated his Oxford lectures on
that subject.

Though Senior had a wide range of opportunity to concern himself
with policy questions in economics, he was particularly concerned to keep
this aspect of his inquiries strictly separated from those of a theoretical
nature. He believed that this separation was essential to the development of
economics as a science, for as long as the science of political economy is
associated with controversial issues of public policy, it cannot develop a
body of universal truths. Thus, his own discussions of social problems were
always undertaken as a moralist or statesman and not as an economist. His
efforts to present economics as a body of generalizations deduced from a
small number of postulates give him the distinction of being, methodologically speaking, the first of the pure theorists in England.

SENIOR'S CONTRIBUTION TO ECONOMICS

The Four Postulates

While the technique of establishing economic laws by the process of
deduction was already well established when Senior wrote his *Outline of the
Science of Political Economy* (1836), he was the first to give explicit
statement to the postulates or axioms on which economic theory is constructed.[4] His list is extremely circumscribed in that it includes only four
postulates from which economic reasoning is properly to proceed. It is
preceded by a definition of wealth as all goods and services which possess
utility and are scarce.

The first of Senior's propositions is: "That every person is desirous to

---

[4] Nassau Senior, *Outline of the Science of Political Economy* (6th ed.; London:
George Allen & Unwin, Ltd., 1872), p. 22.

obtain, with as little sacrifice as possible, as much as is possible of the articles of wealth." This proposition was, of course, an integral part of economics long before Senior's explicit formulation. The only difference derives from his definition of wealth as including services as well as material goods. While this conception of wealth obscures the difference between the stock of tangible goods and the flow of money income, it has the advantage of facilitating inquiry into the pricing of services as well as goods. It also facilitates more specific attention to the role of demand in the pricing process than was given by Ricardo. Senior was extremely critical of Ricardo's failure to deal more specifically with utility and demand in the pricing process and considered his premise on the nature of human choice as a basis for constructing a theory of value which would take cognizance of utility.

Senior's three remaining propositions are significant for the theory of production and distribution as well as value. His second proposition is as follows: "That the Population of the World, or, in other words the number of persons inhabiting it, is limited only by moral or physical evil, or by a fear of a deficiency of those articles of wealth which the habits of the individuals of each class of its inhabitants lead them to require." Though this proposition is reminiscent of Malthus, Senior did not accept the popular doctrine that population tended to expand more rapidly than the food-producing potential of land. He maintained instead that with the advance of civilization, there is a natural tendency for subsistence to increase in a greater ratio than population. The basis for the difference between his position and Malthus' on this matter is his third proposition, which is stated as follows: "That the powers of labour, and of the other instruments of production which produce wealth, may be indefinitely increased by using their products as the means of further production." This proposition, as will be seen, is also the basis of Senior's theory of capital and interest, which was to broaden significantly the theory of the cost of production by adding abstinence as a separate factor of production. It is fundamental to Senior's conception of increasing returns in manufacturing as the result of the application of additional labor. In contrast, the application of additional labor in agriculture results in diminishing returns. Thus the fourth proposition is: "That agricultural skill remaining the same, additional labor employed on the land within a given district produces in general a less proportionate return, in other words, that though, with every increase of the labor bestowed, the aggregate return is increased, the increase of the return is not in proportion to the increase of the labor."

Though these four propositions had already been stated by Senior in his lectures, they assumed a new importance in his *Outline of the Science of Political Economy,* published in 1836, apparently because Senior became impressed with the desirability of separating economic science from questions of policy. Although Senior had earlier conceived of economics as dealing with the "art" as well as the science of wealth, he now conceived of it as "the science which treats the nature, the production and the distribution of Wealth."[5] The significance of this definition is that it limited economics exclusively to pure theory in order to make it an exact science based on the four postulates and the definition of wealth noted above. Within this definition of the scope of economics, all questions of policy are part of the science of legislation and are not the concern of the economist qua economist.

Capital and Its Return

There are two aspects to Senior's contribution to the theory of capital and its return: first, his explanation of the relationship between capital and what he termed abstinence; second, his explanation of the productivity of waiting. While he is better known for his concept of abstinence than for his explanation of the gain to be derived from roundabout production, the latter concept, although it is not fully developed, is a new idea in English thinking, whereas the desirability of waiting is not. The desirability of waiting was, after all, inherent in Smith's concept of parsimony and in Ricardo's explanation of why the values of commodities produced with more fixed capital or more durable capital deviated from their labor quantity. What Ricardo did not see is that the use of capital, besides entailing a longer waiting period until the final product matures, is also more productive and that the return on capital is related to the productivity of waiting as well as to the real cost or disutility of waiting. He thus failed to recognize what is the substance of Senior's third postulate, namely: "That the powers of Labour and other instruments which produce wealth may be indefinitely increased by using their products as means of further production." While it is, of course, not true that the use of intermediate products can indefinitely increase the productivity of labor and natural agents, this proposition gives expression to the idea of roundabout production. The productivity of waiting derives from the greater productivity of the roundabout method and thus provides a basis for explaining the demand for capital.

The supply of capital depends on abstinence; abstinence expresses "the conduct of a person who either abstains from the unproductive use of what he can command, or designedly prefers the production of remote to that of immediate results." While the second part of this definition implies that abstinence is waiting in the Ricardian sense, the first part implies that revenues are permanently being withdrawn from consumption in order to create intermediate products. It is on this basis that Senior regards abstinence itself rather than the capital goods it creates as a separate factor of production. "By the word abstinence, we wish to express that agent, distinct from labour and the agency of nature, the concurrence

---

[5] *Ibid.,* p. 1.

of which is necessary to the existence of capital, and which stands in the same relation to profit as labour does to wages."[6] The significance of this statement is that it specifically makes capital a distinct factor of production, the cost of which must be included along with wages as part of the total cost of production. It thus completes the destruction of the view that labor cost is the only cost. Actually, Ricardo himself initiated this destruction when he observed that the values of commodities which are produced with more fixed capital must deviate from their labor value because the producer must be compensated in consequence of the greater lapse of time before his product can come to market.

An obvious weakness of Senior's abstinence theory is the implication that saving is always associated with disutility. The savings of persons in the higher income groups may involve little, if any, sacrifice; nor are business savings amenable to an explanation in terms of personal sacrifice. Thus the abstinence theory does not provide a satisfactory explanation of the scarcity of capital. Neither does it provide a satisfactory explanation of the interest rate. It is merely a theory of the supply of savings which must be coordinated with a theory of the demand for investment funds. While Senior's conception of the productivity of capital pointed in this direction, the interaction of demand and supply forces was not examined until Alfred Marshall integrated the waiting theory of interest with the productivity theory.

Value and Distribution

Senior's theory of abstinence is significant for his theory of value because it results in a broadening of the concept of cost to include the cost of capital as well as the cost of labor. Moreover, Senior conceived of costs not merely in a money sense but in a real sense, i.e., as payments for the sacrifices incurred in producing goods. Although this conception of cost could have been fruitful in explaining the distributive shares, Senior unfortunately adhered to the wage fund doctrine and confined himself to an examination of the relative proportions of rent, profit, and wages.

Senior's inquiry into the value problem also entails an attempt to introduce utility as a value determinant by insisting that value depends not only on the difficulty of acquiring goods as reflected in their labor and abstinence costs, but also on utility. However, while he recognized that the utility of additional units of one and the same good diminishes as additional units are acquired, he did not undertand the relationship between scarcity and the utility of the marginal unit. Thus the relationship between utility and demand was not explored in a way which sheds much light on price determination. His discussion of monopoly prices is, for example, designed to illustrate that prices will equal costs of production only under competi-

---

[6] *Ibid.,* pp. 58–59.

tion. But he does not show that utility limits in any way the extent of the deviation.

His analysis of monopoly price does, however, lead in another direction. Because monopoly returns are essentially a surplus, Senior included them in his concept of rent. He also suggested that when a worker receives an "extraordinary" remuneration because of extraordinary natural talents, the surplus may be termed rent. He thus anticipated the generalization of the Ricardian theory of rent which was to be fully developed subsequently by Alfred Marshall in his analysis of quasi-rent.

In summary, then, it would seem that Senior had a number of potentially fruitful ideas. But his most substantive contribution is in the area of capital theory. His analysis in this area led not only to the broadening of the concept of cost of production but also to an abstinence theory of interest.

MILL'S *PRINCIPLES OF POLITICAL ECONOMY*

The Laws of Production and Distribution

Mill's *Principles of Political Economy* enjoyed a position of unchallenged leadership from the time of its publication in 1848 until the publication of Marshall's treatise in 1890. It was Mill's object in writing this book to modernize *The Wealth of Nations* in the light of "the more extended knowledge and improved ideas of the present age," and to examine economic principles with respect to "their application to social philosophy."[7] It is the latter objective which sets the tone of the book. Mill is less concerned with theoretical analysis for its own sake than with the application of the economic doctrines of Malthus and Ricardo, in which he had been steeped since childhood, to the solution of the problems of the age. Thus, he is led at the very outset of his work to distinguish between the laws of production and those of distribution. The laws governing the production of wealth are physical truths, whereas "those of Distribution are partly of human institution. . . . But though governments of nations have the power of deciding what institutions shall exist, they cannot arbitrarily determine how those institutions shall work. The conditions on which the power they possess over the distribution of wealth is dependent, . . . are as much a subject for scientific inquiry as any of the physical laws of nature."[8] This distinction between the laws of production and the laws of distribution became the vehicle by which Mill reconciled his concern for reform with Malthusian and Ricardian economic principles. Analytically speaking, the distinction is, of course, completely unacceptable, because it implies that the income shares the factors receive are independent of the process of production and

---

[7] John Stuart Mill, *Principles of Political Economy,* edited by W. J. Ashley. (London: Longmans, Green & Co., Inc., 1923), Preface.

[8] *Ibid.,* Preliminary Remarks.

the determination of exchange values. But from the standpoint of Mill's reform objectives, the distinction enables him to tackle questions of social justice on a different basis than questions of productive efficiency.

Production

Book I of Mill's *Principles* treats the various aspects of production and begins with the identification of labor and natural agents as the two requisites of production. He perpetuates the distinction between productive and unproductive labor, and defines labor as productive if it results in the creation of wealth.[9] The latter is conceived of as the stock of the products of past labor. While nonproductive labor may be as useful or more useful than productive labor, "it does not render the community, and the world at large, richer in material products but poorer by all that is consumed by the labourers while so employed."[10] Similarly, consumption is productive or unproductive if it contributes directly or indirectly to the maintenance of productive labor.

The significance of Mill's distinction between productive and unproductive labor and consumption is that it leads directly to his theory of capital. While labor and natural agents are the primary requisites of production, all but the most primitive operations also require an accumulated stock of the products of past labor. Labor is maintained out of the wage fund, whose size depends on the decision of capitalists to expend their earnings on advances to productive labor rather than in unproductive consumption. Thus, Mill, like Ricardo, maintained that the demand for labor is enhanced by the capitalists' abstinence, for wages represent the advances which capitalists make to workers.

Since the wage fund is part of circulating capital, the Ricardian question of the effect on employment of increasing the ratio of fixed to circulating capital is examined, though, unlike Ricardo, Mill focuses his attention on fixed capital devoted to land. His conclusion, too, is different from Ricardo's, for he concludes that improvements in production are seldom injurious, even temporarily, to the working class in the aggregate.[11] The basis for this conclusion is not, however, the compensation principle, which Mill regards as fallacious, on the ground that a demand for commodities is not a demand for labor.[12] According to his reasoning, employment has been maintained in industries like cotton manufactures and printing not because of machine-engendered cost reductions which facilitate the absorption of displaced labor, but by the accumulation of additional savings which have made possible increases in circulating capital in addition to the in-

---

9 *Ibid.*, p. 45.
10 *Ibid.*, p. 49.
11 *Ibid.*, p. 97.
12 *Ibid.*, pp. 79–90.

crease in fixed capital. However, he also maintains that if the "sinking or fixing of capital in machinery or useful works were ever to proceed at such a pace as to impair materially the funds for the maintenance of labour, it would be incumbent on legislators to take measures for moderating its rapidity. . . ."[13]

The causes and advantages of large-scale production in achieving increasing returns to scale are also examined by Mill with considerable insight. The test, says Mill, of the relative productive efficiency of large-scale versus small-scale establishments in the same business is the ability to sell more cheaply.[14] However, large-scale production is necessarily accompanied by the existence of large capital in few hands. The result may then be higher rather than lower prices, for "where competitors are so few, they always end up by agreeing not to compete."[15] Mill therefore suggests that when a firm produces its output under conditions of natural monopoly, it is best to treat it as a public utility.

Though Mill appreciates the possibilities and significance of increasing returns to scale in manufacturing, he is nevertheless a true Ricardian in pronouncing the law of diminishing returns to labor in agriculture as "the most significant proposition in political economy. Were the law different, nearly all the phenomena of the production and distribution of wealth would be other than they are."[16] This law operates because a given quantity of land is cultivated in a "given state of agricultural skill and knowledge." Though he agreed with Henry Carey, Ricardo's American critic, that the order of cultivation does not always proceed from the best lands to the poorest, but may proceed from the poorest to the best, he maintained that diminishing returns will ultimately assert itself because land is fixed in quantity. Though this tendency may be temporarily controlled or offset as man gains control over nature, the limited supply of land, along with the deficiency of capital, presents fundamental impediments to the increase of production. Thus, his statement of the principle of diminishing returns emphasizes that, given the state of the arts in agriculture, diminishing returns will eventually be experienced, regardless of the order in which lands are cultivated. Economic progress is therefore dependent on maintaining a sufficiently rapid rate of technical improvement in agriculture to offset the tendency toward diminishing returns.

Distribution

While the modern reader would expect the subject of exchange value to be treated immediately after production, Mill's examination of the

---

13 *Ibid.*, p. 99.
14 *Ibid.*, p. 143.
15 *Ibid.*
16 *Ibid.*, p. 177.

distributive shares precedes his discussion of exchange value. Since he regards these shares as the result of human institutions, he apparently considers their determination as unrelated to the price-making forces that operate in commodity markets. His opening chapter, "On Property," examines the origin of private property and proceeds to an extremely sympathetic discussion of socialism and communism. He observes that if "the choice were to be made between Communism with all its choices, and the present [1852] state of society with all its sufferings and injustices; if the institution of private property necessarily carried with it as a consequence, that the produce of labour should be apportioned as we now see it, almost in an inverse ratio to the labour . . . if this or Communism were the alternative, all the difficulties, great or small of Communism would be but as dust in the balance."[17] Mill is not, however, prepared to take an unequivocal stand in favor of communism, feeling that we must first consider "the regime of individual property, not as it is, but as it might be made."[18] His zeal as a reformer of the present system is nowhere in greater evidence than in this statement.

Mill takes the position that the basic tenet of the institution of property is the right of each person to the "exclusive disposal of what he or she may have produced by their own exertions. . . ."[19] Thus, each is entitled to the product of his labor and his abstinence.[20] When the institution of private property prevails, the division of the produce among the various claimants is determined primarily by competition, though it may be modified by custom. Wages are regulated primarily by competition, that is, by the supply and demand for labor. Though he was subsequently to recant the doctrine of the wages fund, Mill maintained in his *Principles,* as did Ricardo before him, that there is a fund of predetermined size which is destined to maintain labor in production which sets a limit, or ceiling, on the size of the annual wage flow. He therefore reasoned that the average wage depends on the number of participants in the market and that there is nothing which can be done, either by government or by labor unions, to raise the wages of labor as a whole. The wages of any particular group may of course be raised, but only at the expense of other groups.

The fallacy of this explanation of the average wage rate, as Mill himself was later to recognize, is that the wage flow may be altered by employers and other nonwage groups. If these groups reduce their own consumption expenditure and divert it to giving more employment, neither

---

[17] *Ibid.,* p. 208.

[18] *Ibid.,* p. 208.

[19] *Ibid.,* p. 218.

[20] While he admits that those who have inherited the savings of others have an advantage, which Mill believes should be curtailed as much as is consistent with justice to those who left their savings to their descendants, he also points out that laborers share in this advantage (*ibid.,* p. 219).

the wage fund nor the flow of wages is predetermined. It was this line of reasoning which led Mill in 1869 to recant the wage fund doctrine and to take the position that it was not inherently impossible for wages to rise to a point at which they absorb not only the funds initially intended for the maintenance of labor, but also funds intended by the capitalist for other businesses and personal expenses.[21] He therefore concluded that even under competition, there are numerous possible wage rates at which the supply of labor can be absorbed. However, since the employer generally has greater bargaining power than the individual employee, the wage bargain will usually be to his advantage. Labor unions can therefore, within limits, raise the wage rate by reducing the disparity between the relative strength of the parties to the wage bargain. Thus the practical significance to Mill of recognizing the fallacy of the wage fund doctrine was that it provided him with a theoretical basis for supporting labor combinations.

Mill's discussion of wages is followed by his inquiry into profits, which are "according to Mr. Senior's well chosen expression, the remuneration of abstinence."[22] The reward for abstinence is more specifically identified as net profit or interest, for gross profit includes also a return for the risks and superintendence of the "undertaker."[23] Thus, Mill, unlike Senior, specifically recognizes that interest and profit are returns which are associated with the performance of different functions. His explanation of the level of the interest rate leaves much to be desired, however, for it proceeds only in terms of abstinence and the supply price of savings. The demand for savings based on the productive services of capital is not part of Mill's thinking. This is evident in his observation that capital, strictly speaking, has no productive power, but only sets productive labor into motion. Thus, while he adopts Senior's concept of abstinence, he apparently does not appreciate the significance of Senior's third postulate in connection with explaining the rate of interest.

Gross profit will, Mill observes, tend to be equalized under competitive conditions because of the transfer of capital from one employment to another. Extraordinary rates of profit can long prevail only under conditions of monopoly. The rate of profit, says Mill, depends, first, upon the size of the product and, secondly, on the proportion of that produce which is obtained by workers in the form of wages. Thus, he arrives at the Ricardian conclusion that the rate of profits depends on wages or, more specifically, on the cost of labor. This, he insists, and accurately, is an important alteration to Ricardo's wording, for it recognizes that there is a difference between wages and the cost of labor. The cost of labor may be at

---

[21] John Stuart Mill, *Some Unsettled Questions on Political Economy* (London: London School of Economics, 1924), p. 108.

[22] Mill, *Principles of Political Economy*, p. 405.

[23] Mill remarks in a footnote that it is regrettable that the French term "entrepreneur" is not familiar in England.

its highest when wages are at their lowest. Labor may be cheap but inefficient, so that the cost of using it is high. Conversely, though wages may be high, labor may be cheap to use if it is efficient, especially if the cost of the commodities it consumes is cheap, as it is in the United States. In this case, high wages and high profits can coexist.

While Mill's observations that it is not wages per se but the cost of using labor that is important, what is missing in his discussion is the role of capital in improving the efficiency of labor. This undoubtedly derives from his conception of capital as consisting primarily of an inventory of wage goods out of which advances are made to workers during the course of the production process. While he subsequently gave up the notion that there is a fixed fund out of which these advances are made, the conclusion that profits and wages vary inversely is conceptually derived from the wage fund model which was at one and the same time a theory of wages and a theory of capital.

Though Mill emphasized the importance of capital accumulation, he believed that the rate of profit tended to a minimum level at which there would be zero net savings. The limited supply of land limits the capacity to increase agricultural output, so that wages and rents increasingly encroach upon profits, which, in turn, limit capital formation and population growth. These tendencies become pronounced in the absence of continued improvements in mankind's control over nature and lead eventually to the stationary state. Mill, however, viewed the stationary state as the millennium, for, unlike Smith and Malthus, he did not conceive of the progressive state, in which life is a continual struggle toward progress, as ideal. The best state for human nature, Mill believed, is one "in which while no one is poor, no one desires to be richer nor has any reason to fear being thrust back by the efforts of others to push themselves forward. . . . There would be as much scope as ever [in the stationary state] for all kinds of mental culture, and moral and social progress; as much room for improving the Art of Living, and much more likelihood of its being improved, when minds ceased to be engrossed by the art of getting on."[24]

Exchange Value

Mill's discussion of exchange value, as already observed, is peculiarly placed, for the matter of factor price determination has already been dealt with in Book II before the problem of exchange value is finally examined in Book III. Mill begins by classifying goods into three categories: (1) commodities which are absolutely limited in supply, (2) commodities whose supply can be indefinitely increased at a constant cost, and (3) commodities whose supply can be indefinitely increased but not without an increase in cost.

The significance of this classification is that it leads to an explanation

---

[24] *Ibid.*, pp. 748–49, 751.

of price which recognizes the relative influence of demand and supply forces in determining price under different circumstances. Thus, in the case of perfectly inelastic supply, demand is relatively more important; while in the case of perfectly elastic supply, supply and the cost of production are relatively more important. Since the supply of commodities in the third class can be augmented only under conditions of increasing cost, their value is governed by the cost of producing them under the least favorable circumstances. While he does not draw demand and supply curves, his discussion leaves no doubt that he conceives of demand and supply in the schedule sense, that is, as a function of price. Hence, he recognizes that the equilibrium price is the price which equates demand and supply. This is a novel conception in English economics and one on which Alfred Marshall was to build in an important way, though Mill, ironically enough, remarked: "Happily, there is nothing in the laws of value which remains for the present [1848] or any future writer to clear up; the theory of the subject is complete."[25]

Though Mill was aware of the law of demand and supply, he nevertheless followed Ricardo in conceiving of short-run prices as being governed by demand and supply, and long-run prices as being determined by costs. Indeed, he categorically states that value depends almost entirely on the quantity of labor required to produce goods, though he includes in the cost of production the cost of conveyance to market. Neither variations in wages nor variations in profits have any effect on value. Nor does rent enter into the cost of production unless the factor in question has a scarcity value, because of the possibility of alternative employment. The latter qualification to Ricardo's rent doctrine is of course important, for land is seldom without alternative uses, though Mill did not develop the significance of this point.

The labor theory of value is, however, qualified by Mill under conditions of joint cost, for when a given production process yields two or more products in fixed proportions, it is impossible to allocate costs on any but an arbitrary basis. The greater the demand for a joint product, the larger the proportion of the total cost which will be covered by the price of the product. Demand and supply conditions for each of the products will establish the price at which the market will be cleared of both, and the sum of the prices established will equal their joint costs of production. This analysis stands as one of Mill's original contributions to economic theory.

Comparative Cost and Reciprocal Demand

Mill's exposition of the principle of comparative advantage proceeded in terms of the comparative effectiveness of labor rather than the comparative labor cost. Ricardo, it will be recalled, took as given the output of each

---

[25] *Ibid.,* p. 436.

commodity in two countries and assumed their respective labor costs to be different. Mill, however, assumed a given input of labor in each of the two countries, so that the comparative efficiency of labor in production is reflected in differing outputs. The product in which a country has the greatest comparative advantage, or the least comparative disadvantage, can then be determined in terms of the comparative efficiency of labor in producing the outputs in question. The barter terms of trade, that is, the rate at which the product of one country will be exchanged for that of a second country, depends on the state of reciprocal demand, and it is the latter principle which explains how the gains from trade will be divided. Ricardo, it will be recalled, simply assumed that the gains from trade will be equally divided.

TABLE 8–1

	Country X				*Country Y*		
Input of Labor	*Total Labor Cost*	*Out-put*	*Average Cost per Unit*	*Input of Labor*	*Total Labor Cost*	*Out-put*	*Average Cost per Unit*
10 hours to A $20		100	$0.20	10 hours to A $20		80	$0.25
10 hours to B $20		400	0.05	10 hours to B $20		40	0.50

The nature of the principle of reciprocal demand and the way in which it supplements the principle of comparative cost may be explained in terms of a simple example which is summarized in Table 8–1. Assume two countries, X and Y, which have different capabilities in terms of labor cost of producing commodities A and B. Assume that in country X, 10 labor-hours, costing $2.00 per hour, can produce 100 units of commodity A at an average cost of 20 cents per unit, or 400 units of commodity B at an average cost per unit of 5 cents. In the absence of trade, both goods would be produced, and their domestic exchange ratio based on labor cost would be $A = 4B$. Assume also that in country Y, 10 labor-hours can produce 80 units of A at an average cost of 25 cents, or 40 units of B at an average cost of 50 cents. If both goods are produced, the domestic exchange ratio between A and B in country Y will be $A = B/2$.

If there is freedom to trade commodities A and B internationally, each country will specialize in producing that commodity which it can produce most efficiently. In the example given, country X can produce both commodities at an absolutely lower real labor cost, but it enjoys a comparative advantage in the production of B. Country Y is at a disadvantage in the production of both commodities, but it has the smallest disadvantage in the production of A. Thus, there is a basis for specialization and trade.

Each country will be willing to trade its specialty for that of another country at any ratio of exchange which improves on that which would obtain if both goods were produced domestically. Thus, country X will trade B for A at any ratio which is better than $A = 4B$; for example, $A = 3B$, $A = 2B$, $A = B$, $A = B/2$. However, the fact that country Y can produce the commodities at a ratio of $A = B/2$ sets a limit to the exchange ratio, for if it is necessary to export more than one unit of A to acquire one-half unit of B by trade, Y will be as well off to produce B domestically. Similarly, country Y will be willing to trade at any ratio which is better than $A = B/2$. But again, the limit to the barter terms of trade is imposed by the ratio of the domestic costs of A and B in the exporting country. Thus the barter terms of trade in this example must necessarily be between $A = 4B$ and $A = B/2$.

The actual barter terms of trade depend, according to Mill's doctrine of reciprocal demand, on the relative strength of the demands which the two countries have for each other's products. In Mill's own words: "It may be considered therefore, as established, that when two countries trade together in two commodities, the exchange value of these commodities relatively to each other will adjust itself to the inclinations and circumstances of the consumers on both sides, in such manner that the quantities required by each country, of the articles which it imports from its neighbor, shall be exactly sufficient to pay for one another."[26] However, it does not follow that the gains from trade will be equally divided. If, for example, country X has a relatively greater demand for commodity A than country Y has for commodity B, the actual rate of barter exchange would favor country Y. That is, Y would be acquiring commodity B by exchanging it for A at a relatively greater saving in terms of labor than that which is enjoyed by country X in importing A from country Y. This idea is expanded by the recognition that the benefit of cost-reducing improvements in the production of a good which is exported may be enjoyed entirely by the importing country if its demand for the product increases proportionately with the reduction in price. Mill thus demonstrates his appreciation of what is today called the price elasticity of demand. Mill also recognized that the benefits from trade are reduced by increases in transportation costs and that transportation costs may make it uneconomical to trade certain goods regardless of their production costs.

CONCLUDING COMMENTS ON MILL AND THE CLASSICAL SYSTEM

Mill and Ricardianism

Though John Stuart Mill examined a number of theoretical issues with genuine originality, the essentials of his theoretical inquiries, particularly as they relate to the determination of factor prices and their long-run

---

[26] *Ibid.*, p. 587.

trends, represent a refinement of Ricardo's principles. The critical element is the labor cost of producing wage goods which are, in the main, the products of agriculture. While technical progress operates to reduce these costs, Mill believed the law of diminishing returns to scale is the most important principle of political economy because of the limited supply of land. His conclusion with respect to the long-run trend of the income shares is therefore necessarily Ricardian, though his conception of the scope for social and moral progress in the stationary state injects an optimistic tone which is conspicuously absent in Ricardo's analysis.

Mill's treatment of value includes a correct statement of the law of demand and supply, and the idea of price as representing the equilibration of demand and supply conceived of in a schedule sense. However, like Ricardo, he apparently thought of supply and demand as determining short-run prices, while costs determine long-run prices, instead of recognizing that the same principle rules in both cases, though demand is relatively less important in the long run because of the elasticity of supply. Thus the role of demand never achieves the importance in Mill's analysis that it does in the analysis of subsequent writers on the value problem such as William Jevons and Alfred Marshall. The notable exception is in his analysis of the barter terms of trade, which he explains with the aid of a distinctly new concept: reciprocal demand. The role of demand is also recognized in his explanation of the prices of commodities produced under conditions of true joint supply. Neither of these problems had been dealt with by Ricardo, and Mill's treatment is both original and correct. Indeed, Mill's theoretical analysis seems at its best when he ventures into an area with which Ricardo had not previously dealt. Elsewhere, Ricardian principles seemed to impose a constraint that stifled originality, though Mill's interest in reform proposals rather than pure theory is undoubtedly another reason why so much of his theoretical analysis emerged as a restatement, though a very refined one, of Ricardo's doctrines.

Economic reform is Mill's essential objective. While he believed that individual and social interests are generally compatible with each other within the framework of a competitive economy, there are numerous exceptions to the laissez-faire principles he recommended. These include taxation of the unearned increment on land, control of the rate at which technological changes are introduced, and social control of natural monopolies. He also emphasized the necessity of worker education, particularly with respect to the importance of controlling their numbers, and favorably regarded labor combinations as contributing to the improvement of the position of the working class. These reforms, clearly premised on the principle of the greatest good for the greatest number, were conceived of as necessary improvements in the system of individual property which functions within the framework of man-made, and therefore alterable, institutions. Thus, his distinction between the laws of production and exchange and the laws of distribution enabled Mill to go beyond pure theory while at the same time adhering to the "immortal principles" of Ricardo. From the standpoint of doctrine, therefore, the work of Ricardo virtually completed the architecture of classical political economy, though Mill gave the doctrine its most refined statement. This system remained substantially intact, commanding respect and attention throughout most of the nineteenth century, though it encountered criticisms and reactions on several fronts. However, except for the efforts of Karl Marx to construct an alternative system on classical foundations, no new system of economic analysis was to emerge until that of the marginal utility economists in the latter part of the nineteenth century.

SUGGESTIONS FOR FURTHER READING

BOWLEY, MARION. *Nassau Senior and Classical Political Economy*. New York: Augustus Kelley, 1949.

MILL, JOHN STUART. *Autobiography*. London: Oxford University Press, 1924.

――――. *Principles of Political Economy*. Edited by W. J. ASHLEY. London: Longmans, Green & Co., Inc., 1923.

――――. *Utilitarianism*. London: Everyman's Library, 1944.

SENIOR, NASSAU. *Outline of the Science of Political Economy*. 6th ed. New York: Augustus Kelley, 1951.

VINER, JACOB. "Bentham and J. S. Mill: The Utilitarian Background," *American Economic Review*, Vol. XXXIX, No. 2 (March, 1949).

――――. *Studies in the Theory of International Trade*, chaps. iii–iv. New York: Harper & Bros., 1937.

Chapter 9

CLASSICAL THEORY
IN REVIEW

Scope and Method

At the beginning of the nineteenth century, it was France and not England that had a school of theoretical economists; the Physiocrats conceived of political economy as the science which sought the laws governing the distribution of wealth. Adam Smith, on the other hand, made virtually no attempt to distinguish between economics as a science and economics as a branch of politics. It was Smith's French disciple, Jean Baptiste Say, who concentrated on the use of the deductive method to derive the laws which govern the production, distribution, and consumption of wealth. His method, as well as his logical arrangement of the subject matter of economics, has become classical. It was probably introduced into England through James Mill, who studied the work of the Physiocrats and was also well acquainted with Say.[1] It was Mill who taught the deductive method to David Ricardo, whose work became the prototype for a school of thinkers who sought to discover universal laws of production, exchange, and distribution by reasoning from premises which were accepted a priori, or which had been previously arrived at by deduction. This tradition continued with the contributions of Nassau Senior, John Stuart Mill, Elliott Cairnes, and J. R. McCulloch. All of these thinkers elaborated and refined in some way the economic principles and methodological tools introduced by the Physiocrats, Smith, and Say, while at the same time avoiding their use to forge a rival system of thought. The use of the term "classical" in connection with their work is therefore intended to convey the virtually universal acceptance of their methodology and economic principles up to approximately 1870, and to distinguish their work from that of the various dissenting schools which made their appearance coincidentally or shortly afterward, not only in England but to a greater extent on the Continent. While the product of their efforts was more rigorous than *The Wealth of Nations,* it also had less popular appeal. Nevertheless, the classicists believed that their laws were a scientifically arrived at and universally applicable body of principles which depicted the operation of the economic system

---

[1] Elie Halévy, *The Growth of Philosophical Radicalism* (New York: Augustus Kelley, 1949), pp. 266–82.

regardless of time, place, or existing institutions. Institutions were regarded as being largely an expression of simple and universal laws of human behavior and therefore irrelevant to the functioning of specific societies. This is in accord with the associationist and hedonistic psychology on which Jeremy Bentham constructed utilitarianism, even though the laws of classical economics do not themselves rest on utilitarian foundations.

The conception of economics as a science which seeks to discover the laws governing the production, exchange, and distribution of wealth, restricted the scope of inquiry more narrowly than that of Adam Smith in *The Wealth of Nations*. Smith was concerned with policy quite as much as he was with analysis. But later members of the classical school generally took the position that for economics to be a science, it must restrict itself to analyzing the functioning of the economy and not intrude into the realm of policy making, where value judgments necessarily come into play and inject a bias. Economists have attempted ever since, at least in principle, to preserve the distinction between pure economics and applied economics. The former seeks only to establish laws, while the latter is normative and seeks to alter the results which emanate from economic laws. Thus the classicists conceived of production and exchange as being governed by immutable laws whose operation they sought to discover. Distribution, on the other hand, has some laws which are not of man's creation which political economy seeks to discover, but it is primarily the result of human institutions. The classicists, therefore, conceived of the laws of distribution as being alterable by human intervention and for this reason different from the laws of production and exchange. This distinction became particularly important in the writings of later classicists such as John Stuart Mill.

The Laws of Classical Economics

While the post-Smithian classical economists were of utilitarian persuasion philosophically, the economic laws they described owe little to utilitarianism. These laws are (1) the law of self interested behavior, (2) the law of value, (3) the law of comparative advantage, (4) the law of diminishing returns, (5) the law of population, (6) the law of wages, (7) the law of capital accumulation, (8) the law of rent, and (9) the law of markets. These laws were regarded as irrevocable but were not viewed as being preordained for the benefit of mankind. They were conceived of as operating in the same impersonal way as physical laws and, unlike the laws of the Physiocrats and Smith, are neither good nor bad, moral nor immoral, in and of themselves. Naturally, not all who are collectively referred to as classical economists dealt exhaustively with each of these laws or accepted all of them without modification.

The law of self-interested behavior refers quite simply to the motivation of man to maximize his monetary gains if he is free to do so. This does not imply that people's only interests are pecuniary, but rather that pecuniary interests have been singled out for special consideration. Thus the classicists envisaged businessmen as seeking to decrease costs to maximize profits and minimize losses, while workers seek to increase wages and work fewer hours, and landlords and moneylenders seek to maximize rent and interest. This view of human behavior owes nothing to utilitarianism, though it is compatible with it. Smith conceived of individuals as acting in precisely the same way, though he derived his conception of human behavior from the philosophy of the natural order rather than hedonistic psychology.

Nor does the classical law of value owe anything to utilitarianism. Cost of production was thought to determine value. Even though Smith and his followers explained the oscillations of market price around natural price in terms of demand and supply, they had little understanding of the relationship between utility and demand. Otherwise Bentham's "felicific calculus" might have added a new dimension to post-Smithian economics by leading to a greater appreciation of utility, if not to a utility theory of value. This, in turn, could have led to an understanding of the conditions of maximum consumer satisfaction and optimum resource allocation. Bentham did, after all, perceive the principle of diminishing marginal utility, which was later to figure so importantly in the thinking of the marginal utility theorists, when he observed that while happiness is associated with the possession of wealth, each addition to an individual's wealth will not produce a corresponding increase in his happiness. On the contrary, "the quantity of happiness produced by a particle of wealth, each particle being of the same magnitude, will be less and less at every particle. The second will produce less than the first, the third less than the second and so on."[2] However, this observation did not lead him to a utility theory of value. The fact that his calculus was nothing more than a table or list of the various sources of human pleasure is probably a major reason why it did not serve as a fruitful beginning for a utility oriented theory of value. The development of this sort of theory took place only after it was perceived that a mathematical calculus, which proceeds in terms of balancing infinitely small increments of utility and disutility, is needed to define the conditions under which consumer satisfactions are maximized.

Conceivably, the orientation of economic analysis to explaining the behavior of businessmen rather than consumers is another reason why the role of utility was so generally ignored by the classicists. While it was shown that the competitive market will lead to an optimum allocation of resources among different industries, the effectiveness of this process was interpreted in the light of monetary gains for the businessman, rather than the maximization of consumers' satisfaction. Thus the classicists chose to develop Smith's labor cost theory of value instead of developing a value theory

---

[2] W. Stark ed. *Jeremy Bentham's Economic Writings op. cit.*, vol. 3 p. 441.

premised on a theory of consumer behavior. Only Say and Senior gave utility a significant role by maintaining that prices are proportional to utilities, but their failure to recognize that it is the utility of the marginal unit that is important prevented them from developing a utility oriented theory of value. Not until the advent of the marginal utility school in the 1870's was the economic problem to be conceived of primarily in terms of the relationship between maximum consumer satisfaction and the allocation of resources among alternative uses. Thus, utilitarianism did not influence the classical theory of value because it did not lead to an examination of the relationship between utility and demand.

The classical explanation of exchange value is, in essence, a cost of production theory. It was recognized, after Smith, that commodities must have utility in order to have value in exchange but, difficulty of attainment was conceived to be the essential determinant of value. Commodities have values which are commensurate with their labor and capital costs and command prices which tend, over time, to reflect production costs including the current rate of wages and profits if competition is free.

The classicists conceived of international trade as being governed by the same laws which govern individual exchange. Like individual exchange, international exchange yields a saving to both participants. If there is freedom to buy in the cheapest market, the tendency will be to buy from abroad those commodities which would impose the greatest costs if produced domestically. The value of a commodity imported from abroad depends on the cost of producing the commodity exported in exchange for it. This is the essence of Ricardo's famous law of comparative cost, which was further elaborated by John Stuart Mill.

The law of diminishing returns holds an especially prominent place in classical thinking. It expresses the relationship between a constant factor, land, and a variable factor, labor, in the production process and leads to the conclusion that there is a limit to the practicality of using additional doses of labor with a given quantity of natural resources. The law of diminishing returns, together with the law of population, according to which population will tend to increase directly with and to the limits of subsistence, led to the classical theory of economic development, which conceived of the tendency toward the stationary state as the irrevocable final stage. It also provided the basis for the pessimistic bent of English economics after Smith. Concern with the pressure which a growing population would put on the food supply led even such an ardent champion of liberty as John Stuart Mill to consider the desirability of restricting liberty in order to reduce the birth rate.

The law of wages conceived of the wage rate as being dependent on the relationship between the number of workers seeking employment and the size of the wage fund available. The wage fund consisted of previously produced wage goods, principally food products, which are advanced to workers during the production process, and was therefore identified with the real capital fund of society. The concept of the wage fund thus provided the basis for the development of an abstinence theory in which interest is conceived of as a reward to those who made present goods available. It also leads to the classical notion that the rate of capital accumulation depends on the willingness of capitalists to curtail unproductive consumption in favor of the productive employment of labor. The only practical mode of raising the level of wages was therefore thought to be encouraging the accumulation of capital or discouraging population growth, or both.

The law of rent emerges because the tendency toward diminishing returns forces a resort to the inferior margin of cultivation, and competition causes price to equal the cost of producing a product on the least productive land in cultivation. A differential surplus, namely, rent, will therefore make its appearance on superior grades of land. This principle is primarily associated with Thomas Malthus and David Ricardo, and was later elaborated by Nassau Senior and John Stuart Mill.

Finally, the classical economists, with the notable exception of Malthus, accepted the proposition known as Say's law of markets, that there cannot be a general glut or overproduction of all goods. According to this proposition, which was introduced into English political economy by James Mill, specific individual goods may be produced in excess of the demand for them, with the consequence that other specific goods are produced in smaller quantity than dictated by demand. But such an occurrence with respect to all goods was regarded as an impossibility because every act of production creates not only goods but also the purchasing power with which to take them off the market. Although it was recognized that income is saved as well as spent, it was further reasoned that savings cannot create a deficiency of aggregate effective demand because the capital which results from savings is also consumed as wage advances are made during the course of the production process. It was on these grounds that the classical economists extended the identity known as Say's law to arrive at the conclusion that a glut of capital is impossible.

The work of Say has not been examined separately because only his concept of the law of markets was incorporated into the principles of classical economics. However, it is worth noting that Say developed other concepts which were subsequently adopted. Specifically, Say, unlike the classicists, accorded a unique role to the entrepreneur who organizes and manages production. He also recognized that factor values, and therefore distribution shares, reflect factor contributions to production. This treatment of the relationship between production and distribution was considerably in advance of the thinking of the English classicists, who treated distribution simply as the sharing of income among the social classes instead of as functional rewards. He also recognized the role of utility as a determinant of value, although he did not have a concept of the margin. But he was in many ways in advance of English writers, and it is unfortunate that the barrier of language prevented Say's work from being more widely studied than was apparently the case.

Classicism as a Theory of Economic Development

In formulating and elaborating the laws noted above, the classical economists believed that they had succeeded in providing a realistic and universal, though abstract, description of the production of goods, the establishment of domestic and international prices, and the distribution of the income of the economy among the three social classes. But they were even more concerned with the long-run trend of wages, profits, and rent. Indeed, the central problem of classical economics after Smith was that of long-run economic development rather than the problem of value and price. The latter was subsequently to become the focal point of neoclassical theory.

Economic development was envisaged in the classical model as the result of population growth and capital accumulation. Population was seen as growing in response to the availability of subsistence, as evidenced by the market rate of wages. The higher the market rate of wages in relation to labor's requirements, the greater the stimulus to population growth. The market rate, in turn, was thought to depend on the initial size of the labor force and the willingness of capitalists to provide the wage fund out of which subsistence is advanced. Growth also required a net accumulation of capital. This required, in the classical model, a sufficiently large total product to leave a residual for profit after the wage requirements of the laboring population and the rental payments of the landlord class have been satisfied. Accumulation was seen as being conducive to progress because it increases production in addition to stimulating population growth.

Continued growth was impossible in the classical model. Eventually, the tendency toward diminishing returns would raise the cost of maintaining the laborer and his family to a level which leaves too small a margin of profit after wages and rents to stimulate further accumulation. The stationary state, in which both population growth and net capital accumulation cease, will then come into existence.

Classicism and Liberalism

The inherent disparity of interests among the receivers of rent, profit, and interest was an important conclusion of post-Smithian thinkers. This dichotomy made the proper role of government an issue. Laissez-faire had been the policy counterpart of Physiocratic as well as Smithian thinking, in which individual conscience was regarded as the instrument through which the ideal of individual freedom under law was to be realized. But once the thesis of the natural harmony of interests fell into discard, another basis for policy recommendations was required. Classical political economists were primarily concerned with the discovery of laws, but insofar as they concerned themselves with matters of policy, Bentham's utilitarianism provided them with the foundation they needed. They accepted Bentham's principle that the greatest good for the greatest number should be the governing consideration and, for the most part, believed that this objective is served by a laissez-faire policy coupled with education and appropriate legislative reforms to reconcile divergent class interests. It is interesting to note in this connection, however, that Bentham himself originally believed that the reforms he sought would be accomplished more quickly under a system of enlightened despotism than by political liberalism. But he later abandoned this view, largely under the influence of James Mill, in favor of a program of reform which called for broader representation in Parliament and universal male suffrage.

Appraisal of Classicism

Classical economic theory attempted to provide, first of all, a simplified model of the operation of the actual economic system. It attempted secondly, to offer a hypothesis concerning its probable future long-run development. Finally, its philosophical and psychological foundations were thought to offer a basis for a policy of economic and political laissez-faire. How well were these objectives satisfied?

The conception of the operation of the economic system which is fundamental to the classical analysis is that its functioning is comparable to a self-correcting physical mechanism which is capable of automatic adjustment to external forces disturbing its equilibrium. This assumption proved to be most valid while the economy was in its preindustrial stage of development. Later, as industrialization altered the system, the assumption of automatic adjustment became less valid and rendered analyses conducted on that assumption less tenable. Malthus' theory of gluts is in the nature of an internal attack on the classical system in this regard. The impact of this theory was, however, greatly softened by the prominence which Says' law of markets assumed in Ricardo's thinking. Ricardo's views on this matter were so persuasive that subsequent analyses of the nature and cause of economic crisis came largely from heretics like Jean Charles Sismondi and Karl Marx.

The classical system was conspicuously successful for a long time in providing a basis for political theory. Philosophically, the roots of its political system stem from John Locke's conception of the natural order in which labor was conceived of as a source of property and consequently as the foundation for all claims to wealth. Intervention of any sort was regarded as violating the property relations of the natural order. Thus, political laissez-faire became the logical counterpart of an economic theory predicated on labor. However, not everyone agreed that the property relations which came into existence in the course of time coincided with the requirements of the natural order.

Benthams' system of utilitarianism, which is a later expression of the philosophy of natural law than Locke's, can be used to lend support to a radical movement as well as a conservative one.[3] The principle of utility provides an unequivocal basis for laissez-faire only if egotistic behavior can be relied on to produce socially altruistic behavior, as would be the case if the same basic desires can be attributed to all men, so that they engage in essentially the same behavior to maximize pleasure and avoid pain. But this presupposes not only that every individual is in fact the best judge of his own interests and that the pleasures and pains of different persons are homogeneous and comparable, but also that individuals commonly and regularly make rational calculations with respect to the pleasures and pains associated with the various modes of behavior open to them. If these conditions are not realized, it is a simple matter to make out a case for state intervention. If, for example, competition cannot be relied upon to assure everyone his just share of society's product, or if general overproduction is possible or if the urge for procreation is so powerful that population tends to multiply without reference to the supply and fertility of land, there is a basis for arguing that the state should properly intervene to improve and correct these conditions.

Bentham himself prescribed that governmental intervention in economic matters be limited, but the limits he suggested were not so narrow as to support the doctrine that there exists natural harmony of interests in a society unregulated by government.[4] While the classical economists who followed him advocated laissez-faire as a general rule, they also recognized that legislation is sometimes required to identify naturally divergent interests and recommended numerous exceptions to laissez-faire on the basis of the principle of utility. The schism between liberalism and intervention is particularly apparent in the writings of John Stuart Mill, but the frequently encountered notion that the classicists regarded the functions of government as being wholly negative is quite erroneous in spite of its persistence.[5] It was, however, the case the classicists made for laissez-faire which, more than its technical analysis, gave it continued authority.

The classical analysis was not conspicuously successful as a theory of economic development. Its shortcomings as regards its visions of the stationary state are evident. The pessimistic results associated with the tendency to diminishing returns and population growth failed to materialize as technological developments, emigration, and birth control alleviated

---

[3] Halévy, *op. cit.*, Part III, chap. 1.

[4] Jacob Viner, "Bentham and J. S. Mill: The Utilitarian Background." *American Economic Review*, Vol. XXXIX, No. 2 (March, 1949); reprinted in *idem, The Long View and the Short* (Glencoe, Ill.: Free Press, 1958).

[5] This question is examined at length by Lionel Robbins, *The Theory of Economic Policy in Classical Political Economy* (New York: Macmillan Co., 1952).

population pressures. These were factors which Malthus, Ricardo, and John Stuart Mill did not foresee. They were essentially unhistorical in their outlook and took it for granted that the behavior they observed among their contemporaries was inherent in human nature and that their conclusions concerning them were valid for all eternity. This is the essence of the criticisms which the German historical school directed against classicism.

The historical school took the position that the laws of the classical school were neither absolute nor perpetually valid either in terms of economic theory or as a basis for policy. They argued that economic laws, if they can be discovered at all, must necessarily be relative to time and place. Because economic laws operate within the framework of constantly changing environments, they argued that it is necessary to replace the classical method of deduction by induction in order to discover the nature of these environments. Induction would, they felt, also shed new light on the motives of human conduct, which, in their view, the classicists interpreted all too simply as being only the product of self-interest. The study of political economy should proceed by collecting a mass of historical data from which generalizations will eventually be drawn. Precisely what the nature of these generalizations will be cannot be determined in advance, for the necessary data must first be assembled.

German scholars such as Gustav Schmoller took the rather extreme position that the historical method is the only way of studying political economy and that nothing of importance can be learned by using the deductive method. He and several of his contemporaries embarked on an ambitious program of study which resulted in the accumulation of a remarkable and most impressive volume of historical detail. But their contribution is primarily of a descriptive character. Their criticisms undoubtedly made deductive economists more selective regarding their premises and more cautious in putting forward their generalizations, but the historical school contributed little to the body of economic analysis. Eventually, the disagreement over methodology (*Methodenstreit*), which reached England but found few enthusiastic adherents, resolved itself as participants to the dispute recognized that both deduction and induction have their place in economic analysis and mutually fructify one another.

The criticism of the socialists against classicism was much more formidable than that of the historicists. Revolutionary in character, the socialist movement was inspired in part by the exploitation and genuine misery which the Industrial Revolution imposed on the working class. But it had still another root, and this one was philosophical. It has already been suggested that the doctrine of the natural order and the natural law governing it could as readily be used to support radical political views as conservative ones. Indeed, the emergence of capitalism, sweeping away as it did feudal institutions and the vested interests of the medieval era, was itself revolutionary. Since capitalism in turn gave rise to new vested interests and abuses, the same liberal philosophy which sired capitalism could now be called upon to sanction further reform. The English socialists for example, started with the Ricardian theory of value but also gave a revolutionary twist to Bentham's utilitarianism. In their interpretation the principle of the greatest good for the greatest number did not lend sanctity to the existing social order but required instead a more egalitarian system of income distribution in which each would receive the whole product of his labor. These early English socialists, as well as their French counterparts, were part of Marx's inspiration. Philosophically, however, Marxian socialism was grounded on the Hegelian dialectic rather than philosophical radicalism. As an economist in the classical tradition, Marx was to forge a system which rivaled the classical one. His analysis of the origin, functioning, and inevitable destruction of the capitalistic system is not only the most complete and best-articulated rival to the classical analysis but also the one having the greatest impact on future generations. As such, the work of Marx is deserving of a separate chapter, which follows.

SUGGESTIONS FOR FURTHER READING

HALÉVY, ELIE. *The Growth of Philosophical Radicalism*. New York: Augustus Kelley, 1949.

LOWE, A. "The Classical Theory of Economic Growth," *Social Research,* (Summer, 1951).

MYINT, HLA. "The Classical View of the Economic Problem," *Economica,* N.S., Vol. XIII (May, 1946); republished in *Spengler and Allen, op. cit.,* pp. 442–53.

―――. *Theories of Welfare Economics,* chap. v. Cambridge: Harvard University Press, 1948.

ROBBINS, LIONEL. *The Theory of Economic Policy in Classical Political Economy*. New York: Macmillan Co., 1952.

SMITH, V. E. "The Classicists Use of Demand," *Journal of Political Economy,* Vol. LIX, No. 3 (June, 1951).

Chapter	THE CONTRIBUTION OF
10	KARL MARX TO ECONOMIC
	ANALYSIS

INTRODUCTION

Life and Times (1818–83)

The name of Karl Marx is not only most intimately associated with the socialist movement, but his ideas have also had a more influential impact than those of any other socialist advocate. It is to him that we may attribute the rise of "scientific" socialism—that distinctively Marxian fusion of philosophy, socialism, and economics put forward as a "revelation" of the ultimate collapse of capitalism and the inevitable triumph of socialism.

Marx was born in the German Rhineland, the son of a moderately well-to-do Jewish lawyer who became a convert to Lutheranism and raised his children in that faith. At 17, Marx entered the University of Bonn to study law, but transferred after a year to the more stimulating atmosphere of the University of Berlin, where his interests became directed primarily to philosophy and history. His religious views now abandoned, he became an avowed atheist and materialist. Intellectually, he was, like many others of his generation, profoundly affected by the ideas of the philosopher Hegel, whose views of the individual, the state, and the mode of historical change were in sharp contrast with the tenets of rationalism which characterized the Age of Enlightenment. Initially, Hegelian ideas led Marx in the direction of what became known as the "higher criticism." The latter sought to examine religious views within the framework of the historical method and was at least partly an outgrowth of the strict control of the Prussian authorities over political inquiry and action. As a result of these curbs, intellectual activity, particularly of a critical nature, became directed toward religious issues.

Intellectually trained but unable to secure a university post, largely because of his unpopular religious views, Marx turned his attention to journalism. He became the editor of the *Rheinische Zeitung* in Cologne, a moderately liberal paper sponsored by business interests. It was in this post that Marx became interested in social and economic questions. The suspension of the newspaper a year later caused him and his wife to take up residence in Paris, which he felt to be a base of operations more congenial to his liberal views. It was here that he made contact with a whole gamut of revolutionary socialist and communist ideas. This was the period during which Marx became a serious student of history, politics, and economics. Pierre Proudhon appears to have initially suggested the possibility of interpreting economic phenomena in Hegelian terms. The latter idea was eventually to become the foundation stone for the whole Marxian system, though Proudhon was later denounced by Marx as an incompetent exponent of the dialectic.

His period in Paris also brought Marx into close personal contact with Friedrich Engels, with whom he had an intellectual and personal association that spanned a lifetime. Engels' family was in the textile business in Barmen (Germany), and he later became the prosperous part-owner of a cotton business in England. His intimate knowledge of economic and social conditions in that country, the basis for his work on *The Condition of the Working Class in England* (1844), was invaluable to Marx. It was also through Engels that he made contact with the English socialists of the day.

Marx's sojourn in Paris was brief, lasting a little more than a year. At the request of the Prussian government, he was expelled from France and moved to Belgium. By this time, his intellectual system had already taken shape, and he turned his attention for the first time to political activity. He helped found a German Workers' Union which joined with other such groups into an international Communist League. Marx and Engels together drafted a statement of principles which they called the *Communist Manifesto* (1848), which became the best known of all Marxist writings and is today available in virtually all languages. A powerful and brilliant document, the *Manifesto* was intended to present a theoretical basis for communism, a critique of utopian socialist movements, and a program of socialist aims and methods for achieving them.

The year 1848 brought many revolutionary uprisings in Europe. The outbreak which took place in France forced the abdication of Louis Philippe and the proclamation of the Second French Republic. Though there were efforts to direct the new government in accordance with socialist principles, the coup of 1852 established Louis Napoleon as Emperor Napoleon III. In all likelihood, Marx's *Manifesto* had little to do with the revolution. Nevertheless, he was deported from Belgium for revolutionary activity, and he returned first to Paris and then briefly to Germany. London became his ultimate refuge, and it was here that he lived the remainder of his life, supported largely by gifts and loans from friends, relatives, and sympathizers (Engels in particular), and stipends from intermittent journalistic activity. The most noteworthy of the latter was his work as foreign correspondent for the *New York Tribune,* an association which lasted from 1851 to the 1860's. This was also the period during which he utilized the facilities of the British Museum to gather material for the first volume of

Das Kapital, which appeared in print in 1867. The remaining two volumes were put together by Engels from partial drafts and notes. This was the trilogy that Marx intended to represent the reconstruction of the science of political economy.

THE BACKGROUND FOR MARXIAN ECONOMIC THEORY

Socialist Thought

Fundamentally, Marxian theory is a theory of capitalist economic development rather than a theory of socialism. Indeed, Marx had remarkably little to say about socialism, the system that he maintained was ultimately to succeed capitalism. However, the Marxian analysis derives partly from the social reform movements of the Enlightenment. The earliest roots of socialism are of course to be found in the ideals of Christian brotherhood; but another and perhaps more important origin is the emergence during the Enlightenment of the idea that human society can be rationally reconstructed to promote the best interests of its members.

There were two broad views as to how this reconstruction might take place. The first, continuing the tradition of classical liberalism, maintained that society's best interests would be served by assuring freedom to its individual members, who, in seeking their own best interests, would automatically also assure the ideal functioning of the whole. Philosophical radicalism was this sort of reform movement. It stressed the preservation of private property rights and individual enterprise within the framework of minimal government functions.[1] The socialist-anarchist movement was similar in its aims but fundamentally different in the modus operandi it visualized to achieve them. It was socialistic in its view that the only rational society is one which substitutes collective for private ownership of the means of production as a foundation for an egalitarian distribution of income. It was anarchistic in its conception of government as the outgrowth of the inequities and abuses of a society in which the property rights of the wealthy required the coercive influence of the state in order to survive. The view of Proudhon is typical. "Property," he said, "is theft"; consequently, the state becomes the agency required to perpetuate it. He reasoned that after private property has been abolished and men have renounced their acquisitive ambitions in favor of cooperation for the common good, government will be abolished because it has no further function to perform.

Pre-Marxian socialism was, like classical liberalism, initially an idealistic movement which attracted intellectual rather than working class support. It had its primary early development in the France of the early nineteenth century, which had not yet experienced an industrial revolution and its associated labor discontent. The Industrial Revolution was still, in the main, an English phenomenon, and it was here, and later in Germany,

---

[1] See Chap. 6 above.

that socialism was to become a mass movement of the working class. It is perhaps worth noting in this regard that the German Workers' Union which Marx helped found while he was in Belgium had no workers in it, but existed primarily to study socialist thought.

It was from these early socialists that Marx acquired many of his ideas. Though many of these ideas were retained and made part of his new system, he criticized these early socialists as "utopian." He agreed with them concerning their aims, shared many of their visions of the future society, but felt they were unrealistic in believing that a major transformation of existing society could be brought about simply by an appeal to reason. The prosperous upper classes, in particular, could never be led by reason alone to accept the reforms proposed by the socialists. Even the workers were not yet ready, in his view, for a radically different society. Nor would they become ready until the evils of the present system greatly worsened their position and thus made them receptive to socialism. It became Marx's aim to demonstrate how this deterioration of the working class would inevitably come about and necessarily call forth socialism. This is the difference between Marx's "scientific" socialism and the earlier (in his view) "utopian" movements. He sought to demonstrate that the advent of socialism will be the inevitable result of an evolutionary process which could be hastened by proper strategy and tactics, and that the approach of the utopians would in fact serve to hinder rather than serve that ultimate aim. Precisely why socialism was inevitable according to Marxian thinking turns upon the use he made of Hegel's philosophy of history.

Hegel's Philosophy of History

The development of the Marxist system appears to have begun with its general philosophy. Marx was still a student at the University of Berlin when he came under the influence of Hegel's philosophy of history. The latter was the first systematic exposition against the philosophy of natural rights. The revolt against reason which began with Rousseau and culminated in Hume's *Treatise of Human Nature* virtually destroyed all claims to validity of the doctrine of natural law and, along with it, its applications to religion, ethics, law, and politics. Specifically, Hume maintained that the concept of reason as used in the system of natural law is ambiguous and cannot, therefore, be a source of knowledge. Immanuel Kant sought to rescue the problem of knowledge from this abyss by effecting a synthesis between rationalism and empiricism. Knowledge, he maintained, is acquired in three ways: via the senses, via the intellect, and via moral will. The knowledge gotten through the senses and the intellect cannot be of the world as it really is, but only as it appears to be, because our minds impose upon these things a quality which has no existence in the things themselves. Thus, it is only through moral will that we can have contact with the real world. Morality belongs to the noumenal world, that is, to the world of reality, whereas science belongs to the phenomenal world, that is, the world as it appears to be. The realms of science and morality are therefore regarded by Kant as autonomous and separate. But this "solution" to the problem posed by Hume made the schism between science and religion more acute by placing one in the realm of fact and the other in the realm of value. Hegel, however, maintained that there is a necessary and logical relationship between them which is demonstrable via the dialectic, the only instrument of analysis through which truth can be discovered.[2]

The dialectic is the self-propulsion of ideas through the process of synthesis. Its origin is to be found in ancient Greek philosophy, in which it referred to the method by which two persons engaged in argument or debate modify, and eventually correct, one another's views until they arrive at a third view which incorporates elements of both. Thus, there is a thesis which is confronted with a conflicting antithesis. The controversy between them leads to corrective argument and modification until a synthesis emerges in which thesis and antithesis are reconciled. This is the method which was used by Plato in his *Dialogues* and which was later an important intellectual tool of the Scholastics.

Hegel's adaptation of the dialectic was little concerned with the opposing ideas of individual human beings. He conceived of the dialectic as the process by which change takes place in the universe. There is, he thought, an inherent pattern according to which this development takes place about which we can learn from the study of history. Under his influence, European scholars came to believe that a knowledge of the past is necessary in order to foresee and influence the future. Conservative and radical thinkers alike embraced anew the study of history; and there followed an age, particularly in Germany but also elsewhere in Europe, in which the historical method became regarded as the only truly scientific one and was applied to virtually all fields of inquiry.

Hegel himself undertook to utilize the dialectic to predict the next stage of German history. The next and inevitable step, he maintained, would be the amalgamation of the several German states under a single monarchy. The new German state would thus be the apex of history. Hegel's political philosophy not only rejected individualism on the ground that it failed to recognize the intimate relationship between the individual and society, but also endowed the state with a spirit all its own. This is the conception of the state which characterized German political theory even into the twentieth century.

Ricardian Economics

Ricardian economics or, more specifically, Ricardo's labor theory of value, was the third source of inspiration for Marx's analysis of the func-

---

[2] Excellent treatments of Hegelian philosophy are available in George Sabine, *A History of Political Theory* (rev. ed., New York: Henry Holt Co., Inc., 1950), and H. B. Acton, *The Illusion of the Epoch,* Boston, Beacon Press, 1957, Part I.

tioning of the capitalistic system. Ricardo, it will be recalled, wrote as follows: "Possessing utility [which he discarded both as a cause and as a measure of value] commodities derive their exchangeable value from two sources: from their scarcity and from the quantity of labour required to obtain them."[3] Scarcity was regarded as being of primary significance when a commodity, like a rare work of art, is not reproducible. Most commodities, however, being the product of labor, can be supplied "almost without any assignable limit, if we are disposed to bestow the labour necessary to obtain them."[4] He then proceeded to reason that rent, as a differential surplus, is not a determinant of exchange value, and that since neither variations in wages or nor variations in profits could affect value in exchange, commodities would be exchanged in proportion to the labor used in their production.

Marx's serious study of economics dates from his early Paris days, and he was greatly impressed with the treatment that Smith, and more particularly Ricardo, gave to labor as the cause of value. The latter were, however, favorably disposed toward competitive capitalism and laissez-faire policy, whereas Marx was hostile to that system in every form, on the ground that the laboring class is exploited by capitalist employers. However, he regarded their labor theory of value as providing an essential foundation for his hypothesis concerning labor exploitation and the eventual destruction of the capitalist system. Indeed, Marx considered himself to be, intellectually speaking, a lineal descendant of the great classical tradition.

THE ORIGIN, NATURE, AND FUNCTIONING OF CAPITALISM

The Economic Interpretation of History

Marx's objective was "to lay bare the economic law of motion of modern society."[5] The prime mover of social change was, he maintained, to be found in changes in the mode of production. This premise was a firm part of his convictions considerably before he published Volume I of *Capital.* In the preface to *A Contribution to the Critique of Political Economy,* he wrote as follows:

The mode of production in material life determines the general character of the social, political and spiritual processes of life. It is not the consciousness of men that determines their existence, but on the contrary, their social existence determines their consciousness. At a certain stage of their development, the material forces of production in society come in conflict with the existing

---

[3] David Ricardo, "Principles of Political Economy and Taxation" in *The Works and Correspondence of David Ricardo, op. cit.,* Vol. I, p. 11.

[4] *Ibid.,* p. 12.

[5] Karl Marx, *Capital,* translated from the 3d German ed. (1883) by Samuel More and Edward Aveling, and edited by Friedrich Engels (Moscow: Foreign Languages Publishing House, 1959), Preface to 1st ed., Vol. I, p. 10.

relations of production, or—what is but a legal expression for the same thing, with the property relations within which they had been at work before. From forms of development of the forces of production these relations turn into their fetters. Then comes the period of social revolution. With the change of the economic foundation the entire immense superstructure is more or less rapidly transformed.[6]

The impetus to social change is thus to be found in the "mode of production." The mode of production prevailing in a particular period is associated with a given set of social relationships which reflect the ownership and use of the material means of production which have developed in the process of social production. As the mode of production becomes altered, as it will in the course of time, new social relationships, more appropriate to the altered production relationship, will be required. It is the contradiction that develops between the altered mode of production and existing social relationships that generates change. This is the Hegelian aspect of Marx's thinking. But unlike Hegel, Marx considered that conflicts are not in the realm of ideas, but in the material world with its existing social system. The mind of man, far from originating the conflicting thesis and antithesis which Hegel stressed, merely perceives the material world around him. This is the essence of Marx's materialism as opposed to Hegel's idealism. The conflicts to be resolved are between social classes— the ruling class of the epoch versus the exploited class. Thus, Marx began the *Communist Manifesto* with the observation that "the history of all hitherto existing society is the history of class struggles."

The economic source of class conflict was also of particular interest to the classicists. This is precisely what Ricardo meant by "the distribution of the produce of the earth." In his view, the basic antagonism between social classes was that which existed between the landlords and the industrial capitalists. It was for this reason that the doctrine of rent loomed so large in the Ricardian analysis. Marx, however, regarded the emphasis on land and rent to be inappropriate in a bourgeois economy, for the latter is a society in which the antagonistic classes are the bourgeoisie and the proletariat. It is the relationship between them which determines the nature of the mode of production and hence of the whole society.

In analyzing the relationship between these two classes, Marx relies heavily on the deductive methodology so strongly associated with Ricardo and his neoclassical followers. The manner of its application is of course different, in that it is oriented toward demonstrating the transitory nature of capitalism. To do this, Marx finds it necessary to isolate the capital-labor relationship from all other social relationships in order to examine its basic character. Reduced to its simplest form, this relationship is one of exchange. The commodity which is being bought and sold Marx identifies as

---

[6] Karl Marx, *A Contribution to the Critique of Political Economy,* translated by N. I. Stone, Chicago, Charles H. Kerr & Co., 1904, p. 11.

"labor power." This commodity, the only one labor has available for sale, is merely one commodity among many, and the exchange relationship that results from its sale is one among many. Thus, Part I of the first volume of *Capital* is entitled "Commodities" and is an analysis of the general phenomenon of exchange. It begins with simple commodity production such as takes place when each individual owns his own means of production and satisfies those wants he cannot fulfill directly by exchanging his surplus with others. Such is not the case under capitalism; here, the ownership of all the means of production is vested in one class, the bourgeoisie, while the work is performed by the members of the proletariat. The means of production and labor power are thus given commodity form, and exchange relationships are involved in their purchase and sale. This is the mode of production that is typical of capitalism.

That the concept of the mode of production does not refer to the technical aspects of production alone should now be obvious. It includes not only the technology surrounding the physical means of production, but also the social relationships deriving from the whole complex of the socioeconomic, political, and cultural institutions which pertain to a given stage of development. This superstructure is a major aspect of the mode of production and therefore plays a role in the historical process. Thus, what is so often referred to as the "economic interpretation of history" is at least as much in the realm of sociology as of economics.

Use Value and Exchange Value

The manner in which the conflict between the mode of production and the superstructure of social organization will make itself felt and the reason why the capitalistic system will eventually become untenable are questions which Marx's economic analysis is intended to answer. His analysis is focused on the value problem. Marx begins by noting that every commodity has a use value and an exchange value. Though he uses these terms in their usual sense, he regards the analysis of use value as lying outside the sphere of political economy because it involves a relation between a consumer and an object of consumption. Political economy, in Marx's view, properly involves only social relations. The study of use values does not come within the province of the political economist because they involve a relationship between a person and an object. But exchange values between goods, though they seemingly do not involve social relationships, are of particular concern to the political economist because every exchange of commodities is also an exchange of labor. Marx thus conceives of the value problem as having a qualitative aspect as well as a quantitative one. It has been suggested that the great originality of Marx's value theory lies in its attempt to deal simultaneously with both.[7]

---

[7] See Paul M. Sweezy, *The Theory of Capitalist Development* (New York: Oxford University Press, 1942).

Marx's insistence that an object can have exchange value only if it represents embodied labor led him to distinguish between value and price. An object like uncultivated land may command a price but is devoid of exchange value because there is no labor congealed in it.[8] While he thought that all value derived from labor, Marx, like Smith and Ricardo before him, was aware that labor is not homogeneous but is sometimes more proficient because of natural ability or superior training. When a more effective worker is employed in a given line of production side by side with one who is less productive, their comparative efficiency is measurable in physical terms. Once the ratio of their output has been established, the two kinds of labor can be reduced to a common denominator, namely, "human labor pure and simple." "Skilled labor counts only as simple labor intensified, or rather, as multiplied simple labor, a given quantity of skilled labor being considered equal to a greater quantity of simple labor."[9] The labor congealed in a commodity is thus measurable in time units which express the proportion of the community's labor force a commodity absorbs. From this, Marx deduces that there is a correspondence between the labor-time ratios involved in the production of two commodities and their exchange ratios.

There is an obvious qualification to this principle: The fact that more labor time is lavished on a commodity does not necessarily give it greater value. Unnecessary or inefficient expenditures of labor time do not enhance value. Only "socially necessary" labor time contributes to value. "The labor time socially necessary is that required to produce an article under the normal conditions of production, and with the average degree of skill and intensity prevalent at this time."[10] Thus, commodities are exchanged for one another at a rate which is determined by the quantity of socially necessary labor each embodies. When this ratio of exchange prevails in the market between any pair of commodities, the producers of neither commodity will have an incentive to shift from the production of one to the production of the other, and the price of each will be proportional to the labor time required to produce it. In other words, if the forces of supply and demand have free play, an equilibrium price which is proportional to labor time will obtain. Competitive market forces, then, are the mechanism through which deviations between market prices and real (labor) values are eliminated. Thus the supply and demand explanation of price determination is really an essential part of the labor theory, though Marx did not always express this point clearly.

Marx did not completely overlook the role of demand in determining exchange values, though it is frequently maintained that he did. He specifically emphasized that use value is a prerequisite for exchange value and

---

[8] Marx, *Capital,* Vol. I, p. 102.

[9] *Ibid.,* p. 44.

[10] *Ibid.,* p. 39.

that therefore the social need for a commodity is the determining factor of the amount of social labor which is to be allocated to a particular type of production. Thus, if too much of a commodity has been produced, or if more labor has been expended than is socially necessary, it will be reflected in a reduced exchange value. Nevertheless, it is true that he did not approach the value problem from the standpoint of consumer choice, any more than did Smith or Ricardo. It has been suggested that to have done so would have been inconsistent with his objective of investigating the causes of social change, for consumer wants, except insofar as they originate in physical requirements, are a reflection of the mode of production and are therefore passive as regards the process of change.[11]

Surplus Value

There is a significant difference between a system of simple commodity production and that which prevails in a capitalistic system. Under simple commodity production, each producer owns his own means of production and sells the product he produces. He exchanges his commodities for money and then reconverts money into commodities. Symbolically, the process is described as $C-M-C$ by Marx. Under capitalism, the means of production are owned by one group of individuals, the capitalists, but actively used in production by another group, the workers. The capitalist, who produces nothing, starts the process with money. He purchases commodities in the form of means of production and labor and, after the completion of the production process, converts the commodities once again into money. Thus the process is $M-C-M'$. M' must necessarily be greater than M in order to make the process worthwhile. The difference between M and M' is the surplus value, the income of the capitalist and the aim of the production process.

Surplus value has its origin in the difference between the value of the commodities workers are able to produce in a given period of production and the value of the labor power they sell the capitalists for use in the production process. Its nature will be most clearly understood if it is recognized that the worker, because of his inability to accumulate capital goods, is unable to utilize his own labor power and therefore has no choice but to sell it to an employer. This commodity, his labor power, is bought and paid for at its going competitive price, which is the market wage rate, and the products produced by the employment of this labor power are also sold at their going competitive prices. Surplus value, therefore, does not originate either from selling commodities above their real value or buying labor power at less than its real value. The worker receives the full value of his labor power. Thus, Marx avoided the moralistic interpretation which the Ricardian socialists gave the labor theory of value when they maintained that labor is robbed of its own fruits.

---

[11] Sweezy, *op. cit.*, p. 51.

It may of course happen that wages and/or commodity prices temporarily deviate from their norms and thereby enhance or diminish profits, but surplus value is a permanent and normal phenomenon of capitalist production. It is neither the product of dishonesty nor monopsonistic or monopolistic power on the part of the capitalist, but merely part of the normal operation of the capitalistic system. The operation of this system, because of capitalist ownership of the means of production, requires the worker to sell his labor power. This is a commodity whose value is determined in precisely the same way as any other, namely, by its socially necessary labor cost.

> The value of labor power is determined, as in the case of every other commodity, by the labor time necessary for the production and consequently, also the reproduction of this special article. . . . Therefore, the labor time requisite for the production of labor power reduces itself to that necessary for the production of those means of subsistence, in other words, the value of labor power is the value of the means of subsistence necessary for the maintenance of the laborer.[12]

In this manner, Marx establishes that the exchange value of labor power is determined by the labor cost of producing the goods that the physical requirements of life demand and the degree of civilization in the country generally regard as essential. Subsistence, in other words, need not be interpreted as the bare minimum for survival, but only as a more or less definite quantity of physical goods which represent the congelation of a given amount of labor power. The worker receives money wages corresponding to the value of his labor power. In short, his labor power is sold for precisely what it is worth. The product the worker produces is in turn also sold for precisely what it is worth, as determined by the labor power absorbed in its production. Thus the laws that regulate the exchange of commodities have in no way been violated; and yet, in the process, surplus value is somehow created.

This surplus value, Marx maintains, arises because the capitalist, in buying labor power and paying its equivalent exchange value, actually receives its use value for an entire working day. Thus, if the average working day is, let us say, twelve hours, and the worker can produce the equivalent of his own subsistence in six hours, then six hours remain during which the worker continues to create new exchange values. The working day is, therefore, divisible into two parts, necessary labor and surplus labor. The output resulting from necessary labor accrues to the worker in the form of his wages; but the product of surplus labor goes, in the form of surplus value, to the capitalist. Under the assumptions made above, the rate of surplus value will be 100 percent. The surplus value realized by the capitalist is indicative of the degree of exploitation.

---

[12] Marx, *Capital,* Vol. I, p. 171.

The rate at which surplus value can be created depends on three factors: the length of the working day, the productivity of labor, and the quantity of commodities comprising the worker's real wage. Individually, or in combination, these factors can be altered by the capitalist to increase surplus value. It is obvious from this that Marx associated the creation of surplus value strictly with labor. That part of the machinery and tools actually used up and the materials utilized in the production process are incapable of creating a surplus, but only transfer an equal value to the final good. These Marx calls "constant capital," represented by the letter c. Only variable capital, v, which represents payments to labor and tends to be equal to labor's subsistence, creates a surplus, s, for v is transformed into labor power. Every commodity produced, therefore, has a total value comprised as follows: $c' + v + s$, where c' represents the used-up portion of constant capital. The rate of surplus value, which measures the extent of exploitation, derives directly from this formulation and is written by Marx as $s' = \dfrac{s}{v}$. To the extent that labor tends to move from low-wage areas to high-wage areas and producers utilize productive techniques as efficient as those used by their competitors, Marx maintains that the rate of surplus value will tend to be the same, not only for all firms within an industry, but also among all the industries in the economy.

The Equalization of Rates of Profit

In Volume I of *Capital,* Marx maintains that the rate of surplus value is equalized. In Volume III of *Capital,* however, it is argued that surplus values are reshuffled among the different industries in such a way that rates of profit rather than rates of surplus value are equalized. In other words, it is the ratio $\dfrac{s}{c + v}$ rather than $\dfrac{s}{v}$ which tends to equality under competitive conditions.

It is more realistic to maintain that rates of profit rather than rates of surplus value tend to be equalized because businessmen are not interested in profit per unit of labor cost, but in profit per unit of total invested capital. Only if the rate at which capital depreciates annually and the turnover rate of inventory were the same in every industry, which it clearly is not, would it be immaterial to conceive of rates of surplus value rather than rates of profit as being equalized. This does, however, appear to vitiate the labor theory of value, for it leads to the conclusion that a commodity will sell not at its labor value, but at its cost of production. Marx's critics have maintained that the problem of transforming values into prices necessarily undermines the entire labor theory of value.[13] Marx himself recognized the problem it posed, for he said: "It would seem

---

[13] See, in particular, Eugen Böhm-Bawerk, *Karl Marx and the Close of His System* (New York: Augustus Kelley, 1949).

therefore, that here the theory of value is incompatible with the actual process, incompatible with the real phenomena of production, and that for this reason any attempt to understand these phenomena should be given up."[14] He did, however, offer a "solution" to the problem. The essence of this solution is that the market transforms values into prices that individually will differ from labor-determined values of commodities. Some capitalists will sell above value and enjoy more surplus value, and others will sell below value and enjoy less surplus value. Capitalists will share in the aggregate of surplus value not in accordance with their variable capital component, but in accordance with their total capital.

TABLE 10–1

Capital Composition by Industry	Surplus Value	Rate of Surplus Value (s/v)	Used Up (c)	Cost Price	Value of Commodities $(c' + v + s)$	Rate of Profit $\left(\frac{s}{c + v}\right)$
1. $80c + 20v$	20	100%	50	70	90	20%
2. $70c + 30v$	30	100	51	81	111	30
3. $60c + 40v$	40	100	51	91	131	40
4. $85c + 15v$	15	100	40	55	70	15
5. $\dfrac{95c + \ 5v}{390c + 110v}$	$\dfrac{5}{110}$	100	10	15	20	5

Marx himself explained the transformation of values into prices by means of a numerical example, reproduced in Table 10–1. He assumed five industries with different organic compositions of capital, with each enjoying the same rate of surplus value, namely, 100 percent. That is, the rate of surplus value is equal throughout the economy to the variable capital component. The capital for each industry is equivalent to 100 and is regarded as a part of one single capital of 500. In the process of production a portion of the constant capital will be "used up" and thus become congealed in the commodity. These figures, indicated in column 4, are arbitrarily selected. The value of the commodities produced by each industry on the basis of socially necessary labor time may now be computed as $c' + v + s$, indicated in column 6. The total value of each of the outputs equals the cost price plus the surplus.

If each industry's commodities were sold at their values, each industry would experience a different rate of profit, as indicated in the last column of Table 10–1. This is, however, incompatible with the operation of competitive forces. These forces, Marx maintains, will tend to redistribute the total amount (110) of surplus value in such a fashion that each producer will receive a share of the aggregate surplus value that will yield him a rate of

---

[14] Marx, *Capital*, Vol. II, p. 151.

profit equivalent to that of his competitors. As shown in Table 10–2, each will receive a rate of profit equal to the average, which is 22 percent. This equalization is brought about by inter-industry capital movements. If the rate of profit is less than the average, as is the case in industries 1, 4, and 5, capital will tend to move out and enter industries 2 and 3, where the rate of profit is higher than average, until the average rate of profit is the same for all.

The implications of the equalization of the rate of profit are twofold. It implies, first of all, that products will be sold not at their value, but at what Marx calls their "price of production." This is determined by

TABLE 10–2

DEVIATION OF PRICES FROM VALUES BASED ON 22 PERCENT PROFIT

Capital Composition by Industry	Cost Price of Com- modities	Value of Com- modities	Price of Com- modities	Rate of Profit	Deviation of Price from Value
1. $80c + 20v$	70	90	92	22	+ 2
2. $70c + 30v$	81	111	103	22	− 8
3. $60c + 40v$	91	131	113	22	−18
4. $85c + 15v$	55	70	77	22	+ 7
5. $95c + 5v$	15	20	37	22	+17

$c' + v + p$. Individual commodity prices will therefore deviate from value. As is shown in Table 10–2, which demonstrates the effects of equal rates of profit of 22 percent on each individual capital of 100, individual prices now will deviate from values by the amounts shown in the last column. It will be noted, however, that these deviations of prices from values cancel one another out. These deviations had their origin in the manner in which profits were distributed throughout the system. Since total profits are equal to total surplus value, and the latter amount is unchanged, the total of the prices of production is the equivalent of the sum of the values. This is the manner in which Marx rescues the labor theory of value from the abyss into which it appears to fall as a result of the problem of transforming values into prices.

Capital Accumulation and the Tendency toward a Falling Rate of Profit

It has already been noted that the rate of profit, which is the ratio of surplus value to total capital, $\frac{s}{c + v}$, is more significant to the capitalist than the rate of surplus value and is the real inducement to investment. The rate of profit depends not only on the rate of surplus value, but also on the organic composition of capital, i.e., the relationship between constant and variable capital. The tendency for the rate of profit to become equal throughout the economy implies not only that commodity prices will deviate from their values, in the manner discussed above, but also that individual capitalists, in order to increase their shares of the aggregate surplus value, will make additions to constant capital which will enhance the productivity of labor.

The original source of capital funds is something Marx explains with his economic interpretation of history. Primitive accumulation, which occurred in England during the late fifteenth and early sixteenth centuries, created, for the first time, the "free" proletarian (in the sense of his being emancipated from the soil and therefore free to sell his labor) and the money-owning capitalist. Describing the demise of the feudal system and the related destruction of the agricultural economy, Marx observes:

> The spoliation of the church's property, the fraudulent alienation of the state domains, the robbery of the common lands, the usurpation of feudal and clan property, and its transformation into modern private property under circumstances of reckless terrorism, were just so many idyllic methods of primitive accumulation. They conquered the field for capitalistic agriculture, made the soil part and parcel of capital, and created for the town industries the necessary supply of a "free" and outlawed proletariat.[15]

After the era of primitive accumulation is over, further accumulation takes place from additions derived from surplus value. The accumulation of capital is accompanied by an increased mechanization in the production process. A given amount of labor, now combined with a greater supply of more efficient equipment, will be able to process a greater volume of raw materials into finished goods. Though labor productivity is enhanced, the organic composition of capital is altered. More and more constant capital relative to total capital is now acquired by the capitalist.

Since only variable capital yields a surplus, the ratio $\dfrac{s}{c + v}$ will fall. From this, Marx deduced his "law of the falling tendency of the rate of profit." The latter naturally tends to dampen the enthusiasm for new investment and encourages the capitalist to seek ways of counteracting it.

Since the rate of profit is a function of both the rate of surplus value and the organic composition of capital, it follows that any factor which tends to raise the rate of surplus value or reduce the constant capital component of total capital will tend to keep the rate of profit from falling. Marx notes six such counteracting factors, the most obvious one of which is the lengthening of the working day, which operates to increase the amount of surplus labor. The speedup has essentially the same effect. The increase in surplus value tends to keep the rate of profit from falling. The technique of cutting wages is not one which Marx seriously entertains, for he assumes that wages, like prices, are determined in a purely competitive market.

---

[15] *Ibid.*, Vol. I, p. 732.

Marx, however, saw a tendency for wages to be depressed downward as a result of the growing constant capital component rather than aggressive employer wage policy. This growth creates a situation of technological unemployment which Marx regards as the primary factor operating to keep wages at subsistence levels. He regarded as a "libel on the human race" the population theory by which Malthus and Ricardo explained the tendency of the market wage to equal the natural wage. He emphasized instead the development of a surplus population. The workers who are set free by machine power constitute an industrial reserve army which depresses the rate of wages and thereby tends to raise the level of surplus value. Technological changes are regarded by Marx not as the fortuitous occurrences that the classicists regarded them to be, but as conscientiously sought-after laborsaving devices necessary to the continued existence of capitalist production. The existence of a reserve army is necessary for the maintenance of surplus value. Thus, Marx observed in the *Communist Manifesto:* "The bourgeosie cannot exist without constantly revolutionizing the instruments of production, and thereby, the relations of production, and with them the whole relations of society." It is in this manner that Marx lays bare an area of inherent conflict within the framework of capitalism, from which he deduces one of the laws of motion of the capitalistic system.

The human aspect of these observations is "the increasing misery of the proletariat." On the one hand, the degree of worker exploitation is enhanced through the speedup and the lengthening of the working day; and on the other, the value of the worker's labor power is depressed through the reduced labor requirements of producing labor's subsistence.[16] It is another of capitalism's internal contradictions that the increasing productivity of labor is associated with increasing exploitation and diminished ability to consume goods.

Capitalist Crisis

The classical economists, as has already been noted, largely assumed away the problem of economic crisis by their acceptance of Say's law.

Marx rejected Say's law because he regarded it as applicable only to a barter economy. In a capitalistic economy, commodities are exchanged first for money and then for one another. In the process, qualitatively different use values represent quantitatively equal exchange values. The exchange value of commodities is transformed into money form and then back again to commodity form. The transformation of commodities into money and back into commodities is not necessarily synchronized with regard to time and place. It is for this reason, Marx maintains, that endogenously created crises are inherent in capitalism. "If the interval in time between two

---

[16] A different interpretation is presented by Thomas Sowell, "Marx's Increasing Misery Doctrine," *American Economic Review,* Vol. L, No. 1 (March, 1960).

complementary phases of the complete metamorphosis of a commodity becomes too great, if the split between the sale and the purchase becomes too pronounced, the intimate connection between them, their oneness, asserts itself by producing a crisis."[17] Thus, Marx regarded crisis as being indicative of and taking the form of a state of general overproduction. Crisis is the process by which equilibrium between the production and circulation of goods is forcibly restored. The actual cause of periods of general overproduction is among the problems to which Marx returned again and again in his various works. Nowhere, however, does he present a systematic and thorough treatment of the subject. He seems more concerned to show, contrary to the fundamental theorem of Says' law, that partial gluts are always possible in a capitalistic system and that, instead of being corrected, they tend to culminate in general overproduction.

Marx offered several hypotheses concerning the manner in which a crisis, which will manifest itself in the form of overproduction, may be precipitated. However, Marxist interpreters and revisionists have considerably more to say on the specific causes of crisis than Marx himself, though in some instances arguments which are in reality the product of a follower have been erroneously attributed to him.[18] His followers extended and embellished hypotheses that may be found in his original works, but which are incompletely developed.[19]

Among the hypotheses suggested by Marx on the matter of crisis is the view that this phenomenon is associated with the declining rate of profit. One interpretation stresses the fact that the growth of accumulation stimulates the demand for labor power, thus raising the level of wages and diminishing profits. Diminished profits, in turn, discourage further accumulation and precipitate a crisis, the immediate cause of which, in more modern terminology, is underinvestment. In other words, an interruption to the circular flow takes place as a result of a decline in the rate of profit below normal. This hypothesis finds its modern counterpart in the Keynesian hypothesis of the declining marginal efficiency of capital, although the Marxian formulation is far less well developed, especially as regards its failure to take into account the significance of the interest rate, the money market, institutional credit arrangements, and the role of expectations. Some writers, such as Maurice H. Dobb, have concluded that Marx regarded the tendency of the rate of profit to fall as the primary explanation of crisis.[20]

---

[17] Marx, *Capital*, Vol. I, pp. 113–14.

[18] Sweezy maintains that ideas put forward by Michael Tugan-Baranowsky have been erroneously attributed to Marx. See Sweezy, *op. cit.*, pp. 159–60.

[19] The subsequent discussion is greatly indebted to the analysis presented by Sweezy, *ibid.*, Part III.

[20] See Maurice H. Dobb, *Political Economy and Capitalism* (New York: International Publishers, 1944), especially chap. iv.

Another hypothesis regarding economic crisis which may be derived from Marx's fragmentary observations is that crisis is traceable to the atomistic character of capitalist production. The essence of this view is that crises originate because individual businessmen have, at best, only partial knowledge of the market they are serving and tend to produce either too much or too little. These errors call forth adjustments, but only small errors can be corrected without general disturbance. Michael Tugan-Baranowsky, especially, is associated with this view.

A third hypothesis regarding crisis, and the most clearly stated by Marx himself, stresses the role of underconsumption. The capitalist, he maintains, creates surplus value in the process of production in the form of commodities. But in order that he may "realize" his surplus value, he must sell his product. However, the consumption of the great mass of the people is restricted by low wage rates and unemployment, with the result that the capitalist has to sell his product at prices below the cost of production. Labor is not less exploited, but the capitalist benefits little from this exploitation. Consumption is further restricted by the tendency to accumulate and expand capital in order to introduce laborsaving technological improvements. These are undertaken in order to improve the level of profits, but the reduction in variable capital relative to constant capital defeats this goal through its impact on the labor component, which is the source of surplus value. The quest for profit is thus the reason for its falling rate. Although this tendency is counteracted from time to time (the problem of timing was not specifically dealt with), it is nevertheless an inexorable tendency which will grow more pronounced as the counteracting forces become attenuated. Thus, crises will become increasingly severe, "putting the existence of the entire bourgeois society on trial each time more threateningly."

Monopoly Capitalism

Marx's entire economic analysis is intended to demonstrate the impossibility of an indefinite expansion of the capitalistic system and the consequent inevitability of a revolutionary period during which the proletariat will overthrow the existing structure of production and its associated social relations and establish in its place a socialistic organization of production. The prelude, in Marx's thinking, to the ultimate overthrow of capitalist production is the change in the organic composition of capital. The proportion between constant and variable capital will grow and the fixed component of constant capital, that is, the proportion in buildings, machinery, and equipment as opposed to raw materials will increase. As a result, there is an increase in the optimum size of the production unit. This implies not only concentration of capital, but what Marx called centralization of capital. "This process differs from the former in this, that it only presupposes a change in the distribution of capital already to hand and functioning; its field of action is therefore not limited by the absolute growth of social wealth, by the absolute limits of accumulation. Capital grows in one place to a huge mass in a single hand because it has in another place been lost by many. This is centralisation proper, as distinct from accumulation and concentration."[21]

The causes of the centralization of capital are only briefly sketched by Marx. The major factor is, of course, the economies inherent in large-scale production. As the optimum-size production unit grows larger, "the larger capitals beat the smaller."[22] In other words, interfirm competition for profits is, in itself, a force of centralization. In addition, the credit system, which Marx conceives of as including not only banks but all financial institutions, facilitates the development of the large corporation, which alters the production structure from one in which there is competition among a large number of producers to competition among a few. In the process of this phase of capitalist development, there is a divorce between the ownership of capital and the entrepreneurial function.[23] The owner of capital becomes a shareholder, and the actual function of the entrepreneur is assumed by professional managers. The ultimate stage in the development of the capitalistic system gets under way when corporations unify in the form of cartels, trusts, and mergers in order to control production and prices. At the same time, there is also the tendency, because of the close relations between the banks and industry, for capital to be concentrated in the form of money and to reach production firms only via the banks. This is the stage of "monopoly capitalism," in which social production is under the virtual control of a single bank or a small group of banks.

During this phase of capitalist development the contradictions of capitalism become even more acute. Monopoly tends to increase the rate of accumulation out of surplus value, since centralization of capital, in decreasing the number of competitors, tends to increase the portion accruing to each one. Monopolists, however, tend to invest in the remaining competitive areas of the economy rather than in their own industry in which the marginal rate of profit is low, though the average rate may still be high. This tends to strengthen the tendency in those sectors toward a declining rate of profit. Also, to the extent that additional monopoly profits are a deduction from labor's share, the tendency toward underconsumption is further strengthened. The declining rate of profit further encourages the adoption of laborsaving technology, with a resultant expansion in the size of the industrial reserve army. Monopoly, therefore, intensifies the contradictions inherent in capitalism and strengthens the forces leading to social

---

[21] Marx, *Capital,* Vol. I, pp. 625–26.

[22] *Ibid.,* p. 626.

[23] This aspect of Marx's work was greatly extended by Rudolf Hilferding in *Das Finanzkapital,* Berlin, Dietz, 1955, (first published 1923).

revolution. "Centralization of the means of production and socialisation of labor at last reach a point where they become incompatible with their capitalist integument. The integument is burst asunder. The knell of capitalist private property sounds. The expropriators are expropriated."[24] Thus the internal contradictions created by capitalist production ultimately make its continuation untenable. Conditions are then ripe for the proletariat to seize the instruments of production and establish socialism, which is the first stage of full communism. This, in Marx's view, could not come about without violent revolution. The question as to precisely what the pattern and tactics of revolution should be or the nature of the proletariat state, while interesting, is not only outside the scope of economic analysis, but is also a matter to which Marx himself gave little expression.

CONCLUDING REMARKS

While Marx's technical apparatus was built on Ricardian foundations, the political implications he derived from the Hegelian interpretation he gave to the labor theory of value made his analysis unacceptable in orthodox circles. Then, too, Marx adhered to the tradition of the labor theory of value at a time when the importance of utility and other cost elements was beginning to be appreciated. His theory therefore met with an attitude of almost complete rejection except among those who sympathized politically. This attitude did not begin to be modified until problems like monopoly, mass unemployment, excess production, and other phenomena which Marx had described became so prevalent that they could no longer be glossed over.

Marx's theory of socially necessary labor as the determinant of value is untenable. But the ultimate use to which he put his theory of value, namely, as the basis for a model in which economic breakdown is ascribed to internal insufficiencies, was a path-breaking conception. Marx's precapitalist model of simple commodity production envisages an economy in which there is no technical progress and no change in the capital-labor ratio. Thus, there is no net accumulation of capital. But his model of a capitalist economy is one in which there is capital accumulation and, consequently, a continuous reduction in the labor requirements of production. This is associated with a declining rate of profit which affects not only the process and composition of capital accumulation but the entire structure of the system. He envisaged constant capital as increasing more rapidly than the output of consumer goods, so that the economic structure will become increasingly disbalanced.

This principle is very suggestive of the later Keynesian conception, in which a declining marginal efficiency of capital causes a lack of effective

---

[24] Marx, *Capital,* Vol. I, p. 763.

demand. But Marx went even further, for his model implies that stable economic growth requires a proportionate expansion of both the consumer and the capital goods industries. Thus the law of capitalist motion which Marx discovered is also surprisingly anticipatory of the principle recently established by modern growth theorists that a growing equilibrium requires that the rate of increase in capacity must equal the rate of increase in income and that both must be expanding at a compound interest rate in order to avoid deflationary tendencies.[25] The change that is required to update Marx's model is, of course, partly substantive, especially insofar as it hinges on the labor theory of value; but once the philosophical and sociological overtones are removed, it is largely terminological. The long underestimated richness of his legacy can best be appreciated if we abstract the Hegelian elements and the sociology of revolution which obscure the contribution of Marx qua economist.

SUGGESTIONS FOR FURTHER READING

BÖHM-BAWERK, EUGEN. *Karl Marx and the Close of His System.* New York: Augustus Kelley, 1949.

LANGE, OSCAR. "Marxian Economics and Modern Economic Theory," *Review of Economic Studies,* Vol. II (June, 1935).

MARX, KARL. *Capital and Other Writings.* Edited by MAX EASTMAN. New York: Modern Library, Inc., 1932.

MAYO, HENRY B. *Introduction to Marxist Theory.* New York: Oxford University Press, 1960.

ROBINSON, JOAN. "Marx and Keynes," *Economica Critica,* 1948. Reprinted in *idem, Collected Economic Papers,* Oxford: Basil Blackwell, 1951.

SOWELL, THOMAS. "Marx's Increasing Misery Doctrine," *American Economic Review,* Vol. L, No. 1 (March, 1960).

SWEEZY, PAUL M. *The Theory of Capitalist Development.* New York: Oxford University Press, 1942.

WINTERNITZ, J. "Values and Prices: A Solution of the So-Called Transformation Problem," *Economic Journal,* Vol. LVIII (June, 1948). See also A. MAYS, "A Note on Winternitz's Solution," *ibid.* (December, 1948).

---

[25] See Chap. 19 below.

Chapter 11

THE FORERUNNERS OF

MARGINALISM

The two decades following the appearance of John Stuart Mill's work were comparatively sterile as far as the development of economic analysis is concerned. It was not until the 1870's that economic analysis was to be revolutionized by the introduction of a new point of view and a powerful new tool. The new point of view concerned the role of utility in the determination of value; the new tool was the concept of the additional or marginal increment.

The concept of the margin is applicable to any measurable magnitude of economic significance. Because it relates to the rate of change in a magnitude—for example, the rate at which cost changes when output changes—it lends itself to mathematical expression and is a more refined tool than is an arithmetical average or total. Its discovery and the development of precision in its use provided the economist with an analytical tool which has since become indispensable. Its initial application was to the kind of analysis which is termed "microeconomic." The concern of microeconomic analysis is to examine particular segments of the economy, such as the individual household, firm, or industry, with a view to explaining individual commodity and factor prices and the allocation of resources among alternative uses. This is the type of economic analysis which predominated from the 1870's into the 1930's and which continues to be a major facet of modern economic analysis.

While the refinement of microeconomic techniques dates from the end of the nineteenth century, there were several thinkers who had a remarkably clear understanding of the concept of the margin and who used it to seek answers to specific questions before marginal analysis came into general vogue. The efforts of Jeremy Bentham to give expression to the concept of marginal utility in the 1840's have already been noted. Jules Dupuit (1804–66) of France used the concept of marginal utility even earlier, while Wilhelm Gossen of Germany (1810–54) gave a remarkably polished statement not only of the principle of diminishing marginal utility, but also of the principle of individual consumer equilibrium, in 1854. Earlier still, the Italian Daniel Bernoulli (1700–1782) had used the concept of marginal increments of income, while Augustin Cournot (1801–77) of France and Johann Heinrich von Thünen of Germany (1780–1850) are remembered for their respective discoveries and applications of the concepts of marginal revenue and marginal productivity.

All of these early and isolated efforts to develop and use the concept of the margin took place, so to speak, before their time. They were scarcely known and little appreciated. Bentham's "felific calculus," it will be recalled, had no effect on the development of value theory in England. The efforts which will be examined here shared a similar fate; they were overlooked in their own time and had to be "rediscovered" after the so-called "marginal revolution" was on its way. They are therefore examined here as a background to the marginal approach which came into general vogue around the 1870's, even though, chronologically speaking, many of the contributions described here antedated John Stuart Mill's *Principles of Political Economy* of 1848.

THE UTILITY CONCEPT BEFORE THE MARGINAL REVOLUTION

The Classical and Early Continental Conception

The concern of classical economists with the problem of exchange value and their failure to perceive any relationship between value in use and value in exchange caused them to overlook the role of utility and demand in the determination of prices. They recognized that a commodity must have value in use in order to have value in exchange, but precisely how the two are related was not understood. The reason was that they conceived of utility as a general characteristic of a commodity rather than as a relationship between a consumer and a unit of a commodity. This was true even of Senior, who was more aware of the subjective aspects of value than most other English thinkers. Thus the "paradox of value" posed by Smith's example of the diamond and the water went unresolved for lack of the concept of the marginal increment.

Continental rather than English thinkers were the first to use the concept of the marginal increment. Daniel Bernoulli was one of its earliest anticipators. His special contribution was his understanding of the significance of the margin as it relates to increments of income. His hypothesis, presented in the 1730's, was that the importance of an additional dollar to an individual is inversely proportional to the number of dollars already in his possession. From this relationship, he deduced that in a situation of uncertainty with respect to future receipts, an individual will not be guided exclusively by the mathematical probability of gain or loss, but will also be influenced by the significance of given gains or losses in terms of his means.[1] He did not, however, explore the concept of the margin as it re-

---

[1] Some of the more sophisticated aspects of economic behavior under conditions of uncertainty have only recently been explored. See, for example, John von Neumann and Oskar Morgenstern, *The Theory of Games and Economic Behavior* (Princeton: Princeton University Press, 1944).

lates to utility, consumer behavior, or the determination of exchange value.

The concept of marginal utility expresses the subjective value or want-satisfying power of an additional unit of a given good to a particular user. The importance an individual attaches to an additional unit of a particular good depends in part on its relative scarcity. The larger the supply of a given commodity, the smaller will be its relative significance at the margin. Thus the reason why water usually commands no price is because its supply is so large relative to the demand for it that the utility of the marginal unit is zero. Professor Joseph A. Schumpeter noted that there were a number of eighteenth-century Italian and French thinkers who understood this paradox of value and that its existence did not, as Smith thought, bar the way to a theory of exchange value based upon value in use.[2] However, while these thinkers realized that utility is more than the condition or prerequisite of value that David Ricardo thought it to be, none of them understood the significance of scarcity, and they thus continued to be confounded by the paradox of value. Although they appreciated the importance of utility, they lacked the concept of the margin. A marginal utility theory of value was therefore unable to germinate from their efforts.

It is interesting to speculate why Continental thinkers were appreciative of the role of utility in the determination of value so much earlier than their English counterparts. One suggested hypothesis is that Protestant theology, with its greater emphasis on the virtue of work, was more compatible with a labor-oriented theory of value than the more subjective doctrine of Catholicism.[3] Its dominance in England may conceivably be a reason for the general lack of interest of the classical economists in consumer wants, while thinkers in Catholic countries like France and Italy placed greater emphasis on utility.

Gossen's Conception of Utility

The German writer Wilhelm Gossen introduced the concept of marginal utility in a publication entitled *Development of the Laws of Human Commerce and of the Consequent Rules of Human Action* (1854). Using the term *Werth* to express utility, Gossen noted that there is no such thing as absolute utility, but rather that *Werth* is a relationship between an object and a person. He observed that as an individual acquires additional units of the same kind of good, each successive act of consumption yields contin-

---

[2] Schumpeter in his *History of Economic Analysis,* specifically mentions the Neapolitan Abbé Ferdinando Galiani (1728–87) and the French Abbé Étienne de Condillac (1714–80) in this connection. J. B. Say, the early nineteenth-century French thinker who is best known for popularizing *The Wealth of Nations,* also appreciated the significance of utility as a value determinant, though he lacked the concept of the margin.

[3] See R. S. Howey, *The Rise of the Marginal Utility School, 1870–1889* (Lawrence: University of Kansas Press, 1960), p. 2.

uously diminishing pleasure up to the point of satiety. This principle later became known as the law of satiable wants, or Gossen's first law.

If we are willing to assume that pleasure or utility can be measured in cardinal numbers, the relationship between increases in consumption and the behavior of total and marginal utility inherent in Gossen's first law may be demonstrated graphically by means of a hypothetical curve of total utility. This is done in Figure 11–1, in which the maximum utility

FIGURE 11–1

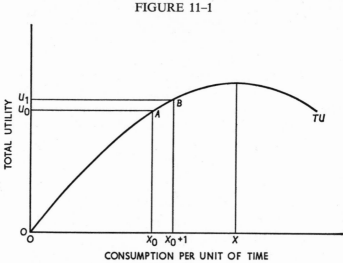

CONSUMPTION PER UNIT OF TIME

derived from the consumption of the commodity in question is reached when quantity OX is consumed per unit of time. The relationship between total utility and marginal utility may be easily perceived from this graph. If an individual is assumed to be taking quantity X_0 per unit of time and he increases his consumption to $X_0 + 1$, his total utility increases from U_0 to U_1. The marginal utility of the unit $X_0 + 1 - X_0$ is therefore $U_1 - U_0$ and is approximately equal to the average slope of the total utility curve between points A and B. If the change in quantity and the utility associated with it are both infinitely small, marginal utility at any given level of consumption is equal to the slope of the total utility curve at that point. Symbolically, the slope of the curve is equal to $\dfrac{dTU}{dX}$. It is evident from the total utility curve that marginal utility decreases as consumption per unit of time increases between O and X. Thus the slope of the total utility curve becomes progressively less until it is zero when quantity OX is consumed, and it is negative beyond that point.

Figure 11–2 derives a marginal utility curve from the total utility curve in Figure 11–1. The marginal utility of each unit of consumption is plotted on the ordinate axis. Since the slope of the total utility curve, as shown in Figure 11–1, is decreasing as consumption level OX is approached, and reaches zero at that level, the marginal utility curve must necessarily slope downward and pass through the horizontal axis when OX units are consumed. The curve MU_x represents the marginal utility for all levels of consumption between O and X per unit of time. This function is significant because it subsequently became the basis for drawing consumer demand curves.

In addition to the law of satiable wants, Gossen is also given credit for formulating a law expressing the optimum allocation of income among alternative uses. Since separate units of the same pleasure-giving good yield different quantities of satisfaction, each individual will, in general, derive

FIGURE 11–2

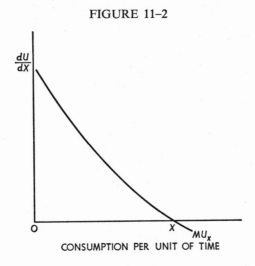

CONSUMPTION PER UNIT OF TIME

utility only from a limited number of such units. Continued consumption beyond this point does not, therefore, continue to add to total satisfaction. From this, Gossen inferred that each person should distribute his available money income among the various goods he consumes in such a manner that the last unit of money spent on each commodity yields an equal degree of satisfaction. His statement of the equimarginal principle as it applies to consumption has become known as Gossen's second law.

While Gossen must be credited with the statement of the basic principles on which the marginal utility theory of value is grounded, the fact is that he did not utilize them in connection with the problem of value and price, and his work attracted virtually no attention until it was rediscovered by William Jevons of England in the 1870's. But this rediscovery came too late to make it a significant force in the development of marginal utility doctrine, though Jevons admitted that "Gossen has completed anticipated me as regards the general principles and method of the theory of Economics."[4]

Dupuit's Conception of Utility

Those who inquired into the monopoly problem, especially as it is associated with large fixed and low variable costs, and therefore increasing returns to scale, are also among the pioneers of the marginal utility analysis. These cost conditions are typical of railroads and other public utilities. Those who dealt with the pricing problems of these industries, therefore, also contributed to the rise of the marginal utility analysis.

The contribution of Jules Dupuit, a French railway engineer, is particularly noteworthy in this connection. The essence of his thinking is contained in an article published in 1844, entitled "On the Measurement of the Utility of Public Works."[5] In this article, he maintained that exchange value cannot be used, as Say suggested it might, as a measure of utility. The utility of everything which is consumed, observed Dupuit, varies according to the person consuming it. This may be illustrated by noting the reaction of consumers to a tax which the government imposes on some commodity. For example, a tax of five sous per bottle of wine will cause its price to rise by that amount but adds nothing to the utility of the product. Thus, if a bottle of wine is bought for 15 sous instead of 10, it is because the buyer finds at least an equivalent utility in it. Were he willing to pay more than 15 sous, but only had to pay that price, the difference would be what Dupuit called *utilité relative,* consumer surplus. He subsequently used this concept as a basis for a theorem on taxation and for a theory of pricing in which he showed that an enterprise which charges a single price to all its customers and sustains a loss might become profitable if it adopted a policy of price discrimination. Such a policy would charge different groups of buyers different prices, depending on the strength of their demands.

Dupuit provided a graphic explanation of his concept of consumer surplus and its relation to price. To do this, he drew a downward-sloping demand curve premised on the principle that the quantity of a commodity purchased tends to increase as the price falls. He conceived the curve to become increasingly elastic as the price falls, like *DD* in Figure 11–3, because each price reduction brings the commodity into a price range which a larger number of consumers can afford.[6] Given a demand schedule for a commodity like *DD,* which Dupuit also took to be a total utility curve,

---

[4] William Jevons, *The Theory of Political Economy,* Preface to 2d ed. (1879).

[5] *Annales des Ponts et Chaussées* (1844). This article was not translated from the French until it was made available in *International Economic Papers,* No. 2 (London and New York: Macmillan & Co., 1952), pp. 83–110.

[6] Dupuit showed price on the horizontal and quantity on the vertical axis. These have been reversed to conform to standard practice in economics today.

the quantity which would be taken at a price of OP would be OM.[7] If a tax is imposed which raises the price of OP_1, the quantity demanded will be OM_1. As shown in Figure 11–3, the tax yield will be accompanied by a loss of utility which is proportional to the square of the tax. From this Dupuit, concluded that the yield of a tax is no measure of the loss it causes society to suffer.

The foregoing conclusion led Dupuit to inquire into the tolls which should be charged for publicly used goods such as canals, bridges, and

FIGURE 11–3

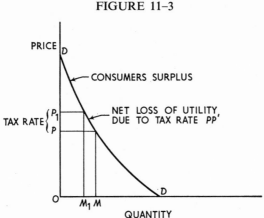

roads. He reasoned that different objectives require that different tolls be charged. If, for example, the objective is to set a toll sufficient to raise a sum of money to cover the cost of capital expended in making a bridge available, then, given a demand curve for its services of $y = f(x)$, Dupuit reasoned that the appropriate toll can be established by solving the equation $A = xy$ where A is the required amount of money. If, on the other hand, the objective is to raise the maximum revenue possible, given the demand for the service, it is necessary to set a toll at which the marginal revenue will be zero. This requires solution of the equation $\dfrac{dyx}{dx} = 0$.[8]

Figure 11–4 helps us to appreciate the difference which results when the first equation rather than the second is used as a basis for establishing a toll rate. If the value of x derived from the first equation is equivalent to Op the total revenue yielded by that rate will be $Ornp$. Granting Dupuit's interpretation of a demand curve as a utility curve, the utility of the bridge

---

[7] Jevons was acquainted with Dupuit's work and recognized its merit as a beginning of the utility approach. Leon Walrás, Jevons' codiscoverer of the marginal utility concept in the 1870's, was, however, quite critical of Dupuit's failure to distinguish between the utility curve and the demand curve.

[8] "On the Measurement of the Utility of Public Works," *op. cit.*, p. 107–8.

to those who use it is the area under the curve denoted by the triangle *pnP,* while the utility which will be lost by the public when this rate, as opposed to a zero rate, is charged is the triangle *nrN.* A maximum revenue of *ORTM* can be achieved by charging the higher toll *OM* as in Part B of Figure 11–4. The utility of the bridge to those who would use it at that rate is equivalent only to the triangle *PMT* while the loss of utility is represented by the triangle *NTR.* From this Dupuit concluded that, ideally, the tolls

FIGURE 11–4

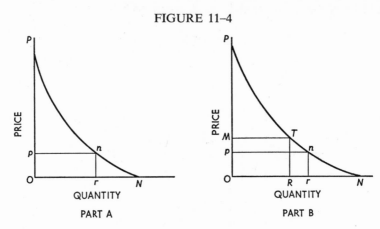

imposed for the services of publicly used goods like bridges, canals, and roads should be set at the lowest rate consistent with providing a revenue which wll cover costs. He also reasoned that if consumers can be grouped according to the utility each category of user derives from the same service it is possible to increase the revenue collected and diminish the loss of utility to consumers by choosing an appropriate combination of tolls.

COST AND REVENUE CONCEPTS BEFORE THE MARGINAL REVOLUTION

The Classical Conception

Just as the classical school made no use of the marginal concept with respect to utility, so it also had no need for it with respect to the cost of production. The classicists generally assumed that production costs are constant, i.e., that additional units of output are produced at the same average cost as preceding units. There was therefore no necessity to deal with a divergence between average and marginal cost.

Marginal cost is the change in total cost associated with an additional unit of output. It is calculated by dividing the increase in total cost associated with the production of added output by the change in output. This measure of cost becomes important whenever it is not realistic to assume that production is associated with a given level of unit costs regardless of the volume which is produced. As a rule, changes in the level of a firm's output will be associated with changes in the average total cost and, therefore, with the marginal cost of output. But this principle was not understood by the classical economists any more than they recognized that the principle of diminishing returns from successive inputs of labor and capital is applicable to all forms of production, and not just to agriculture. While their recognition of the operation of the latter principle in agriculture marked the beginning of marginal analysis in productivity theory, classical analysis did not explore the behavior of cost as output changes. They could not, therefore, discover the concept of marginal cost. But if, instead of examining merely the change in output associated with the application of successive doses of labor or capital to a given quantity of land, which is what Ricardo did in explaining the emergence of rent, they had also examined the effect of output changes in terms of additions to cost, they would have discovered the concept of marginal cost.

Nor did the classical economists have an appreciation of the concept of marginal revenue. Marginal revenue identifies the change in total revenue which is associated with the sale of an additional unit of output. Since the classical analysis of price assumed a purely competitive market, the individual firm is implicitly assumed to be able to sell additional units of output without having to reduce its selling price. Expressed in modern terminology, the classicists thought of a firm as being confronted with an infinitely elastic demand curve. Under these conditions, the marginal revenue which can be gotten from the sale of output is necessarily equal to its average revenue. Thus the emergence of the concept of marginal revenue was delayed until attention was directed to the problem of determining price in a market which is not purely competitive.

Cournot and Marginal Revenue

The first to appreciate the nature and significance of additional increments of revenue with respect to the behavior of the individual firm was Augustin Cournot, who developed the concept in connection with his analysis of monopoly profit maximization.[9] He recognized that increments of revenue are related to increments of demand, and his mathematical training enabled him to perceive the demand for a commodity as a function of its price. Accordingly, he wrote the demand function as $q = f(p)$. Although he made no effort to relate demand to utility, he apparently realized, taking the demand for a commodity as a whole, that more would be bought only at a lower price, so that the demand function for an industry would be negatively sloped, i.e., $\frac{dq}{dp} < 0$. In the case of pure monopoly, which Cournot thought of as the polar opposite of "illimited competition"

---

[9] Augustin Cournot, *Researches into the Mathematical Principles of the Theory of Wealth* (1838), translated by Nathaniel Bacon (New York: Macmillan Co., 1897).

(our pure competition), the firm is the entire industry, so that the monopolist is confronted with the same demand curve as the industry. However, while price is a parameter of action to a pure competitor who maximizes profits by adjusting output, a monopolist can maximize profits with respect to variations in either price or output. Given the demand curve, he can select the output he wishes to sell and let consumers determine the price, or he can set the price and let consumers determine the quantity they will take. His demand curve $q = f(p)$, therefore, has a unique inverse, $p = f(q)$. Thus, if a monopolist's selling price is p and his demand curve is $p = f(q)$, his total revenue may be written as $R = p(q)$. It may also be expressed functionally as $R = R(q)$. His total cost may also be expressed as a function of output. Thus, $C = C(q)$. The difference between total revenue and total cost is profit. This difference is maximized when the additional revenue associated with an extra increment of output is equal to the additional cost of that increment. It follows that a monopolist will maximize profit when he sets a price which equates the first derivative of total revenue with the first derivative of total cost or, what amounts to the same thing, when marginal revenue equals marginal cost.[10]

Although Cournot did not refer to the first derivative of total revenue as marginal revenue, his proof that profits are maximized when $MR = MC$ is a fundamental which is now contained in every textbook on economic principles. It was, however, neglected after Cournot initially introduced it in his *Researches* in 1838. This is due partly to Alfred Marshall's subsequent analysis of monopoly profit maximization in terms of the monopolist's total net revenue rather than in marginal terms. Marshall's procedure, coupled with the fact that neoclassical price analysis, until the 1930's, was typically conducted under the assumption that the structure of the market is purely competitive, accounts for the neglect, subsequent to Cournot, of the concept of marginal revenue.

Although Cournot recognized that a monopolist can set the price for his product in such a way as to maximize his total revenue by offering to sell that volume of output at which marginal revenue will equal marginal cost, he apparently failed to appreciate the additional opportunities for adding to total profits that are inherent in discriminatory pricing. This is the policy of offering a product or service to different groups of demanders at different prices, rather than at the same price, depending upon the strength of their demands. Total profits will then be maximized when the marginal revenue in each separate market is equated to marginal cost. The success of this type of policy depends, of course, on the ability of the monopolist to segregate his buyers according to the urgency (elasticity) of their demands

---

[10] $P = R(q) - C(q)$, where P is profit
$$\frac{dP}{dq} = R'(q) - C'(q) = 0$$
$$R'(q) = C'(q)$$

and his ability to keep those who are able to buy from him at low prices from reselling to those to whom the product is made available only at higher prices. There was already a lively appreciation of this aspect of the theory of price discrimination by Dupuit and others in the applied fields, transportation in particular.

Cournot on Duopoly

Cournot sketched out the kinds of market conditions which lie between pure monopoly and what he termed "illimited competition" (our pure competition). His most famous case was that of duopoly—two competing monopolists whom he assumed to be selling a costless homogeneous commodity (water from a mineral spring). Assuming, to begin with, that one seller is in possession of the entire market, he proceeded to examine what will happen if a second seller enters to compete with the first. Cournot's explanation of the nature of the ultimate equilibrium position derived from the assumptions he made about the behavior of the two rivals.

Cournot assumed that neither seller has the power to name a price. But each has the power to adjust the quantity he offers for sale and, as a result, influences buyers bidding for his product. Thus a rival who enters the market to compete with a former monopolist is conceived to offer that quantity which will maximize his total revenue, on the assumption that the former monopolist will not alter the quantity he offers for sale. But, says Cournot, this assumption on the part of the newcomer will prove to be invalid, for his sales cut into the former monopolist's market and force him to make adjustments in price and output. These adjustments are similarly assumed by Cournot to be made on the invalid premise that the rival seller will not alter his output. Each seller in his turn will always have to adjust to the new situation created by the change his rival makes in the quantity offered for sale. This will necessitate corresponding adjustments by his rival until a stable equilibrium is reached. He reasoned that in an equilibrium situation the amount offered in any market which is not purely competitive can be determined according to the formula $\dfrac{n}{(n+1)}$ times the competitive output. Thus, the amount offered in a duopoly equilibrium is equal to two thirds the competitive output, with half the amount being offered by each of the sellers.[11] The equilibrium price will be below the monopoly price and above the competitive price, and any departure from this level will cause its reestablishment as a result of "a series of reactions, constantly declining in amplitude."

----

[11] Cournot's formula $\dfrac{n}{(n+1)}$ times the competitive output is applicable to any number of sellers. Competitive output is approached as the number of sellers (n) increases; whereas when the number of sellers decreases, the monopolistic situation is approached. Monopoly output is half the competitive output.

The Cournot solution of the duopoly problem is only one among several that are possible, for there are numerous behavior assumptions which might be made. Cournot assumed that a duopolist maximizes his profit on the basis of a conjectual variation of zero with respect to the rival's output. His solution was subsequently criticized by Joseph Bertrand, who offered an alternative solution based on the assumption that each seller tries to maximize his profit, on the assumption that his rival will not alter his price.

Actually, neither Cournot's solution nor Bertrand's is based on realistic assumptions, for duopolists, as well as oligopolists, are likely to realize that their decisions with respect to both price and output are interdependent. Various behavior patterns may result from this interdependence. For example, the monopolists may agree to cooperate and both set a monopoly price, or they may engage in a price war designed to drive the competitor out of business. This is why it has often been said that the problem posed by Cournot is indeterminate. That is, there is no general solution possible without introducing further assumptions about the behavior of the two competitors.

PRODUCTIVITY AND DISTRIBUTION THEORY BEFORE THE MARGINAL REVOLUTION

The Classical Theory

It has already been noted that the observation of the tendency toward diminishing returns on land marked the beginning of marginal productivity theory, but failed to develop the concept of marginal cost. Ricardo, as well as Malthus, understood that if additional doses of labor and capital are applied to a given land area, output will increase at a decreasing rate, beyond a certain point. These observations were made in connection with the emergence of rent and the apparent tendency of this share of income to increase. The unique social and political implications of the rent problem undoubtedly helped to obscure the fact that the principle of diminishing returns, or productivity, is equally applicable to labor and capital. Thus the classicists simply treated the problem of distribution as the sharing of the social income among the three main economic classes of society. No attempt was made to explain income shares from a functional point of view, that is, as a problem of valuing the services of factors in the production process under conditions of competition or monopoly.

Von Thünen and the Marginal Product

A brilliant pioneer effort was made by a little-known German thinker, Johann Heinrich von Thünen, to explain factor rewards in terms of the contributions that marginal increments make to the total product. This explanation was developed in conjunction with his effort to explain the location of different kinds of agricultural production in relation to the market. His analysis, as set forth in his leading work, *Der Isolierte Staat* (*The Isolated State*) (1826), supposes a city surrounded by uniformly fertile agricultural land which is isolated by an impenetrable wilderness from the rest of the world. The problem which von Thünen postulates is that of explaining to what use the land will be put as the distance from the city increases. He reasoned that the further lands are removed from the city, the less intensive production will become. The more distant areas will concentrate on products that are relatively nonperishable and yet valuable enough to bear the cost of transportation to market. He depicted the location of the different types of production which will develop with varying degrees of proximity to a city by a series of concentric circles. The lands represented by the first circle, immediately surrounding the city, are devoted to garden and dairy products which are highly perishable and/or difficult to transport. The lands represented by the next circle are devoted to forests which provide fuel and building materials. Beyond that, one encounters various kinds of extensive farming and, in areas still farther away from the city, stock raising.

The principle involved in this example is that production must be guided by the additional or marginal cost incurred by moving away from the market. Von Thünen concluded that the added application of a factor should stop when the additional cost exactly equals the value of the added product and that the return to a factor is determined by the productivity of the last unit employed. Thus, he anticipated the marginal productivity theory of factor rewards, though he never used the term, in the process of developing his location theory. His contributions were, however, largely unnoticed; and it was not until the 1890's, as will be seen in Chapter 13, that the marginal productivity principle was rediscovered and the theory of distribution revolutionized.

CONCLUDING REMARKS

Two observations appear to be in order with respect to early efforts to develop the marginal concept as an analytical tool. The first is that while the concept of the margin is obviously applicable to any magnitude of economic significance, such as utility, cost, revenue, and productivity, not one of the individuals who pioneered in its use perceived the possibility of its general application. Bernoulli understood the concept of the margin and applied it to increments of income. Gossen and Dupuit appreciated the concept of marginal utility and its relationship to consumer behavior. Cournot developed the concept of marginal revenue and its relationship to marginal cost in a profit-maximizing situation. Von Thünen understood the relationship between additional applications of a factor of production and its marginal output, and used these concepts as a basis for developing a theory of location and an explanation of factor rewards. However, all understood the concept of the margin and its significance only in relation to a particular problem. They therefore failed to develop the marginal concept as a general analytical tool.

A second and perhaps related observation is that their embryonic efforts failed to bear fruit; indeed, as is so often the case, essential truths had to be rediscovered or developed anew by others before they could become incorporated into the body of economic analysis. Thus the reconstruction of the theory of value and distribution was delayed until the 1870's, when the marginal concept was reintroduced through the virtually simultaneous and independent efforts of William Jevons in England, Leon Walrás in Switzerland, and Carl Menger in Austria. The contributions of this trilogy will be examined in the next chapter.

SUGGESTIONS FOR FURTHER READING

COURNOT, AUGUSTIN. *Researches into the Mathematical Principles of the Theory of Wealth* (1838). Translated by NATHANIEL BACON. New York: Macmillan Co., 1897.

DUPUIT, JULES. "On the Measurement of the Utility of Public Works," *Annales des Ponts et Chaussées* (1844). Published in *International Economic Papers,* No. 2. London and New York: Macmillan & Co., 1952, pp. 83–110.

HOUGHTON, R. W. "A Note on the Early History of Consumer's Surplus," *Economica,* N.S., Vol. XXV (February, 1958), pp. 49–57.

LEIGH, ARTHUR H. "Von Thünen's Theory of Distribution and the Advent of Marginal Analysis," *Journal of Political Economy,* Vol. LIV (December, 1946). Reprinted in JOSEPH J. SPENGLER and W. ALLEN, eds. *Essays in Economic Thought: Aristotle to Marshall.* Chicago: Rand McNally & Co., 1960.

Chapter 12

CONTRIBUTIONS TO THE MARGINAL UTILITY THEORY OF VALUE

The first area of economic theory to be revolutionized through the rediscovery of the marginal concept was the theory of value. William Jevons, Carl Menger, and Leon Walrás independently formulated a theory of exchange value based on the principle of diminishing utility. Jevons' work, *The Theory of Political Economy,* first appeared in 1871, although he had already preceded it with *Notice of a General Mathematical Theory of Political Economy.* Menger's *Grundsätze der Volkswirtschaftslehre* appeared in the same year, while Walrás' *Eléments d'economie Politique Pure Ou Theorie de la Richesse Sociale* appeared in 1874.

Jevons was only 24 years old and a graduate student at the University of London when he adopted the concept of marginal utility into his thinking. His private correspondence indicates that he arrived at the marginal utility principle as early as 1860, which is an earlier date than the initial efforts of either Carl Menger or Leon Walrás. Although his theory of production and distribution is essentially classical, his subjective theory of value and its exposition in mathematical terms set it apart from the classical tradition. But, the classical school of thought was so dominant in England that Jevons attracted few followers to build on ideas he introduced.

By comparison, Carl Menger of Austria fared significantly better than Jevons, for a whole group of able economists, generally referred to as the "Austrian school," followed in his footsteps. Friedrich von Wieser and Eugen Böhm-Bawerk are the most notable. Though Menger's own writings are little known, largely because of the barrier of language, he laid the foundation for theoretical work in Germany and Austria. While he did not have to triumph over an established theoretical tradition, he was confronted with the tradition of the historical school, and engaged in a lengthy methodological dispute with Gustav Schmoller, who was the acknowledged leader of that school. The success of Menger's followers, Friedrich von Wieser and Eugen Böhm-Bawerk, is perhaps ample proof that the case he made for theoretical economics won adherents. They are members of the "second generation" of marginalists, and discussion of their works will be undertaken, along with that of other marginalist contributions to distribution theory, in Chapter 14 below.

Leon Walrás was the most mathematically inclined of all the marginal utility economists and lavished his greatest concern on the formulation of his general equilibrium equations. This is his great contribution to economic theory; and in the opinion of Professor Joseph A. Schumpeter, at least, it has earned him the distinction of being rated as the greatest of the pure theorists. Walrás built on the work of Quesnay, Condillac, Say, Cournot, and his father Augustin Walrás, who was a professor of philosophy and an economist in his own right. It was from his father that he drew the notion of the general interdependence of all social phenomena; from Quesnay, the idea of the general equilibrium of the economic system; and from Say, the notion that value derives from utility and scarcity rather than cost of production. It was his hope to produce separate volumes in the fields of price theory, applied theory, and social economy; but unfortunately, his work in the latter two fields did not develop into treatises. Walrás invited a young Italian nobleman, Vilfredo Pareto, who left his country because of political disturbances, to succeed him at Lausanne. Pareto adopted Walrás' concept of the general equilibrium of the static state and developed a technique, already introduced by Francis Edgeworth and known as an indifference curve, as an analytical tool for the purpose of defining the nature of the economic optimum. Since the indifference curve technique has come into general use only since the 1930's, particularly in connection with the theory of rational consumer behavior and welfare theory, Pareto's contribution will be examined in a subsequent chapter along with recent developments in microeconomic theory.

The present chapter will treat only the first generation of marginal utility economists: Jevons, Menger, and Walrás. The principle which unites their efforts is their emphasis on the role of marginal utility as opposed to cost of production as the determinant of exchange value. While there are individual differences among them with respect to particular aspects of the value problem and, in the case of Walrás, a difference of approach as well, there are sufficient similarities to warrant treatment of their contributions in terms of the subject matter which, in its entirety, represents the principles they labored to set forth.

THE THEORY OF CONSUMER BEHAVIOR

Subjective Value

Because of the introspective nature of utility, the marginal utility economists considered inquiry into the subjective value of goods as a necessary beginning. Only Walrás neglected this as a first step and introduced his analysis of utility after his presentation of the theory of exchange value. Jevons, however, observed that investigation of the "nature and conditions of utility . . . doubtless furnishes the true key to the problem of Economics.[1] Since "the whole theory of Economics depends upon a

---

[1] William Jevons, *The Theory of Political Economy* (5th ed.; New York: Kelley and Millman, 1957), p. 46.

correct theory of consumption,"[2] "we must necessarily examine the character of the wants and desires of men."[3] Bentham's influence is apparent in Jevons' definition of a commodity as "any object or, it may be, any action or service which can afford pleasure or ward off pain," while utility is "the abstract quality whereby an object serves our purposes, and becomes entitled to rank as a commodity." Utility is not an intrinsic characteristic of a commodity, but is "a circumstance of things arising out of their relationship to man's requirements."[4]

Menger gives even more detailed attention than Jevons to the subjective aspects of value. In his inquiry into what he terms *Güterqualität* (prerequisites for status as goods), he notes that there must be a human want for an object and that it must have characteristics which will satisfy this want.[5] Further, consumers must be aware of its want-satisfying power and have the object at their disposal. *Güterqualität* is thus seen as deriving from human wants. Because objects having *Güterqualität* are generally in smaller supply than the needs (*Bedarf*) for them, people will economize in their use. The individual will therefore classify his wants in accordance with their importance. Menger illustrates this hypothesis with an arithmetical example which presents a hierarchy of wants from the point of view of an individual consumer designated by Roman numerals from I to X as in Table 12–1. Arabic numbers listed in each column represent the satisfaction associated with a unit increase in the stock of goods acquired to satisfy that want. Declining numerical values were selected to represent the diminishing want-satisfying power of additional units of the same good. No additions are made to any stock when the utility of the marginal increment becomes zero.

TABLE 12–1

I	II	III	IV	V	VI	VII	VIII	IX	X
10	9	8	7	6	5	4	3	2	1
9	8	7	6	5	4	3	2	1	0
8	7	6	5	4	3	2	1	0	
7	6	5	4	3	2	1	0		
6	5	4	3	2	1	0			
5	4	3	2	1	0				
4	3	2	1	0					
3	2	1	0						
2	1	0							
1	0								
0									

---

[2] *Ibid.*, p. 47.

[3] *Ibid.*, p. 46.

[4] *Ibid.*, p. 43.

[5] Carl Menger, *Grundsätze der Volkswirtschaftslehre*, Vol. I, Reprint No. 17 (London: London School of Economics, 1870), p. 3.

Adherents of the marginal utility concept, Jevons and Walrás in particular, were fully aware that utility is in the realm of psychics and that it has no direct or measurable relationship to time or space. Walrás, however, proceeded boldly and suggested:

We need only assume that such a direct and measurable relationship does exist, and we shall find ourselves in a position to give an exact mathematical account of the respective influences on prices of extensive utility, intensive utility and the initial stock possessed.

I shall, therefore, assume the existence of a standard measure of intensity of wants or intensive utility, which is applicable not only to similar units of the same kind of wealth, but also to different units of wealth.[6]

Jevons proceeded more cautiously. He suggested that although the measurement of utility was not yet possible, it might become so at a future time.[7] He noted that in the field of economics, numerical data are both abundant and precise, but we do not yet know how to use them.[8] However, his subsequent discussions imply, as did those of his contemporaries, that utility can be measured in cardinal terms. Indeed, even though Edgeworth and Pareto both developed, in the 1880's, the technique of indifference curves, which merely assumes that utilities can be ranked ordinarily, the assumption that utility is cardinally measurable was typical of neoclassical economics until the 1930's.

Both Jevons and Walrás conceived of the marginal utility of a commodity as a diminishing function of only the quantity of that particular commodity—for example, $U_a = f(A)$, $U_b = f(B)$, etc. They also assumed that these functions are additive and wrote the total utility of an individual as $f(A) + f(B) + f(C) + \ldots$. Single variable utility functions, however, ignore the very real possibility that the utilities of some commodities, at least, are interrelated rather than independent of the quantities and prices of other goods, changes in income (and therefore the marginal utility of money), and other peoples' utility functions. Commodities may be complementary to one another or rivals of one another. In the case of complementarity, the more of a given good acquired by a consumer, the higher his marginal utility curve for a complementary good becomes. Or if commodities are rivals (substitutes), the more a consumer acquires of one of them, the lower is the marginal utility for the second (rival) good. The assumption of universal independence of utility functions also has the implication that there are no "inferior" goods, that is, goods of a kind of which less is purchased as income increases. Yet, there are many goods, particularly if

---

[6] Leon Walrás, *Elements of Pure Economics,* translated by William Jaffé (London: George Allen and Unwin, Ltd., 1954), p. 11.

[7] Jevons, *op. cit.,* p. 9.

[8] *Ibid.,* p. 12.

commodity classifications are narrowly defined, which are inferior for certain income ranges. There is also the possibility that the utility of a commodity to a given individual is affected by the quantities consumed by other people. None of these issues were, however, successfully dealt with in this stage of the development of marginal utility theory. The only problem that was successfully dealt with during this period was that inherent in assuming that utility is cardinally measurable. Both Pareto and the English mathematical economist Edgeworth tried to circumvent the measurability problem by means of the indifference curve. However, as already noted, this technique did not come into general use until the 1930's. Examination is therefore postponed until Chapter 17 below.

The negative counterpart of utility is disutility. In the process of gaining utility, an individual necessarily makes sacrifices or, in other words, incurs disutilities. In the language of Jevons: "To satisfy our wants to the utmost with the least effort, to procure the greatest amount of what is desirable at the expense of the least that is undesirable, in other words, to maximize pleasure, is the problem of Economics."[9]

The significance of this principle in explaining how maximum pleasure is achieved in a barter situation or in the utilization of income is obvious. In a barter situation the individual will continue to trade units of a given commodity from his stock for units of another good as long as the utility he gains from the exchange exceeds the disutility he incurs in sacrificing the units he gives up. Thus, if the individual is conceived to start with quantities of several goods, as in Menger's example, exchange will enable him to maximize his position by trading units from his fixed stock until he has acquired a combination which yields the same satisfaction at the margin of all his wants. Each consuming individual reaches his optimum or equilibrium position when he has equated the marginal utilities of each of the various goods in its various possible uses. The same principle pertains to the expenditure of money income. The consumer is viewed as arranging his hierarchy of preferences for present and future goods and services in his own mind and distributing his money income in such a way as to maximize the total satisfaction he can get. This necessarily involves him in calculating not only the utility he expects from an additional unit of a good, but also the disutility associated with giving up an additional dollar of income. This is the way in which marginal utility economists sought to explain how rational consumer choices underlie the demand behavior in the market, and therefore the formation of price.

Exchange Value

Jevons was less concerned than Menger with investigating the subjective side of value and proceeded early in his analysis to deal with the

---

[9] *Ibid.,* p. 37.

problem of exchange value. His approach is in terms of two individuals each with a stock of goods (corn and beef). Having recognized that the additional utility acquired by an individual decreases with each increase in total supply, he explains that exchange will take place until both individual maximize their positions by bartering units from their given stock in exchange for the commodity they do not have, until exchange is no longer profitable. His concern is to deduce the limits of exchange and define the nature of the equilibrium position. This is achieved when the ratio of exchange of any two commodities is the reciprocal of the ratio of the final degrees of utility of the quantities of the commodity available for consumption after the exchange is completed.[10]

Following Jevons' notations, let a denote a quantity of corn held by one person, while b denotes a quantity of beef held by a second. Each exchanges successive small increments of the commodity he has for successive small increments of the commodity he does not have. If x of corn is traded for y of beef and the market is purely competitive, there will only be one ratio of exchange, that is $\dfrac{dy}{dx} = \dfrac{y}{x}$. After exchange has taken place, one person will have $(a - x)$ of corn and y of beef, and the second will have x of corn and $(b - y)$ of beef. If now $\phi_1(a - x)$ and $\psi_1(y)$ are the marginal utilities of beef and corn to the first person, while $\phi_2(x)$ and $\psi_2(b - y)$ are the marginal utilities of corn and beef to the second person, the conditions of maximum satisfaction for each of the two parties in a barter exchange is expressed by the following equation:

$$\frac{\phi(a - x)}{\psi_1(y)} = \frac{y}{x} = \frac{\phi_2 x}{\psi_2(b - y)}$$

This equation expresses the principle that neither party to an exchange of two goods will be satisfied unless the ratio of the marginal utilities between them is inversely proportional to their ratio of exchange.[11]

While Jevon's example was intended to demonstrate the limits of barter exchange, the equimarginal principle easily explains also how a consumer will allocate his income to maximize his total satisfaction. Given his income, the rational consumer will allocate it among two or more goods in such a way that the marginal utility if the last cent spent on good A is equal to that of the last cent spent on good B. If this were not the case, the consumer could add to his total satisfaction by buying more of the commodity that offers greater marginal utility per additional expenditure because the loss of utility associated with giving up a unit of the second good would be less than the gain gotten from buying more of the first. This

---

[10] *Ibid.*, p. 95.
[11] *Ibid.*, p. 100.

principle is of course applicable for any number of goods the consumer might buy.

Rational allocation of money income does not imply that a consumer will spend the same dollar amount on every commodity. Rather, it means that differences in expenditures must be balanced by differences in utility, so that if the expenditure on good A is twice as high as on good B, the marginal utility associated with good A will be twice as high as that associated with good B. In other words, the marginal utility of the expenditure on any good is found by dividing the price of the good into its marginal utility. The marginal utilities of the goods themselves would be equated only in the event that their prices are the same. Thus, it may be concluded that a consumer who makes a rational allocation of expenditures on any pair of goods acquires them in proportions which will make

$$\frac{\text{Marginal utility of good A}}{\text{Price of good A}} = \frac{\text{Marginal utility of good B}}{\text{Price of good B}}$$

which is the same as making

$$\frac{\text{Marginal utility of good A}}{\text{Marginal utility of good B}} = \frac{\text{Price of good A}}{\text{Price of good B}}$$

This is a conclusion which is not dependent on the cardinal measurement of utility. That is, even if utility cannot be measured directly in terms of real numbers, the expression of quantities in terms of a ratio has the effect of eliminating the unit of measurement. Thus the principle laid down by the marginal utility theorists concerning the maximization of satisfaction was not vitiated by subsequent work in demand theory, which introduced a system of ordinal ranking of consumer preferences for the older analysis, with its implicit assumption of cardinally measurable utility.

The Derivation of Individual Demand Curves

Besides enabling us to analyze individual consumer behavior, the principle of the optimal allocation of income can also be used to derive individual consumer demand curves. Cournot, as we have already noted, drew demand curves without the substructure of utility theory. Menger virtually ignored the relationship between demand and utility, and simply set demand prices which he assumed represented marginal utilities. Jevons, on the other hand, drew demand curves which he regarded as depicting individual utility curves when he assumed a constant marginal utility of money. Only Walrás correctly perceived the relationship between utility and demand, although it must be pointed out that his discussion of marginal utility (*rareté*) is presented subsequent to his analysis of demand curves and equilibrium market conditions.

Walrás' primary objective was to demonstrate the establishment of general equilibrium, that is, to show that the prices of m commodities and n factors (land, labor, and capital) are mutually determined. The first portion of his analysis, however, is devoted to the solution of the two-commodity exchange problem. He introduces the theorem of maximum utility, which, in substance, holds that an individual maximizes satisfaction by equating the ratios of marginal utility and price for all commodities. If there are m commodities, and one is selected as a *numéraire* in terms of which all other prices are expressed, so that $P_1 = 1$, the individual will maximize his satisfaction when

$$MU_1 = \frac{MU_2}{P_2} = \frac{MU_3}{P_3} = \ \cdots \ \frac{MU_n}{P_n}$$

FIGURE 12–1

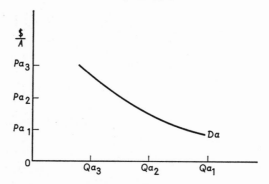

That a price reduction will increase the quantity demanded, while a price increase will decrease the quantity demanded, follows directly from this rule. Postulating a market in which there are definite quantities of only two goods, and in which the price of one good is expressed in terms of units of the other, Walrás showed how to establish a consumer demand curve for either good. He followed the standard mathematical procedure of placing the independent variable, the price, on the abscissa and the quantities demanded on the ordinate as the dependent variable. The derivation of a consumer's demand curve for a commodity, say A, begins with his initial equilibrium position. The coordinate of the initial price, Pa_1, and the quantity, Qa_1, taken at that price constitute one point on the demand curve shown in Figure 12–1, which follows the economist's practice of placing price on the ordinate axis.[12] The problem is now to establish other price-quantity relationships with respect to commodity A. If the price of A is assumed to increase to Pa_2, a consumer who buys the same quantity at the higher price as he did initially would be left with less income to spend on commodity B. It would also mean that the marginal

---

[12] The procedure of placing price on the ordinate axis and quantity on the abscissa was introduced by Alfred Marshall.

utility per dollar expended on A would have decreased, whereas the marginal utility of a dollar's worth of the now smaller quantity of B at an unchanged price would have increased. That is:

$$\frac{MU_{Qa_2}}{Pa_2} < \frac{MU_{Qb_1}}{Pb_1}.$$

The purchase of the same quantity of good A, after the price has risen to Pa_2, will not maximize the consumer's satisfaction. He can improve his position by transferring a part of his expenditures to commodity B as long as the marginal utility of a dollar's worth of A is less than a dollar's worth of B. This transfer will continue until he has again equalized the marginal utility of his expenditure on both commodities—in other words, when

$$\frac{MU_{Qa_2}}{Pa_2} = \frac{MU_{Qb_2}}{Pb_1}.$$

The relationship between the quantity Qa_2 and the price Pa_2 yields a second point on the consumer's demand curve for A. This procedure may then be repeated until a whole series of price-quantity relationships for commodity A is obtained. These price-quantity combinations constitute a demand schedule and may be presented graphically as in Figure 12–1. It should not be inferred, however, that Walrás conceived of an individual's demand for a given commodity as a function of its price alone. Cournot, and later Marshall, defined the demand curve as $D = f(p)$, a form which continues to be used in present-day partial equilibrium analysis. Walrás' demand function is the relationship between the quantity of a commodity and all prices.[13] Only money income and tastes are assumed constant, whereas the Marshallian demand curve assumes also that all prices other than that of the commodity are held constant.

THE THEORY OF PRICE DETERMINATION

The Concept of the Trading Body

While Jevons' equation $\dfrac{\phi_1(a - x)}{\psi_1 y} = \dfrac{y}{x} = \dfrac{\phi_2 x}{\psi_2(b - y)}$ was designed to illustrate equilibrium in the case of an isolated exchange taking place at fixed prices, he attempted to make a transition from the subjective valuations of two trading individuals to multiple exchange and the formation of market price. To do this, he employed the concepts of the trading body and the law of indifference. The trading body is comprised of the aggregate of buyers and sellers of a commodity in a purely competitive market, and the law of indifference implies that only one price can prevail for a given commodity in a competitive market. These concepts were used by Jevons to extend the conclusion arrived at with respect to the nature of the equilibrium

---

[13] See his general equilibrium analysis below.

achieved by two traders to the case of a large number of traders engaged in multiple exchange.

His approach involves some rather obvious difficulties, even apart from the fact that it is possible that the relative utilities of the two commodities to either or both traders may be such as to preclude all exchange. The latter limitation is recognized in his discussion of the "Failure of the Equations of Exchange."[14] He is also aware that utility functions may not be continuous, although his analysis proceeds on the premise that marginal utilities vary continuously with variations in the quantities held. However, he maintains that while the single individual may not vary the quantity he buys with every small variation in price, this will not be true of a large number of individuals. The concept of the trading body, the composition of which may range from the single individual to the sum total of a country's inhabitants, poses other difficulties. It implicitly assumes that the utilities of different individuals are additive, which Jevons himself recognized is not possible.[15] Moreover, the equilibrium rate of exchange is assumed as given at the outset, rather than explained, so that the analysis begs the question of price determination. What Jevons' analysis really amounts to, therefore, is a definition of consumer equilibrium with given supplies. Only within the framework of given stocks of commodities do utility functions determine exchange ratios or relative prices.

Jevons himself seemed to sense these limitations. While he stated categorically "that value depends solely on the final degree of utility," he amended this principle by asserting: "Cost of production determines supply; supply determines the final degree of utility."[16] Thus, it would seem that while Jevons emphasized the role of utility in determining exchange value, he was groping toward an analysis of price which would also take the role of supply into account. The marginal utility explanation of market price is valid only when supplies are given. It is capable only of demonstrating that each consumer with given tastes and income maximizes his utility position relative to given prices so as to obtain the same marginal utility per dollar expended on every product he buys. It omits the whole problem of variations over time in supply and cost of production, and their effect on exchange value. Yet, it is obvious that just as each consumer maximizes utility, so each producer maximizes his profit position within the framework of factor prices by employing factors in proportions that will yield an equal marginal value product per dollar of factor outlays. This is the sort of analysis which was to be undertaken by Alfred Marshall, who solved the problem of the determination of particular prices without resorting to the fiction of the trading body by explaining that the price of a

---

[14] Jevons, *op. cit.*, pp. 118–27.

[15] *Ibid.*, p. 21.

[16] *Ibid.*

commodity is determined by the interaction of the schedule of demand for it and its schedule of supply.

General Equilibrium Analysis

The general equilibrium analysis is an alternative approach to that used by Marshall to the problem of price determination. The rationale for this method was clearly perceived by Cournot, who wrote that "for a complete and rigorous solution of the problems relative to some parts of the economic system it is indispensable to take the entire system into consideration."[17]

Although Cournot recognized the necessity of considering the economic system as a whole, it was Leon Walrás who constructed a mathematical system to demonstrate general equilibrium. His analysis, instead of embracing only two commodities and seeking to establish the equilibrium rate of exchange between them, is broadened to include simultaneous equilibria in all commodity and factor markets. Like a partial analysis, a general equilibrium analysis is constructed on the basis of certain assumptions. In Walrás' system, these "givens" are (1) the quantities of m finished goods to be consumed in a given period of time; (2) the supplies of n factors of production which may be offered for hire in the factor market or employed directly by their owners; (3) the technical coefficients of production, that is, specific combinations of land, labor, and capital which are required by technical considerations to produce finished goods; and (4) the marginal utility or *rareté* functions of individuals for goods and self-employed factor services. These are the data of Walrás' system.

The system seeks to determine four sets of unknowns: the quantities of n productive services offered for sale, the quantities of m finished goods demanded, the prices of n productive services, and the prices of m finished goods. In practice, of course, quantities and prices are determined in the marketplace through the interaction of demand and supply forces. But Walrás demonstrated that, given the necessary data, it is possible to achieve a solution mathematically. If one of the commodities whose prices we seek to establish is chosen as a common denominator (or *numéraire*) in terms of which all prices are expressed, so that $P_a = 1$, there is one less price to be established, so that there are $2m + 2n - 1$ unknowns to be determined. Therefore, $2m + 2n - 1$ independent equations must be written. Thus the solution of Walrás' general equilibrium equations is precisely like the solution of a system of simultaneous equations.

The achievement of general equilibrium in all markets is premised on the achievement of simultaneous individual equilibria. Assuming that the

---

[17] Augustin Cournot, *Researches into the Mathematical Principles of the Theory of Wealth* (1838), translated by Nathaniel Bacon (New York: Macmillan Co., 1897), p. 127.

quantities of productive resources available to be supplied by each household is known once commodity and factor prices are established, two conditions must be satisfied for each individual consumer of finished goods or supplier of resources to be in a state of general equilibrium. Both of these conditions can be given expression in terms of an equation. The first is that the marginal utilities of the finished goods bought and the productive services of self-owned factors retained by individuals for their own use must be proportional to their prices. If this condition is not satisfied, maximum satisfaction from expenditures is not achieved. The second condition derives from the fact that every individual is subject to a budget constraint imposed by the requirement that individual expenditures must equal individual receipts. The individual budget equations, together with the marginal utility equations, determine the quantity of each good bought or factor retained by the household for its own use. These consumer equations express the optimum allocation of income for each individual among alternative goods and services when their prices and the marginal utilities consumers derive from them are given. By contrast, Jevons' equation of the ratio of exchange only expressed the conditions of maximum satisfaction for two parties to a barter exchange.

Consumer utility and budget equations provide part of the information needed to define the conditions of general equilibrium for the economy as a whole. Individual demands for each good, expressed as a function of all commodity and factor prices, are aggregated into a group of market demand equations. There are m such equations, each of which is a summation of individual consumer demand equations for each good. Unlike a particular equilibrium analysis in which the demand for each good is expressed as a function of its price alone, each of the m equations of demand in the Walrásian general equilibrium analysis is expressed as a function of all commodity and factor prices. Similarly, individual supply equations for productive resources, expressed as a function of individual commodity and factor prices, are aggregated to provide a group of equations of factor supplies. There are n such equations.

The technical coefficients of production, which are one of the data of Walrás' system, and the demands for finished goods establish the quantity of each resource required to produce each good. Since Walrás assumed full employment, it is axiomatic that the sum of these requirements is equal to the total supply of each resource. This, too, may be expressed in terms of a group of equations which are n in number. A final group of equations expresses equality between the prices of consumer goods and their average costs of production. Since one of these goods is the *numéraire,* there are $m - 1$ such equations. Summing up, then, there are $2m + 2n - 1$ independent equations to solve for the same number of unknowns, so that the system is determinate.

The preceding verbal description of the Walrásian system may be supplemented by a symbolic presentation. Let the quantity of finished goods to be consumed be designated as

$$a, b, \ldots m$$

Let the supply of factors used to produce these goods be designated as

$$s_{f_1}, s_{f_2}, \ldots s_{f_n}$$

Let the technical coefficients, i.e., the quantities of the various factors f_1, f_2, . . . f_n that enter into the production of finished goods $a, b, \ldots m$ be designated as

$$a_{f_1}, a_{f_2}, \ldots a_{f_n}$$
$$b_{f_1}, b_{f_2}, \ldots b_{f_n}$$
$$\cdot \cdot \cdot \cdot \cdot \cdot \cdot \cdot \cdot$$
$$m_{f_1}, m_{f_2}, \ldots m_{f_n}$$

Let the quantities of finished goods demanded be designated as

$$d_a, d_b, \ldots d_m$$

and let the demands for the services of owner-employed factors be designated as

$$d_{f_1}, d_{f_2}, \ldots d_{f_n}$$

The marginal utility or *rareté* functions of each of the m consumer goods and n productive services retained by owners are

$$u_a = \phi_a(d_a)$$
$$u_b = \phi_b(d_b)$$
$$\cdot \cdot \cdot \cdot \cdot \cdot \cdot \cdot \cdot \cdot$$
$$u_m = \phi_m(d_m)$$
$$u_{f_1} = \phi_{f_1}(s_{f_1} - d_f)$$
$$u_{f_2} = \phi_{f_2}(s_{f_2} - d_{f_2})$$
$$\cdot \cdot \cdot \cdot \cdot \cdot \cdot \cdot \cdot \cdot$$
$$u_{f_n} = \phi_{f_n}(s_{f_n} - d_{f_n})$$

Assuming that the price of good A is the *numéraire*, the unknowns to be determined are $2m + 2n - 1$ in number. An equal number of independent equations must therefore be written. The individual is, first of all, subject to a budget equation which expresses equality between his expenditure and his income:

$$(s_{f_1} - d_{f_1})p_{f_1} + (s_{f_2} - d_{f_2})p_{f_2} + \ldots (s_{f_n} - d_{f_n})p_{f_n} = d_a + d_b p_b + \ldots d_m p_m$$

Maximum satisfaction requires that the marginal utilities of goods and services be proportional to their prices. There are $m - 1$ equations for commodities, as follows:

$$\phi_b(d_b) = p_b \phi_a(d_a)$$
$$\phi_c(d_c) = p_c \phi_a(d_a)$$
$$\cdot \cdot \cdot \cdot \cdot \cdot \cdot \cdot \cdot \cdot$$
$$\phi_m(d_m) = p_m \phi_a(d_a)$$

and n equations for factor services, as follows:

$$\phi_{f_1}(s_{f_1} - d_{f_1}) = p_1\phi_a(d_a)$$
$$\phi_{f_2}(s_{f_2} - d_{f_2}) = p_2\phi_a(d_a)$$
$$\cdots\cdots\cdots\cdots$$
$$\phi_{f_n}(s_{f_n} - d_{f_n}) = p_n\phi_a(d_a)$$

No equation is required for good *a*, which is the *numéraire*. The total number of equations is $n + m - 1$, which is sufficient to determine n unknown factor supply functions, as follows:

$$s_{f_1} = f_1(p_{f_1}, p_{f_2}, \ldots p_{f_n}, p_b, p_c, \ldots p_m)$$
$$s_{f_1} = f_2(p_{f_1}, p_{f_2}, \ldots p_{f_n}, p_b, p_c, \ldots p_m)$$
$$\cdots\cdots\cdots\cdots\cdots\cdots\cdots$$
$$s_{f_n} = f_n(p_{f_1}, p_{f_2}, \ldots p_{f_n}, p_b, p_c, \ldots p_m)$$

and $m - 1$ unknown demand functions, as follows:

$$d_b = f_b(p_{f_1}, p_{f_2}, \ldots p_{f_n}, p_b, p_c, \ldots p_m)$$
$$d_c = f_c(p_{f_1}, p_{f_2}, \ldots p_{f_n}, p_b, p_c, \ldots p_m)$$
$$\cdots\cdots\cdots\cdots\cdots\cdots\cdots$$
$$d_m = f_m(p_{f_1}, p_{f_2}, \ldots p_{f_n}, p_b, p_c, \ldots p_m)$$

The summation of individual demand and supply functions results in two of the four sets of equations Walrás required to define the conditions of general equilibrium for the economy as a whole. There are n equations of supply for productive services, as follows:

$$S_{f_1} = \Sigma s_{f_1} = F_{f_1}(p_{f_1}, p_{f_2}, \ldots p_{f_n}, p_b, p_c, \ldots p_n)$$
$$S_{f_2} = \Sigma s_{f_2} = \ldots\ldots\ldots\ldots\ldots\ldots\ldots$$
$$\cdots\cdots\cdots\cdots\cdots\cdots\cdots$$
$$S_{f_n} = \Sigma s_{f_n} = \ldots\ldots\ldots\ldots\ldots\ldots\ldots$$

There are also $m - 1$ equations of demand for finished goods, as follows:

$$D_b = \Sigma d_b = F_b(p_{f_1}, p_{f_2}, \ldots p_{f_n}, p_b, p_c, \ldots p_m)$$
$$D_c = \Sigma d_c = \ldots\ldots\ldots\ldots\ldots\ldots\ldots$$
$$\cdots\cdots\cdots\cdots\cdots\cdots\cdots$$
$$D_m = \Sigma d_m = \ldots\ldots\ldots\ldots\ldots\ldots\ldots$$

The third group of n equations expresses equality between the quantity of productive services employed to produce each good, given the technical coefficients of production, and the quantity offered:

$$a_{f_1}D_a + b_{f_1}D_b + \ldots m_{f_1}D_m = S_{f_1}$$
$$a_{f_2}D_a + b_{f_2}D_b + \ldots m_{f_2}D_m = S_{f_2}$$
$$\cdots\cdots\cdots\cdots\cdots\cdots\cdots$$
$$a_{f_n}D_a + b_{f_n}D_b + \ldots m_{f_n}D_m = S_{f_n}$$

Finally, the fourth group of equations expresses equality between the prices of m consumer goods and their average costs of production. Thus, there are m equations, as follows:

$$a_{f_1}p_{f_1} + a_{f_2}p_{f_2} + \ldots a_{f_n}p_{f_n} = 1$$
$$b_{f_1}p_{f_1} + b_{f_2}p_{f_2} + \ldots b_{f_n}p_{f_n} = p_b$$
$$\cdots\cdots\cdots\cdots\cdots\cdots\cdots$$
$$m_{f_1}p_{f_1} + m_{f_2}p_{f_2} + \ldots m_{f_n}p_{f_n} = p_m$$

Summing up, there are $2m + 2n - 1$ independent equations to solve for the same number of unknowns. The determinateness of the system is assured by the equality of the number of independent equations with the number of unknowns. This demonstration has become the inspiration for all subsequent work on general equilibrium.

It is not difficult to appreciate some of the problems inherent in the general equilibrium approach. To establish and solve such a system of equations is certainly to perform Herculean labor. Furthermore, equality between the number of equations and the number of unknowns will not necessarily mean that there will be a single positive solution. Sets of simultaneous equations may have multiple solutions or may be satisfied by zero or negative prices, which imply that the good is either a free good or a nuisance good. Negative prices for goods are more easily accomodated in the equations than negative factor prices, for the latter imply that factors are paying firms to employ them. Yet, it is obvious that if factor supplies and technical coefficients of production are fixed, as Walrás assumed them to be, it may not always be possible to satisfy the market-clearing equations at positive factor prices.

Walrás took his analysis a step beyond demonstrating the determinacy of a general market equilibrium. He tried to show that the problem for which he gave a theoretical explanation is that which is, in practice, solved in the market by the mechanism of free competition through a process of recontracting. People are presumed to come to the market with certain stocks of commodities and certain dispositions to trade, from which a set of prices will emerge. If demand and supply are equal at these prices, there is an immediate equilibrium. If, on the other hand, demand and supply are not equal, people will recontract until none of the parties see any advantage in further recontracting. The price ultimately established by this process is the equilibrium price.

The two cardinal points in Walrás' description of exchange equilibrium are (1) that the amounts demanded and supplied by particular individuals depend on the system of market prices and (2) that there must be an equilibrium between demand and supply in particular markets. What Walrás does not make clear in his analysis of exchange equilibrium is whether exchanges do or do not take place at the prices originally proposed if these prices are not equilibrium prices. If there is no actual exchange until the equilibrium prices are reached by bidding, Walrás' explanation of the way in which a position of stable equilibrium is reached seems unrealistic. But if exchanges do take place at prices which are not equilibrium prices, the final equilibrium prices are bound to be affected by them. That is, the final position of equilibrium is not independent of the path followed to reach the equilibrium position.[18]

---

[18] John R. Hicks, "Leon Walrás," *Econometrica*, Vol. II, 1934, pp. 338–48.

CONCLUDING REMARKS

The threads of the preceding examination may now be drawn together to see what positive contribution to economic analysis was made by the marginal utility theorists and how they differed from their classical predecessors. The most significant contribution is their use of the marginal utility apparatus to deduce the exchange ratios that will establish themselves between commodities in competitive markets. In so doing, they established the nexus between value in use and value in exchange which Smith, Ricardo, and Marx failed to recognize. Their analysis thus marks a clear departure from labor and cost of production theories of value. While they did not emphasize the weaknesses of the labor theory of value as a basis for advancing their views on marginal utility, they pointed out that a labor theory of value is deficient in several respects. They noted first that a large expenditure for labor will not necessarily result in a high commodity value, because future demands may be inaccurately forecast. They also noted that a labor theory of value lacked generality, for it does not explain the value of land or objects like works of art that exist in permanently fixed supply. While the role of marginal utility appears somewhat less obvious in Walrás' analysis than in that of Menger and Jevons, because it is overshadowed by the theory of general equilibrium, Walrás nevertheless regarded the notion of *rareté* as fundamental, for it constituted the basis for his demand functions and thus the whole production process.

The preoccupation of the marginal utility economists with the theory of exchange made it appear that the theory of maximizing behavior was a special case rather than a tool of general application. However, the subsequent development of marginal economics consisted primarily of the extension of the marginal principle to the theory of production and distribution. The concepts of marginal and total utility have significance not only in relation to consumer goods but also in relation to producer goods. These goods do not satisfy human wants directly, but are transformed into objects of want satisfaction in the production process. Menger called them "goods of a higher order," which differ from consumer goods only in terms of their nearness to the final user. Their value is therefore dependent on the marginal utility of the goods in whose production they assist. Though Menger himself was too preoccupied with the problem of subjective value to make the transition to the problem of factor valuation, and therefore income distribution, his ranking of goods into various "orders" became the basis for later important analysis which demonstrated how the productive contribution of separate factors to the utility of the total product could be isolated. This is the route by which later Austrians were to discover the principle of imputation.

It is something of an enigma that the marginal productivity theory was not clearly developed alongside the theory of subjective value. It seems that once the revolutionary concept of explaining the value of consumer goods in terms of marginal utility theory was developed, the next logical step would have been to explain how the values of the productive services themselves are determined. Yet, it was approximately twenty years later that the marginal productivity theory finally made its appearance. As in the case of marginal utility, it also appeared more or less simultaneously in several countries. These developments will be treated in the chapter which follows.

SUGGESTIONS FOR FURTHER READING

HICKS, JOHN R.   "Leon Walrás," *Econometrica,* Vol. II (1934).

HOWEY, R. S.   *The Rise of the Marginal Utility School, 1870–1899.* Lawrence: University of Kansas Press, 1960.

HUTCHISON, T. W.   *A Review of Economic Doctrines, 1870–1929,* particularly chaps. i, ii, vi, ix, and xiii. Oxford: Clarendon Press, 1953.

JEVONS, WILLIAM.   *The Theory of Political Economy.* 5th ed. New York: Kelley and Millman, Inc., 1957.

KEYNES, JOHN MAYNARD.   "William Stanley Jevons," *Journal of the Royal Statistical Society,* Vol. XLIX (1936).

MENGER, CARL.   *Principles of Economics,* tr. and ed. by JAMES DINGWALL and BERT F. HOSELITZ, Glencoe: Free Press, 1950.

ROBBINS, LIONEL.   "The Place of Jevons in the History of Economic Thought," *Manchester School,* Vol. VII (1935).

STIGLER, GEORGE.   "The Development of Utility Theory," *Journal of Political Economy,* Vol. LVIII Nos. 4 and 5 (August and October, 1950). Reprinted in JOSEPH SPENGLER and W. ALLEN eds., *Essays in Economic Thought: Aristotle to Marshall.* Chicago: Rand McNally & Co., 1960.

————.   "The Economics of Carl Menger," *Journal of Political Economy,* Vol. XLV (April, 1937). Reprinted in JOSEPH J. SPENGLER and W. ALLEN, *Essays in Economic Thought: Aristotle to Marshall.* Chicago: Rand McNally & Co., 1960.

WALRÁS, LEON.   *Elements of Pure Economics.* Translated by WILLIAM JAFFÉ. London: George Allen and Unwin, Ltd., 1954, particularly Lessons 8–13.

Chapter 13 | CONTRIBUTIONS TO THE THEORY OF DISTRIBUTION

INTRODUCTION

The State of Distribution Theory in 1870

The rapid advance of theoretical economics during the 1870's was largely concentrated on the problem of value. Little, if any, work had been done with respect to reformulating the theory of distribution. Indeed, there was no separate and distinct theory of distribution in the 1870's in the sense of a body of principles which explained the division of the economy's product among those who perform different functions in the production process or supply different factors. The problem of distribution was still being approached in the classical manner, which viewed rent, wages, and profits as the income shares of the three main social classes rather than as functional returns to productive factors which are, at one and the same time, costs of production and factor incomes. What was needed, therefore, to bridge this hiatus was the formulation of a theory of distribution which was integrated with the theory of value.

While this integration was not quickly accomplished, nor carried through by the original proponents of the marginal utility theory of value, it was apparent that once the value of a consumer good had been explained according to the marginal utility principle, the next logical step was to explain the values of the factors which cooperated in its production. When conceived in this manner, the problem of distribution is essentially a matter of allocating the value of a product among the factors according to their respective contributions. Thus the new approach to the theory of distribution became to relate the income shares of land, labor, and capital to their productive contributions. The leading theory is known as the marginal productivity theory of income distribution. Stated briefly, the theory maintains that in the long run, under perfect competition, factors of production will tend to receive a real rate of return which is determined by and equal to their marginal productivity. The Austrian theory of imputation, which extends the marginal utility theory of value to the factors of production, is an alternative though not entirely dissimilar approach.

The approach of the marginalists to the problem of explaining the distributive shares reflects, at least in a general way, the economic and social changes that accompanied the evolution of industrial capitalism.

There was little evidence that the dismal Malthusian and Ricardian proph-ecies were being fulfilled. In general, the real wages of labor were rising, and rates of profit did not exhibit significant downward pressure; nor was rent increasing relative to other income shares. On the contrary, immigra-tion, falling birth rates, and freer trade were reducing population pressures, while, at the same time, technological improvements such as Thomas Malthus and David Ricardo had never envisioned were greatly improving production potentials in both industry and agriculture. The vision of the "stationary state" therefore receded, and the doctrine of economic har-mony, as being inherent in the functioning of a system guided by self-interest, gained new adherents. Thus, there was a revival of the optimism that had characterized the thinking of the late eighteenth century, but which was unable to survive the stern realities of the first part of the nineteenth. This spirit of optimism again found expression in the doctrine of laissez-faire, though few economists sought to present a philosophical basis for their views. Indeed, the scope of economics was becoming more narrow and specialized. In the process, economic analysis became increasingly abstract and technical. Though it gained greatly in precision, it lost much of the commonsense quality upon which the "realism," and therefore public ac-ceptance of its conclusions, rested. The older political economy had a much wider appeal than the new, more technical body of principles, which, while it did not actually fall into disrepute, nevertheless had less prestige and consequently less influence.

Though the businessmen of the community and economists generally continued to adhere to the laissez-faire tradition, they did so with a differ-ence worth noting. To businessmen, the principle of lassez-faire implied, in the main, freedom from public interference to pursue profit making activi-ties. Consequently, they were generally in opposition to free trade and to antimonopoly policies of government, as well as to the bulk of regulations that would further the interests and objectives of the working class. Econo-mists, on the other hand, were almost unanimous in supporting free trade, public control of monopolies, and legislation generally favorable to the working class. However, it is only fair to note that theoretical economists after John Stuart Mill were much more concerned with the formulation of economic laws than with policy prescriptions. They also tended to deduce conclusions from assumptions about the institutional setting and human behavior which did not always coincide with observable reality. Though this process of abstraction was intended to facilitate the establishment of propositions which represented only a first approximation to the truth, and which therefore required amendment and qualification, there was often a tendency to overlook the tentative nature of the conclusions. The ideal thus tended to be equated with reality; and as a result, the body of economics which developed after Mill frequently appeared to have an apologetic bias in favor of the system of private capitalism.

The Contributors to Distribution Theory after 1870

The contributors to distribution theory as it developed after 1870 concerned themselves with three major questions. The first of these is the theory of production, the second is the explanation of factor rewards according to their productive contributions at the margin, and the third is the special problem of capital and interest. The origin of capital and the nature of its return became of such special concern that it warrants separate consideration. This will be done in the chapter immediately following.

With the exception of Francis Edgeworth, Philip Wicksteed, and Alfred Marshall, all of the leading contributors to the development of distribution theory after 1870 were non-English. Chief among them was the Austrian, Friedrich von Wieser, who followed in the tradition established by Carl Menger and the American John Bates Clark. Other important contributions came from the Swedish economist Knut Wicksell, much of whose work was Austrian in inspiration. Except for Marshall, these individuals made their most substantive contributions in the area of distribution theory and the necessarily related area of production theory. Other than Marshall and Wicksell, none attempted a comprehensive treatise concerning the whole subject matter of economics in the manner of Smith, Ricardo and Mill. Only Alfred Marshall was sufficiently inspirational and persuasive to stimulate what may be termed a "school." While their contributions are of major importance in the aggregate, it is only Marshall's work which, because of its nature and impact, seems to demand a separate chapter. The present chapter will devote itself, therefore, primarily to the Austrian and American contributions to the development of distribution theory during the closing decades of the nineteenth century and the first decades of the twentieth century. The only English contributions which will be examined are those of Edgeworth and Wicksteed which bear on the subject matter. Marshall's work will be examined in its entirety in a subsequent chapter.[1]

Friedrich von Wieser (1851–1926) was, like many young Germans and Austrians from the upper class, trained in law and destined for a career as a civil servant. After his discovery of Menger's *Grundsätze der Volkswirtschaftslehre,* he came to view economics as the most useful vehicle for studying social relationships. While it appeared that von Wieser's early concern with social problems would lead him in the direction of applied economics, he in fact turned his attention more and more to purely theoretical work. He adopted Menger's subjective approach, according to which utility is the basis for economic action, and proceeded to build a theory of the determination of the values of the factors of production and their

---

[1] The indispensable reference on the contributions of most of these thinkers is George Stigler, *Production and Distribution Theories* (New York: Macmillan Co., 1941).

allocation among alternative uses on that foundation. Beyond this, he tried, in his *Social Economics,* to integrate economic theory with a theory of society which conceived of individuals as being linked to society through the process of exchange. This work gives him the distinction of being the only one of the Austrians to produce a full-fledged treatise.

Knut Wicksell (1851–1926) was approaching 40 when he came into economics out of mathematics and philosophy. Living in an era and in a society that was still predominantly conservative, Wicksell was an outspoken social reformer and champion of unpopular causes and unorthodox views. Nevertheless, his ability as a theorist won him the respect of others in his profession. His principal works are *Value, Capital and Rent* (1893); *Interest and Prices* (1898; translated in 1936); and *Lectures on Political Economy* (two volumes, published in 1901 and 1906; translated in 1934–35).

Wicksell was in many respects close to the Austrian tradition, particularly in the area of interest theory. He was a thoroughgoing marginalist who successfully integrated the utility theory of value with the marginal productivity theory of distribution. His special contribution to the theory of distribution, for which he shares the honor of discovery with Philip Wicksteed, is the theorem concerning the exhaustion of the product.

John Bates Clark (1847–1938) is the most distinguished American contributor to the development of distribution theory during the period under consideration. He is also a theorist whose contributions to theoretical economics as a whole can be rated as among the most original and significant to have come out of this country.

Clark brought to economics a lifelong interest in philosophy and ethics acquired in his undergraduate days at Brown University and Amherst College. This philosophic bent led him to the view that the economic aspects of life cannot be divorced from questions of morality. From 1895 well into the 1920's, he was Professor of Economics at Columbia University, where he contributed to periodical literature besides publishing three books: *The Philosophy of Wealth* (1885), *The Distribution of Wealth* (1899), and *Essentials of Economic Theory* (1907). His reputation rests chiefly on *The Distribution of Wealth,* in which he presented the hypothesis that the functional distribution of income will be determined in the long run under static and perfectly competitive conditions according to the principle of factor productivity at the margin.

Most of Clark's work aligns him with the orthodox tradition of English economists and makes him an intellectual cousin of his English contemporary, Alfred Marshall. There appears to be little, especially as regards his mature work, to mark his contribution as distinctively American. The early Clark, as reflected in his first work, *The Philosophy of Wealth,* gave promise of a departure from English tradition in its criticism of the assumptions on which classical analysis rested. In it, Clark undertook to question the premise that man's economic behavior is motivated by material self-interest and urged the necessity of a more valid psychological basis for economic inquiry. He also questioned the inherent desirability of competition as the regulator of economic life and introduced into economics the Spencerian conception that society is an organic whole. While many of these ideas were novel when Clark introduced them into economics, the body of economic analysis which he ultimately perfected and which is given expression in *The Distribution of Wealth* places him, in terms of viewpoint, in the ranks of the English orthodox thinkers who believed that competitive forces could be relied upon to work economic justice and social harmony. Thus, while Clark gave promise of leading the revolt against the body of orthodox economics, it was in fact his student, Thorstein Veblen, who became the most prominent critic of received doctrine.

THE THEORY OF PRODUCTION

Production Functions and the Laws of Return in the Short Run

All of the contributions to the theory of distribution which were made during the period under consideration seek to relate the income shares of land, labor, and capital to their productive contributions at the margin. The theory of distribution is therefore necessarily related to the theory of production. The latter is concerned with the relationship between factor inputs and product outputs. Leon Walrás was the first to express these relationships in the form of a mathematical function, although the concept of a production function is implicit in von Thünen's thinking as well as in the classical theory of diminishing returns. Walrás' initial assumption with respect to the nature of the production function was that the coefficients of production are fixed, so that there is only one possible combination of inputs which will yield any product. The significance of this assumption from the standpoint of the theory of distribution is that it makes it impossible to isolate the productive contribution of any individual factor. It is interesting to note that Walrás never did arrive at a theory which related the distributive shares to the marginal productivities of their factors, even though he eventually introduced the concept of variable proportions into his theory of production.

It is only in the very short run that the extreme situation in which factor substitution is a complete impossibility is likely to be encountered. It is more than likely that at least one of the inputs will be variable. The classical theory of rent assumed a production function of this sort. It recognized that the presence of a fixed factor imposes a constraint on the production process and deduced that returns to the variable factor will increase at a decreasing rate. The operation of this law accounted for the emergence of rent as a differential surplus on better than marginal land.

This analysis had its short comings both as a theory of production and as a theory of distribution. Not only did it fail to distinguish between diminishing average and marginal product, but it also implied that the law of diminishing returns applied only to land and agricultural output. Classical theorists therefore failed to recognize that it is possible to generalize Ricardo's theory of rent and conceive of the return to any factor either as a differential product or as the equivalent of its marginal product, depending upon whether that factor is a fixed constant or a variable in the production function.

TABLE 13–1

RETURNS FROM VARYING AMOUNTS OF LABOR AND EQUIPMENT APPLIED (IN SMALL DOSES) TO A GIVEN PLOT OF LAND

Day's Labor of Man with Team and Tools	Total Crop in Bushels	Increments Due to Successive Doses	Bushels per Day's Labor
..	...	..	....
13	220	..	16.92
14	244	24	17.43
15	270	26	18.00
16	294	24	18.38
17	317	23	18.65
18	339	22	18.83
19	360	21	18.95
20	380	20	19.00
21	396	16	18.86

While the classical theorists stated the law of diminishing returns, Francis Edgeworth is credited with making a clear-cut distinction between proportional and incremental changes in the output which can be gotten from a variable factor.[2] He also made it plain that when for any reason it is not possible to vary all factor inputs, diminishing returns are due to the change in the ratio in which the factors are used. In order to demonstrate the distinction between diminishing average and marginal returns, he assumed that successive small doses of labor and capital are applied to a given plot of land and that the total output, marginal output, and average output behave as recorded in Table 13–1. This table provides a clear demonstration that there is a difference between diminishing marginal returns and diminishing average returns, though the two were usually confused.[3]

The behavior of marginal product and average product when the land-to-labor ratio is varied may also be shown graphically. Figure 13–1

---

[2] Francis Edgeworth, *Collected Papers Relating to Political Economy,* Vol. I (London: Macmillan & Co., 1925), p. 68.

[3] Even Alfred Marshall was among those who confused the two concepts. See Chap. 15, p. 259.

plots the labor-to-land ratios from Table 13–1 on the horizontal axis, and the average and marginal product associated with varying the labor-to-land ratio on the vertical axis. It is evident that as long as additional increments of a variable factor can cause total output to increase at an increasing rate, both marginal and average output will increase, and the marginal physical product of the variable factor will be greater than its average product. The marginal product curve will then be above the average product curve.

FIGURE 13–1

AVERAGE AND MARGINAL PRODUCT OF A VARIABLE FACTOR

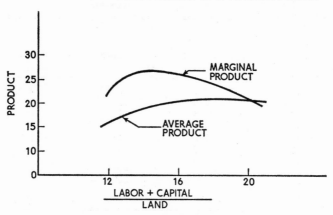

When additional units of the variable factor can no longer raise the total product at an increasing rate, as is the case in Edgeworth's example after the application of the fifteenth dose of labor and equipment, the marginal product will diminish, and the marginal product curve will slope downward. When additional inputs of the variable factor can no longer raise the average product beyond the maximum already reached, the average product of the variable factor will equal the marginal product. Beyond that point, additional applications of the variable factor will cause the average product to diminish. This takes place, in Edgeworth's example, with the application of the twenty-first dose of labor and equipment to a given plot of land. The marginal physical product is then smaller than the average product.

While Table 13–1 and Figure 13–1 do not show it, additional applications of the variable factor to a given amount of a fixed factor will, at some point, be associated with an absolute decrease in total product. The average product of the variable factor will then decrease, and the marginal product will be negative.

Edgeworth's distinction between diminishing average productivity and diminishing marginal productivity is fundamental to understanding the behavior of production costs in the short run. It is also fundamental to an understanding of entrepreneurial demands for factors of production. Just as a consumer maximizes his gains by allocating his income among alternative uses until the ratios of the marginal utilities of the goods he consumes are equal to the ratios of their prices, so a producer maximizes his gains from his factor inputs when he equates the ratios of the marginal revenue products of the factors he hires to the ratios of their prices.

Euler's Theorem and Returns to Scale

Philip Wicksteed appears to have been the first to appreciate the fact that when it is not possible to vary all factor inputs, the laws of return are different from those which govern when all inputs are variable.[4] The output possibilities when all factors are variable are commonly described today by the term "returns to scale." There are three possibilities: constant returns, increasing returns, and decreasing returns.

If a proportionate increase in all factor inputs increases output proportionately, the returns to scale are obviously constant. The production function in this case also satisfies the requirement which the mathematician Leonhard Euler laid down in his theorem concerning linear homogeneity. A function is linearly homogeneous if the multiplication of every variable it contains by a given real number increases the value of the total function by the same multiple. Applying this principle to the relationship between factor inputs and the resulting product, a production function is homogeneously linear if a given increase in all factor inputs increases the total product in precisely the same proportion. If, however, a proportionate increase in all factor inputs increases output more than proportionately, the returns to scale are increasing. Conversely, if a proportionate increase in all factor inputs increases output less than proportionately, the returns to scale are decreasing.

Wicksteed was especially concerned with the bearing which returns to scale have on the problem of "coordinating" the laws of distribution.[5] He conceived of the latter problem as involving the demonstration that each of the distributive shares is governed by the principle of marginal productivity, and that the total product which is distributed is the exact sum of the shares which that principle assigns to each of the several factors. He appreciated that it is only in the case of constant returns that it is possible to pay each factor the equivalent of its marginal product and exactly exhaust the total product. That is, when returns to scale are constant, the marginal product of the factors is independent of the absolute amount of the factors employed. A proportionate change in the quantity of all factors does not, there-

---

[4] Philip Wicksteed, *The Commonsense of Political Economy,* edited by Lionel Robbins (London: George Routledge & Sons, Ltd., 1935), p. 529.

[5] Philip Wicksteed, *An Essay on the Co-ordination of the Laws of Distribution* (London: Macmillan & Co., 1894).

fore, affect their marginal product. Thus the increase in the total product resulting from additional quantities of all factors is precisely equal to the sum of the marginal products of each of the separate factors. The problem Wicksteed posed concerning the exhaustion of the total product thus revealed an essential link between the theory of production and the theory of distribution, though this link was not equally apparent to all the thinkers who sought to relate factor incomes to their productive contributions.

THE THEORY OF IMPUTATION

Menger's Theory of Negative Imputation

Carl Menger was the first economist to consider the problem of the valuation of the factors of production on the basis of their contributions to the value of their products. He conceived of factors of production as goods of a higher order whose value is determined by imputation from the anticipated value of the goods of a lower order in whose production they serve. Menger thought that the correct procedure for establishing this value was to withdraw one unit of a good of a higher order from production and observe the effect on total output. The loss in the total product is the marginal product of the variable factor in question, and the utility of the product which is forgone establishes the value of the unit of the good of a higher order in the production process. This value may also be conceived of as the alternative or opportunity cost of using the factor in the production of some other good. This alternative cost is equal to the difference in want satisfaction incidental to the withdrawal of a unit of the resource in question.

Within the framework of Menger's reasoning, it is immaterial whether the factors are used in fixed proportions or variable proportions. In the case of fixed proportions the withdrawal of a unit of one resource necessitates the employment of some portion of cooperating resources elsewhere. The total loss of product minus the product produced by the complementary factors in their new employment establishes the loss of utility, and thus the value, of the variable factor. In the more usual case of variable factor proportions, Menger implies that the withdrawal of one unit of a factor necessitates a rearrangement of complementary factors. The resulting loss of utility associated with the reduction of the product determines the value of the withdrawn factor unit. What is not made clear in Menger's analysis is the effect which the tendency toward diminishing returns exerts on output when the input of one variable resource is altered. Nor does he examine the problem as to whether his method of valuing the factors will result in payments which will exactly exhaust the total product. This is a question which was to be a major issue of the marginal productivity theory of distribution. Also absent from Menger's theory of distribution is a theory of capital. That is, he does not distinguish between capital goods themselves and the services they render. However, Menger's explanation of the value of productive factors, as far as it went, was significantly better than any previously offered hypothesis.

Von Wieser's Theory of Positive Imputation

Friedrich von Wieser extended Menger's theory of imputation by emphasizing that the process identifies the economic contribution rather than the physical contribution of a factor. He also maintained that Menger's procedure of valuing the factors by negative imputation is inaccurate. The withdrawal of a unit of any one agent reduces the productivity of remaining agents. Therefore the loss of total product is not due just to the withdrawal of an individual unit of the factor in question. Factor payments established on the basis of the product loss will therefore result in the distribution of shares which are greater in the aggregate than the total product. Hence, he proposed the alternative method of positive imputation, which measures the product gained by retaining a unit of the factor in question.

He assumed that factors are combined in fixed proportions in each industry, though these proportions vary from one industry to another. By assuming that the values of the factors are simply reflections of the marginal utility of consumer goods, and therefore equal to the value of the product, von Wieser was able to demonstrate that factor payments just exhaust the final product. However, this procedure does not prove that a factor's reward is determined by the value of its marginal product, because the separate productivity of a factor cannot be imputed at all when factors are combined in fixed proportions. A factor's marginal product can be isolated only if proportions are variable and substitution is possible. Otherwise, the concept of marginal product is without meaning.

A further limitation of the Austrian theory of imputation is its interpretation of the marginal value product of a factor as a reflection of consumer satisfaction in an aggregate sense. A concept of social marginal utility implies that individual utilities are additive. Moreover, the Austrian formulation implies that marginal utility and commodity value are the basis for determining factor prices, whereas the relationship is a reciprocal one because consumer incomes, which are derived from the sale of productive services, also underlie the demands for commodities.

THE MARGINAL PRODUCTIVITY THEORY OF DISTRIBUTION

Generalization of Ricardo's Theory of Rent

The marginal productivity theory is an alternative hypothesis to the Austrian theory of imputation for explaining the functional distribution of income. The individual most closely associated with this theory is John Bates Clark, who gave this hypothesis its fullest exposition in *The Distribu-*

tion of Wealth (1899). He had already formulated, independently of Jevons, Menger, and Walrás, the hypothesis that the value of a commodity expresses the utility of the marginal unit to society as a whole. Examination of the problem of distribution was therefore the logical sequel to his inquiry into the problem of value.

The starting point of the marginal productivity theory of distribution is the demand for and the supply of the factors to individual hiring firms. Firms are assumed to have production functions in which factor proportions are variable and in which the contribution of the variable factor to the total product increases at a decreasing rate beyond a certain point, with the result that added inputs then cause the marginal physical product curve to be downward-sloping. Given a competitive market price for its product, the marginal physical product curve of a variable factor can be translated into a marginal revenue product curve by multiplication, i.e., $MPP(P) = MRP$. This curve is also the firm's demand curve for the factor in question because it indicates the revenue an additional unit of that factor will add.

Firms are also assumed to be confronted with factor supply curves which are perfectly elastic at the ruling market price. In other words, the factor market is assumed to be purely competitive. If, in addition, each firm is assumed to hire its factors in profit-maximizing proportions, each variable factor will be employed until the marginal revenue product it produces is equal to its price of hire. Since all factor inputs are variable in the long run, all factors will by employed in proportions which will make the ratio of their marginal revenue products equal to the ratio of their prices. The marginal productivity theory is, therefore, from the point of view of an individual firm, a theory of employment.

The market demand curve for a homogeneous factor represents the summation of the demand curves of individual firms with the necessary adjustment in the market price of the commodity being sold. The commodity price is, of course, no longer a parameter when the analysis is extended from the individual firm to the industry as a whole. Since the market price of a competitively produced product will fall as output is increased, the industry demand curve for a factor will fall more rapidly than the marginal revenue product curve of a factor to a firm. Given the supply of the factor which is available for employment, the productivity theory therefore establishes the market price per unit which will tend to prevail for a homogeneous factor in a static state. According to Clark's conception, a static state would exist "if labor and capital were to remain fixed in quantity, if improvements in the mode of production were to stop, if the consolidation of capital were to cease and if the wants of consumers were never to vary."[6]

Both Clark and Wicksteed recognized that the marginal productivity

---

[6] John Bates Clark, *The Distribution of Wealth* (London and New York: Macmillan & Co., 1899), Preface.

theory of distribution is a generalization of Ricardo's theory of rent.[7] Ricardo's theory viewed rent as the differential surplus which appears on land as a result of the difference between the value of the total product and the value of the marginal product of labor and capital in their intramarginal applications. There is no rent at the margin of cultivation because the marginal product of capital and labor is exhausted by wages and interest. In his case, land is assumed to be the fixed factor to which variable labor-capital inputs are applied. The surplus he called rent arises because the payment to the variable factor is determined by productivity of labor and capital at the margin.

FIGURE 13–2

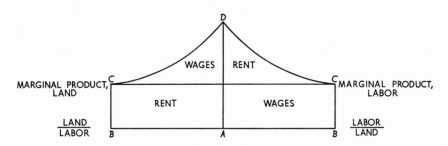

Wicksteed and Clark showed that if the inputs of capital and labor are assumed to be fixed and land is the variable factor, rent is the marginal product of land, while interest and wages constitute the residual surplus. Figure 13–2 represents the gist of their reasoning graphically. The right-hand portion of the diagram shows the classical case in which a fixed quantity of land is combined with increasing quantities of a given grade of labor. The curve *DC* represents the diminishing marginal product of labor. Since all units of labor are assumed to be homogeneous, and therefore perfect substitutes, the marginal productivity curve of labor establishes *BC* as the demand price per unit. Thus the rectangle labeled "Wages" represents labor's share of the total product on the basis of its productive contribution when the total product is *ABCD*. The area under the marginal productivity curve is, therefore, the return to land as the fixed factor. Rent is thus a differential surplus which remains after the payment of wages at a rate established by the marginal productivity of labor.

The left-hand portion of the diagram utilizes the same vertical axis to facilitate comparison and assumes labor as the fixed factor and land as the variable factor. It has also been assumed that the same total product,

———
[7] Wicksteed's generalization of Ricardo's theorem appears in *An Essay on the Co-ordination of the Laws of Distribution.* Clark's first exposition is in "Possibility of a Scientific Law of Wages," in *Publications of the American Economic Association,* Vol. IV, No. 1 (1889); also "Distribution as Determined by the Law of Rent," *Quarterly Journal of Economics,* Vol. V (Oct. 1890–July 91), pp. 289–318.

ABCD, is produced by varying land as by varying labor, and that the productivity curve is now that of land. In this case, rent is determined by the marginal productivity of land, while wages are a residual surplus. From this, Wicksteed and Clark deduced that all factors will be rewarded according to their marginal productivities, and that the total product will be exhausted when each factor is paid the equivalent of its marginal product. Proof of this proposition was, however, not provided by either Clark or Wicksteed, but by A. W. Flux in his review of Wicksteed's book.[8] Flux recognized that the distribution of factor rewards whose sum will equal the sum of the marginal products of the factors is consistent with production functions which are linearly homogeneous.

Wicksell and the Adding-Up Problem

Some of the most penetrating observations on the "adding-up problem," as the question of whether the total product is exactly exhausted by factor rewards equal to their marginal products has become known, were made by the Swedish economist Knut Wicksell. He recognized that the sum of the marginal products will equal the total product if the production function is homogeneous and linear, or if the presence of pure competition causes firms to achieve optimum size in the long run.[9] The entry and exodus of firms in response to short-run profits or losses will result in a tendency for firms to operate at an output level which is consistent with the lowest point of their long-run average cost curve. When output is at this level, it will coincide with that point on the production function which is linear and homogeneous. Thus, even if the production function as a whole is not linearly homogeneous, Euler's theorem applies at the long-run, least-cost point, for at this point returns are constant.

If either increasing returns to scale or decreasing returns to scale prevail, the payment of the factors in accordance with the value of their marginal products cannot exactly exhaust the value of the total product. That this is necessarily the case can easily be seen in terms of long-run return to outlay. In the case of increasing returns, the marginal return to outlay is greater than the average return; while in the case of decreasing returns, it is smaller. Thus, in the case of increasing returns, the value of the total product is too small to reward all factors according to the value of their marginal products; and in the case of decreasing returns, a surplus will remain after the factors have received rewards equal to the value of their marginal products. However, Wicksell maintained that neither of these situations is likely to prevail in the long run under competition because of the tendency for firms to achieve optimum size and therefore to operate under conditions of long-run constant cost. Instead of conceiving of in-

---

[8] In *Economic Journal,* Vol. IV, June 1894, p. 305.

[9] Knut Wicksell, *Lectures on Political Economy* (New York: Macmillan Co., 1934), Vol. I, pp. 126–31.

creasing returns, decreasing returns, and constant returns as being mutually exclusive situations, Wicksell regarded these conditions as governing different phases of a firms' long-run cost curve. While increasing returns are likely to prevail in the initial phases of a firm's expansion, decreasing returns will assert themselves beyond some point. The transitional phase, in which these forces are balanced, is the stage of constant returns and costs, which is the optimum long-run condition for a firm under pure competition. The output at which long-run marginal cost equals long-run marginal revenue is also the one at which total cost equals total revenue. Therefore the payment of the factors according to the value of their marginal product would exactly exhaust the value of the total product.

Clark's Ethical Interpretation of the Marginal Productivity Theory

The "natural laws" of income distribution which Clark sought to formulate in *The Distribution of Wealth* are those which would operate in a static state from which all changes have been abstracted. These laws, if they were able to work without friction, "would give to every agent of production the amount of wealth that agent creates."[10] Thus, Clark's conception of the problem of functional distribution was, at the very outset, placed squarely in the realm of ethics. The position taken was that if everyone receives precisely the value of what he or the resources he owns creates, there is no basis for grievance. If, on the other hand, a factor does not receive its full product, there is "institutional robbery" and therefore a potentially disruptive condition in the society. Hence, in Clark's view, an understanding of the laws of distribution is basic to providing insight into the "right of society to exist in its present form, and the probability that it will continue so to exist. . . ."[11]

While Clark's earlier work, *The Philosophy of Wealth,* questioned the efficiency and justice of competition in the economic sphere, a fundamental change of attitude is evident in *The Distribution of Wealth* with respect to the role of competitive forces as a beneficial influence. In the earlier volume, he conceived of competition as being self-destructive and the immorality of the marketplace as being incompatible with economic justice and social harmony. In the later volume, competition is viewed in a different light, namely, as the force which "insures to the public the utmost that the existing power of man can give in the way of efficient service."[12]

The logic by which Clark came ultimately to have faith in competition as a perfect regulatory mechanism is not difficult to perceive. Competition forces product prices to equal costs of production. Pure profits are therefore absent because all the changes associated with entrepreneurial risk are

---

[10] Clark, *The Distribution of Wealth,* Preface, p. v.

[11] *Ibid.,* p. 3.

[12] *Ibid.,* p. 77.

absent and the entrepreneurial function is reduced to that of a special kind of labor. Incomes which accrue in excess of contractual costs and imputed wages and interest to the owners exist only because they are imperfectly eliminated by competitive forces, or because new frictions develop. These frictions are the source of what Frank Knight, writing during the 1920's, called "uncertainty."[13] In Knight's view, it is the entrepreneur's uncertainty about the demand for his product, and therefore the price at which he can sell it, that causes him to hire productive factors, not on the basis of the actual value of their marginal products, but on the basis of expected value. Profits or losses thus materialize if actual product values diverge from those which are anticipated.

Competition also forces all factor rewards to be equal to the value of the factor's marginal product. The fact that entrepreneurial demands for factors are based on their marginal revenue product rather than their marginal value product creates no difficulty within Clark's framework of perfect competition, for in this case the two are equal. Thus, Clark argued that in the static state, competition among workers would keep the wage rate from rising above the point at which the value of the marginal product of labor equals the marginal revenue product of labor, while competition among employers would prevent it from being less. Competition among the suppliers of capital funds and those who demand them would likewise assure that the interest rate is neither more nor less than that at which the value of the marginal product of capital is equal to the marginal revenue product of capital.

A further reason for Clark's laudatory attitude toward competition stems from the relationship between the natural laws of distribution and the natural laws of value. Although Clark does not systematically develop a theory of value, he accepts as correct the Ricardo-Mill view that the natural price of a commodity is its cost price.[14] But whereas the classicists conceived of prices as being determined by cost of production in the long run, Clark conceived of price as being an indication of the social cost of acquisition of commodities. Money costs, therefore, reflect the pain and sacrifice incurred by factors in production. These costs are measured subjectively by individuals, as are the utilities of goods. The market, however, transforms individual costs into social costs and individual utilities into social utilities. The "universal law" of economics is that costs and benefits are everywhere equalized. The social organism as a whole is visualized as capable of rationally weighing the social marginal utility of goods against the social marginal cost of acquiring them and maximizing the social welfare by balancing them one against the other. Thus the static state constitutes the ideal for Clark in much the same way that the natural order

---

[13] Frank Knight, *Risk, Uncertainty and Profit* (Boston and New York, Houghton Mifflin Co., 1921).

[14] Clark, *The Distribution of Wealth*, p. 230.

was ideal for the thinkers of the eighteenth century. The major impediment, in his view, to the attainment of this millennium is the growth of monopoly power and the consequent necessity for government regulation to hold its spread in check.

Limitations of the Marginal Productivity Theory of Distribution

The marginal productivity theory of income distribution maintained that in the long run under perfect competition, all factors of production, including entrepreneurs, tend to receive a real rate of return equal to the "social value" of their marginal physical product. Since the profits of enterpreneurs tend to be no higher than normal, i.e., they tend to equal the marginal productivity of that kind of labor, the total product of society is exactly exhausted by the payments made to the factors.

This theory is premised on the behavior of an individual firm under perfect competition with respect to the purchase of a single variable factor when all other factor inputs and their prices and the state of the arts are fixed. In this case a firm is always confronted with a given sales price for its output, so that its total revenue is a function of its output. Its marginal revenue, therefore, expresses the share of the sales proceeds of a firm which will be available to pay any given factor of production.

The marginal productivity theory was not, however, intended simply as a theory of the behavior of the individual firm with respect to the employment of a homogeneous factor at the going market price. It was also intended as a theory of per unit price determination. There are limitations inherent in its use for this purpose. Specifically, the marginal productivity theory neglects completely the influence of factor supplies in determining factor prices. The marginal productivity of a factor explains the demand for a factor, but a complete theory of factor price determination must also consider the economic and social factors which determine factor supplies. This is precisely why Alfred Marshall, the foremost English contributor of the period, shied away from a marginal productivity theory of distribution in favor of a theory which recognized the interaction of demand and supply forces.

A much more formidable difficulty is encountered in making the transition from the demand for a variable factor by a firm to the demand by an industry, and from there to the demand by the economy. The marginal revenue product of a factor to a given firm is calculated on the basis of an assumed product price. This price is itself premised on a given product demand curve, which is drawn up on the assumption that consumer preferences, the prices of other goods, and the level of income are given. The latter assumption poses a special difficulty for the theory of income determination because every change in the marginal revenue product of a factor, and therefore in its compensation, must necessarily affect the product demand curves of the firms in the economy. This must, in turn, affect the marginal revenue product on which the demand for the factor depends. Nevertheless, marginal productivity theory implicitly ignores the interdependence of factor demand curves and product demand curves.[15] This is the reason why John Maynard Keynes, writing during the 1930's, objected to wage cuts as a suitable method for dealing with the problem of mass unemployment. A wage cut will cause an individual firm to employ additional workers until the marginal revenue product of labor equals the new wage rate because the demand for its product is not likely to be affected. But if wage rates everywhere are reduced, product demand curves, and therefore the demand for labor itself, are altered, so that the derivation of industry and market demand curves for a factor cannot be accomplished by the simple process of summing up individual firms' factor demand curves. Marginal productivity theory has a microeconomic bias which limits the validity of the conclusions it can yield when its application is extended. What the marginal productivity principle provides is not an explanation of factor prices but rather a basis for understanding an employer's demand for a particular factor of production at a given market price.

The normative implications inherent in the marginal productivity theory have been another source of criticism. The theory implies that if a factor is compensated according to the value of its marginal product, it is receiving a just payment. Yet, when a firm hires a factor in a market which is not purely competitive or sells its product in a market which is not purely competitive, the value of its marginal product (i.e., the marginal physical product multiplied by the sale price of the good) is not equal to its marginal revenue product (i.e., the marginal physical product multiplied by the marginal revenue the sale of a product yields). It follows that the absence of pure competition, either in the product market or in the factor market, is associated with "exploitation" in the sense that the marginal increment of the factor cannot then receive a compensation which is equivalent to the value of its marginal product.[16]

CONCLUDING REMARKS

The formulation of a theory of the exchange value of commodities on the basis of the principle of marginal utility eventually led to the development of parallel theories of factor rewards based on the principle of marginal productivity. The Austrian theory of imputation, which derives the values of higher order goods from their contributions to the social marginal utility, is a direct extension of the theory of value introduced by Carl Menger. The marginal productivity theory of distribution, which is associated most closely with John Bates Clark, is an alternative hypothesis

---

[15] Sidney Weintraub, *An Approach to the Theory of Income Distribution* (Philadelphia: Chilton Co., 1958), chap. i.

[16] See chapter 16 below.

which relates the price per unit of a homogeneous factor of production to the value of the product it produces in its marginal application. This theory is premised on the assumption that factor proportions are variable and that the return to the variable factor will increase at a decreasing rate beyond a certain point. It is therefore a generalization of Ricardo's theory of rent, in that any factor, not just land, may be the fixed factor whose return appears as a differential surplus which remains after the variable factor is paid at a rate which is established by its marginal productivity.

In Clark's interpretation, the payment of factor rewards which are determined according to the marginal productivity principle is consistent with the natural law of income distribution. In his view, every agent is justly compensated when it receives the equivalent of its own product; and the payment of each factor according to the value of its marginal product will, in the competitive long-run static state, exactly exhaust the total product.

Looked at from the point of view of the individual firm, marginal productivity theory is essentially a theory of factor employment. Looked at from the point of view of the market as a whole, it purports to explain the per unit price of a homogeneous factor in a competitive market. It is in this respect that the validity of its conclusions are most limited. Specifically, the price of a particular factor cannot be explained without reference to the supply of the factor. Nor is it sound to explain the price of a factor in terms of a factor demand curve which is itself premised on a given product demand curve when product demand curves and factor demand curves are in fact interdependent. The microeconomic bias of the marginal productivity theory, therefore, limits its usefulness in explaining the level of factor rewards, though it is a valid principle for explaining the extent to which a firm will employ a particular factor at a given price.

While the whole theory of distribution was substantially reconstructed after 1870 with the application of the marginal principle to the explanation of factor rewards, some of the most substantive contributions to the development of distribution theory were made in the area of capital and interest theory. Again, progress is largely the result of Austrian, American, and Swedish contributions. Specifically, the leading contributors to the development of the theory of capital and interest were Eugen Böhm-Bawerk, Irving Fisher, and Knut Wicksell. Their contributions are examined in the chapter which follows.

SUGGESTIONS FOR FURTHER READING

CASSELS, JOHN M. "On the Law of Variable Proportions," in *Explorations in Economics*. New York: McGraw-Hill Book Co., Inc., 1936. Reprinted in *Readings in the Theory of Income Distribution* (Philadelphia: Blakiston Co., 1949).

CLARK, JOHN BATES. *The Distribution of Wealth*. London and New York: Macmillan & Co., 1899.

CLARK, J. M. "Distribution," *Encyclopedia of the Social Sciences*, Vol. V (1931). Reprinted in *Readings in the Theory of Income Distribution*. Philadelphia: Blakiston Co., 1949.

DOUGLAS, PAUL H. *The Theory of Wages*, chaps. i–ii. New York: Macmillan Co., 1934.

HUTCHISON, T. W. *A Review of Economic Doctrines, 1870–1929*, particularly chaps. v, x, xv, and xvi. Oxford: Clarendon Press, 1953.

STIGLER, GEORGE. "Production and Distribution in the Short Run," *Journal of Political Economy*, Vol. XLVII (June, 1939). Reprinted in *Readings in the Theory of Income Distribution*. Philadelphia: Blakiston Co., 1949.

———. *Production and Distribution Theories*, chaps. i–vii and xii. New York: Macmillan Co., 1941.

UHR, CARL G. *The Economic Doctrines of Knut Wicksell*, chap. iv. Berkeley: University of California Press, 1960.

WEINTRAUB, SIDNEY. *An Approach to the Theory of Income Distribution*, Philadelphia: Chilton Co., 1958.

Chapter 14

CONTRIBUTIONS TO THE THEORY OF CAPITAL, INTEREST, AND THE PRICE LEVEL

INTRODUCTION

The least satisfactory aspect of the theory of distribution during the closing decades of the nineteenth century concerned the return to capital. Interest and profit were still not clearly distinguished from each other, nor was there agreement about the nature and origin of capital. Several reasons suggest themselves for the continued identification of interest and profit. The first is that Adam Smith, though he clearly distinguished between profit and interest, conceived of interest as being a derivative of profit. Secondly, the fact that entrepreneurs were usually also capitalists obliterated their functional differences in practice, and this was undoubtedly reflected in attempts at explanation. Also significant is the fact that capital itself was conceived of largely as a stock of wage goods out of which advances were made to workers, rather than as a stock of producer goods used for further production. Thus the relationship of the return on capital to the lengthening of the time span of the production process and abstinence was understandably more apparent and more emphasized than its relationship to the productivity of capital, though an appreciation of the greater productivity of roundabout methods of production was by no means absent from classical analysis. Indeed, this is the essence of Nassau Senior's third postulate, though he associated the existence of profit more precisely with abstinence than with the productivity of capital. Senior's explanation of profit was, of course, obviously unacceptable to those who held a labor theory of value. The latter rejected the idea that capital—or "abstinence," as Senior called it—is a separate factor of production and interpreted interest as well as profit as a form of surplus value. No effective rebuttal had yet been made to this line of reasoning.

Another matter requiring clarification concerned the effect of capital accumulation and invention on the distributive shares in the economy. The question as to whether accumulation and invention had a beneficial or adverse affect on particular classes had originally been posed by David Ricardo in his famous chapter, "On Machinery." There was also the question as to whether interest is an income uniquely related to capital goods or a flow of income which reflects the capitalized value of any asset which yields an output or a service over a period of time. If the latter is the case, there is no real difference between the income of natural agents and capital goods or between the income from capital goods and that derived from securities and other capital assets.

Still another question concerning interest which was examined during this period became a matter of great importance during the 1930's. This is the question of whether interest is a monetary or nonmonetary phenomenon. The interest theories of the classical writers were nonmonetary. Unlike their mercantilist predecessors, who conceived of the interest rate as reflecting changes in the value of money, classical writers thought of changes in the quantity of money as affecting only the general price level. The classical conception of interest as a nonmonetary phenomenon continued to be the predominant point of view throughout the latter part of the nineteenth century and on into the twentieth century. Not until the depression of the 1930's was the conception of interest as a monetary phenomenon revived and acclaimed anew.

Contributors to the Theory of Capital and Interest

The individuals who are especially remembered for their efforts with respect to the theory of capital and interest, and the relationship between movements of the interest rate and the general price level, are the Austrian Eugen Böhm-Bawerk; his Swedish follower, Knut Wicksell; and the American Irving Fisher. The earliest contributor was Böhm-Bawerk, who, in true Austrian tradition, developed his theory of interest as an aspect of the theory of imputation. Böhm-Bawerk (1851–1914) was a close boyhood friend and later a brother-in-law of Friedrich von Wieser. He devoted most of his adult life to public service as the Austrian Minister of Finance, so that his career as an academician, especially during the middle years of his life, was sandwiched in among his official duties. As a younger man, before entering the civil service, he taught for eight years at the University of Innsbruck. In his later years, he returned to teaching once more at the University of Vienna. Like von Wieser, his interest in economics was theoretical; his primary subject of inquiry was the theory of capital and interest.

While Böhm-Bawerk was well aware of the sociological and political aspects of the problems of capital and interest, they were of no concern to him with respect to examining their role in economic activity. He was a pure scientist who sought general economic laws that would be universally valid for any economic system. The essential characteristic of capitalism resides, in his opinion, in its employment of roundabout as opposed to direct methods of production. The ownership of capital is a purely incidental question. Any economic system which employs roundabout methods of production is capitalistic, and a net return to capital will exist regardless of institutional characteristics. Thus the theoretical problem which he posed, and to which he sought an answer, was essentially the same as that posed by Marx, namely: Why does surplus value accrue in an endless stream to capital? However, Böhm-Bawerk rejected the Marxian contention that interest and profit are manifestations of the exploitation inherent in capitalism, and formulated an alternative explanation on the basis of Menger's marginal utility theory.

While Böhm-Bawerk's hypothesis was intended to be neutral, his explanation of the circumstances which give rise to interest provided an implicit justification for its receipt by the capitalists of society. It therefore had political and sociological overtones which made it sympathetic to the capitalistic system. Joseph A. Schumpeter's well-known description of Böhm-Bawerk as the bourgeois Karl Marx is thus particularly appropriate.

Böhm-Bawerk's work in the theory of capital and interest was a source of stimulus to Wicksell, whose contribution to the general theory of production and distribution was examined in the preceding chapter. But Wicksell had neither the intellect nor the temperament of a mere follower. The originality of his thought is nowhere more in evidence than in his theory of capital and interest, particularly as it relates to the area of monetary theory. These contributions were begun during his graduate school days and came to full fruition during the period between 1900 and 1916 while he held the chair of political economy at Lund University in Sweden.

Irving Fisher (1867–1947) was a statistician and mathematician as well as an economic theorist. All of his work aimed at advancing economic theory in relation to mathematics and statistics. This objective was already evident in his first work, *Mathematical Investigations in the Theory of Value and Prices* (1892), which first appeared as his Ph.D. thesis. He is perhaps best known for *The Purchasing Power of Money* (1911), in which he attempted to measure the elements in the equation of exchange in order to test the relationship between changes in the quantity of money and changes in the general price level.

From the standpoint of the development of distribution theory, Fisher's special contribution is in the area of the theory of the interest rate. His ideas are given their most fully developed exposition in *The Theory of Interest*, which was published in 1930 as a revision of his earlier volume, *The Rate of Interest* (1907). The central idea of this book, which is dedicated to both Böhm-Bawerk and the latter's forerunner, John Rae, is that interest is not a separate form of income but is an element common to all income shares which accrue over a period of time.

BÖHM-BAWERK'S AGIO THEORY OF INTEREST

The Value of Present versus Future Goods

The development of interest theory and the necessarily related area of capital theory emerged, during the period under consideration, as a special aspect of distribution theory. Interest theory during this period sought, in the main, to explain the real rate of remuneration of capital relative to the prices of other factors of production and was little concerned with the relationship between changes in the interest rate and the general price level or changes in the level of aggregate income, output, and employment.

The earliest of these nonmonetary theories of interest is Böhm-Bawerk's agio theory. His point of departure was Menger's marginal utility theory of value, to which he added his own solution, different from von Wieser's, of the imputation problem. His theory of capital and interest was developed within this typically Austrian conception of the problem of valuation. It was presented in a three-volume magnum opus entitled *Capital and Interest,* whose first volume, *History and Criticism of Interest Theories,* appeared in 1884 and set the groundwork for the two subsequent volumes. This volume presents a detailed review and criticism of all the theories on the subject of interest which had been previously formulated. It thus provides the background for Böhm-Bawerk's definitive statement of his own views on capital and interest in his *Positive Theory of Capital,* which was published in 1889 as the second volume of his triology.

The key to the problem of capital as a means of production and as a source of a net return is, in Böhm-Bawerk's view, an understanding of the nature of the production process in which the original factors, labor and resources, transform matter into want-satisfying goods. These may be consumer goods or "produced means of production." When production proceeds with the aid of produced means of production, the same input of original factors results in a larger total product than when direct methods of production are employed. This observation, which was not completely original with Böhm-Bawerk, but which had never been given detailed formulation before, became one of the pillars of his theory of capital and interest. He reasoned that the net return to capital must result from the effect which the greater productivity of the roundabout method has on the formation of value and also must be related to the postponement of consumption inherent in roundabout production. This is the reason why he sees the problem of capital and interest as part of the broader problem of value. Goods have value only because they have utility; the want-satisfying power of a particular unit of a given good depends not only on the total quantity which is available, but also on the dimension of time in which it is available.

Capital goods are, in Böhm-Bawerk's view, not original and independent factors of production, but are simply intermediate products which yield final goods after a period of waiting. The more capitalistic, or roundabout, a process of production is, the longer will be the interval of waiting time which will elapse before the final goods emerge from the production process. Any good which is available in the present has a greater value than an equal quantity of the same kind available at some time in the future. Present goods, therefore, command an agio, or premium, over future goods.

The Three Reasons for Interest

Böhm-Bawerk advanced three separate reasons for the higher value placed on present goods. The first two are of a psychological nature and are relevant to the demand for consumer loans, namely, the hope which most people entertain of being better able to provide for future wants and the all too human tendency to underestimate future wants. These factors reinforce one another and enhance the value of present goods. The third reason for the greater value of present goods is technical rather than psychological and relates to the demand for producer loans. Presently available goods are "technically superior" instruments for the satisfaction of human wants and therefore yield a higher utility than future goods. Böhm-Bawerk illustrates this principle with an example intended to demonstrate that the want-satisfying power of any presently available productive resource, say 30 days of labor, is greater than that of 30 days of labor used in the same production process which will become available in a year's time.[1] By the same reasoning, 30 days of labor which became available last month are technically superior to the same quantity which became available only this month. Precisely the same principle applies to the utilities which are produced by capital goods. Unless there is a change in the state of the arts which will enhance the productivity of still-to-be-produced capital goods, those capital goods which are already on hand are "technically superior" to those which are not yet available because the time interval which must elapse before they generate finished goods is shorter than that which would necessarily elapse if these intermediate products were not yet available. Thus, presently available intermediate goods have a greater value productivity and are therefore technically superior with respect to want satisfaction than those not yet available. Hence, their use in time-consuming roundabout methods of production will yield a product which contains a surplus value.

The concept of the period of production is an integral part of the Austrian theory of capital. If only the third reason for interest were operative, the greater productivity of the roundabout method would result in an infinitely long period of production. The operation of the first and second reasons, however, which cause the value of future goods to be discounted in the present, implies that the period of production cannot be infinitely long. It is therefore the interaction between the first two and the third of Böhm-Bawerk's "three grounds" which will determine the optimum length of the production period in terms of its yield of present value. Thus the agio in the exchange of present for future goods derives, on the one hand from the fact that for psychological reasons future values are discounted in the present and, on the other, from the fact that the roundabout method of production yields a greater value product. It is precisely because

---

[1] Eugen Böhm-Bawerk, *Capital and Interest,* Vol. II: *Positive Theory of Capital,* trans. G. D. Huncke (South Holland, Ill.: Liberaterian Press, 1959), pp. 273–89.

the three grounds for the value agio of present over future goods are not equally operative for all individuals that there is a market for exchanging present against future goods. The preference at the margin for present versus future goods is objectively expressed in the rate of interest. This rate is the price phenomenon which reflects the difference in value between present and future commodities.

The Forms of Interest

Böhm-Bawerk considers the simplest manifestation of interest to be that which arises in connection with consumer loans. A borrower, in order to acquire present goods, finds he must pay interest to the lender who makes the funds available. However, the principle form in which interest manifests itself is as a profit to entrepreneurs. The latter buy remote goods, such as raw materials, tools, machines, and the use of land and labor, and transform them into finished products ready for consumption. For performing this function, they receive, in addition to the compensation for their managerial services, a gain which is proportioned to the amount of capital invested in their business. This gain, which has variously been called "profit," "surplus value," and "natural interest on capital," arises, according to Böhm-Bawerk, from the fact that the goods of remote rank which the businessman transforms are, economically speaking, future commodities. They are incapable of satisfying wants in their present form and need to be transformed into consumption goods in order to do so. They are, in effect, therefore, future commodities which have a lower present value than they will have when the transformation process is complete. The increase in value is, according to Böhm-Bawerk, the profit of capital.[2] Profit is therefore a price agio which appears in exchange transactions between capitalists, on the one hand, and workers and landlords who own the original means of production, on the other. Differently expressed, profit is a discount from the money value of the future marginal product of the original means of production. It follows that even in a socialist society the value of a worker is the equivalent only of the discounted value of his product rather than the whole product, and the same is true of land. That is, both rent and wages are the monetary expression of the marginal products of a given quantity of labor and land discounted to the present. This would, in Böhm-Bawerk's view, be equally true in a socialist society, for labor and land can in any case receive only the present or discounted value of their future product.[3]

---

[2] *Ibid.*, pp. 299–302.

[3] The American theorist Frank Taussig combined the marginal productivity theory of factor rewards with Böhm-Bawerk's theory of time preference to develop the hypothesis that competitive wages tend to be equal to the discounted value of labor's marginal product because wages represent an advance made by employers against the finished product. See *Wages and Capital* (New York: Appleton & Co., 1898).

FISHER'S THEORY OF INTEREST

The Nature of Interest

The issue as to whether the "third reason" which Böhm-Bawerk advanced as a basis for a positive rate of interest is really independent of the other two has given rise to a considerable body of literature.[4] Böhm-Bawerk himself regarded it as a separate reason, though others, Irving Fisher in particular, have argued that a positive rate of interest could not arise from this reason alone. Fisher's argument was that the greater productivity of roundabout methods of production explains only the willingness of borrowers to pay a premium. But the necessity of paying a premium derives from the first two reasons, which explain why people discount the future.

The distinctive features of Fisher's theory of interest derive from his conception of interest as "an index of the community's preference for a dollar of present over a dollar of future income." This notion was first advanced in *The Rate of Interest* (1907), the revision of which in 1930 as *The Theory of Interest* resulted in "the peak achievement, so far as perfection within its own frame is concerned, of the literature of interest."[5] Fisher suggested that the nature of interest and its determinatuon can best be understood if interest is conceived of in relation to income rather than capital because "capital wealth is merely the means to the end called income, while capital value is merely the capitalization of expected income."[6] He therefore objected to that part of Böhm-Bawerk's explanation of interest which is based on what the latter called the technical superiority of present goods. He objected not only to the concept of the production period but also to the thesis that the longer the average period of production, the larger the final product will be. But he considered Böhm-Bawerk's fatal error to be the notion that the greater productivity of lengthier processes over shorter ones, which makes present goods technically superior to future goods, is an independent cause of interest.[7] Fisher did not deny the technical superiority of present goods in Böhm-Bawerk's sense of the term, but maintained that this is not an independent cause of interest but one which operates through its effect on wants and the provision for them in the present and in the future. The fact that capital is productive will not,

---

[4] See, in particular, Böhm-Bawerk, *op. cit.,* pp. 260–75; Irving Fisher, *The Theory of Interest* (New York: Macmillan Co., 1930), pp. 476–85; Guy Arvidsson, "On the Reasons for a Rate of Interest," trans. A. Williams, in *International Economic Papers,* No. 6 (New York: Macmillan Co., 1956), pp. 23–33, from *Ekonomisk Tidschrift,* March, 1953.

[5] Joseph A. Schumpeter, *Ten Great Economists* (London: Oxford University Press, 1965), p. 230.

[6] Fisher, *op. cit.,* p. 61.

[7] Irving Fisher, *The Rate of Interest* (New York: The Macmillan Co., 1907), p. 55.

in and of itself, cause people to prefer income today in preference to income tomorrow. But the productivity of capital will affect the relative abundance of present and future goods, and therefore the willingness of people to pay a premium for income available today instead of in the future. Thus, Fisher sees the interest rate of being determined by the actions of people to alter the time flow of their income receipts.

Individual Equilibrium

The alteration of the time flow of the income stream is made possible by the existence of a loan market and a market in which capital assets can be purchased and sold. Thus, Fisher sees the interest rate as being determined in part by a subjective element analogous to Böhm-Bawerk's first and second grounds which he calls "human impatience." This factor interacts with an objective factor which Fisher calls the "principle of investment opportunity." It is the interaction of these two factors which determines the rate of interest to which each individual adjusts himself, and therefore the time flow of his income according to his degree of impatience and his opportunity for investment.

Fisher's demonstration of the way in which these factors interact begins on an individual level with an examination of adjustments to an already established rate of interest and proceeds to an explanation of market equilibrium. For an individual, the adjustment is a matter of altering the time shape of his income stream to bring his marginal preference rate into harmony with an already established interest rate. If his preference rate is above the market rate, he will "sell some of his surplus future income in return for an addition to his meager present income, i.e., he will borrow. . . . On the other hand, the man, whose temperament or whose income stream or both give him a preference rate below the market rate, will buy future income with some of his abundant present income, i.e., he will lend."[8] One's income stream can also be modified by selecting among investment opportunities which offer alternative ways of utilizing resources such as capital, land, labor, or money to produce an income stream.[9] The relative attractiveness of alternative investment opportunities depends on the rate of interest which prevails. Fisher calls the hypothetical rate of interest which will equalize the present worth of two investment options the "rate of return over cost." Individuals select those investment opportunities which maximize the present worth of their income stream by equating the expected marginal rate of return over cost with the rate of interest. Changing expectations, which reflect individual estimates of the technical possibilities of alternative investments as well as their imagination and courage, cause shifts among alternative investment opportunities.

Fisher supplemented his description of the way in which an individual

---

8 Fisher, *The Theory of Interest,* p. 104.

9 *Ibid.,* p. 151.

adjusts his rates of time preference, or impatience, and his opportunities for investment to the real rate of interest confronting him with geometric demonstrations like those of Figure 14–1, in which absolute amounts of this year's income are measured along the horizontal axis and equivalent amounts of next year's income on the vertical axis.[10] Part A of Figure 14–1 shows that in the absence of a market in which an individual can lend, borrow, and invest, the modification of the time incidence of his income stream is impossible. Thus the income position of an individual who has a certain real income at present and an expected claim to an equivalent amount of future income can be denoted by some point, *P,* along the vector which represents a constant income stream. Additional points along this

FIGURE 14–1

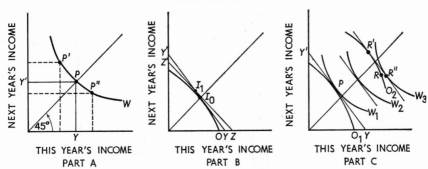

| THIS YEAR'S INCOME | THIS YEAR'S INCOME | THIS YEAR'S INCOME |
| PART A | PART B | PART C |

vector represent larger or smaller combinations of present and future income. But if there is no market in which he can trade some of this year's income for some of next year's, or vice versa, his income combination will always lie along this line, no matter what his preferences about the time incidence of his income may be.

There are any number of possible combinations of real present and future income with which the individual might be equally well satisfied. He may, for example, be willing to sacrifice, either by lending or investing, two units of this year's income for three units of next year's. This willingness is represented by point *P'* in Part A of Figure 14–1. Or he may be willing to sacrifice one unit of next year's income in exchange for an addition of two units to this year's income, as represented by point *P''.* The connection of a series of these points results in a curve like *W,* which Fisher called a "willingness line." There will be a whole family of willingness lines for each individual in which more preferred combinations of this year's and next year's income will be to the right of *W* and less preferred combinations to the left. Fisher drew his willingness lines, which might also be called

---

[10] A lucid graphic description of Fisher's interest theory is included in J. W. Conard, *An Introduction to the Theory of Interest* (Berkeley: University of California Press, 1959), chap. iv.

"indifference curves," convex to the origin, on the assumption that present income is preferred to future income.

Whether an individual will alter the time flow of his income depends on his degree of impatience, his investment opportunities, and the interest rate to which he must adjust himself. Fisher's graphic demonstration of an individual's possibility for altering the time flow of his income stream utilized what he called an "investment opportunity curve." Such a curve is an "envelope," like the one marked *"O"* in Part B of Figure 14–1, of the most profitable investments among which an individual can choose. Each such curve is concave to the origin because of the principle of diminishing returns from investment. Given the rate of interest, it will be profitable for an individual to invest in real capital goods along his opportunity curve until the rate of return over cost is equal to the rate of interest. Assuming an interest rate of $Y'Y$, this equality exists when the opportunity curve is tangent at I_1 to the interest line. If, however, the opportunity curve is tangent to an interest line like $Z'Z$ at I_0, which coincides with the constant income line, there will be no inducement to invest because the expected rate of return over cost is zero.

But the investment opportunity curve only illustrates the range of possibilities which are open to an individual to alter the time flow of his income by investing. His inclination to avail himself of these opportunities is shown by the slope of his willingness line at its point of tangency with the interest rate line. A willingness line like W_3 in Part C of Figure 14–1, which has a slope greater than unity, indicates a positive time preference; i.e., the individual will borrow. If the point of tangency intersects the vector representing the constant income stream, as is the case when an individual willingness curve is like W_2, the individual's time preference at interest rate $Y'Y$ is neutral. Such an individual will neither borrow nor lend nor invest at that rate. Individuals whose willingness lines are like W_1, which has an absolute slope less than one at its intersection with the line representing a constant income stream, have a negative time preference at interest rate $Y'Y$. If such individuals are also confronted with an investment opportunity curve like O_1, they will optimize the stream of present and future income by (1) investing an amount of present income which will yield an expected rate of return equal to the rate of interest and (2) lending an amount of present income to acquire a claim on additional future income. This reduces this year's income until its present value is equal to the interest rate. Thus the individual will have maximized his position with respect to borrowing, lending, saving, and investing to alter the time flow of his income when his willingness curve and his investment opportunity curve are tangent to each other and the interest line at point P, as is the case for willingness curve W_1 and opportunity curve O_1 in Part C of Figure 14–1.

The double adjustment pictured with the help of the investment opportunity line and willingness line W_1 is only one among many. Another individual might begin with an income combination of R. Given the interest line, he will first move along the investment opportunity line to point R', where the opportunity line is tangent to the interest line. He will then move along the interest line to R'', where the interest line is tangent to a willingness line. That is, given the rate of interest, the individual will shift in such manner that the marginal rate of return over cost and the marginal rate of time preference will both be equal to the market rate of interest. The sequence of this adjustment is that the point of tangency on the investment opportunity line is always found first. This is because "there is only one opportunity line and only one point on it at which the slope corresponds to the rate of interest, while there are an infinite number of W lines with a point on each having that slope or direction."[11]

Market Equilibrium

In a purely competitive market in which income streams can be freely modified by lending, borrowing, and investing, expected rates of return over cost and rates of impatience for present over future income for all individuals will become equal to each other and the rate of interest at the margin. From the standpoint of the market as a whole, the exploitation of alternative investment opportunities is the objective factor which interacts with the impatience principle to establish the rate of interest. "The more we invest and postpone our gratification, the lower the investment opportunity rate becomes, but the greater the impatience rate; the more we spend and hasten our gratification, the lower the impatience rate becomes but the higher the opportunity rate."[12] Individuals' adjustments to differentials in these rates will ultimately push all impatience rates and all opportunity rates to equality. When this equality obtains, the real rate of interest is in equilibrium and exactly reflects the premium that people are willing to pay for present as opposed to future income.

Whether this rate will be positive "depends entirely on the conformation of the O curve and the W curves of each person in the loan market."[13] If the slope of both the willingness and the opportunity curves is greater than unity at their point of tangency with each other, the real rate of interest will be positive. By the same logic, Fisher concluded that the real rate could be zero only if the slope of both the willingness curve and the investment opportunity curve were unity at their point of tangency because the degree of time preference is then neutral and the net productivity of capital zero.

Real and Money Rates of Interest and the Price Level

Fisher also investigated the relationship between the real and the money rates of interest. The relationship between these two rates depends,

---

[11] Fisher, *The Theory of Interest*, p. 272.

[12] *Ibid.*, p. 177.

[13] *Ibid.*, p. 283.

he thought, on the behavior of the general price level, whose determination he fully investigated in *The Purchasing Power of Money* (1911).

His explanation of changes in the general price level sought to relate the price level (P) with the quantity of money in circulation (M), its velocity of circulation (V), and the volume of trade (T). The statistical measurement of these components led him to introduce checking deposits (M') and their velocity (V'), so that his equation of exchange reads $MV + M'V' = PT$. His statistical studies concluded that in virtually all cases of substantial price change, the active variable in the equation of exchange was M, the quantity of money in circulation. One basis for this conclusion is that P is "normally the one absolutely passive element in the equation of exchange."[14] In addition, V and V', which reflect the spending habits of the community, are short-run constants. Moreover, autonomous variations in M' cannot take place because there is a stable relationship between primary money, bank reserves, and the volume of checking deposits. Thus, Fisher concluded that changes in the quantity of money are the source of changes in the general price level.

What bearing does a change in the general price level have on money rates of interest? Fisher's inquiry into the interaction of the impatience principle and the investment opportunity principle explained only the phenomenon of the real rate of interest. Yet the behavior of real and money rates is obviously related. Fisher reasoned that if there is no change in the general price level, the money rate of interest on a risk-free loan will be equal to the real rate of interest. If, however, the price level is changing, this will be reflected in the behavior of the money rate. More specifically, the money rate of interest on a risk-free loan will be equal, says Fisher, to the real rate as determined by the opportunity to invest, plus or minus the change in the general price level.[15]

WICKSELL'S THEORY OF CAPITAL AND INTEREST

Capital Accumulation and the Distributive Shares

Wicksell's concern with the theory of capital and interest is the outgrowth of his examination of Böhm-Bawerk's works. His critical examination and restatement of the latter's theory is a contribution in and of itself, particularly as it relates to his introduction of the concept of the capital structure. The capital structure reflects the "height" and the "width" of the land and labor inputs invested in real capital goods. The width of the capital structure is the number of input units invested, while its height reflects the length of time over which such inputs must remain invested before the maturation of their services in production. The economic value

---

[14] Irving Fisher, *The Purchasing Power of Money* (Second ed., 1922) New York: The Macmillan Company, p. 172.

[15] Fisher, *The Theory of Interest*, chap. xix.

of this structure can be determined by multiplying the input units by the relevant rate of wages and rent, and then applying the rate of interest, properly compounded, over the average length of the investment period. Or expressed in terms of Böhm-Bawerk's agio principle, the value of a capital structure is equal to the discounted value of the products which the invested inputs yield until they mature.

The usefulness of Wicksell's concept of the capital structure is that it provided new insight into the effect of capital accumulation and invention on national income and the relationship between the distributive shares. He reasoned that, given a constant supply of labor and land, net investment initially expands the capital structure by extending its width. Subsequent expansion extends its height; i.e., in more modern terminology, it is "capital-deepening" as opposed to "capital-widening." Expansion of the capital structure always increases the national income by the marginal product of new investment. But it will affect the share going to capitalists differently from that going to workers and landowners. Capital widening, i.e., net investment which proportionately increases capitals regardless of their maturity, decreases the marginal productivity of capital so that the interest rate tends to fall while wages and rents tend to rise. This was essentially the conclusion of the classical economists, too. Eventually, however, accumulation increases the height or intensity of capital as well as the width because the profitability of investments of longer maturity becomes relatively greater as wages and rents rise. This effect, Wicksell maintained, serves to retard their further increase and slows down the reduction of the relative share going to capital. It cannot, however, stop the increase in the share going to land and labor or prevent the decline in the relative share going to capital.

Wicksell also examined the effect of technological change on the distributive shares. He reasoned that even in the absence of net investment, technological improvements always increase national income if there is perfect competition because they increase the average and marginal productivity of all factors, although not all are affected equally. Even though labor may experience hardship because of displacement by capital and a consequent fall in wages, it will find employment elsewhere. Thus, Wicksell concluded that invention does not in and of itself seriously reduce labor's share of the national income because of its productivity-enhancing nature. It will, however, injure labor if it serves to make long-term capital absolutely more profitable than before. Net investment will then result in the relative deepening of capital. When this occurs, a smaller quantity of capital will be used in current production, so that its marginal productivity rises both relatively and absolutely. If the supply of land and labor is constant, this has the effect of reversing the downward trend of the interest rate and the increase in rent and wages which normally results when there is net capital accumulation. Wicksell thus concluded that "the capitalist saver is fundamentally the friend of labor though the technical inventor is not infrequently its enemy."[16]

The Wicksell Effect

Wicksell's analysis of the effect of net accumulation led him to the conclusion that in addition to technical invention, there is still another factor which tends to halt the downward trend of the interest rate. The classicists, it will be recalled, anticipated that the trend toward a zero rate of interest would accompany the tendency toward a stationary state. Wicksell argued that a zero rate of interest would not come about in an economy in which there is capital formation. Part of the increase in real capital is continually absorbed, Wicksell argued, by rising rents and wages, so that the quantity of capital never gets large enough to reduce its marginal productivity to zero. This principle is generally referred to as the "Wicksell effect."

Wicksell utilized the principle of the partial absorption of the product of capital by labor and land in the form of rising wages and rents as the basis for his argument that the marginal productivity principle applies in a different way to real capital than it does to labor and land. According to the marginal productivity principle, or "von Thünen's law," as Wicksell called it, every factor will tend to receive the equivalent of its marginal social product. An increase in real capital results in an increase in output which is its social marginal product. The social marginal productivity rate of real capital is determined by dividing the increment of output by the increase in real capital. According to von Thünen's law, the rate of interest should tend to be equal to the social marginal productivity rate of real capital. But this is not the case, according to Wicksell, because part of the social marginal productivity of capital is absorbed by rising wages and rents. The quantity of capital actually created is smaller than it would have been if part of net saving had not been absorbed in this manner. The rate of interest therefore tends to be equal not to the marginal social product of capital, but to the somewhat smaller marginal product of the real capital actually created. Thus, Wicksell concluded, von Thünen's law cannot apply to real capital for the economy as a whole, but can only apply on a microeconomic level.

The reason why the application of von Thünen's law is qualified only in the case of capital and not in the case of labor and land is not far to seek. It is the result of the valuation process. Wicksell conceives of the value of the capital stock as being determined by its physical size multiplied by the rate of wages and rent relevant to the labor and land inputs which comprise it, discounted to the present. Thus, when the stock of capital increases, given a constant supply of labor and capital, it alters the rate of wages and rent and thus its own value.

---

[16] Knut Wicksell, *Lectures on Political Economy* (2 vols., 1901 and 1906; translated 1934–35) (New York: Macmillan Co., 1934), Vol. I, p. 164.

The Indirect Mechanism of Price Change

Wicksell's greatest contribution was his pioneering effort in the integration of monetary analysis with real analysis. Monetary analysis, in Wicksell's day, was largely concerned with the behavior of the general price level and proceeded on the implicit assumption that changes in the value of money are unrelated to real phenomena such as the level of output and employment. Changes in the price level and the value of money were thought to reflect only changes in the quantity of money and its velocity. The level of output, on the other hand, was thought to depend on the supply of resources and the state of the arts that determined the efficiency of their use at full employment. The acceptance of Say's law made it axiomatic that the resources of the economy would always tend to be fully employed.

It was Wicksell's contention that monetary phenomena and real phenomena are interrelated in that changes in the general price level take place not directly, as implied by the quantity theories of money, but indirectly as a result of changes in the interest rate. He took the position that any theory of money worthy of the name must show the interrelationship between changes in the quantity of money, the interest rate, and the price level.[17] To demonstrate these interrelationships, he conceived of a natural rate of interest and a market rate of interest. The natural rate of interest is the rate at which the demand for loan capital, which reflects the demand for capital for investment purposes, is equal to the supply of savings. It is also the rate which corresponds to the yield on newly created capital. The market rate of interest is the money rate charged by banks. Unlike the natural rate, its level can be objectively determined. Whether it coincides with the natural rate or diverges from it can, Wicksell believed, be inferred from the behavior of price.

If, for example, there is an increase in the demand schedule for funds, reflecting perhaps innovation and an improvement in the marginal productivity of capital, it will cause the natural rate of interest to rise. There is, however, no reason for the market rate of interest to rise as long as banks have excess reserves. The rise in the natural or real rate above the money rate "will provide a stimulus to trade and production and alter the relation between supply and demand for goods and productive services."[18] That is, the total demand for goods increases as a result of an increase in investment demand. The expansion of bank credit is the source of this increased demand. It enables the businessman receiving these credits to bid factors away from the consumer goods industries. The rise in factor prices increases factor income at a time when fewer consumer goods are available

---

[17] *Ibid.*, Vol. II (1935), p. 160.

[18] Knut Wicksell, *Interest and Prices* (1899) trans. Richard F. Kahn (London, 1936). (Reprinted New York: A. M. Kelly, 1965), p. 89.

because factors have been diverted to the capital goods industries. Rising consumer goods prices deprive the consumer of increased real consumption out of higher incomes; they create a situation of "forced saving," which may moderate the price rise. However, the expansion made possible by the divergence of the natural rate and the money rate of interest is cumulative and self-perpetuating in a pure credit system. That is, the rise in prices will continue indefinitely unless a shortage of reserves forces the bank rate up to the market rate. This will eventually happen under gold standard conditions because the loss of specie by external drain as well as internal drain into currency circulation will ultimately bring about a shortage of reserves. Such shortages will cause banks to raise the market rate. Their action will bring the expansion to a halt.[19] Needless to say, such an expansion could never have gotten started within the framework of a banking system requiring 100 percent reserves.

Wicksell's analysis also demonstrated how a reduction of the natural rate below the market rate would produce a cumulative contraction. The demand for investment funds is diminished in this situation. Falling factor prices and incomes are accompanied by reduced employment and production. The contraction is cumulative because the deficiency of demand associated with falling factor incomes offsets the stimulus arising from falling money costs. Demand will remain insufficient until either investment demand or consumption increases, and this cannot take place so long as the banks absorb funds. This requires either that the market rate of interest is reduced to the natural rate or that the natural rate rises until it is above the market rate. The implication of Wicksell's analysis is, therefore, that if the monetary authority will act to prevent divergences between the natural rate of interest and the market rate, it can prevent cumulative expansion and contraction and achieve a stable price level. The existence of a stable price level is indicative of and consistent with a monetary equilibrium in which money is "neutral."

Wicksell's conception of a divergence between the market rate and the natural rate of interest may be thought of in terms of savings and investment magnitudes as they exist ex ante and as they are realized ex post. Ex ante phenomena are those which refer to planned magnitudes of income, saving, investment, and consumption. Ex post phenomena refer to realized magnitudes, as opposed to those which are merely planned or expected. A natural rate of interest above the market rate implies an excess of planned investment over planned savings out of expected incomes. As was subsequently shown by writers of the modern Swedish school, an ex ante excess of planned investment creates an expansionary process.[20] Conversely, if ex ante investment is smaller than savings, a cumulative contrac-

---

[19] Wicksell, *Lectures,* Vol. II, pp. 200–201.

[20] See, in particular, Gunnar Myrdal, *Monetary Equilibrium* (London: W. Hodge and Co., 1939); and Eric Lindahl, *Studies in the Theory of Money and Capital* (New York: Farrar and Rinehart, 1939).

tion will be initiated. In either case the process of expansion or contraction is accompanied by changes in the level of realized income. The volume of savings that are actually realized at the new income level will be such that they are equal to realized investment. Savings and investment are always equal ex post, though they may well diverge ex ante. Such an ex ante divergence appears to be what Wicksell had in mind when he conceived of inequality between the natural rate and the market rate, and the process of cumulative expansion or contraction which he envisioned as resulting.

One difficulty in Wicksell's analysis derives from the implicit assumption that the economy is fully employed when the expansion initiated by the divergence of the natural rate from the market rate begins. If there are unemployed resources, the expansion of the capital goods sector will not bid up factor prices. Nor will it necessitate the cutback in consumer goods output which leads to forced saving when the increased factor incomes are expended for diminishing supplies of consumer goods. Thus the usefulness of this portion of the analysis is limited to those periods during which an economy has reached full-employment levels. Until this point is reached, or bottlenecks develop in key sectors, inflationary pressures will not manifest themselves.

In spite of this shortcoming, Wicksell's analysis is a major innovation in several respects. First, it is intended to demonstrate that the price level changes not directly, as is implied by the quantity theory of money, but indirectly as a result of changes in the rate of interest. Secondly, by relating changes in investment to changes in the interest rate, and therefore factor and commodity prices, it provides an explanation of the process of income determination. It is to be noted, however, that it presents an income theory which emphasizes only changes in investment demand. The level of consumption expenditures is ignored. Wicksell's emphasis on fluctuations in the marginal productivity of capital, coupled with the lagging response of the market rate of interest, was itself only a theory of cumulative expansion and contraction, but it became a foundation for subsequent monetary theories of the business cycle.[21] It also paved the way for a variety of analyses, such as those of the Swedish economists and Sir Dennis Robertson, which conceived of divergences between saving and investment as the source of cumulative expansion and contraction.[22]

Though the concept of the natural and market rates of interest was introduced before the turn of the century, and made fundamental to the hypothesis that changes in the quantity of money influence the price level only indirectly through the interest rate, this line of reasoning had little impact on the English-speaking world. Alfred Marshall's emphasis on the

---

[21] A variety of monetary theories of the cycle developed in the period after 1900. See T. W. Hutchison, *A Review of Economic Doctrines, 1870–1929* (Oxford: Clarendon Press, 1953), pp. 390–97.

[22] A useful comparison of these two approaches is to be found in Alvin Hansen, *Business Cycles and National Income* (New York: W. W. Norton & Co., Inc., 1951), Appendix, p. 606.

direct connection between money and prices, in the manner of Richard Cantillon and David Hume, had much greater impact. As a consequence, the monetary theory inherent in neoclassical macroeconomic analysis is that of the quantity theory. Within its framework, the level of commodity and factor prices was thought to be determined exclusively by monetary forces. Such forces were, however, regarded as having no effect on the real magnitudes of the economy such as output (real income), employment, and the exchange values of goods and services in terms of each other. As will be seen in the chapter on the contribution of Marshall, which follows, the neoclassical theory of employment and output proceeds in real terms because it was taken for granted that monetary changes cannot produce changes in real magnitudes.

CONCLUDING REMARKS

While the whole theory of distribution was substantially reconstructed after 1870 with the application of the marginal principle to the explanation of factor rewards, some of the most substantive contributions to the development of distribution theory were made in the area of capital and interest theory. The earliest contributor was Eugen Böhm-Bawerk, who developed his theory of interest as an aspect of the theory of imputation. He conceived of capital goods as goods of a higher order which come into existence as a result of roundabout methods of production. Roundabout methods of production are, on the one hand, more productive than direct methods; on the other hand, they involve the postponement of consumption. It follows that since present goods have a greater value than a like amount and kind of future goods, the creation of capital goods and their use in roundabout methods of production gives rise to a product which contains a surplus value, or agio. The principal form of this agio is as profit to businessmen who transform remote goods into consumer goods. Since the technical superiority of roundabout methods of production is, in Böhm-Bawerk's view, the source of the net return to capital, profit would exist even in a socialist state, though not as an individual source of income.

Irving Fisher's disagreement with Böhm-Bawerk's explanation of the determination of the real rate of interest turned upon the question of whether the technical superiority of the roundabout method of production, taken by itself, would account for the existence of a positive rate of interest. Fisher maintained that the subjective factor of "impatience," which is essentially the equivalent of Böhm-Bawerk's explanation of the preference for present over future goods, interacts with the rate of return over cost from investment opportunity to determine the real rate of interest. The eclectic nature of Fisher's theory of interest distinguishes his work from both the Austrian and the marginal productivity theories *and* aligns it more closely to that of the great English eclectic, Alfred Marshall.

While Böhm-Bawerk and Fisher were concerned with the nature of capital and the determination of the real rate of interest, the Swedish economist Knut Wicksell pioneered in examining the relationship between changes in the interest rate, the money supply, and the level of output and employment. The more typical approach of his contempories was to separate their inquiry into the determination of the interest rate from their examination of the general price level and the level of employment. More specifially, the problem of explaining output was virtually assumed away by the acceptance of Say's law. The problem of the general price level was deferred to a separate chapter on money, and the problem of investment was incidental to that of explaining interest as an income share. The rate of interest was conceived of as a rate of return to physical capital, while the money rate was simply a derivative of the real rate.

The possibility of a divergence between these rates had not gone unrecognized, but Wicksell was the first to perceive its significance. His analysis of the cumulative process of expansion and contraction as a result of a divergence between the bank rate and the real rate of interest served, in the first instance, as a first step in the integration of real and monetary analysis. This integration was not, however, fully accomplished until the publication in 1936 of John Maynard Keynes's *General Theory of Employment, Interest and Money.* Wicksell's pioneering effort also served to stimulate monetary analysis per se, as well as a variety of business cycle theories which sought to explain cyclical fluctuations in terms of internal disturbances, particularly to the capital structure, caused by monetary factors.

SUGGESTIONS FOR FURTHER READING

BÖHM-BAWERK, EUGEN.   *Capital and Interest,* Vol. II: *Positive Theory of Capital.* Translated by G. D. HUNCKE. South Holland, Ill.: Liberterian Press, 1959.

CONARD, J. W.   *An Introduction to the Theory of Interest,* chaps. i–iv. Berkeley: University of California Press, 1959.

FISHER, IRVING.   *The Theory of Interest.* New York: Macmillan Co., 1930.

HUTCHISON, T. W.   *A Review of Economic Doctrine, 1870–1929,* chaps. x–xi and xv–xvi. Oxford: Clarendon Press, 1953.

STIGLER, GEORGE.   *Production and Distribution Theories,* chaps. viii and x–xi. New York: Macmillan Co., 1941.

UHR, CARL G.   *The Economic Doctrines of Knut Wicksell,* chaps. v–vii. Berkeley: University of California Press, 1960.

———.   "Knut Wicksell: A Centennial Evaluation," *American Economic Review,* Vol. XLI, No. 4 (December, 1951). Reprinted in JOSEPH J. SPENGLER and W. ALLEN, eds., *Essays in Economic Thought: Aristotle to Marshall.* Chicago: Rand McNally & Co., 1960.

WICKSELL, KNUT.   *Lectures on Political Economy,* Vol. I. New York: Macmillan Co., 1934.

Chapter 15

THE CONTRIBUTION OF ALFRED MARSHALL TO ECONOMIC ANALYSIS

INTRODUCTION

Life and Times (1842–1924)

Until he came under the influence of Darwinian ideas, Alfred Marshall planned to make the ministry his lifetime work. He became instead a mathematician who developed an interest in economics after reading John Stuart Mill's work on political economy. Like Mill, he was a reformer at heart and devoted himself with an almost religious zeal to the problems of human improvement. These he approached with a utilitarian spirit inherited from Mill and an analytical approach firmly anchored in Ricardianism.

Marshall came into economics at a time when the influence of the classical tradition was on the wane. The twist which Marx gave to Ricardian doctrines, coupled with the attack of the German historical school and the reaction of the marginal utility school, contributed to its deterioration. While Marshall believed in the essential validity of Ricardo's principles, he recognized that utility must be accorded a greater role in the determination of value and that the evolutionary approach derived from Darwin's thesis could be utilized to revitalize Ricardian economics. He thus founded a new tradition known as "neoclassicism" and became the fountainhead from which much of modern economic thought and analysis springs. Even those who later reacted against the tradition he founded employed concepts and analytical tools which are Marshallian in origin.

His greatest theoretical work, and the source of most of this chapter, is his *Principles of Economics,* published in 1890. The success of this treatise was so great that for many decades afterward it almost totally eclipsed works of lesser stature. The study of economics became perforce, in the United States as well as in England, the study of Marshall's *Principles.* It is generally agreed that it is unfortunate that he devoted so much time to its original formulation that publication was delayed until 1890, and that he labored over seven revisions, none of them substantive, instead of turning his attention to other work. His other publications are *Industry and Trade* (1919), which is a historical study of the development of industry and has little analysis; *Money, Credit and Commerce* (1923); and a brief book which he coauthored before the *Principles* with his wife, Mary Paley Marshall, in addition to numerous occasional papers and lectures.[1]

PRINCIPLES OF ECONOMICS

Objectives

Marshall begins the *Principles of Economics* with the observation that "political economy or economics is the study of mankind in the ordinary business of life; it examines that part of individual and social action which is most closely connected with the attainment and with the use of the material requisites of well-being."[2] Unlike Nassau Senior, therefore, he intends to study economics as a science of human behavior rather than as a science of wealth.

He is concerned, above all, that his analysis be scientific, that is, that it shall bring to light such regularities or patterns of orderliness as are inherent in economic phenomena. Once discovered, these regularities can be given expression in the form of generalizations or laws describing the behavior of the economic forces which have been examined. The primary aim of the *Principles* is, therefore, to study the economic aspects of human behavior in order to derive the laws governing the functioning of the economic system.

Though the primary aim of the *Principles* is the analysis of the functioning of the economic system, Marshall believed that the system he was analyzing reflected the progress of western civilization, not only in terms of material achievement but also in the improvement of human character. To him, the present system is the product of a gradual but progressive extension of individual independence, freedom, and competitiveness. Though fully aware that competition can have negative results both from a social and from an individual standpoint, he regarded the rivalry of men against one another as the source not only of economic gain but, equally important, the source of a wholesome effect on individual character and behavior. He believed that as individuals gain in freedom, they also become more rational in their goals and decision making, more sportsmanlike and socially conscious in their behavior, so that in seeking their own success, they also promote the common good. The study of economics can contribute to this progress because the laws it discovers constitute more than knowledge for its own sake; they also contribute to the solution of social problems.[3] Humanitarian motives thus pervade all Marshall's inquiries. He is interested not only in that which is, but equally in

---

[1] Consult Arthur C. Pigou (ed.), *Memorials of Alfred Marshall* (London: Macmillan & Co., 1925), pp. 500–508 for a list of Marshall's writings.

[2] Alfred Marshall, *Principles of Economics* (8th ed.; London: Macmillan & Co., 1920), p. 1. (This work is hereafter cited in the footnotes as *Principles.*)

[3] *Ibid.*, p. 42, margin.

that which ought to be. His pure analysis of the economy's functioning is therefore frequently interspersed with what Schumpeter has called Marshall's "Victorian moralizing."

Methodology

Marshall recognizes that the complexity of the economic system he is studying is so great and the motives of human behavior so diverse that it is necessary to devise techniques for their systematic study. This requires that the number of variables be reduced to manageable proportions and that some method be devised to subject their behavior to measurement. Accordingly, Marshall introduces the method of abstraction to single out one variable or sector of the economy at a time, on the assumption that its behavior is incapable of exerting any appreciable influence on the rest of the economy. This does not necessarily imply that the rest of the economy remains unchanged, but rather that if the small sector being analyzed is subjected to an external change, it adjusts itself without producing more than a negligible effect on the rest of the economy. This is Marshall's principle of the negligibility of indirect effects. By invoking this principle, all of the effects and countereffects which take place in the real world between a sector and the rest of the economy are impounded by the assumption ceterus paribus, other things remaining equal.

The regularities Marshall is seeking can be discovered only if the forces which underlie them can be subjected to measurement. Since these forces are themselves the product of human behavior, which is governed by a wide variety of motives, the economist must abstract those human motives which lend themselves to objective measurement. Not all motives are measurable; hence, they defy scientific investigation. But, Marshall observed, fortunately for the problem at hand, so much of man's life is oriented to the pursuit of economic gain that economic motives, at least, become measurable in terms of a single common denominator: money. He notes that this common denominator is probably unreliable when applied to single individuals for whom the marginal utility of money is different, but its application to the large group or social organism is valid because it involves a sufficiently large number of individuals to average out differences in income. For the group as a whole, therefore, Marshall conceives of economic motives as being measurable in terms of money.[4] This is not to say that economic motives are unique, but rather that those motives which underlie action in the marketplace give rise to results that are measurable in terms of market prices. Thus the primary area of inquiry with respect to the discovery of the regularities in economic activity Marshall was seeking became the study of prices—commodity as well as factor.

Marshalls' famous Book V of the *Principles* has become the classic

---

[4] *Ibid.*, p. 19.

example of the use of the technique of abstraction to investigate the interaction of demand and supply forces to explain the emergence of an equilibrium price. Here, he treats the individual industry that is so small relative to the rest of the economy that he can draw up industry demand and supply curves which are completely independent of one another. That is, it is assumed that indirect effects are so negligible that changes in the quantity of output produced by the industry do not have a sufficient impact on the incomes earned in that industry to shift even the demand curve for its product, much less the aggregate demand for output as a whole. The assumption of an industry which is such a miniscule part of the whole implies that the market is perfect; the industry supply curve is comprised of the outputs of a large number of small firms. These outputs are perfectly homogeneous from the point of view of the buyers, so that the industry faces a definite market demand curve which, when set against the supply curve, will result in a single market price for all buyers. This schematic is, of course, most satisfactory when we are satisfied with approximations, when it is not necessary to take specifically into consideration the effect which a change in the conditions of production surrounding one commodity will have on national income, and via national income on the demand for some other commodity.

The use of the term "competition" in connection with Marshall's *Principles* can be confusing to modern students of economics who are already conversant with the more precise terms of "pure competition" and "perfect competition." He himself thought that the term "competition" is not well suited to describe the special characteristics of industrial life in the modern age.[5] He suggested "Freedom of Industry and Enterprise" or, more briefly, "Economic Freedom," because these terms are devoid of moral implications. It would be convenient if Marshall had committed himself to the precise assumptions on which he constructed his analytical model of the industry. Such assumptions are, however, nowhere precisely set forth; on the contrary, he avoided them in the belief that each real problem investigated would require modifications in the model. Marshall's followers, rather than Marshall himself, have supplied us with such rigorous concepts as pure and perfect competition.

The concept of pure competition, as it is used in modern economics, involves rather precise requirements with respect to both the demand side and the supply side of the market. It requires, on the demand side, that the commodity is one which absorbs only a small portion of the consumer's income and on which the total expenditures constitute only a small part of the nation's income. It requires, on the supply side, a sufficiently large number of small selling units offering a homogeneous product, so that only one selling price can emerge as a result of the interaction of demand and

---

[5] *Ibid.*, p. 9.

supply forces. The concept of perfect competition is even more rigorous, requiring, in addition, perfect knowledge on the part of market participants and perfect mobility of buyers and resources. It represents an ideal set of circumstances which, if they existed, would facilitate the perfect functioning of the economy. The precise results which would obtain under these conditions were subsequently to be detailed by the modern welfare school.[6]

Marshall's concept of economic freedom was considerably less refined than these more modern concepts. But he conceived himself as describing the functioning of an economy within the framework of enough of the elements of what is conceived as pure competition to make the typical firm an insignificant part of the whole industry. Each individual firm produces such a small portion of the total market output that output variations cannot affect either the total supply of the product or the price which emerges.

The passage of time poses a major difficulty in the explanation of prices because the strength and the relative importance of the forces operating both on the side of demand and on the side of supply may change. Marshall has too keen an appreciation of the impact of change to ignore these possibilities. Reasoning from unchanging static assumptions would result in an analysis incompatible with change. On the other hand, he is committed to uncovering regularities, that is, to explaining the "normal" behavior of prices. The method he chooses is therefore a compromise which does not eliminate change but reduces it to manageable proportions by introducing the assumptions of the "stationary state." In the stationary state, consumer tastes and production techniques remain unchanged. Population and capital are allowed to increase slowly and at the same rate. Business enterprises grow and decline, but always there will be certain firms which may be regarded as being representative of the others in an industry. Change is therefore not entirely absent, but has been abstracted from sufficiently to show how prices would be adjusted in the long run if the conditions under which they are determined are sufficiently stable to allow these forces the opportunity to work themselves out. There are times when Marshall seems to imply that the long-run results he describes actually occur in the real world.[7] But except for occasional lapses, he reminds his reader that his concept of the stationary state is an analytical construct designed to cope with the many variables operating in the real world. For while Marshall aimed at realism, his method was to start with simplifying assumptions. He singled out variables and impounded them; that is, he treated them as data in order to arrive at conclusions that represented tendencies or, at least, first approximations.

He recognized that these generalizations must necessarily be modified

---

[6] See Chap. 17 below.

[7] See Claude W. Guillebaud, "Davenport on Marshall," *Economic Journal,* Vol. XLVII (March, 1937), p. 35.

as the passage of time alters the institutional framework of behavior, and therefore behavior itself. Marshall's sense of history kept him from inferring that the generalizations economists arrive at are universal and permanent. "That part of economic doctrine which alone can claim universality, has no dogmas. It is not a body of concrete truth, but an engine for the discovery of concrete truth."[8] Thus, when he spoke of long-run normal laws, paralleling the classical conception of long-run natural laws, he was conceiving of abstract analytical propositions which are indicative of tendencies in the economic system rather than concrete truths which express actualities. He never lost sight of the complexity and changeability of the universe within which economic forces operate, and the consequent difficulty of arriving at valid generalizations. His reluctance to claim universality for economic propositions is evident in his paper "The Old Generation of Economists and the New," in which he maintains that qualitative analysis, by which he meant deductive analyses, "will not show the resultant drift of forces. . . . The achievement of quantitative analysis stands over for the twentieth century."[9]

These observations appear to suggest that in Marshall's view, pure theory has been carried as far as it fruitfully can be for the present, besides being unable to yield universal or permanent laws. In fact, he frequently depreciated even the present significance of pure analysis; for example, he hesitated to publish his diagrammatic analyses, fearing that "if separated from all concrete study of actual conditions they might seem to claim a more direct bearing on real problems than they in fact had."[10] He regarded theory as essential, but he warned against regarding it as economics "proper." What is today conceived of as economic principles Marshall regarded as "a very small part of economics proper." However, much of modern microeconomic analysis has developed out of Marshall's theory of value and distribution.

THE THEORY OF DEMAND

Utility and Demand

While Marshall's theory of value is fully developed in Book V, which treats the "General Relations of Demand, Supply and Value," the analysis presented there is predicated on the two books which precede it. Book III, "On Wants and Their Satisfaction," begins with the observation that insufficient attention has been paid to demand and consumption until just recently. He was alluding here, in particular, to Jevons, who "did excellent service by calling attention to it [the demand side of the theory of value]

---

[8] Pigou, *op. cit.,* p. 159.
[9] *Ibid.,* p. 30.
[10] *Ibid.,* p. 21.

and developing it."[11] But while Marshall regarded consumer wants and their satisfaction as an important part of the theory of value and was himself an important contributor to the development of demand theory, he believed that to accord the dominant role to marginal utility in the explanation of value was to commit a serious error. Ricardo, he agreed, tended to slight the role of demand; but he did not, as Jevons maintained, think of value as being governed by cost of production without reference to demand. Thus, while the theory of utility and demand supplemented and rounded out the classical analysis, the Ricardian emphasis on cost of production remained, for Marshall, the fundamental basis for explaining long-run normal values. His analysis was therefore designed to demonstrate the *interaction* of demand and supply forces. As a result of this approach, he has frequently been thought of as a synthesizer of the Ricardian cost-oriented type of analysis with the newer approach of the marginal utility theorists. Marshall himself was, however, irritated at being cast in the role of an eclectic, though his failure to publish earlier his own work on utility and demand makes such an interpretation understandable, even though incorrect.[12]

Demand Schedules and Curves

Marshall proceeds with his analysis of demand by translating the law of diminishing utility into terms of price. He reasons that the larger the quantity of a commodity a person has, the smaller (other things being equal) will be the price he will pay for a little more of it. Impounded in the phrase "other things being equal" is the assumption that the amount of money the individual has available and its purchasing power remain constant. By assuming a constant marginal utility of money, and thereby ruling out any income effects resulting from price changes, the marginal utility curve for a commodity is converted into a demand schedule and then into a demand curve.

The demand of any individual for certain commodities may be discontinuous, that is, it will not always vary continuously for every small change in price. However, the aggregate demand of many persons on a market will vary continuously with changes in price. The inverse relationship between price and the quantity which will be taken per unit of time gives the demand curve a characteristic downward slope to the right.[13] It is also the basis for the generalization known as the law of demand: "The amount demanded increases with a fall in price and diminishes with a rise in

---

[11] *Principles,* Appendix I.

[12] See, for example, Joseph A. Schumpeter's discussion of Marshall's originality in *History of Economic Analysis* (London: Oxford University Press, 1954), pp. 835–40.

[13] Marshall introduced the now standard practice of putting price on the ordinate axis.

price."[14] Thus, there will be a movement along a *given* demand curve as a result of a change in the price of the commodity itself if none of the other factors which can influence the demand for it—for example, tastes, or the prices of other goods—have changed. Only if the factors which have been held constant in defining a given demand situation become altered does the position, and perhaps shape of the demand curve itself, change. In a schedule sense, this means that buyers will be willing to buy either more or less of the commodity per unit of time at every possible price. This will shift the entire demand schedule from its original position, either upward to the right or downward to the left.

Consumer Surplus

The concept of consumer surplus is a distinctively Marshallian idea which was destined to figure importantly in what later became known as "welfare economics." Marshall himself used the concept in more than one sense. He first defined it as the monetary value of the utility a consumer gains when the price at which he can purchase a good is lower than the price he would pay rather than go without it. He then proceeds to add individual surpluses together in order to arrive at the consumer surplus as the area under a market demand curve, given the price of a commodity. Figure 15–1 shows the area $DA'p_1$ as the consumer surplus when the

FIGURE 15–1

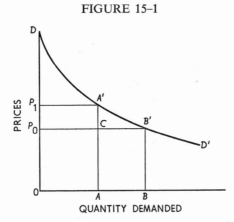

market price is p_1 and the area $DB'p_0$ as the surplus when the price is p_0.

If a demand curve is asymptotic to the price axis, so that it is not tangent at D, as in Figure 15–1, the consumer surplus cannot be calculated as the area under the demand curve because the integral under the curve is infinite. Marshall was of course aware of this difficulty and avoided it by concentrating on the change in consumer surplus when price changes from one level to another. This change is represented by the triangle $A'CB'$ in

---

[14] *Principles,* p. 99.

Figure 15–1. This is the sense in which Marshall used the concept of consumer surplus in his tax subsidy analysis. This application of the consumer surplus concept will be examined later in connection with the price and output results of increasing- and decreasing-cost industries.

The main criticisms of Marshall's attempt to measure consumer surplus are that it treats individual utilities as being additive, and that it assumes that the marginal utility of money remains constant as the price of a good changes. The latter assumption rules out changes in real income resulting from price changes, as well as substitution effects between the good in question and other goods consumers might buy. This assumption is obviously valid only if the good is a very unimportant item in all budgets; otherwise, changes in its price will have income as well as substitution effects. Many modern economists have therefore avoided both the concept or marginal utility and that of consumer surplus by utilizing the indifference curve technique of Francis Edgeworth and Vilfredo Pareto.[15]

Price Elasticity of Demand

While the law of demand expresses the inverse relationship between the demand for a commodity and its price, it does not indicate how sensitive the demand for a commodity is to a change in price. The concept of the price elasticity of demand is needed to supply this sort of information. The simplest way to determine whether the demand for a particular commodity is elastic or not is to observe the behavior of total expenditures when the price of the good in question is changed. If total expenditures are greater at a lower price than at a higher price, the demand is elastic. Conversely, if total expenditure is smaller at a lower price, the demand for the good is inelastic. The limitation of this method is that it cannot indicate the degree of demand elasticity or inelasticity.

Demand elasticity can also be measured by the slope of the demand curve, that is, by relating the change in price to the change in quantity as the initial price is assumed to change. For example, if a 10-cent price reduction results in a 500-pound increase in the quantity demanded, the slope of that portion of the demand curve is $\frac{-10}{500}$ or $\frac{-1}{50}$. However, if the unit in terms of which prices are measured is changed from cents to dollars, the slope of the same segment of the demand curve is $\frac{\frac{-1}{10}}{500}$ or $\frac{-1}{5,000}$. A change in the unit of measurement thus produces a very great decrease in the slope of the demand curve, yet there has been no change in the demand curve itself. A similar alteration of slope would result from altering the unit in terms of which quantities are measured—for example, a shift from pounds to bushels.

---

[15] See Chap. 17 below.

It is because the measurement of elasticity by the slope of the curve is unreliable that Marshall defined elasticity as the percentage change in quantity demanded divided by the percentage change in the price when both changes are infinitely small.[16] In symbols, then:

$$E_d = \frac{\dfrac{dQ}{Q}}{\dfrac{dP}{P}} = \frac{dQ}{dP} \cdot \frac{P}{Q}$$

Because the resulting number (coefficient) is derived by dividing one percentage by another, it is independent of the units in terms of which prices and quantities are measured. The coefficient denoting elasticity will always be negative, since price change and quantity change take place in opposite directions and therefore have different signs. However, in speaking of demand elasticity, it is customary to ignore signs and refer to the numerical values of elasticity magnitudes simply as equal to one, greater than one, or smaller than one. When elasticity equals one, it is referred to as unitary elasticity. When elasticity is greater than one, demand is said to be elastic; and when it is less than one, it is said to be inelastic.

The Marshallian formula is now a standard analytical tool for calculating the degree of sensitivity of the demand for a commodity to a change in its price. It lends itself to measuring elasticity either at any point on a given demand curve or between two points on a demand curve. The latter measurement involves the computation of what is known as "arc elasticity." However, the application of the formula to computing elasticity between two points on a demand curve will result in two different elasticity coefficients, depending on the direction in which the change is measured.[17] The further apart these points are, the greater will be the discrepancy between

---

[16] *Principles,* Mathematical Appendix, Note III.

[17] This can be easily verified by measuring elasticity from point *A* to *B* and then from *B* to *A* using the data in the accompanying table:

	Price	*Quantity*
A	$2.00	100,000
B	1.00	200,000

Using the formula to measure elasticity from point *A* to *B,* the demand is elastic:

$$E_d = \frac{\dfrac{100,000}{100,000}}{-\dfrac{1}{2}} = \frac{1}{-\dfrac{1}{2}} = -2$$

But measuring from *B* to *A,* it is inelastic:

$$E_d = \frac{\dfrac{-100,000}{200,000}}{\dfrac{1}{1}} = \frac{-\dfrac{1}{2}}{1} = -\frac{1}{2}$$

the resulting elasticity coefficients.[18] Greater precision can therefore be achieved if price-quantity data are sufficiently continuous to result in any two points *A* and *B* which are very close together on the curve. This is precisely why Marshall's elasticity formula is intended to measure very small changes in price and quantity.

THE THEORY OF PRODUCTION

The theory of production is the foundation for the analysis of costs and the supplies of goods. It is also fundamental to explaining the pricing of the factors, their allocation among alternative uses in the economy, and the distribution of the economy's product among the various claimants. Thus, Marshall's discussion of the agents of production and the laws of return under which they operate is placed in Book IV before the analysis of price determination, which is the burden of Book V, and the analysis of income distribution in Book VI.

The laws of return are significant in the short run and in the long run, but not in the market period, which, since the time of Marshall, is conceived of as a situation in which the available output has already been produced and is on hand. Physical supply in this period cannot be increased, and it can be decreased only by sale or destruction. During the short run, however, the supply of a product may be varied by altering some, though not all, of the factor inputs required to produce output. The long run is a period during which the supply of a product can be varied by altering all of the factor inputs. Only those changes in output associated with economic growth or decline are absent.

The Laws of Return in the Short Run

Since a production unit is always confronted with one or more fixed factors and a given state of technology in the short run, its production function is governed by the law of diminishing returns. Marshall, like his classical predecessors, examined this tendency with respect to agricultural production and concluded that when land is a fixed constant in the production function, "the application of increased capital and labor to land will add a less than proportionate amount to the produce raised, unless there be meanwhile an increase in the skill of the individual cultivator."[19] This "final statement" of the law of diminishing returns thus emphasizes that *average* output begins to decline after a certain quantity of the variable factor (labor) has been employed in conjunction with a given quantity of the

---

[18] This discrepancy may be reduced by modifying the formula for calculating elasticity as follows: Calculate the change in price from the lower of the two prices and the change in quantity from the smaller of the two quantities. This results in an average of the two results obtained in the original formula. For the problem given in note 17, elasticity would be −1.

[19] *Principles*, p. 153.

fixed factor (land). He also states the principle in its marginal sense; "a continued increase in the application of capital and labor to land must ultimately result in a diminution . . . of the extra produce which can be obtained by a given extra amount of capital and labor."[20] However, the distinction between these two concepts is not so clear in Marshall's analysis as in Edgeworth's.[21]

Marshall's treatment of diminishing returns has been termed "disappointing" because he restricted its operation to agriculture. But he undoubtedly knew that any variable factor of production will yield diminishing marginal returns if it is combined in production with a given quantity of a fixed factor.[22] This is implied by his principle of substitution, according to which the desire to maximize profits causes the businessman to substitute less expensive for more expensive factors. It is precisely because one factor is not a perfect substitute for another that diminishing returns occur. If the ratio of a variable factor, A, to a fixed factor, B, is progressively increased, A becomes a less effective substitute for B, and returns to the variable factor increase at a decreasing rate. According to the principle of substitution, a firm will alter the proportions in which it uses its variable inputs in order to achieve the least-cost combination. It will experiment with different combinations of its variable factors until it achieves the greatest revenue product for a given expenditure. Given the cost of its variable factors, it will maximize its product (minimize its cost) by distributing its factor expenditures in such a way that the marginal revenue product of a dollar's worth of one factor is exactly equal to the marginal revenue product of a dollar's worth of each of its other variable factors. Thus, if P_a and P_b are the prices of factors A and B, the total product will be maximized with a given expenditure when

$$\frac{MPP_a}{P_a} = \frac{MPP_b}{P_b}$$

A firm's demand curve for a factor is therefore related to its marginal productivity in much the same way as a consumer demand curve is related to marginal utility. The best combination of variable resources depends on the respective marginal physical products of these resources, the cost at which they can be employed and the price at which the product they produce can be sold. To minimize the cost of a given amount of product or, conversely, to maximize the product which can be gotten from a given expenditure requires that variable factors be combined so that the ratio of the marginal revenue product for each factor to price is equal. This principle is analogous to that previously examined with respect to the

---

[20] *Ibid.*

[21] Edgeworth is generally given credit for the earliest clear distinction between proportionate and diminishing marginal returns. See Chap. 13 above.

[22] George Stigler, *Production and Distribution Theories* (New York: Macmillan Co., 1941), pp. 66–67.

maximization of consumer satisfaction. The consumer maximizes his satisfaction by distributing his income among different goods so as to equate the marginal utility of each dollar's worth of goods purchased. A firm achieves its objective of maximizing its product (minimizing its cost) by distributing its expenditures so as to equate the marginal revenue product of each dollar's worth of variable resources it purchases.

Because the marginal productivity of a factor underlies the demand for it, it will also affect in an important way the price the factor will be able to command in the market. The marginal productivity principle therefore serves to integrate Marshall's theory of value with his theory of income distribution. It enters into the theory of value through its effect on the cost and supply of commodity outputs, and it enters into the theory of distribution through its effect on factor demands.

The Laws of Return in the Long Run

Marshall's concern with the laws of return in the long run was to establish a basis for depicting the long-run supply curve of an industry. He identified three possible output behavior patterns which might result when an industry expands in the long run. In the case of constant return, output will increase proportionately with an increase in factor input; in the case of increasing return, the increase in output will be proportionally greater than the increase in factor input; in the case of diminishing return, it will be proportionately smaller. Increasing and diminishing returns were conceived of as forces which "press constantly against one another";[23] ". . . the part which nature plays in production shows a tendency to diminishing return, the part which man plays shows a tendency to increasing return."[24] When the two forces are balanced, there is a tendency toward constant returns.[25]

Marshall distinguished between external and internal economies which facilitate the production of a proportionately larger output with a given increase in expenditures. External economies are those which result from the general progress of the industrial environment and enable the firms of an expanding industry to experience decreasing costs. The development of better transportation and marketing facilities, and improvements in resource-furnishing industries, are possible sources of such economies which Marshall specifically mentions.[26] Internal economies are those which accrue to a firm as it enlarges its size to achieve greater advantages of large-scale production and organization.[27] Marshall observed that "an increase of labor and capital leads generally to improved organization, which increases the efficiency of the work of labor and capital."

---

[23] *Principles,* p. 319.

[24] *Ibid.,* p. 318.

[25] *Ibid.,* p. 310.

[26] *Ibid.,* p. 317.

[27] *Ibid.,* p. 318.

It is not clear from the preceding statements that Marshall conceived of the laws of return in the long run as relating strictly to the results associated with changes in *all* factor inputs, i.e., to changes in scale. Only in the case of increasing returns resulting from internal economies is it clear that a change in the scale of production is involved. Increasing returns resulting from external economies, that is, "the general progress of the industrial environment," may or may not involve a change in scale. But, diminishing returns is a short run phenomenon which occurs because a change in scale is not possible. In the short run, as has already been noted, the impossibility of varying all factor inputs results in a production function which is governed by the law of diminishing returns beyond some point. It is therefore not possible for the tendency toward diminishing returns and increasing returns to "press against one another" in the manner conceived by Marshall, as these tendencies are operative in different time periods.[28]

Marshall's distinction between internal and external economies as the source of increasing returns in the long run has important implications with respect to competitive tendencies in the economy. He was aware that a condition of increasing returns is incompatible with competition. "Insofar as the economies of production on a large scale are 'internal,' i.e., belonging to the internal organization of individual firms, the weaker firms must speedily be driven out of existence by the stronger." However, he did not think it possible for such economies to continue indefinitely. "The continued existence of weaker firms is an evidence that a strong firm cannot indefinitely increase its output, partly because of the difficulty of extending its market and partly because the strength of a firm is not permanent."[29] The reason, he suggested, is that the growth of individual enterprises would be limited by the probably inferior business talents of the descendants of present business leaders.[30] He also envisaged increased difficulties of marketing as limiting the possibilities for securing advantages of large-scale production.[31] Increasing long-run returns were therefore attributed by Marshall to the presence of external rather than internal economies. The basis for subsequent disagreement with this conclusion is discussed in the next chapter.

COSTS OF PRODUCTION AND SUPPLY

Real Costs and Money Costs

Examination of Marshall's inquiry into production costs is a logical extension of the preceding inquiry into his theory of production. Except in the short run, when the supply of a good has already been produced, costs

---

[28] See Stigler, *op. cit.*, p. 68.
[29] *Principles*, pp. 808–9 n.
[30] *Ibid.*, p. 316.
[31] *Ibid.*, pp. 286–87.

of production underlie the supply schedules of firms and industries. While these costs are necessarily monetary, Marshall is also concerned with the real costs imposed by the disutilities of labor and the "abstinences or rather the waitings required for saving the capital" required to produce capital goods.[32] All factors of production except land, which is a free gift of nature requiring neither abstinence nor labor effort, impose a real cost when they are used in production. The money costs of production are, then, in Marshall's view, the prices which must be paid "in order to call forth an adequate supply of the efforts and waitings that are required for making it; or, in other words, they are its [a commodity's] supply price."[33] This emphasis on the subjective or psychological aspects of cost reflects a continuation of the utilitarian philosophy of the classicists. Insofar as the classicists explained money costs, they referred them back to the discomforts of labor and saving. Marshall followed this tradition, adding also the effort and waiting of the labor of enterprise.[34] Some "normal" rate of profit is therefore included by Marshall as part of the cost of producing a commodity.

The money costs of production consist of prime costs and supplementary costs. Prime costs, or operating expenses, vary directly with output, whereas supplementary costs are standing charges which do not vary with output. Marshall's classification corresponds to the current distinction between variable and fixed costs. In the short run, the inputs represented by supplementary costs are fixed. Only variable inputs, and therefore prime costs, are subject to change. In the long run, all inputs, and therefore all costs, are variable.

Diminishing Returns and Short-Run Cost Behavior

Although Marshall's discussion of diminishing returns implies that it is a land law, he is aware that the employment of increasing quantities of any variable input which is used in conjunction with a fixed factor will yield diminishing returns and that this will be reflected in the behavior of all average and marginal costs of production. Average prime costs reach their minimum when marginal physical product is at a maximum and rise as marginal physical product diminishes. Marginal costs, which fall and rise more sharply than average prime costs, also reach their minimum when marginal physical product is at its maximum and then rise as marginal physical product diminishes. Since marginal cost represents the additional cost a firm incurs in supplying one additional unit of output, the marginal cost at each level of output is the firm's supply price of that output, except for those outputs for which marginal cost is less than average prime cost. Production of the profit-maximizing (loss-minimizing) output (i.e.,

[32] *Ibid.,* p. 339.
[33] *Ibid.*
[34] *Ibid.,* p. 362.

$MC = MR$) will therefore cause the firm to be producing on the rising portion of its marginal cost curve. Its short-run supply curve will therefore be rising.

While Marshall did not make cost calculations of the sort which have now become standard in most texts on economic principles or draw the cost curves these calculations describe, such calculations are implicit in his distinction between prime and supplementary costs. They are also useful in understanding why Marshall drew upward-sloping industry supply curves for the short run. Since the industry supply curve is a summation of individual firms' supply curves, it must be positively inclined in the short run. This is not necessarily the case in the long run. But in the short run the presence of fixed factors in the firm's production function confronts it with rising marginal costs in consequence of the tendency toward diminishing marginal returns to the variable factors. Individual firms and the industry as a whole will therefore offer larger quantities only at higher prices. The typical upward slope of the supply schedule of a purely competitive industry in the short run reflects this relationship.

Long-Run Cost and Supply Curves

There is no reason to assume that the cost curves of individual firms are the same in the short run, even though all firms are assumed to purchase factors in a purely competitive market. Some firms may enjoy lower costs because of superior capital equipment, more favorable location, or better management. These advantages will yield what Marshall terms "quasi rents" in the short run. These incomes accrue in the short run from using factors that are fixed in supply and are akin to the economic rent of land. In the long run, however, quasi rents will tend to be eliminated, either through an increase in the supply of a reproducible factor or, in the case of one which is not reproducible, through a price rise which results from competitive bidding for its use. In the long run under competition, therefore, each firm will tend to produce along identical cost curves which include the quasi rents of the short run. These costs may be explicit or imputed, depending on whether the firm hires the factor in the open market or owns it.

Marshall himself did not examine the long-run cost curves of the individual firm, but dealt only with the long-run supply curve of the entire industry.[35] He conceived of the shape of the industry supply curve in the long run as depending on whether it is one of constant returns (constant cost), decreasing returns (increasing cost), or increasing returns (decreas-

---

[35] This problem was later dealt with by Jacob Viner in his article, "Cost Curves and Supply Curves," *Zeitschrift für Nationalökonomie,* Vol. III (1931), pp. 23–46; republished in Kenneth E. Boulding and George Stigler (eds.), *Readings in Price Theory,* Vol. VI (Homewood, Ill.: Richard D. Irwin, Inc., 1952) and in R. V. Clemence ed., *Readings in Economic Analysis,* Reading, Mass.: Addison-Wesley Publishing Co., Inc., 1950, Vol. II.

ing cost). The predominant tendency in each industry will manifest itself in the experience of what Marshall terms the "representative firm." This is a firm which "has had a fairly long life, and fair success, which is managed with normal ability and which has normal access to the economies, external and internal, which belong to that aggregate volume of production; account being taken of the class of goods produced, the conditions of marketing them and the economic environment."[36] This firm is not an actual firm, but rather an analytical tool which Marshall conceived of for the purpose of identifying cost of production, and therefore the supply schedule of a commodity, in the long run. "[The] normal supply price of any amount of that commodity may be taken to be its normal expenses of production (including gross earnings of management) by that firm."[37] Thus, Marshall examines the long-run supply curve of the industry with reference to the costs of the representative firm.

The concept of the representative firm is presented within the framework of a biological analogy. The life cycles of business firms are compared to those of trees in a forest, which first grow to maturity and then decay. During its growth phase, a firm will enjoy internal economies of scale; in its declining phase, these economies will be offset by diseconomies which limit its growth potential and its ability to experience decreasing costs as a result of internal economies. A firm therefore cannot, in Marshall's view, expand its size to an extent which will enable it to dominate an industry. Competition remains pure, and an increase in the output of the industry in the long run results from an increase in the number of firms rather than an increase in the size of firms.

Given pure competition, the long-run supply curve of an industry may be constant, upward-sloping, or downward-sloping as the industry expands in size to accommodate an increase in demand. The case of constant cost implies that the internal and external economies of production are canceled out by internal and external diseconomies. Increasing quantities of the product can therefore be supplied at a constant long-run average cost.

The long-run supply curve may also be upward-sloping. This will be the case, for example, if the expansion of the industry raises the average cost curve of each firm, because the increasing scarcity of a nonreproducible factor increases the cost of using it. The quasi rents which accrued as a producer's surplus in the short run are capitalized in the long run and become embodied in long-run cost curves and supply curves when the supply of factors which gave rise to them is less than infinitely elastic. Increasing quantities of the product can then be supplied only at increasing long-run average costs, and the industry supply curve will be upward-sloping.

---

[36] *Principles*, p. 317.
[37] *Ibid.*, p. 343.

Marshall believed that the long-run supply curve could also be downward-sloping in a competitive industry. This kind of supply curve would obtain, he believed, when the availability of external economies to the firms enables them to experience falling average costs as the industry expands in size. Since external economies reflect input or output advantages which accrue to the firms in the industry, but which cannot be charged for by any factor, they have the effect of reducing costs rather than creating rents. Therefore, increasing quantities of the product can be supplied at decreasing long-run costs.

Decreasing costs deriving from external economies must not be confused with decreasing costs associated with internal economies. Internal economies are under the control of the firm and can be achieved by enlarging its scale of plant. External economies are those which accrue to firms in an industry from its general expansion. But these forces are outside the control of the firm, which is merely the beneficiary of gains or improvements in which all firms share, but for which no factor of production can charge a price. The chapter which follows will discuss the difficulty of identifying the source of such external economies and the reasons for which later economists questioned and eventually rejected Marshall's explanation of decreasing long-run cost.

THE THEORY OF PRICE DETERMINATION

Prices Which Deviate from Cost of Production

In Marshall's view, price is governed neither by cost of production alone nor by marginal utility alone, but by the interaction of these forces as they express themselves in the demand for and the supply of a good. Normally, the price of a commodity will, Marshall believed, tend to be equal to its long-run cost of production. That is, the longer the relevant period of time, the more accurately is it possible to adjust supply to changes in demand when there is freedom of enterprise. It follows that there are three cases in which the price of a product will reflect the state of the demand for it rather than its cost of production. One of these, namely, the case of competitive price determination in the market period, requires little elaboration. When the supply of a commodity has already been produced, the force of demand will necessarily be relatively more important than supply in determining price, so that there is no necessary tendency for price to approximate the cost of production. However, Marshall's explanation of the reason why long-run price bears no necessary relationship to price in the case of true joint supply or in the case of monopoly warrants separate examination.

Marshall reformulated Mill's principle that the individual prices of products produced in fixed proportions cannot be governed by the cost of producing them because these individual costs cannot be determined. That is, if two or more products are produced in fixed proportions, the marginal cost of one product no longer exists. We can speak only of the marginal cost of a combined unit of production, i.e., the marginal cost of a bushel of wheat and so many pounds of straw, but we cannot separate the cost of the wheat from the cost of the straw. Thus, Marshall concluded that the price of a particular joint product will be governed, even in the long run, by the relative intensity of the market demand for it rather than its cost of production. Further, whenever a change in the demand for one joint product induces a change in the joint supply, their prices will vary inversely with each other. Marshall showed that if, for example, there is an increase in the demand for wool, the supply of both wool and mutton will increase as the high price of wool stimulates the production of sheep. The increased cost of output is as attributable to the extra output of mutton as it is to the extra output of wool, but since there is no change in the demand for mutton, its price must fall. Uniform prices for two jointly produced products would result only in these accidental cases in which the demand schedules for both of the jointly produced products are exactly alike. Only the case of joint cost with variable proportions presents no unusual value problem because it is possible to assign a separate supply price to each of the products.[38]

Marshall likewise noted that in a monopoly situation the cost of producing is no guide to the price which will be charged. "The prima facie interest of the owner of a monopoly is clearly to adjust the supply to the demand not in such a way that the price at which he can sell his commodity shall just cover its expenses of production, but in such a way as to afford him the greatest possible total net revenue."[39] The price a monopolist will charge, given the demand schedule for his product, may be determined, Marshall tells us, by calculating the monopoly revenue associated with the production and sale of various quantities of output. In order to calculate what portion of the total revenue will be the monopoly net revenue at every level of output, it is necessary to draw up a supply schedule which represents the normal expenses of production of each of the several amounts supplied, including the interest on all capital and managerial salaries. For small outputs, the supply price, or average cost, will be high, so that the supply curve will be above the demand curve; for larger outputs, average cost of production will diminish, and the supply curve will therefore lie below the demand curve before it ultimately rises again. If the supply price of each quantity of output is subtracted from the corresponding demand price, the differential which remains is the monopoly net revenue. The object of the monopolist is to select that volume of output

---

[38] *Principles*, p. 388.
[39] *Ibid.*, pp. 477–88.

which, given the demand for the product, will make the aggregate net revenue the greatest.

Marshall's method of finding the price-quantity combination at which monopoly net revenue is at a maximum will produce the same results as Cournot's method of equating the first derivative of total cost with the first derivative of total revenue.[40] Net revenue is at a maximum when marginal revenue and marginal cost are equal. That is, we can measure monopoly profit as the difference between average cost and average revenue multiplied by output. Or alternatively, we can measure monopoly profit as the difference between the area lying under the marginal revenue curve (aggregate revenue) and the area lying under the marginal cost curve (aggregate

FIGURE 15–2

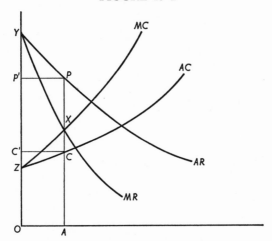

cost). Thus, in Figure 15–2, monopoly profit is equal to the area YXZ and to the area $P'PCC'$ when output OA is produced at an average cost of AC.

Long-Run Competitive Price Determination

In the absence of monopoly and production under joint supply, the long-run or normal price of a commodity, as Marshall calls it, will be equal to the cost of production, including the normal earnings of management, of the representative firm. This is the competitive equilibrium toward which the industries in the economy are always moving. His emphasis on the predominant influence of cost of production in the determination of value in the long run led him to conclude "that the foundations of the theory as they were left by Ricardo remain intact; that much has been added to them,

---

[40] This was demonstrated by Joan Robinson, *Economics of Imperfect Competition* (London: Macmillan and Co., Ltd., 1933), p. 56.

and that very much has been built upon them, but that little has been taken from them."[41] This is as much of a concession as he was willing to make to the marginal utility theory of value. He accorded utility a role, but by no means the dominant one, in the determination of competitive price. The longer the period of time under consideration, the greater the influence of cost of production on price. In the long run, when all the forces of adjustment have had time to work themselves out, price will be equal to the cost of producing the supply needed to satisfy the demand for the product.

The long-run cost tendencies which prevail, coupled with the demand for an industry's product, determine whether the long-run price will be higher, lower, or the same as an industry expands or contracts in response to changes in demand. A change in demand will cause output to expand or contract in the long run in a constant-cost industry, but the long-run equilibrium price will be neither higher nor lower than that which prevailed in the short run.

If, on the other hand, the firms in an industry experience external economies as they expand their factor inputs, the industry's long-run supply curve will slope upward, and it will produce a larger output at a higher cost than previously if increases in demand cause it to expand. Conversely, if external economies cause resource prices, and therefore the cost curves of an industry, to decrease as its scale is increased, an increase in demand will enable the industry to produce a larger output than before at a lower price. Marshall regarded these cases as constituting a possible basis for interfering with the free operation of the price mechanism through a system of taxes and subsidies. His analysis of the effect of imposing a tax or granting a subsidy in different industries clearly demonstrates that he did not share the position of the classical and utility schools that welfare is always maximized under free competition. When production takes place under long-run increasing cost or long-run decreasing cost, there will be a loss in economic welfare under laissez-faire conditions. These cases lend themselves best, Marshall believed, to the partial type of analysis in which it is possible to concentrate on net changes in economic welfare as a result of given changes in particular sectors of the economy, the rest of the system being assumed constant. Marshall measures these changes in terms of the effect which altered opportunities to buy or sell a particular commodity have on the surpluses consumers are able to reap. The change in consumer surplus is measured in terms of a sum of money which will offset the gain or loss resulting from price changes brought about by the imposition of a tax or the granting of a subsidy in industries operating with different laws of return.

The effects a tax or subsidy will have is most clear-cut in a constant-cost industry. This is illustrated in Figure 15–3, in which the imposition of a tax raises the long-run supply curve to *ss*. The demand curve *DD* will

---

[41] *Ibid.*, p. 503.

then cut the supply curve at *W* and output will be contracted from *OB* to *OA*. Consumer surplus will be reduced from *DYS* before the tax to *DWs* after the tax. The loss in consumer surplus due to the tax is therefore *sWYS*, while tax receipts are *sWXS*. Thus the loss of consumer surplus is greater than the tax receipts by the amount *WXY*. This triangle on the graph represents the net loss to the community.

The effect of a subsidy given to the same commodity can be demonstrated by similar logic. Assume *ss* as the original supply curve and *SS* as the new supply curve that results when a subsidy of *sZYS* facilitates an expansion of output from *OA* to *OB*. In this case the gain in consumer surplus is smaller than the subsidy spent to acquire it, and the triangle *WYZ* represents the net loss to the community. Marshall concludes, there-

FIGURE 15-3

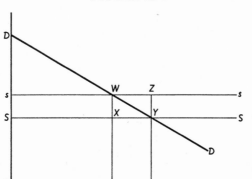

fore, that the imposition of a tax or the granting of a subsidy to a constant-cost industry can make no positive contribution to the economic well-being of consumers.

It may be desirable, however, to tax an industry which operates under diminishing returns and subsidize one which operates under increasing returns. A tax will be beneficial in an industry subject to sharply diminishing returns because in this case a small reduction in output is associated with a substantial reduction in cost, so that the receipts from the tax will be greater than the loss in consumer surplus. Conversely, a subsidy will increase welfare in an industry operating under increasing returns if a small increase in output is associated with a considerable reduction in cost, for here the gain in consumer surplus will be greater than the amount spent on the subsidy. Thus, Marshall concludes that it might be "for the advantage of the community that the government should levy taxes on commodities which obey the laws of diminishing returns, and devote part of the proceeds to bounties on commodities which obey the law of increasing returns."[42] He

---

[42] *Ibid.*, p. 475.

warns, however, that his analysis does not, in and of itself, "afford a valid ground for government interference."

THE PRICING OF PRODUCTIVE FACTORS

Distribution Theory in Relation to Value Theory

Marshall's theory of distribution, as already observed, is an application of his theory of value to the pricing of the factors of production. Factor prices are envisaged as being determined through the interaction of demand and supply forces precisely as are commodity prices. The prices that rule in the factor markets are, at one and the same time, costs of production to the businessmen who give them employment and incomes to the factors. Since, under free competition, long-run commodity prices are equal to production costs, they are also equal, in the aggregate, to long-run factor incomes. Thus, Marshall established an interdependence or complementarity between value theory and distribution theory that was absent in the thinking of his classical predecessors. He also included organization, or enterprise, in his classification of the factors of production, along with land, labor, and capital. The incomes of these factors, which in the aggregate constitute the national dividend, are rent, wages, interest, and profit. Each of these shares, with the exception of the profit residuum, is a market-determined price which needs to be explained in terms of the demand and supply conditions which are operative in the long run as well as in shorter periods.

Marginal Productivity and Factor Demand

Marshall emphasized that the demand for a factor of production by a firm or industry is a derived demand which depends on the value of its services in the production of output. Since the employment of increasing quantities of a variable resource which is combined with one or more fixed resources will result in diminishing marginal returns to that resource beyond some point, it follows that the marginal revenue which the sale of its output yields will also diminish beyond some point. A firm's demand curve for a variable resource will therefore be downward-sloping. The market demand curve for a factor is also downward-sloping. All firms using a given variable factor will experience diminishing returns beyond some point as they employ greater quantities of it. But in addition, the increased product of a variable factor employed by all the firms in an industry is likely to depress the sale price of the product, and hence the marginal revenue product of the variable factor. A market demand curve for a factor cannot, therefore, be drawn on the basis of an assumed product price as is done for a single firm.

While the marginal revenue product of a factor governs the demand for it, it does not, in Marshall's view, explain the price it will command any more than utility governs the price of a commodity. An explanation of the distributive shares therefore requires an examination of the factors influencing the supply of various productive agents, for the interaction of demand and supply forces governs factor prices as well as commodity prices. "The nominal value of everything, whether it be a particular kind of labor or capital or anything else, rests, like the keystone of an arch, balanced in equilibrium between the contending pressures of its two opposing sides; the forces of demand press on the one side, and those of supply on the other."[43]

The Supply of Productive Factors

Time is relevant to the examination of the supply of productive factors, just as it is with respect to the supply of commodities. Marshall maintained that while the short-run supply of the factors is for all practical purposes fixed, the long-run supply of reproducible factors exhibits a reflex influence of remuneration.[44] Thus the supply of labor in the aggregate and of each grade, including that of enterprise and organization, is conceived of as a positive function of the wage rate, and the supply of savings and capital is seen as being responsive to the interest rate.

Turning specifically to the supply of labor, Marshall recognizes that there are complex sociological influences at work which he examines with great insight. But he maintains that in the long run the supply of various kinds of labor responds to economic factors. His emphasis on the functional relationship between the remuneration of labor and its supply is somewhat reminiscent of Malthus's position. However, unlike Malthus, he conceived of the growth of the labor supply as including not merely the increase in numbers, but also the additional quantity of labor associated with the increased efficiency that accompanies a rising standard of life.

Marshall's explanation of the motives for saving and the supply of capital also emphasizes the reflex influence of remuneration on supply. Thus, he states that "a rise in the rate of interest offered for capital . . . tends to increase the volume of savings. . . . It is a nearly universal rule that a rise in the rate increases the desire to save; and it often increases the power to save."[45] Although it is recognized that the motives for saving are very complex and that the rate of interest frequently has little effect on individual savings, the long-run supply of savings in the aggregate is seen as being responsive to a rise in the demand price for it. Only land and other gifts of nature are unique in that their supply in a settled country is fixed even in the long run, so that earnings have no influence on their supply.

The Pricing of Productive Factors

Because the rewards of reproducible factors are similar to that of land when their supplies are relatively fixed, as they are in the short run, it is

---

[43] *Ibid.*, p. 526.
[44] *Ibid.*, Book VI, chap. ii.
[45] *Ibid.*, p. 236.

convenient to examine land rent first and then proceed to the incomes of the other factors. Because the supply of land is fixed in a settled country, Marshall envisages the various parcels that make up the total supply as being transferred from one use to another as the demands, supplies, and prices of various crops alter the opportunity for gain. The active factor determining the uses to which land will be put is the relative demand for the various crops it can produce. "Each crop strives against others for the possession of the land; and if any one crop shows signs of being more remunerative than before relatively to others, the cultivators will devote more of their land and resources to it."[46] Thus the rent secured from any one use must equal that possible from any other use in an equilibrium situation. Therefore, from the point of view of the individual landowner, land is not notably different from capital, for free capital can be invested either in land or in industrial equipment. In either case, the income is a rate of return on an investment whose value is established by capitalizing the income it yields.

Where land is leased to a tenant, the payment he must make for its use is obviously related to the return the owner could earn by cultivating it himself. The rent he pays is therefore one of the costs which must be covered by the market price of his product. This conclusion is at odds with the Ricardian dictum that rent is price-determined rather than price-determining. The notion that rent is not a cost of production is valid only within the framework of the implicit Ricardian hypothesis that land is used only to produce the raw products of labor's subsistence and that it has no alternative use. Since the long-run price of any agricultural commodity must cover the cost of the marginal application of the labor and capital required to produce it, all units of land on which labor and capital are not marginal yield a surplus which is rent in the Ricardian sense. Conceived of in this way, Marshall agreed, rent is not a cost of production and exerts no influence on price. However, when rent is looked at from a private point of view, it is not a surplus but a competitive price which must be paid in order to bid land away from an alternative use.

The difference between Ricardo's treatment of rent and Marshall's stems largely from the problems with which they dealt. Ricardo, it will be recalled, was primarily concerned with explaining the incomes of various social classes, particularly as they were affected by the Corn Laws. He conceived of rent as making its appearance when population growth required less fertile or less well-situated land to be taken out of idleness and used in the production of raw produce. His concern was not with the rent paid by particular agricultural products for particular fields, but with the rent paid by raw produce as a whole for agricultural land as a whole. Competing uses of land for different kinds of raw products, or for nonagri-

---

[46] *Ibid.,* p. 435.

cultural uses, were not considered because his concern was only to determine the laws which regulate the distribution of the produce of the earth among the three social classes under the names of rent, profit, and wages.

Marshall, however, was concerned primarily with the problem of exchange value as it applies to commodities and factors of production. Since the problem of exchange value always relates to particular commodities, Marshall recognized that part of the expense of producing a commodity is the competitive price it is necessary to pay for land in order to take it away from other uses. In this case, rent is a necessary payment; in the other, it is not. Thus, it is the difference in the hypotheses from which they started which is at the root of the issue as to whether rent is a cause or an effect of price. Marshall's own conclusion was that "it is wisest not to say that 'Rent does not enter into the cost of production because that will confuse many people.' But it is wicked to say that 'Rent *does* enter into the cost of production,' because that is sure to be applied in such a way as to lead to the denial of subtle truths. . . ."[47]

In the short run, the rewards of labor and capital are governed by essentially the same principles as the rent of land. Since their supply is relatively fixed, the demand for them is the primary factor governing their remuneration. Their marginal productivity rules the demand for them, and the application of each factor to its profitable margin of use causes the marginal increment of each factor to earn a reward equivalent to its addition to the value of the total product. Competition among homogeneous units of the same factor will operate to secure the same reward for each increment of a factor as the marginal one, since all units are interchangeable. Short-run factor rewards are therefore adjusted by the current market situation without reference to the cost of producing the factor. They may thus exceed the cost of bringing the factors to maket, so that a surplus in the form of quasi rent is contained in their prices.

However, the tendency of short-run factor rewards to equal the contribution of the factor at its margin of employment is not, in Marshall's view, a theory of distribution. It merely serves to "throw into a clear light the action of one of the causes" which govern factor rewards. This cause operates on the demand side. But supply forces must also be taken into account. Thus, Marshall's theory of distribution is not a marginal productivity theory of distribution, but one which holds that we must look to the margin to discover the forces which govern the determination of factor rewards. Supply forces as well as those of demand are operative.

Unlike land, labor and capital are reproducible. While the reflex action will be slow, their supply will tend to increase with their remuneration. With respect to labor, the marginal productivity of each grade will govern the demand for it, so that wages will tend to equal the marginal

---

[47] Pigou, *op. cit.*, p. 436 (from letter to Francis Edgeworth).

revenue product of labor. At the same time, however, wages also bear an indirect and complex relationship to the cost of rearing and training labor, and therefore to its supply. Thus, Marshall, unlike the classicists, does not see the real wage of labor as a constant determined in the long run by the cost of producing raw produce at the margin. Resorting once more to static assumptions, he concludes that if the economic conditions of a country remain stable for a sufficiently long period of time, the adjustment of the supply of labor to the demand for it will cause human beings to earn an amount which corresponds fairly well to their cost of rearing and training.[48] It follows that there is a separate rate of wages for each grade of labor which depends in the long run on the amount of that grade demanded and supplied.

Demand and supply forces are similarly at work in the determination of the income of capital. Such capital may be free capital which is available for new investment, or capital which has already been invested in concrete appliances. The present rate of interest reflects the temporary equilibration of the current demand for and supply of funds. Because the supply of capital is relatively fixed its short run earnings are not necessarily equal to the present rate of interest. Its earnings reflect the market values of its products and are comparable to the earnings of land. Such earnings are properly conceived of as quasi rents rather than interest, though they can be expressed as a percent by capitalizing them at the current rate of interest.

The long run earnings of capital reflect the influence of altered supplies of industrial equipment over time. Types of capital yielding high returns will tend to be augmented in the long run, while those which yield relatively lower earnings will be decreased in supply. As a result, all types of capital will tend to yield a normal rate of return in the long run which corresponds to the additional amount of value product created by the capital applied at the margin.

Marshall's theory of profits involves much the same reasoning as his inquiry into wages and interest. Each industry will tend to evolve the type of organization which provides the greatest opportunity for profit at the margin of advantage. That portion of profit which represents the "wages of management" is governed by the same principle as governs the determination of wages. These are the normal profits which are part of the normal costs of production and which therefore enter into the long-run supply prices of goods. Pure profits exist under competitive conditions only as a short-run phenomenon. Like other quasi rents, they tend to be eliminated, so that there remains in the long run only the normal rate of profit which is required to attract entrepreneurial ability of the appropriate type into each industry. Thus, we see that Marshall's theory of distribution is an integral

---

[48] *Principles,* p. 577.

part of "a continuous thread running through and connecting the applications of the general theory of the equilibrium of demand and supply to different periods of time. . . ."

MACROECONOMIC ASPECTS OF MARSHALL'S ANALYSIS

Acceptance of Say's Law

Since Marshall's analysis is almost wholly microeconomic in character and is little concerned with the behavior of the economy as a whole, it seems appropriate to reflect briefly on the reasons for his apparent lack of interest in what is today called macroeconomic analysis. Macroeconomic analysis, it will be recalled, began with the Physiocrats. The *Tableau Economique* was concerned not only with the allocation of resources, but also with the size of the net product. While the Physiocratic theory of the unique productivity of land and the prime importance of consumption in maintaining the circular flow was subsequently found unacceptable, it is nevertheless to the Physiocrats that we are indebted for a fundamental concept of macroeconomic analysis. This is the concept that production creates incomes which constitute the source from which the circular flow is maintained. Say's law itself is derived from this basic relationship, though it was directed against those aspects of the Physiocratic analysis which Say regarded as untenable.

The conclusions which Ricardo and Mill drew from Say's law effectively limited further macroeconomic analysis on the part of their classical contemporaries and followers because they used it as the basis for their conclusion that overproduction for the economy as a whole is an impossibility and that there cannot be an overaccumulation of capital. Marshall, like his classical forebears, was much more interested in the "normal" equilibrium tendencies of the economy than in its tendency to generate crises and cycles. He paid but limited attention to the problem of oscillations in trade in his treatise on economic principles. Say's law with respect to the impossibility of overproduction for the economy as a whole was implicitly accepted. He also concluded that the labor resources of the economy would tend to be fully employed because the wage rate reductions associated with unemployment would induce businessmen to substitute less expensive factors of production for those that are more expensive.

Although the conclusions derived from Say's law were not based on careful analysis, Marshall nevertheless implicitly made them a premise of his analysis of value and distribution. That is, by assuming full employment and related levels of output and income, Marshall and the thinkers who followed him made their main analytical problem that of price determination and the allocation of resources among alternative uses. The problem of levels of resource use was therefore virtually assumed away. Consequently, it was left to the proponents of the underconsumption doctrine, such as

John A. Hobson, Wilhelm Roscher, and Thorstein Veblen, and the proponents of the disproportionate investment doctrine, such as Michael Tugan-Baranowsky, Arthur Spietoff, and Joseph A. Schumpeter, to challenge Say's law and give the problem of crisis its place in the economic theory of the period between approximately 1870 and 1914.[49]

The Theory of the General Price Level

Though Marshall concerned himself primarily with the explanation of individual commodity and factor prices, he also examined the relationship between the general price level (P), the quantity of money in circulation (M), its velocity of circulation (V), and the volume of trade (T). The formulation of the relationship among these magnitudes which is best known in America is the transactions version of the quantity theory of money which was introduced by Irving Fisher.[50] Fisher emphasized changes in the quantity of money as the causal factor of changes in the general price level, while Marshall's formulation emphasized changes in the use of money as a store of value. His emphasis is premised on the fact that the public holds some portion of the annual money value of goods and services in its cash balances at any moment of time.

Marshall thought that the essential reason why people demand cash or, in modern terminology, have a preference for liquidity is to bridge the time gap between the receipt of money income and its disbursement. If the demand for money for transactions purposes is such that the money stock turns over (say) at a rate of four times a year, the equivalent of one fourth of the annual money value of output will be in cash balances at any moment of time. Thus the demand for cash, which Marshall represented by the letter k, is the reciprocal of V, the velocity of circulation, or $\frac{1}{V}$. By substituting k for velocity in the equation of exchange, Marshall's formulation reads $M = PTk$, where M is the quantity of money at any instant of time and $PT \cdot k$ is the average level of prices, given the volume of trade and the demand for cash to satisfy transaction needs.

Marshall's introduction of cash balances into the equation of exchange has the obvious advantage of facilitating the examination of changes in the price level initiated by changes in the liquidity preferences of the public as well as changes which are initiated by alterations in the quantity of money itself. However, Marshall's introduction of the k factor did not lead

---

[49] Since business cycle theory has historically been on the periphery of economic theory, examination of the historical development of this branch of economic analysis has been omitted from this work. A lucid account of the developments of this period is available in T. W. Hutchison, *A Review of Economic Doctrines, 1870–1929* (Oxford: Clarendon Press, 1953). Selected contemporary developments are examined in Chapter 19 below.

[50] Irving Fisher, *The Purchasing Power of Money* (New York: The Macmillan Co., 1911 revised 1922).

to any different conclusions than those associated with Fisher's quantity theory. This is because k in the Marshallian formulation, like V in the Fisher formulation, is a stable factor. The demand for money for transactions purposes is a function of the level of income and institutional factors such as the frequency of the pay period. It is therefore not subject to autonomous variations which will affect the general price level independently of the quantity of money.

While Marshall also conceived of an asset demand for money, that is, a demand for money to satisfy the speculative acquisition of money assets, he made virtually nothing of it, and it was practically forgotten by his followers. However, his introduction of the concept of a demand for cash balances was a step toward the Keynesian conception, in which primary emphasis was to be given to the speculative motive for holding cash. The latter was to make the demand for cash a function of interest rates (bond prices) and, by showing the relationship between interest rates and the investment demand schedule, integrate monetary theory with the theory of income and output. But until this was done, monetary theory dwelt largely in a compartment separate from the theory of income, output, and employment, and its content was virtually limited to the quantity theory of money.

CONCLUDING REMARKS

While Marshall intended to complete and generalize Mill's exposition of Ricardo's theory of value and distribution with the aid of mathematical techniques, he actually produced, as our presentation has shown, a more complete transformation than he himself originally anticipated. The main features of this transformation consist of (1) the explicit introduction of demand equations in the explanation of commodity values; (2) recognition that the technical coefficients of production are not fixed but vary with the costs of factor substitution at the margin, and that this will affect the marginal cost of producing a commodity in the short run; (3) inquiry into the laws of return which govern cost of production in the long run; (4) recognition that the real wage of labor is not a constant which depends on the cost of producing raw produce at the margin, and that there is a separate wage rate for each grade of labor which depends in the long run on the amount of that grade demanded and the amount supplied; (5) recognition that the return to capital is distinct from that of organization; and (6) recognition that factor prices and commodity prices are interrelated, and that the theories of value and distribution are therefore different aspects of a single problem.

While Marshall chose to conduct his analysis with the aid of the partial equilibrium technique, he also developed concepts which have led outside its confines. The concept of demand elasticity, particularly in such modern developments as cross elasticity and income elasticity, the principle of substitution, and consumer surplus all lead toward the exploration of interrelationships. So do his concepts of joint demand, joint supply, composite demand, and composite supply. His treatment of these cases in his Note XXI leads him to the formulation of equations of the Walrásian type and the conclusion that "however complex the problem may become, we can see that it is theoretically determinate, because the number of unknowns is always exactly equal to the number of equations which we obtain." Marshall himself saw the general equilibrium analysis of the Walrásian type as the logical complement of his partial analysis. But even within the framework of his partial analysis, the principle of substitution at the margin—involving as it does the balancing of small increments of payments and satisfaction, costs and receipts, effort and income, by consumers, producers, and factors—provides the connecting link among all sectors of the economy. Thus the principle of interdependence and mutual determination pervades every aspect of Marshall's analysis, even though the technique of abstraction is employed to reduce the number of variables to manageable proportions.

Marshall also went beyond Ricardo and Mill in emphasizing the efforts and sacrifices which constitute the real costs of production and the satisfactions of consumption. Ricardo and Mill consistently thought of costs in objective rather than in subjective terms. But Marshall emphasized the psychological factors which underlie behavior in the marketplace and considered them measurable in terms of money. Though the first edition of the *Principles* equated optimizing behavior with the hedonistic pleasure-maximizing, pain minimizing choices of utilitarian ethics, subsequent editions sought to avoid the terminology of Benthamism, if not the spirit.

While Marshall examined the nature and sources of monopoly power, most of his analysis was conducted within the framework of the assumption that there is "freedom of industry and enterprise"—not perfect competition but pure competition of the atomistic variety in which there are a sufficiently large number of small economic units to prevent any one of them from exerting a dominant force in the market. He believed in the power of competitive forces to overcome the forces leading to monopoly. He also valued competition as a stimulus to individual initiative and achievement, and believed it would lead to social progress more surely than any form of socialism. He was not, however, opposed to reform measures so long as they did not tend to stultify individual opportunities for growth.

The main departure which modern theory has made from the *Principles* has been in the realm of macroeconomics. Whereas Marshall regarded money as a passive factor with respect to the level of economic activity and accepted the conclusions inherent in Say's law, modern macroeconomic theorists explain the determination of output on non-Sayian assumptions. Their concern is, therefore, to explain the level of resource use rather than the allocation of resources. Even though many Marshallian concepts and tools are indispensable to their analysis, much of the inspiration for modern macroeconomic analysis derives from contributions to the theory of economic crisis and business fluctuation which were made by persons not associated with the neoclassical tradition. Neoclassical theorists literally assumed away the whole problem of explaining economic fluctuations as a result of their acceptance of Say's law; and in their preoccupation with real phenomena, they also failed to appreciate the role of monetary phenomena in the determination of real magnitudes. It is not until the "Keynesian revolution" that the role of money and interest rates with respect to the level of employment and income began to be understood. But once this understanding was gained, its practical significance became so great that microeconomic analysis was almost shunted aside as macroeconomic analysis came to dominate contemporary economic theory.

Microeconomic analysis has, however, not stood still but has developed in two directions, one of which is Marshallian in inspiration while the other is a continuation of the Walrásian tradition. Marshall's continued influence manifests itself primarily in modern price theory. While the emphasis today is on the firm rather than on the industry, modern theories of monopolistic and imperfect competition are not nearly so much revolutionary as they are evolutionary. These developments are examined in the next chapter, which opens our inquiry into contemporary developments in economic theory. Chapter 16 examines those aspects of modern microeconomic analysis which are of Continental rather than English inspiration. while Chapters 17 and 18 complete our inquiry into the mainstreams of contemporary economic theory by examining the developments which have taken place in macroeconomic analysis as a result of the Keynesian revolution.

SUGGESTIONS FOR FURTHER READING

GUILLEBAUD, CLAUDE W. (ed.). *Marshall's Principles of Economics,* Vol. II, "Editorial Introduction." 9th ed. London: Macmillan & Co., 1961.

HUTCHISON, T. W. *A Review of Economic Doctrines, 1870–1919,* chap. iv. Oxford: Clarendon Press, 1953.

KEYNES, JOHN MAYNARD. "Alfred Marshall, 1842–1924," *Economic Journal,* Vol. XXXIV (September, 1924), pp. 311–72. Reprinted in ARTHUR C. PIGOU (ed.), *Memorials of Alfred Marshall.* London: Macmillan & Co., 1925, pp. 1–65.

———. *Essays in Biography.* Rev. ed. London: Rupert Hart-Davis, 1951.

MARSHALL, ALFRED. *Principles of Economics,* in particular Book V. 8th ed. London: Macmillan & Co., 1920.

PIGOU, ARTHUR C. (ed.). *Memorials of Alfred Marshall.* London: Macmillan & Co., 1925.

SHOVE, G. F. "The Place of Marshall's 'Principles' in the Development of

Economic Thought," *Economic Journal,* Vol. LII (December, 1942). Reprinted in JOSEPH J. SPENGLER and W. ALLEN, eds. *Essays in Economic Thought: Aristotle to Marshall.* Chicago: Rand McNally & Co., 1960.

STIGLER, GEORGE. *Production and Distribution Theories,* chap. iv. New York: Macmillan Co., 1941.

VINER, JACOB. "Cost Curves and Supply Curves," *Zeitschrift für Nationalökonomie,* Vol. III (1931). Reprinted in R. V. CLEMENCE, ed., *Readings in Economic Analysis.* Reading, Mass.: Addison-Wesley Publishing Co., Inc., 1950, Vol. II and in GEORGE STIGLER and KENNETH BOULDING, eds., *Readings in Price Theory,* Vol. VI, Homewood, Ill.: Richard D. Irwin, Inc., 1952.

WOLFE, J. N. "Marshall and the Trade Cycle," *Oxford Economic Papers,* February, 1956.

Chapter 16

CONTEMPORARY CONTRIBUTIONS TO THE THEORY OF NONPERFECT COMPETITION

INTRODUCTION

The Nature of Contemporary Microeconomic Analysis

Contemporary theorists have done considerable work in refining and extending the analyses of the marginalists whose works have been examined in the preceding four chapters. Their efforts have, on the one hand, continued the tradition of particular price analysis by refining the work of Augustin Cournot and Alfred Marshall and extending the scope of their efforts by examining in detail the price behavior of firms which are neither pure monopolists nor pure competitors. They have, on the other hand, also continued the general equilibrium approach of Leon Walrás and his successor, Vilfredo Pareto. Both the modern theory of optimal consumer and producer behavior and what has come to be called "welfare theory" owe a great deal to the approach of the marginal utility school and the fact that the thinkers who followed Walrás broadened their inquiry into individual optimizing behavior to embrace the economy as a whole in their general equilibrium of the static state under perfect competition. By contrast, our present understanding of price determination is largely Marshallian in inspiration and rests hardly at all on either the marginal utility theory of value or the concept of general equilibrium. Yet, taken as a whole, modern microeconomic analysis continues both the Marshallian tradition of particular price analysis and the Walrásian general equilibrium approach with its relatively greater orientation to the problem of consumer satisfaction. This chapter will concern itself with contemporary refinements in the theory of monopoly and the theory of monopolistic or imperfect competition. The burden of the next chapter will be the theory of optimal consumer and producer behavior and modern welfare economics.

One cannot help but speculate whether the more rigorous treatment of imperfectly competitive market structures by contemporary theorists was "triggered" by concern with the problem of "big business." It is certainly true that in this country, at least, there was renewed public concern over the concentration of economic power during the 1920's and 1930's, and many institutional studies of the problem appeared at that time.[1] Still, no one could have been more concerned with the problem of monopoly than Marshall or John Bates Clark, though both conducted their theoretical analyses on the premise that most markets approximate "free competition." While the problem of big business and its regulation may indeed have been more pressing in the 1930's than it was fifty or so years earlier, there is no evidence that the new theoretical developments in the area of price theory were in any way a response to the challenge created by this aspect of the institutional environment. If any environmental influences were at work in stimulating their development, they were derived from the intellectual rather than the institutional environment. In particular, greater interest in mathematical economics focused attention on the work of Cournot, whose *Researches into the Mathematical Principles of the Theory of Wealth* (1838) was then nearing its one-hundredth anniversary. Cournot's theory of monopoly and his conclusion that a monopolist will maximize profit when he equates the first derivative of total revenue (i.e., marginal revenue) to the first derivative of total cost (i.e., marginal cost) was the first major achievement of mathematical economics. It is understandable that a wider study of Cournot's work stimulated a more rigorous classification of market structures along the lines he suggested, along with greater terminological precision and development of new analytical concepts. The gaps in Marshall's analysis, particularly as they relate to pricing situations intermediate between competition and monopoly, also attracted able minds. More recently, it is the problem of oligopoly, or competition among a few sellers, which has been of greatest interest in the area of price theory. The paragraphs which follow will provide acquaintance with the names and brief biographical information about the main contributors to price theory since Marshall.

The Contributors to Modern Price Theory

With respect to the theory of monopoly, the improvement since Cournot has been mainly in terms of exposition. The main substantive contributions have been the theory of monopoly price discrimination and the development of the case of monopsony, or buyer monopoly, to parallel the traditional case of seller monopoly. With respect to the theory of monopoly price discrimination, the most substantial contributions have come from the late Arthur C. Pigou (1877–1959) and Joan Robinson (1903–   ).

Pigou was Marshall's most eminent student and succeeded him in the

---

[1] Claire Wilcox, *Competition and Monopoly in American Industry,* Temporary National Economic Committee Monograph No. 21 (Washington, D.C.: U.S. Government Printing Office, 1941); A. A. Berle and G. C. Means, *The Corporation and Private Property* (New York: Commerce Clearing House, Inc., 1932); and Frank Fetter, *Masquerade of Monopoly* (New York: Harcourt Brace & Co., 1931).

chair of economics at Cambridge University. He was particularly concerned with the problem of maximizing social and economic welfare, and his *Economics of Welfare,* which first appeared in 1920, is today a classic. His examination of the nature and results of monopoly pricing is conducted within the framework of his welfare analysis. He was also concerned with a variety of other theoretical issues in economics, among them business cycles and the problem of unemployment. His disagreement with John Maynard Keynes with respect to the nature of the unemployment problem and the most effective way of dealing with it is one of the most significant controversies in the history of economic analysis.

Other than Pigou's, the most substantive contribution to the theory of monopoly pricing is to be found in Robinson's *Economics of Imperfect Competition* (1933), which is also concerned with the analysis of pricing situations which lie in the "gray area" between pure monopoly and pure competition. Mrs. Robinson, of Cambridge University, is perhaps the only woman to achieve recognition as an economic theorist. It is she who rediscovered Cournot's first derivative of total revenue and christened it "marginal revenue," and whose simple yet elegant geometry popularized the use of marginal cost and marginal revenue curves in price analysis. She has also made the most substantial contribution of any contemporary writer since Pigou to the theory of monopoly price discrimination, besides developing the case of monopsony, or buyer monopoly, to parallel the traditional case of seller monopoly.

Her contributions are not, however, limited to the field of price theory. She is equally accomplished in the area of macroeconomic theory. Her *Introduction to the Theory of Employment* (1937) was the earliest effort to present the gist of Keynes's theory on an elementary level, and she also authored *Essays on the Theory of Employment* (1936), in which she examines the application of Keynesian theory to particular problems. Her most recent work in this area, besides numerous articles and essays, is *The Accumulation of Capital* (1960), in which she has demonstrated the construction of a model of secular growth. Her essays on a wide variety of theoretical subjects are to be found in *Collected Essays of Joan Robinson* (1951), and she has also written *An Essay in Marxian Economics* (1942), besides her recent philosophical essay which has been published under the title *Economic Philosophies* (1962).

It is not, however, the theory of monopoly but the theory of monopolistic competition which constitutes the main refinement and extension of the work of Cournot and Marshall. Although both Cournot and Marshall examined monopoly behavior with respect to price, this case was regarded as one which is seldom encountered in the real world. Marshall lavished almost all of his concern on firms which produced their products under conditions of free competition, even though he noted, in his *Industry and Trade,* that competition and monopoly are "interlaced." Nowhere, however,

284 · DEVELOPMENT OF ECONOMIC ANALYSIS

did he examine the nature of this interlacing or its significance for price determination. It was not until the 1920's and early 1930's that there emerged a growing concern with the gaps in Marshall's work, particularly with respect to pricing situations intermediate between competition and monopoly. The most vulnerable part of his analysis proved to be the resort to "external economies" as a device for reconciling increasing returns with the assumption of pure competition. Their inherent incompatibility was clearly pointed out by Piero Sraffa (1898–   ) in his now classic article of 1926 on the laws of return.[2] Sraffa, an Italian who emigrated to England, where he studied under Marshall, eventually taught at Cambridge. His most distinguished work is his recent edition of Ricardo's collected works and personal correspondence. But he is equally well known for his provocative article on the laws of return, which focused analytical attention on the main "dark spots" in the Marshallian theory of value and urged its reconstruction. Even though he did not participate further in bringing about this reconstruction, the keenness of his observations on the technical shortcomings of Marshall's long-run supply curve are alone sufficient to secure him a place among contemporary contributors to value theory.

Sraffa's article had already appeared when Edward Chamberlin (1899–   ), still a graduate student at Harvard in 1927, submitted a doctoral dissertation in which he undertook to examine the determination of prices in markets in which monopolistic and competitive elements are "blended." This dissertation was published in 1933 under the title of *The Theory of Monopolistic Competition*. Because it appeared so nearly at the same time as Joan Robinson's *Economics of Imperfect Competition* was published in England, both writers are equally recognized as pioneers in the theory of pricing situations that are intermediate between pure competition and pure monopoly. Unlike Robinson, Chamberlin, who is now Professor of Economics at Harvard, has devoted his professional efforts almost exclusively to exploring the various ramifications of his original thesis, including the implications of the theory of monopolistic competition for the theory of distribution.

While the leading contributions to contemporary literature on price theory are those of Chamberlin and Robinson, a third contribution was published in Germany during the same period. Heinrich von Stackelberg (1905–46) published his *Marktform und Gleichgewicht (Market Structures and Equilibrium)*, which is especially concerned with duopoly and oligopoly, in 1934.[3] The date of this work thus coincides with the period during which the National Socialist Party was achieving full power in the third Reich. It is interesting to note that von Stackelberg's conclusions with

---

[2] Piero Sraffa, "The Laws of Return under Competitive Conditions," *Economic Journal,* Vol. XXXVI (December, 1926).

[3] Translated as *Theory of the Market Economy* by Allen T. Peacock (New York: Oxford University Press, 1952).

respect to the proper role of the state in oligopolistic markets is compatible with the policies of the Nazi Party, although von Stackelberg supported them by economic analysis.

Original contributions to the literature of price theory have been scant since the three leading works of the 1930's. One contribution of note since that time was made at the close of the decade by Robert Triffin (1911–). His *Monopolistic Competition and General Equilibrium Theory* (1940), provides an analytical comparison of the works of Chamberlin, Robinson, von Stackelberg and others and suggests that the theory of monopolistic competition may provide the bridge which is needed to reconcile the particular equilibrium approach of Marshall with the general equilibrium approach of Walrás. However, the most significant theoretical development of recent years may prove to be that which derives from the application of the principle of game theory to economic behavior. This development is associated primarily with John von Neumann (1903–56) and Oskar Morgenstern (1902–) of Princeton.

John von Neumann was a Hungarian who taught briefly in Germany after obtaining his doctorate at Budapest in 1926. His interest in the mathematical treatment of the theory conflict had already been established in 1928, when he presented a paper to the Mathematics Society in Göttingen, Germany. He came to Princeton in 1930 and was later a member of the Atomic Energy Commission. His untimely death at the age of only 53 was a loss to both the natural and the social sciences. His coauthor on *The Theory of Games and Economic Behavior* (1944), Oskar Morgenstern, came from Germany to the United States and Princeton University in 1938. Together, they pioneered in the application of the theory of strategy, previously found useful in the formulation of military tactics and political policies, to the study of economic behavior.

SOME "DARK SPOTS" IN NEOCLASSICAL VALUE THEORY

Assumptions concerning the Firm's Demand Curve

While Marshall's theory of value is unquestionably superior to its predecessors, it nevertheless has certain shortcomings which made themselves increasingly apparent as time went on. One of these is the implicit assumption that most firms produce and sell their products under conditions of "free competition," that is, in markets in which they must accept a price determined by the interaction of forces outside their individual control as a parameter of action. The individual firm was conceived to have an infinitely elastic demand for its product at the going market price. Unless a firm was a monopolist, there was therefore no need to single it out for separate examination because its experience was essentially that of every other firm in its industry. Thus, Marshall solved the problem of determining the equilibrium price of a commodity in terms of the industry as a whole by setting an industry supply curve, which was conceived of as a simple summation of the supply curves of a large number of firms producing an essentially homogeneous commodity, against an industry demand curve, constructed by the summation of individual demand curves for a given product.

The shortcoming of this procedure is that it does not take into account the fact that buyers are not indifferent with respect to the seller from whom they buy a particular commodity. The causes for their preferences are, as Sraffa observed in his 1926 article, extremely diverse and "may range from long custom, personal acquaintance, confidence in the quality of the product, proximity, knowledge of particular requirements and the possibility of obtaining credit, to the reputation of a trademark, or sign or a name with high traditions, or to such special features of modeling or design in the product as, without constituting it a distinct commodity intended for the satisfaction of particular needs—have for their principle purpose that of distinguishing it from the products of other firms." Joan Robinson, in *The Economics of Imperfect Competition,* made essentially the same observations with respect to the causes of buyer preferences and termed the existence of such preferences as the source of "imperfect" competition.[4] Edward Chamberlin likewise cites essentially the same factors as creating what he terms "product differentiation," the effect of which is to distinguish significantly the goods of one seller from those of his rivals so that there exists a market in which there is "monopolistic competition."[5]

Regardless of the particular method a seller employs to attract and hold customers, the effect of such techniques is always to make the demand curve of the individual seller less than perfectly elastic. This effect was succinctly expressed by Sraffa in his observation that "the peculiarity of the case of the firm which does not possess an actual monopoly but merely has a particular market is that, in the demand schedule for the goods produced by it, the possible buyers are entered in descending order according to the price which each of them is prepared to pay, not rather than go entirely without, but rather than not buy it from that particular producer instead of elsewhere."[6] That product differentiation will cause the demand curve of an individual seller to diverge from the horizontal position it would have if no seller had any individual control over price was similarly pointed out by Chamberlin and Robinson.[7]

Product differentiation also has the effect of making a firm's demand

---

[4] Joan Robinson, *The Economics of Imperfect Competition* (London: Macmillan & Co., 1933), pp. 89–90 (subsequently cited as *Imperfect Competition*).

[5] Edward Chamberlin, *The Theory of Monopolistic Competition* (Cambridge, Mass.: Harvard University Press, 1933, revised 1948), p. 8 (subsequently cited as *Monopolistic Competition*).

[6] Sraffa, "The Laws of Return," p. 546.

[7] *Monopolistic Competition*, p. 71; *Imperfect Competition*, p. 21.

curve and its cost curves interdependent, for the firm's demand curve then depends partly on the expenditure it makes to attract customers. Chamberlin, in particular, has distinguished between selling costs and production costs, and has pointed out that the existence of selling expenditures is prima facie evidence that the market is not one in which there is pure competition.[8] If a seller conducts a successful selling effort, "this means a shift of the demand curve for his product upward and to the right."[9] The position and slope of the demand curve of an individual seller depend not only on his product but also on the extent to which he can, by his selling expense, build up preferences for his particular output as opposed to that of his rivals. It follows that when there is product differentiation, the sales and cost curves, and therefore the profits of rival firms, are interdependent in various degrees. Thus, there arises what Chamberlin has chosen to call the "group problem." His *Theory of Monopolistic Competition* lavishes great attention on defining the nature of group equilibrium and examining the mode of its establishment. Robinson's *Economics of Imperfect Competition,* though it parallels in many ways Chamberlin's work, is not concerned directly with the group problem at all, although it describes the phenomenon of product differentiation in almost the same language as Chamberlin.

Assumptions regarding the Laws of Return

An equally troublesome feature of the Marshallian analysis, along with his assumptions regarding the demand curve confronting the typical firm, is his treatment of the long-run laws of return and their effect on the industry supply curve. Marshall, it will be recalled, conceived of the possibility of long-run constant, decreasing, and increasing returns. He recognized that if it were possible for an individual firm, as distinct from an industry as a whole, to experience economies which would give it increasing returns to scale in the long run, free competition would be destroyed. He did not, however, believe that the economies from which increasing returns might derive are exclusively available to any one firm. He thought them to be the result of external economies equally available to all and therefore compatible with the continuation of competition. This conclusion was, in Sraffa's view, such a vulnerable part of Marshall's analysis of the long-run supply curve that he was led to make the following observation in his 1926 article:

In the tranquil view which the modern theory of value presents us there is one dark spot which disturbs the harmony of the whole. This is represented by the supply curve, based upon the laws of increasing and diminishing returns. That its foundations are less solid than those of the other portions of the

---

[8] *Monopolistic Competition,* chap. vi.

[9] *Ibid.,* chap. vii, p. 130.

structure is generally recognized. That they are so weak as to be unable to support the weight imposed on them is a doubt which slumbers beneath the consciousness of many, but which most succeed in silently suppressing.[10]

The crucial question with respect to the long-run supply curve of a particular industry was, as Sraffa viewed the matter, the compatibility of Marshall's explanation of the tendency toward long-run increasing and decreasing supply price with his insistence on a particular equilibrium analysis. Particular equilibrium methodology requires that variations in output or demand in one industry have neither a direct nor an indirect effect on any other industry. Such long-run independence is unlikely, Sraffa contended, in industries subject to either diminishing or increasing returns because, in these cases, changes in the output of the commodity in question have an effect on the cost of using factors that also enter into the production of other commodities. The requirements of a particular equilibrium methodology are thus violated. He objected for the same reason to Marshall's reliance on external economies which result from the general progress of the industrial environment as a means of explaining why some industries are able to enjoy long-run increasing returns. Such economies would of course be compatible with the continuation of competitive conditions because they are equally available to all the firms in an industry. This is precisely the source of their appeal to Marshall; but, maintained Sraffa, a particular equilibrium analysis requires that the economies from which long-run decreasing costs derive be *internal* to the industry, even though they are external to the individual firms. "The only economies which could be taken into consideration would be such as occupy an intermediate position between these two extremes; but it is just in the middle that nothing, or almost nothing, is to be found. Those economies which are external from the point of view of the individual firm but internal as regards the industry in its aggregate, constitute precisely the class which is most seldom met with."[11] Sraffa therefore advised that we "abandon the path of free competition and turn in the opposite direction, namely, towards monopoly."

While very few undertakings fit the case of pure monopoly, he believed that the theory of monopoly could provide a guide to the relationship between price and the quantity which can be sold when competition is absent for other reasons. The theory of monopoly is, therefore, useful to us in studying those cases in the real world, and they are in majority, which do not fit either the case of pure competition or pure monopoly but are "scattered along the intermediate zone." He also suggested that the task of reconstructing the theory of value could be immediately begun, for an

---

[10] Sraffa, "The Laws of Return," p. 536.

[11] *Ibid.*, p. 540.

analytical tool equal to the task was already at hand in Marshall's concept of "monopoly net revenue."

The Monopoly Net Revenue Curve

Joan Robinson was among those who responded to Sraffa's urging that the time had come to reconstruct the theory of value. However, she regarded Marshall's tool of monopoly net revenue as being unsatisfactory because "it introduces an artificial cleavage between monopoly and competition."[12] The firm under free competition maximizes profits or minimizes losses by equating its marginal cost to price. But since price (average revenue) is equal to marginal revenue in this case, the firm also equates marginal cost and marginal revenue. A monopolist will do precisely the same thing, although this is obscured when expressed in terms of monopoly net revenue. Actually, it matters not in the least whether we say, as did Marshall, that a monopolist maximizes profit by maximizing his net revenue or whether we say, as did Cournot, that a monopolist will maximize profit when he sets a price which will equate the first derivative of total revenue (marginal revenue) with the first derivative of total cost (marginal cost). However, the latter expression has the advantage of being a principle which is equally applicable to competition and monopoly or any market structure combining elements of both.

Robinson sought to facilitate understanding of the problem of price determination by introducing the concept of marginal revenue and demonstrating the relationship between the average and marginal revenue curves of a monopoly firm as opposed to a purely competitive firm. Their difference derives, she explained, from the fact that under conditions of pure competition the individual firm does not depress the market price by offering additional units for sale, with the result that its demand curve is infinitely elastic. Since there is no change in average revenue regardless of the volume of sales, marginal revenue does not change either. It is, therefore, graphically a horizontal line which is identical with that of average revenue. A monopolist, on the other hand, is supplying the total market, and his demand curve has the same characteristics as the industry demand curve for a purely competitive market. It is the summation of the demand curves of individual consumers and is therefore downward-sloping. The price a monopolist can get for an additional unit of output is always less than can be gotten for a smaller volume. Average revenue declines as output increases, so that marginal revenue will be less than average revenue. Graphically, therefore, the marginal revenue curve will lie below the average revenue curve.[13]

---

[12] *Imperfect Competition*, p. 54.
[13] *Ibid.*, pp. 52–54.

Robinson's discovery of the marginal revenue curve has greatly facilitated both the verbal and the graphical exposition of the behavior of a firm as it maximizes profit or minimizes losses. It is much simpler to say that a firm equates marginal revenue and marginal cost than that it equates the first derivative of total revenue with the first derivative of total cost. In addition, the intersection of the marginal cost and marginal revenue curves as the determinant of a firm's output facilitates a much clearer graphic representation of the behavior of a firm than one which proceeds by means of average revenue and average cost. Chamberlin's diagrams in *The Theory of Monopolistic Competition* depict the behavior of firms with the help of average curves only. This diagrammatic technique is cumbersome in comparison with Robinson's, which employs marginal curves. Her terminology and her geometry have become standard for the profession. Robinson herself demonstrated the finesse with which her tool lends itself to examining the nature and implications of monopoly price determination, particularly in the case of discriminating monopoly and buyer's monopoly. The equilibrium of the firm as distinct from the equilibrium of the group is her main concern and her main contribution to the extension of the neoclassical theory of value. It is therefore convenient to examine further what contemporary theorists have accomplished with respect to eliminating the "dark spots" in neoclassical value theory under two headings: The first is "Equilibrium of the Firm," which focuses on the individual seller of commodities in isolation from any rivals it may have. The second is "Equilibrium of the Group," which examines the impact rival sellers and buyers have on one another's behavior.

EQUILIBRIUM OF THE FIRM

The Conditions of Stable Equilibrium

Chamberlin and Robinson clearly reflect the Marshallian origins of their work in their concern with establishment of equilibrium. Marshall's analysis was of course conducted almost wholly in terms of the industry, the notable exception being the case of monopoly, in which the firm is the industry. Contemporary theorists, on the other hand, having discarded the notion that the firms of an industry have infinitely elastic demand curves, are concerned with the individual firm as a separate entity. Robinson, following Sraffa's suggestion, proceeds by allowing the theory of monopoly to "swallow up" the analysis of competition. It is, however, not the behavior of the pure monopolist that Robinson is concerned with, but rather the behavior of a firm which is a monopolist of its own particular product. The equilibrium position of such a firm is necessarily affected by the nature of the reaction which its price-output decisions have on its competitors. Some method must therefore be devised to deal with the problem of interdependence.

It is in the latter respect that there is a striking difference between the approach of Robinson and that of Chamberlin. Whereas Chamberlin is concerned with analyzing the nature of interdependence and the effect which the price-output decisions of one firm will have on those of its rivals, and therefore on the equilibrium of the group, Robinson makes the implicit assumption that every firm in the group but one is in equilibrium. It is thus possible for her to study in isolation the movement of that firm toward an equilibrium position, guided by the objective of maximizing its monetary profits. It is for this reason that her analysis leaves the impression of being concerned with simple monopoly.

Since the individual firm is conceived to move toward its equilibrium position guided by the objective of maximizing its monetary profits, the first condition which must be satisfied is that its marginal revenue must equal marginal cost. Satisfaction of this condition will not, however, assure a stable equilibrium. Obviously, if the production of a larger output than the one at which $MC = MR$ adds more to total revenue than to total cost, it will pay a firm to expand. Robinson has therefore shown that equality between marginal cost and marginal revenue is only a first-order condition. The stability of monopoly equilibrium depends also on the relationship between the marginal revenue and marginal cost curves of a firm. A stable monopoly equilibrium requires as its second condition that the production of a larger output than that at which $MC = MR$ adds more to total cost than to total revenue, so that a further expansion of output is unprofitable.

Since the marginal revenue curve of a firm will be downward-sloping, unless it is a pure competitor, the second-order condition specified by Robinson for a stable equilibrium of a firm is satisfied if marginal cost is increasing or, at least, decreasing less rapidly than marginal revenue.[14] In either case the MC curve cuts the MR curve from below, as in Part A and Part B of Figure 16–1. If MC cuts MR from above, as in Part C of Figure

FIGURE 16–1

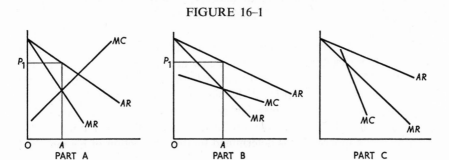

PART A   PART B   PART C

[14] For a mathematical approach to this and other aspects of pricing under non-perfect competition see Henderson, James M. and Quandt, Richard E., *Microeconomic Theory*, New York: McGraw-Hill Book Co. Inc., 1958, Chap. 6.

16–1, so that *MC* lies below *MR* for outputs larger than that at which *MC* = *MR,* the second-order condition is not satisfied; i.e., the maximum profit is indeterminate, and there is no stable equilibrium price or output.

Equilibrium When Monopoly Price Discrimination Is Possible

Monopoly price discrimination, or the practice of charging different prices to different buyers of a product or service, is the ultimate as a technique for profit maximization. It is possible only if a seller who is in a position to control his selling price has the additional power of distinguishing among his customers on the basis of differences in their demand elasticities. Customers having different demand elasticities for a particular product or service, as, for example, is the case with respect to most users of public utility service, enable a seller to group his buyers according to their demand elasticities and to charge a different price to each. The essential requirement for discrimination is the effective segregation of the various parts of the total market. Pigou has shown that this depends on the nontransferability of various units of output and demand from one market to another.[15]

Pigou was, during the 1920's, greatly interested in the special price problems of railroads and showed that the factor of nontransferability is significant in explaining why a discriminatory price structure prevails in this field. A shipper who buys transportation service generally cannot resell a part of the service to some other shipper to whom the railroad has quoted a higher rate.[16] The same factor explains discriminatory rate patterns in the sale of public utility services generally. For example, gas or electric power is sold to industrial users at a lower rate than to residential users; but they cannot redistribute it, at least not without considerable expense, to residential users. Thus the ability of a utility to maintain a policy of price discrimination derives from the fact that ready transference of service from customer to customer is impossible. If units of a product or service were transferable from one market to another, a monopolist would, for all practical purposes, be forced to adhere to a single-price system.

A monopolist who can effectively segregate his markets and who is not subject to public regulation can maximize his returns by charging high prices to those customers whose demands are least elastic, while at the same time cultivating sales to buyers whose demands are more elastic through the offer of low prices.[17] Robinson has demonstrated that profits will be at a maximum when marginal revenue in each submarket is equal to the marginal cost of the whole product. That is, the total output of a discriminating monopolist is determined by the intersection of his marginal

---

[15] Arthur C. Pigou, *Wealth and Welfare* (London: Macmillan & Co., 1912), chap. xxvii.

[16] The freight forwarder does perform this function to a limited extent.

[17] *Imperfect Competition,* chap. xv.

cost curve and the aggregate marginal revenue curve. This is shown in Figure 16–2, in which MR_1 is the marginal revenue curve in the market having a less elastic demand and MR_2 is the marginal revenue curve in the market having a more elastic demand.[18] They are derived from demand curves D_1 and D_2. The lateral summation of both demand curves results in the aggregate demand curve, AD. The aggregate marginal revenue curve, AMR, is obtained by summing MR_1 and MR_2. The total output is therefore OC, which is determined by the intersection of the aggregate marginal revenue curve with the marginal cost curve. It is comprised of output OA, sold at price P_2 to those whose demands are relatively more elastic, and OB, sold at P_1 to those whose demands are relatively less elastic. This is the output which maximizes profit for the discriminating monopolist, since marginal revenue in each market is equal to the marginal cost of the whole output. Monopoly net revenue for output OC is the area under the aggregate marginal revenue curve (total revenue) minus the area under the marginal cost curve (total costs).

FIGURE 16–2

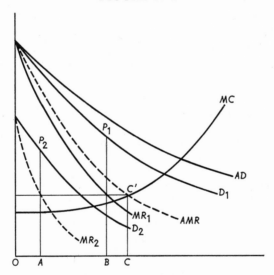

Pigou and Robinson have also examined the welfare effects of monopoly price discrimination. Their general conclusion is that if production takes place under conditions of decreasing average cost, discrimination actually contributes to the welfare of consumers instead of being detrimental to their interests because it may result in the offer of a larger output. If a monopolist is able to segregate his consumers into distinct market groups which he charges different prices, his output may be either equal to, greater than, or smaller than it would be if a single monopoly price were charged.

---

[18] *Ibid.*, pp. 182–83, Fig. 61.

Output will be larger under price discrimination if the shape of the more elastic demand curve is concave while the less elastic curve is convex or linear. In this case the expansion in output sold in the first market at a price lower than the single monopoly price will be greater than the reduction in output sold in the second market at a price higher than the single monopoly price. This is so because discrimination results in an aggregate marginal revenue curve which is above the simple monopoly marginal revenue curve.[19] But if demand curves in both markets are linear, the aggregate marginal revenue curve will equal the simple monopoly marginal revenue curve, and output will be no larger than it would be under a single monopoly price. The only difference will be in the way in which output is allocated between the two markets and the price which is charged in each.

THE EQUILIBRIUM OF THE GROUP

Chamberlin's Concept of Small and Large Groups

The duopoly models of Augustin Cournot and Joseph Bertrand, which were discussed in Chapter 11, are a convenient beginning to an inquiry into what has become known as the "group problem." It will be recalled that Cournot's and Bertrand's models were based on the highly artificial assumption of a conjectural variation of zero with respect to the behavior of competing duopolists. That is, each hypothesized a case in which the solution derives from the assumption that a duopolist behaves as though his rivals' behavior is independent of his own. Cournot hypothesized two sellers of a costless homogeneous commodity, each of whom tries to maximize his net revenue on the assumption that his competitor will not alter *the quantity* he offers for sale. Bertrand, ostensibly criticizing Cournot's solution to the duopoly problem, created a different model in which the competitors behaved on the assumption that, regardless of the rival's action, the other would keep his *price* unchanged.

The oligopoly case is an extension of the duopoly problem in which there are more than two sellers but the number is sufficiently small so that each seller realizes that his own behavior will influence not only the price at which he can sell, but also his rivals' price policies. The solution to the small-group or oligopoly problem depends on the assumptions the particular model makes with respect to the behavior of the various participants. The first among the several models we shall examine is that of Edward Chamberlin.

Chamberlin simplified the problem of analyzing the behavior of the group by assuming that all the firms have identical cost and demand functions. The group can then be described in terms of a single firm which

---

[19] *Ibid.*, pp. 190–93.

is representative of all firms. The essential difference between the small group and the large group is to be found in the reaction pattern which any individual firm will stimulate among its competitors when it alters either its price, its product, or its selling expenses.[20] Chamberlin pictures this reaction pattern in terms of the elasticity and movement of the sales or demand curve confronting the individual firm. The demand curve confronting the representative firm depends on whether its sales are a function solely of its own price, or also of the prices charged by its competitors. The curve *dd* in Figure 16–3 shows how much the representative firm thinks it can sell at all possible prices, provided other firms keep their prices fixed instead of responding to price changes it might initiate. This kind of curve is associated only with a large group because in a case like this the impact of a price change by one firm on its competitors is likely to be negligible. The large group is in this sense akin to pure competition. But it is also akin to monopoly, in that each seller has a negatively sloped demand curve for his

FIGURE 16–3

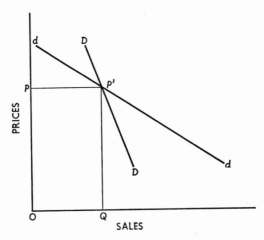

particular product. Chamberlin therefore introduced the term "monopolistic competition" to describe it. He reasoned that if there is monopolistic competition, a price cut will significantly increase the sales of the firm that introduces it because the cut draws away customers from rivals. But the effect of the price cut is spread over so many competitors that the volume of sales it draws away from any one firm is too small to cause any one to alter its policy.

The *DD* curve in Figure 16–3, on the other hand, shows how much the representative firm thinks it can sell at all possible prices if its competitors always charge the same price it charges. This curve is drawn on the

---

[20] *Monopolistic Competition*, pp. 81–104.

assumption that if a particular firm alters its price, say from *OP,* an identical change is made by every other firm in the group. The result is a sales curve which is less elastic than the *dd* curve which would confront the firm if it were able to alter its price and not call forth a similar price change by its competitors. If the market were comprised of only one firm, *DD* and *dd* would be the same curve. But where there is more than one firm, the *DD* curve represents the actual market share the representative firm will enjoy at every possible price it might charge if competing firms charge exactly the same price it charges.[21] This will be the case only if the group is small.

Figure 16–3 also sheds some light on the tendency for oligopoly prices to remain rigid once they have been determined. Paul M. Sweezy suggested that in an oligopoly situation a seller is not confronted with the entire length of *DD* but with a "kinked" demand curve like *dP'D.*[22] If an oligopolist can raise his price above *OP* without his rivals following suit, but finds that the sales curve confronting him at prices above this level is a highly elastic curve like *dP'*, a price increase cannot gain him a larger share of the market. If, on the other hand, he reduces his price below *OP,* only to find that his rivals do the same, a price cut will not increase his share of the market. Thus the demand curve confronting him at prices below *OP* is the relatively inelastic curve *P'D* in Figure 16–3. Sweezy therefore reasoned that because there is no incentive in a case like this either to raise or to lower price from *OP,* once an oligopolistic seller has fixed his price at this level, he will tend to keep it rigid, and so will his rivals.

Chamberlin's Equilibrium Analysis

Given its sales and cost curves, the representative firm of the group will behave in such a way as to maximize profits. While Chamberlin's diagrams demonstrate its behavior with the aid of average revenue and average cost curves, the same thing can be more conveniently illustrated with diagrams which also show the now standard marginal cost and marginal revenue curves. Thus, if *DD = AR* in Figure 16–4 is the sales curve of the representative firm in a small group, and *SMC* and *SAC* are its short-run cost curves, output *OQ* will be offered for sale at a price of *OP* per unit on the assumption that rivals sell at an identical price.

At a price of *OP,* there will be a pure profit equivalent to the area *CC'P'P.* Whether pure profit will continue to be enjoyed depends on the entry of new firms into the market in response to higher than normal

---

[21] *Ibid.,* pp. 83–85.

[22] Paul M. Sweezy, "Demand under Conditions of Oligopoly," *Journal of Political Economy,* Vol. XLVII (August, 1939); also reprinted in Kenneth E. Boulding and George Stigler, *Readings in Price Theory,* Vol. VI (Homewood, Ill.: Richard D. Irwin, Inc., 1952). See also the empirical study by George Stigler on the basis of which the latter denies the existence of the kinked oligopoly demand curve ("The Kinky Oligopoly Demand Curve and Rigid Prices," *Journal of Political Economy,* Vol. LV [October, 1947]).

FIGURE 16–4

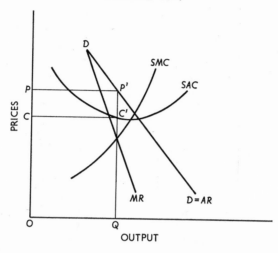

profits. If entry into the group is free, newcomers will encroach on the sales of existing sellers until pure profit has been eliminated. Thus, a long-run equilibrium with only normal profit is possible when the group is small. However, the very existence of a small group usually implies that entry is restricted in some way. Chamberlin therefore conceives of small-group equilibrium as being compatible with any level of pure profit, even in the long run.

If, on the other hand, a group is large, new firms tend to be attracted by the presence of pure profits precisely as is the case when competition is pure. Thus, if there are pure profits, the group will move to a position of equilibrium in which pure profit is eliminated. Chamberlin pictured this move via the demand curve of the representative firm. Equilibrium is achieved when a sufficient number of new firms have entered to shift $DD = AR$ to a level at which it is tangent to the average cost curve, as in Figure 16–5, so that price equals long-run average cost. Total cost will then equal revenue, so that only a normal profit is made and net revenue is zero.

For the firm and the group both to be in equilibrium in the long run, it is necessary that it be unprofitable to alter output from existing capacity; i.e., neither exit from nor entry into the group can occur. This requires that price equal short-run and long-run average cost, and that short-run and long-run marginal costs are increasing and equal to marginal revenue. This is shown in Figure 16–5, in which the curve $DD = AR$ is tangent to both the long-run and the short-run average cost curves. Short-run and long-run marginal costs are equal to marginal revenue at output OQ, and price is equal to both long-run and short-run average cost at QP'. Thus, total revenue and total cost are both equal to $OQP'P$, and net revenue is zero.

FIGURE 16-5

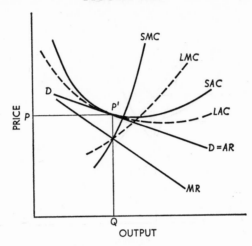

Chamberlin conceives of this result as being possible only if the group is large. If the group is small, which implies that entry is restricted, any level of positive profits can persist even in the long run.

In addition to the insight it provides into the difference between the behavior of oligopolistic firms and those which are monopolistically competitive, the preceding analysis also shows that the equilibrium output of firms producing under monopolistic competition cannot be optimal. This is because the demand curve will always be tangent to the average cost curve somewhere to the left of its lowest point, as in Figure 16-5. Price equals average cost but not marginal cost, as is the case under pure competition. Thus, in comparison with pure competition, the firm under monopolistic competition necessarily produces a smaller output at a higher average cost.[23]

Robinson, unlike Chamberlin, draws no distinction between the large group and the small group. Yet, her conception of "full equilibrium," as expressed in the following quotation, coincides with Chamberlin's tangency solution for large-group equilibrium: "Full equilibrium . . . requires the double condition that marginal revenue is equal to marginal cost and that average revenue is equal to average cost. The double condition of full equilibrium can only be fulfilled when the individual demand curve of the firm is tangent to its average cost curve."[24] While she does not specifically limit the applicability of the tangency solution by distinguishing between the large group and the small one, she does recognize indirectly the effect which the absence of free entry has on profits. She observes that "in trades into which there is no possibility of entry, . . . there is no upper limit to

---

[23] *Monopolistic Competition*, pp. 113–16.
[24] *Imperfect Competition*, p. 94.

profit, though there must be a lower limit at the level of profits which is just sufficient to maintain the existing number of firms in business."[25]

Robinson's definition of costs provides another possible way of reconciling her generalized tangency solution with pure profits. Her treatment of costs includes not only normal profits but also entrepreneurial and factor rents.[26] Chamberlin also includes factor rents and the wages of management as costs, but he has a less inclusive definition of normal profit than she does. Thus, the differences between Robinson's exposition and Chamberlin's of the requirements for equilibrium in the firm and industry appear to be mainly terminological in spite of the differences between them in the presentation of the olegopoly case.

The von Stackelberg Approach

Unlike Chamberlin and Robinson, Heinrich von Stackelberg was particularly concerned with the problem of few sellers. His *Marktform und Gleichgewicht* begins with the relatively simple case of duopoly and then proceeds to oligopoly, and finally to the additional complication of product differentiation.

In the case of two sellers, von Stackelberg conceived of each as being confronted with the alternative of leadership or following the lead of his rival. The profit of each is a function of the output levels of both; but, unlike Cournot and Bertrand, who assumed conjectural variations of zero with respect to quantity and price, von Stackelberg assumes that both sellers are aware of their mutual interdependence. A follower will adjust his output to maximize his profit, given the decision of his rival, whom he assumes to be a leader with respect to output. The leader, on the other hand, maximizes his profit on the assumption that his rival acts the part of the follower.

An equilibrium solution is possible in the case of duopoly under von Stackelberg's assumption if one seller desires to assume a position of leadership while the other desires to be a follower, and both act accordingly. But if both wish to be followers and behave as though the rival is the leader, neither can realize his expectations. Similarly, if both decide that maximum profit is to be made by assuming the role of the leader, there will be disequilibrium. One of the two must change his behavior pattern and act as a follower before equilibrium can be reached.

Von Stackelberg believed that the usual market result in duopoly is one of disequilibrium rather than equilibrium. This implies that there is inherent conflict which can be resolved only by collusion or a fight to the finish in which one of the sellers is forced to yield to the leadership of the other. Disequilibrium and destructive competition are even more likely in

---

[25] *Ibid.*

[26] *Ibid.*, p. 125.

the case of oligopoly. The interdependence among firms in this situation is such that the interplay of their actions cannot result in any economic equilibrium. This is the basis for von Stackelberg's view that direct action by the state or organizations like cartels is necessary to achieve equilibrium. While the validity of this analysis cannot be judged on an a priori basis, the appeal of his implicit defense for intervention by an authoritarian state was obviously compatible with the philosophy and techniques of the German National Socialist Party of the 1930's.

MONOPOLISTIC AND IMPERFECT COMPETITION AND THE PRODUCTIVITY THEORY OF DISTRIBUTION

Monopolistic Competition and Factor Exploitation

In general, a factor of production is said to be exploited if the payment it receives is less than its marginal physical product valued at its selling price.[27] Chamberlin examined the effect of monopolistic competition in the selling market on the relationship between factor payments and their marginal productivities. Marginal productivity, it will be recalled, may refer to the marginal physical product, the marginal value product, or the marginal revenue product of a factor. The marginal value product is computed by multiplying the marginal physical product of a factor by the selling price of the good it produces. The marginal revenue product is computed by multiplying the factor's marginal physical product by the marginal revenue derived from the sale of an extra unit of the good it produces. When competition is pure in both the product and the factor market, the marginal value product of a factor is equal to its marginal revenue product. It is this relationship which has led Chamberlin to observe that under conditions of monopolistic competition the distributive shares of the factors are necessarily smaller than the values of their marginal product.[28]

A firm selling its product in a monopolistically competitive market but buying its factors in a purely competitve one, will employ each factor until

$$\frac{MRP_{f_a}}{P_{f_a}} = \frac{MRP_{f_b}}{P_{f_b}} \cdots = \frac{MRP_{f_n}}{P_{f_n}}$$

But because of the downward slope of its demand curve, the marginal value product of each factor it employs will exceed its marginal revenue product. In buying more of a factor, say labor, the entrepeneur is guided by the latter rather than the former. It follows that it will be unprofitable and often not possible for a firm whose selling market is monopolistically competitive to pay any of its factors the value of their marginal products.

---

[27] Arthur C. Pigou, *Economics of Welfare* (4th ed.; London: Macmillan & Co., 1952), p. 549.

[28] *Monopolistic Competition,* 1948 edition, chapter VIII.

It will be impossible if competition has pushed a firm's demand curve to a position of tangency with its cost curve, for all surplus profit will then have been eliminated. When there is monopolistic competition, the *MRP* curves of all factors will lie below their respective *MVP* curves, with the result that each receives less than the value of its marginal product. Yet if there is no pure profit the total paid to them is exactly equal to the total product valued at its selling price. There is nothing left over after all have been paid, although each factor apparently produces more than it gets.

This does not, however, imply that factors are being exploited in the usual sense of the term, for the tangency solution means that there are no pure profits. Chamberlin has therefore argued that to define exploitation as a payment which is less than a factor's marginal value product is appropriate only under conditions of pure competition. If competition is not pure, the relationship between the total product and the marginal product is such that it is impossible to pay all factors the full value of their marginal products without exceeding the amount available for distribution.

While the discrepancy between marginal value products and marginal revenue products does not imply factor exploitation in the usual sense, it does reenforce another observation made in regard to the social implications of deviations from pure competition. This is the observation that the resources employed at the margin have a greater value to society than they do to the firm and that the firm is underemploying its inputs. This is consistent with the observation previously made that the equilibrium output of a firm selling in a market which is not purely competitive is less than optimal.

Monopsony and Factor Exploitation

Robinson has investigated the effect of buyer monopoly or "monopsony" on the relationship between factor rewards and their marginal productivities.[29] Her analysis proceeds by paralleling with respect to the explanation of factor prices all of the analytical concepts and tools which were found useful in examining commodity price determination. Her first fundamental observation is that the factor supply curves confronting a monopsonistic buyer cannot be infinitely elastic any more than the product demand curve confronting a seller who is not a pure competitor can be infinitely elastic. She has shown that when a firm is a monopsonist in the purchase of a factor, it is confronted with an upward-sloping factor supply curve. The average and marginal cost curves of the factor to the firm are therefore also upward-sloping.[30] The upward slope of the average and marginal cost curves of a monopsonistic buyer of a factor is significant because it alters not only the quantity of that factor which will be hired in

---

[29] *Imperfect Competition*, chap. xviii.
[30] *Ibid.*, p. 220.

an equilibrium situation but also the relationship between the marginal return to that factor and its marginal value product. When the marginal cost of hiring a factor lies above its average cost, as is the case when there is not pure competition in the factor market, the firm will employ a smaller quantity of the factor that it would under pure competition, and the price which it pays for its hire will be less than the value of its marginal product.[31]

FIGURE 16-6

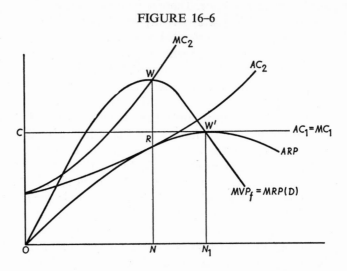

This is illustrated in Figure 16–6 which assumes pure competition in the selling market for a particular product and monopsony in the market in which a factor, f, required for its production is purchased. ARP_f and $MVP_f = MRP_f$ show the average and marginal increments of value added by additional inputs of the variable factor when it is used with other fixed inputs. $MVP_f = MRP_f$ because pure competition in the product market is associated with $P = MR$. The downward-sloping portion of the curve $MVP_f = MRP_f$ is the firm's demand curve for the variable factor. Together with the factor supply curve, it determines the quantity of f the firm will hire. In a purely competitive factor market the supply curve of f is the perfectly elastic curve $AC_1 = MC_1$. In a long-run equilibrium situation, $AC_1 = MC_1$ will be tangent to the average revenue product curve at its maximum level. The firm will maximize its gains from employing the variable factor when it equates the marginal cost of its hire with the marginal revenue product which can be gotten from the sale of its product. It will therefore hire quantity ON_1, for which it will pay $OC = N_1W^1$ per unit. This payment is equivalent to both the average revenue product and the marginal revenue product of the factor.

A monopsonistic buyer would, however, be confronted with upward-sloping average and marginal cost curves like AC_2 and MC_2.

---

[31] *Ibid.*, p. 250.

Therefore the tangency of the average cost curve to the average product curve of the factor in a long-run equilibrium situation will be somewhere to the left of its maximum level. This is because the factor market is not pure. The firm's most profitable level of factor employment will of course be that at which its marginal cost is equal to the factor's marginal revenue product. But a monopsonistic buyer would employ only quantity ON of the factor, as opposed to the larger quantity ON_1 which would be bought by a competitive buyer. It would pay the factor a reward equal to NR, its average product. However, the average revenue product of the factor is less than NW, its marginal revenue product. Thus, there will be monopsonistic exploitation in the amount of WR, which is the amount by which the value of the marginal revenue product of ON units of the factor exceeds NR, its price of employment.

Robinson suggests that these observations bear in an important way on the problem of factor exploitation. If the factor in question is labor, Robinson has shown that exploitation can be reduced or eliminated and employment increased by introducing a minimum wage at which the supply of labor will be perfectly elastic.[32] In a situation such as that depicted in Figure 16–6, an enforced minimum wage rate of OC will eliminate exploitation and result in the employment of ON_1 men which is the same as that which would obtain under pure competition.

FURTHER REFINEMENTS IN THE THEORY OF MONOPOLISTIC COMPETITION AND OLIGOPOLY

Monopolistic Competition and General Equilibrium

Robert Triffin, writing in 1940, suggested that because the theory of group equilibrium involves interdependencies among firms, it "begins to bridge the canyon which has for years separated" the particular equilibrium economics of Alfred Marshall from the Walrásian general equilibrium system of economic theory.[33] Firms selling similar but differentiated products are interdependent with respect to their sales curves, and firms employing the same factors or factors which are competitive with each other are interdependent with respect to their cost curves. Triffin expressed the degree of such interdependence between firms in terms of cross elasticities.

The cross (price) elasticity of demand for a good is the percentage change in the quantity demanded of that good which results in response to a percentage change in the price of *another* good, the price of the first good remaining constant.[34] Given p_i, the price of good i, the change in q_i, the

---

[32] *Ibid.*, chap. xxvi, pp. 295–96.

[33] Robert Triffin, *Monopolistic Competition and General Equilibrium Theory* (Cambridge: Harvard University Press, 1940), Introduction.

[34] Price elasticity expresses the quantity demanded of a commodity as a function of *its* price only. It assumes other prices as given. Cross elasticity specifically introduces one or more other prices into the demand equation.

quantity of good i demanded when p_j is changed, is the cross elasticity of the demand for good i with respect to the price of good j. If goods i and j are produced by different firms, the interdependence of their sales curves may be given expression as a partial derivative.[35] The cross elasticity of the demand for q_i with respect to p_j is

$$e_{p_j} = \frac{\delta q_i}{\delta p_j} \cdot \frac{p_j}{q_i}$$

and the cross elasticity of the demand for q_j with respect to p_i is

$$e_{p_i} = \frac{\delta q_j}{\delta p_i} \cdot \frac{p_i}{q_i}$$

This formulation lends itself equally well to expressing the interdependence of firms with respect to factor purchases. All that is required is to conceive of the quantity variables as representing the amounts of factors rather than commodities and the price variables as representing factor rather than commodity prices.

The advantage of this formulation is, according to Triffin, that it lends itself to describing and classifying the whole gamut of cases from pure monopoly to pure competition without the need to distinguish between the large group and the small group in terms of such a nebulous criterion as the number of competitors. If the value of the coefficient approaches zero, firm i is independent of the price changes of firm j; and if this independence also exists with respect to each and every other firm, the case is one of isolated selling, or *pure monopoly*. The extreme opposite case is the one in which the slightest cut in the price of good j, the price of good i remaining unchanged, reduces the sales of good i to zero by shifting all its customers to firm j. In this case the value of the coefficient approaches infinity, which indicates that from the standpoint of consumers the firms are selling the same commodity. Irrespective of the number of firms among which such a relationship exists, Triffin here refers to the general category of *homogeneous competition*.

Triffin classifies the cases which are intermediate between isolated selling and homogeneous competition as heterogeneous competition. This classification includes all the cases in which a change in p_i, p_j remaining unchanged, or vice versa, affects the volume of the other's sales but does not reduce it to zero because customers do not respond exclusively to price when the products are differentiated. This category, then, embraces Robinson's imperfect competition and Chamberlin's monopolistic competition.

Triffin's is, of course, only one possible classification which may be made of market structures. It is, however, one which avoids the use of the nebulous term "industry" and its Chamberlinian equivalent, "group." For Marshall the concept of the industry performed several distinct functions which it cannot perform when the assumption of pure competition is

---

[35] Triffin, *op. cit.*, pp. 99–108.

dropped. When products are differentiated, it is no longer possible to talk of an industry as being comprised of firms producing identical or even similar products which compete with each other. Triffin pointed out that every firm competes with all other firms in the economy, but with different degrees of closeness.[36] Thus, there may be keener competition between the demand for Chevrolets and trips abroad than there is between Chevrolets and Rolls Royces. He therefore questions that there is anything to be gained by limiting the investigation to a group of close competitors, such as is generally called a group or industry, except in an empirical study.

The Theory of Games and Price Determination

A still more recent effort to develop an approach to the price problem which is sufficiently general to enable it to encompass the entire spectrum of market structures involves the application of the principles of game theory to the behavior of market participants. This approach grew largely out of the limitations of existing price theory with respect to the problems of oligopoly. Comparison of the approaches of Cournot, Bertrand, Chamberlin, and von Stackelberg make it apparent that the solution of the small-group problem depends on the strategy which participants with conflicting interests are assumed to follow. The assumption of Cournot and Bertrand of a conjectural variation of zero is only one possible assumption. So, too, is Chamberlin's assumption that a price change by any one seller is immediately imitated by all. A given seller is likely to have several alternative modes of behavior open to him. Accordingly, John von Neumann and Oskar Morgenstern, in *The Theory of Games and Economic Behavior,* undertook to demonstrate that the theory of games can provide various equilibrium solutions on the basis of various possible assumptions concerning the behavior of market rivals. Each of these strategies results in different "payoffs," and a participant must select among them without necessarily knowing what counterstrategies his rivals will select. We are therefore confronted with the problem of determining what is rational behavior for all participants under all conceivable conditions.

It is possible that the strategies of the participants will not produce a stable equilibrium situation but will result in a situation of inherent instability such as von Stackelberg described. A stable equilibrium will obtain only if the policies of rivals happen to be mutually compatible in terms of what each wishes to achieve. The achievement of an equilibrium in duopoly can be most easily demonstrated in terms of a two-person zero-sum game. A zero-sum game is one in which the sum of the market shares which two players have together is necessarily 100 percent. The gain any one competitor is able to make is always the exact equivalent of the loss of the other. Let us assume, for example, that firm A has three strategies under consideration for increasing its share of the market. Strategy 1, let us say, is to

---

[36] *Ibid.,* p. 88.

reduce its price; strategy 2 is to improve its product; strategy 3 is to advertise its product. The same alternative strategies are also open to firm B, its rival. Looking at the game from the standpoint of firm A, it is apparent that A's share of the market, or "payoff," is determined by the strategy it chooses and the strategy chosen by its competitor. Each possible combination of strategies by A and B will result in a "payoff matrix" such as is shown in Figure 16–7. Thus, if firm A chooses its strategy 1, it may estimate that if B likewise chooses strategy 1, this combination of move and countermove will give it 25 percent of the market. This is recorded at the junction of column 1 and row 1. B's payoff is obviously 75 percent and need not be recorded separately. Similarly, A may calculate that if it employs its strategy 3 and B employs its strategy 2, this will give it 45 percent of the market. The payoff matrix summarizes the results which derive from each possible combination of strategy choices by A and B.

FIGURE 16–7

		B's Strategy		
		1	2	3
	1	25	20	30
A's Strategy	2	10	30	20
	3	80	45	40

Whether or not the game has an equilibrium or saddle point depends on the structure of the payoff matrix.[37] Firm A could, for example, approach the game cautiously and assume that whatever strategy it chooses, its rival will always choose that counterstrategy which will cause it to have a minimum payoff. It will therefore choose the strategy which will give it the maximum minimum gain or, more simply, the *maximin*. The minimum payoff from adopting strategy 1 would be 20 percent, and the minimum payoff from strategy 2 would be only 10 percent. Thus a payoff of 40 percent, which is the lowest payoff which can be gotten from strategy 3, means that strategy 3 will be chosen because it provides the maximum minimum or maximin gain.

Firm B could, conceivably, be equally pessimistic concerning the probable counterstrategy of its rival. However, the assumption that A's strategy will always be such as to reduce its payoff to a minimum will, in a two-person game, actually leave A with a large payoff. If B adopts strategy

---

[37] The equilibrium point of a payoff matrix is technically known as a "saddle point" because of the shape of the curve which results from geometric presentation.

1, the worst payoff is the one which gives A 80 percent. Similarly, if it adopts strategy 2, the worst possible game for B is that which will give A 45 percent of the market, whereas the worst possible result from strategy 3 for B is that A will also follow strategy 3 and get 40 percent of the market. Therefore, from B's point of view, its best possible choice, or *minimax* strategy, is strategy 3, which is likewise firm A's *maximin* strategy. The game therefore has an equilibrium point of 40 because of the coincidence of payoffs in the strategies of A and B. It is of course possible that the maximin strategy combination of one participant and the minimax strategy combination of the second participant will not coincide. In such a case, there is no equilibrium point, and the situation is indeterminate.

The two-person, zero-sum game is the simplest and has been studied most extensively, but it is not, of course, the most realistic. Nonconstant-sum and many-person games are much more likely to be encountered in practice. The many-person game is so complicated that while it has stimulated considerable literature, it has not yet produced an analysis comparable to that for the two-person game, so that its significance for price theory cannot as yet be assessed. The nonconstant-sum game, on the other hand, is understood well enough to shed some light on the tendency toward collusion in an oligopoly situation. The principles of game theory indicate that there will be cooperation if it will increase the payoff of both players and not reduce the share of either. This helps to explain why, for example, a seller may publicize his policy changes instead of maintaining secrecy, as would be expected in a zero-sum game. Disclosure of information may well be a means for inducing rivals to follow suit to the mutual advantage of all. One has only to think in terms of cartel agreements with respect to output and profits to verify the realism of this conclusion. On the other hand, a nonconstant-sum game may also cause both players to make choices which will be mutually disadvantageous.

Even though the application of game theory to economic behavior is still in its early stages, the development has progressed far enough so that it may be possible even now to move away from models in which marginal cost and marginal revenue are conceived to be the primary factors determining price and output. Further, models which are based on the principles of game theory seem in many ways more suitable for describing the reality of the market than current economic models which parallel the models of theoretical physics. It has been suggested that "it is more plausible to compare the sparring and jockeying between large automobile companies to a game of poker with its bluffing, its bids and overbids, or equivalently, to a military situation than to some mechanical process such as a dance of molecules."[38] Whether or not game theory will eventually yield a more

---

[38] Oskar Morgenstern, "Oligopoly, Monopolistic Competition and the Theory of Games," *American Economic Review,* Supplement, Vol. XXXVIII, No. 2, (May, 1948), pp. 10–18.

generalized theory of price determination remains, of course, to be seen. But there is no question that the principles of game theory have already made it possible to visualize the price problem on a more sophisticated level than that which derived from traditional theory.

CONCLUDING REMARKS

Modern price theory is very largely a refinement of the work of Cournot and Marshall. These sources of inspiration are plainly evident in its treatment of the price problem as an optimizing problem within a static particular equilibrium framework. Its basic principle of optimal behavior is that the economic unit is guided by the relationship between marginal cost and marginal revenue. This implies that whenever possible, a firm will continue to engage in a particular activity until the net gain at the margin is zero. If there are several activities, then, ideally, they should all be pursued until they yield the same marginal return.

The fundamental role of marginal analysis in modern price theory has raised the question as to whether businessmen actually employ marginal principles in their decision making. Fritz Machlup has, for example, taken the position that businessmen employ marginal concepts without being aware of it.[39] Empirical studies of the pricing behavior of firms and the objectives they pursue are, however, still inconclusive.[40] Taken by itself, marginal analysis is, of course, only a tool for achieving optimal results. But what constitutes the best objective to seek is something else again. The basic premise of price theory continues to be that businessmen are concerned first and foremost with the maximization of profit. Obviously, however, firms may also have objectives other than maximizing the difference between total cost and total revenue. William Baumol has, for example, argued that the principle objective of corporate managers, who are chiefly responsible for decision making in most corporations today, is to maximize *sales* revenue.[41] That is, subject to the constraint of a sufficient level of profits to maintain a satisfactory dividend policy, Baumol conceives of plant managers as willing to sacrifice profits in the interests of greater sales revenue. A recent study on the relationship between executive incomes and sales appears to support his hypothesis, but a positive relationship between profits and incomes is also compatible with the findings of this study.[42] Thus the profit maximization thesis has not been shown to be empirically invalid, although its validity has been seriously challenged.

[39] Fritz Machlup, "Marginal Analysis and Empirical Research," *American Economic Review*, Vol. XXXVI, No. 4 (September, 1946).

[40] A. D. H. Caplan *et al.*, *Pricing in Big Business: A Case Study Approach* (Washington, D.C.: Brookings Institution, 1958).

[41] William Baumol, *Business Behavior, Value and Growth* (New York: Macmillan Co., 1959).

[42] Joseph W. McGuire *et al.*, "Executive Incomes, Sales and Profits," *American Economic Review*, Vol. LII, No. 4 (September, 1962).

The price-output relationships which modern price theorists conceive to result as firms seek to maximize their profits depend very much on the structure of the market. Interest has centered primarily on those market situations which lie intermediate between pure competition and pure monopoly, i.e., monopolistic competition and oligopoly. Most modern theorists, following Chamberlin, conceive of a monopolistically competitive market as one in which each firm is in competition with so many rival producers of close substitutes that its long run equilibrium position, like that of the pure competitor, is one in which there are no pure profits even though each is a monopolist of its own product. The oligopoly situation has, however, defied such neat packaging and it is in this area that modern price theory encounters its main difficulties.

The main feature of oligopoly is the interdependence of firms with respect to their decision making. Every businessman in a market which is dominated by a few large firms knows that, in varying degrees, he will influence his rivals by his decision and, in turn, be influenced by them. Theorists from Cournot and Bertrand to Chamberlin, Robinson and Stackelberg have constructed models based on different premises with respect to the behavior of rivals. Given their respective premises, each has provided a "solution" compatible with profit maximization. Each of these solutions is, however, only one of a wide variety of possible solutions each of which is perfectly tenable under the assumptions made.

The wide variety of behavior patterns which are possible in oligopolistic markets is presumably the reason why it has been so difficult to obtain empirical support for particular oligopoly models. It is, on the other hand, also a reason why game theory may be promising as a method of studying the optimizing behavior of business firms. The principles of game theory demonstrate that rationality in an oligopoly situation does not necessarily require the maximization of net profits. Oligopoly is also compatible with achieving the maximum payoff, and the payoff may consist of a certain percentage of sales revenues, or a particular share of the market, or a particular return on invested capital and so forth. Thus, game theory may eventually help to resolve some of the seeming inconsistencies between the profit maximizing assumptions of price theory and empirical observations about business behavior.

SUGGESTIONS FOR FURTHER READING

BURNS, A. R. *Decline of Competition.* New York: McGraw-Hill Book Co., Inc., 1936.

CHAMBERLIN, EDWARD. *The Theory of Monopolistic Competition.* 8th ed. Cambridge: Harvard University Press, 1962.

FELLNER, WILLIAM. *Competition among the Few.* New York: A. A. Knopf, Inc., 1949.

MORGENSTERN, OSKAR. "Oligopoly, Monopolistic Competition and the

Theory of Games," *American Economic Review,* Supplement, Vol. XXXVIII No. 2 (May, 1948).

ROBINSON, JOAN. *The Economics of Imperfect Competition.* London: Macmillan & Co., 1933.

SRAFFA, PIERO. "The Laws of Return under Competitive Conditions," *Economic Journal,* Vol. XXXVI (December, 1926). Reprinted in GEORGE STIGLER and KENNETH E. BOULDING (eds.), *Readings in Price Theory,* Vol. VI. Homewood, Ill.: Richard D. Irwin, Inc., 1952.

SWEEZY, PAUL M. "Demand under Conditions of Oligopoly," *Journal of Political Economy,* Vol. XLVII (August, 1939). Reprinted in GEORGE STIGLER and KENNETH E. BOULDING (eds.), *Readings in Price Theory,* Vol. VI. Homewood, Ill.: Richard D. Irwin, Inc., 1952.

TRIFFIN, ROBERT. *Monopolistic Competition and General Equilibrium Theory,* chaps. i–iii. Cambridge: Harvard University Press, 1940.

CONTEMPORARY CONTRIBU-
Chapter TIONS TO THE THEORY OF
17 OPTIMAL BEHAVIOR AND
WELFARE ECONOMICS

INTRODUCTION

The Paretian Origins

While the theories of monopolistic and imperfect competition are Marshallian in inspiration, many contemporary contributions to the theory of optimal behavior and economic welfare are the direct outgrowth of the work of Vilfredo Pareto (1848–1923). Pareto was born in Paris of French-Italian parentage, but lived most of his early life in Italy, where he earned an engineering degree and eventually held a managerial position with the Italian Iron Works. His training in mathematics, which facilitated his later contributions to economic theory, was an integral part of his education as an engineer. He also had a particular interest in politics and sociology, and most of his later work is sociological in nature. It was, in fact, his extreme displeasure with the political and social developments of his native Italy before the turn of the century that caused him to emigrate to Switzerland, where, in 1893, he became Leon Walrás' successor at Lausanne. In view of his antisocialist leanings, it is ironic that his main contribution to economic theory, namely, the definition of the marginal conditions of the economic optimum, later proved as valuable to socialist thinkers as to those of more orthodox persuasion.

The general equilibrium approach of Walrás and Pareto, and their special orientation to the problem of optimization, is today fundamental to the theory of rational consumer and producer behavior and the body of principles which has become known as "modern welfare theory." According to I. M. D. Little, this body of thought owes virtually nothing to Alfred Marshall and the English tradition.[1] English welfare economics is very different from that which was developed by Continental thinkers. The latter followed Walrás and extended their inquiry into individual optimizing behavior to examine the general equilibrium of the static state under perfect competition. The English economists, on the other hand, preferred partial to general equilibrium analysis. They were also less concerned with the realization of the economic optimum under the idealized conditions of

---

[1] I. M. D. Little, *A Critique of Welfare Economics* (2d ed.; Oxford: Clarendon Press, 1957), chap. vi. See also Hla Myint, *Theories of Welfare Economics* (Cambridge: Harvard University Press, 1948), chap. vi.

perfect competition than in understanding divergences from the optimum which may take place under the less stringent, though more realistic, conditions of pure competition. Arthur C. Pigou's recognition of the possibility of divergences between marginal social costs and benefits and marginal private costs and benefits, which will be discussed later in this chapter, proceeds along these lines.

Pareto conceived of welfare as being maximized when the resources of the community are used in such a manner that their reallocation would not enable any individual to improve his position except at the expense of someone else[2]. This optimal situation requires the simultaneous achievement of both a subjective optimum and a physical optimum. This is partly a matter of achieving a level of employment which is in some sense "ideal," partly a matter of achieving an ideal allocation of resources among various products, and partly a matter of achieving an ideal distribution of products among consumers. The latter condition implies also, in a money economy, an ideal distribution of money income.

These aspects of economic welfare are of course not mutually exclusive, for shifting levels of aggregate employment are usually associated with changes in the pattern of resource allocation and income distribution. However, welfare economics is concerned with the allocation of resources rather than with shifting levels of resource use. The assumption of full employment is therefore implicit in welfare analysis. It seeks to examine the efficiency with which resources are used to satisfy given wants with a given distribution of income. The reason why the distribution of income is assumed to be given is not far to seek. Unless we have objective evidence that individual capacities to enjoy goods differ, we can only conclude that an equal distribution is optimal. But even this involves value judgments which, from the time of the classicists, have generally been considered inadmissible for theoretical economics. Welfare theorists from the classics to the present have therefore generally separated questions of efficiency from questions of ethics by divorcing the welfare aspects of production and exchange from those of income distribution.

Contemporary Contributors

Although the inspiration for much of the modern theory of consumer and producer behavior and modern welfare theory is Continental in origin, the leading contributor to both of these contemporary developments is, interestingly enough, an Englishman. The refinement of modern utility and equilibrium analysis is in large measure attributable to Sir John R. Hicks's *Value and Capital* (1939). Hicks (1904–   ), of Oxford University, presently holds the Drummond Chair of Political Economy. While *Value and Capital* is his major work to date, Hicks has made many other contributions

---

[2] The concept of the social optimum is introduced in chapter vi of Pareto's *Manual,* and the marginal conditions are developed in the mathematical appendix, where they are used to demonstrate that perfect competition maximizes welfare.

to the literature of economics, some of which will be examined in a subsequent chapter. Our immediate interest in his work, however, is in connection with the theory of consumer and producer behavior and economic welfare. It is very largely due to Hicks that the Paretian technique of the indifference curve has become a standard tool of modern microeconomic analysis. He used this tool to demonstrate that it is possible to examine consumer behavior without resorting to the assumption that utility is a cardinally measurable magnitude. He maintained that it is possible, once the idea of utility and diminishing marginal utility has been discarded, to formulate a theory of demand independently of the sensationalist psychology on which earlier formulations rested and, as will be shown, to separate the income effects and the substitution effects of price change. Hicks's rejection of the concept of cardinally measurable utility in favor of ordinal ranking generated more than a decade of controversy between the cardinalists and the ordinalists concerning the question as to whether the technique of the indifference curve, in spite of the claims made for it, really avoided cardinal measurement.[3] Also at issue was the question as to how the information about consumer behavior needed to construct a preference hypothesis might be arrived at.

Another source of contemporary contributions to welfare theory is from writers whose primary concern is with the cognate field of socialist economics. The aim of these writers has been to provide a theoretical basis for the functioning of a central planning board charged with the responsibility of allocating scarce resources among alternative uses in a socialist state. They have leaned heavily on the work of Pareto and his compatriot Enrico Barone. Barone's work was written in 1908, but not translated until 1935. He examined the nature of general equilibrium under perfect competition and, although not himself a socialist, suggested how the planning board might duplicate the competitive solution. More recently, a number of writers on socialism such as Abba P. Lerner, Oscar Lange, and Abram Bergson have concerned themselves explicitly with restating the optimum conditions of production and exchange. A number of other writers have concerned themselves with the practical realization of optimal conditions of production and exchange by introducing a method of establishing prices known as marginal cost pricing. A leading contributor to the large literature which has developed on marginal cost pricing is Harold Hotelling.

CONTEMPORARY DEMAND THEORY

Indifference Curves and Optimum Allocation of Income

The marginal utility theorists established the principle that a consumer maximizes his satisfaction from a given income when he spends it in such manner as to make

---

[3] See, for example, Dennis Robertson, "Utility and All What?" *Economic Journal,* Vol. LXIV, No. 256 (Dec. 1954).

$$\frac{MU_x}{P_x} = \frac{MU_y}{P_y}$$

The indifference technique provides an alternative method for determining the optimum allocation of a consumer's income between two goods, say X and Y, given his income and the prices of the two goods. In Figure 17–1 the indifference curves labeled I, II, and III represent increasingly preferable combinations of two goods, X and Y, to a hypothetical consumer. Hicks has demonstrated that all indifference curves must slope downward and be convex to the origin of an indifference map such as shown in Figure 17–1. The reason is that the marginal rate of substitution of X for Y, which is the amount of Y the consumer is willing to give up for an extra unit of X, decreases as more of X is acquired.[4] The ratio between his income and the prices of the two goods determines the quantity of either or both which he could purchase. Thus a line of attainable combinations is drawn by joining the point on the vertical axis which represents the expenditure of all his income, I, on good Y at a price of P_{y_1} to the point on the horizontal axis which represents the expenditure of the entire income, I, on good X at a price of P_{x_1}. The second line on the diagram, drawn from point $\frac{I}{P_{y_1}}$ on the vertical axis to point $\frac{I}{P_{x_2}}$ on the horizontal axis, has no relevence to this discussion and will be explained presently.

The slope of the line of attainable combinations indicates the quantity of X the consumer would *have* to give up in order to obtain a unit of Y, given his income and price constraints. The slope of his indifference curve however, expresses his *willingness* to give up X for Y. Thus, while the consumer can purchase any combination of X and Y permitted by his income, such as those represented by points *A, B,* or *C,* the optimum allocation of his income requires that he choose that combination which gives him the greatest total satisfaction. This is the combination at which the marginal rate of substitution of X for Y is equal to the ratio of their prices. In Figure 17–1, it is the combination that obtains at *B,* the point of tangency between the price line and his highest indifference curve. Thus, given the prices of the two goods, and given his income, a consumer with an indifference map such as shown in Figure 17–1 maximizes his satis-

---

[4] John R. Hicks, *Value and Capital* (2d ed.; Oxford: Clarendon Press, 1946), chap. ii.

If an indifference curve were concave to the origin, the satisfaction of the marginal conditions would define a position of minimum satisfaction for a consumer rather than maximum satisfaction, for in such cases a consumer could improve his position by moving from the point of tangency between the price line and an indifference curve to either axis. The convexity of indifference curves is associated with the diminishing marginal rate of substitution between commodities. This condition is a second-order requirement, whereas the marginal conditions are of the first order. See *ibid.,* chap. ii; also J. Henderson and Richard Quandt, *Microeconomic Theory* (New York: McGraw-Hill Book Co., Inc., 1958), chap. ii, Sec. 2–2.

FIGURE 17–1

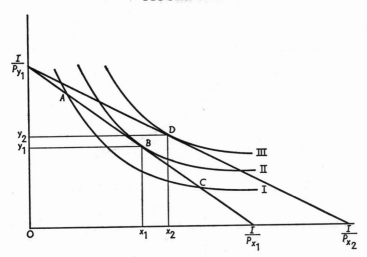

faction when he takes quantities O_{x_1} and O_{y_1} of goods X and Y, because this combination places him on the highest possible indifference curve. However, unlike the older marginal utility analysis, satisfaction is not equated with specific measurable quantities of utility.

Derivation of a Demand Curve

Hicks has shown that the concept of diminishing marginal utility is not essential to the construction of consumer demand curves. The typical downward slope of a demand curve may be derived with the aid of a family of indifference curves and various assumed budget constraints. For example, one point on an individual demand curve for commodity X may be derived from the indifference map in Figure 17–1. Given his income and the prices of goods X and Y, the quantity of commodity X which a hypothetical consumer would buy at price P_{x_1} is O_{x_1}. This price-quantity relationship is therefore one point on the individual's demand curve for X, as shown in Figure 17–2.

In order to demonstrate that more X will be taken at a lower price, its price may be assumed to fall to P_{x_2}. Given his income, a consumer having an indifference map such as that shown in Figure 17–1 can now purchase more of a good X at a lower price. Thus, there will be a new line of attainable combinations drawn from point $\dfrac{I}{P_{y_1}}$, which represents the ratio between the consumer's income and the price of good Y, to the point $\dfrac{I}{P_{x_2}}$, which represents the ratio between his income and the new price of good X. The new price line is tangent to the higher indifference curve

FIGURE 17–2

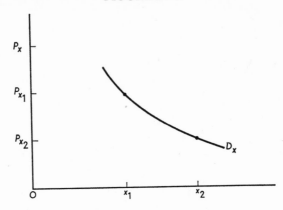

III at D, and quantities O_{y_2} and O_{x_2} represent the optimum allocation of the consumer's income between goods X and Y. The relationship between the lower price, P_{x_2}, and the larger quantity, O_{x_2}, is now a second point on the demand curve in Figure 17–2. This operation may be repeated using other assumed prices of X to establish other points of the demand curve. This demonstration, provided by Hicks, shows that downward-sloping demand curves can be drawn independently of the assumption of diminishing marginal utility and the notion of utility measurable in cardinal terms.

Although the advocates of the indifference curve approach claim that the notion of measurable utility is avoided by using the concept of the marginal rate of substitution, the critics of this approach maintain that the assumption of measurable utility and diminishing marginal utility is no less implicit in the new formulation than it is in the older one. They point out that a consumer cannot know which of several combinations are a matter of indifference to him unless he is able to estimate the amount of utility they represent and that there is a set of marginal utility curves underlying every set of indifference curves. Further, if the analysis is generalized so that the marginal rate of substitution expresses the relationship between one good and the best combination of other goods, this is the same thing as establishing the marginal rate of substitution between that good and money. The marginal rate of substitution then expresses the utility of that good in terms of the best combination of other goods or in dollars.

Separation of Income and Substitution Effects

Even if the indifference curve approach does not really avoid the assumption of measurable utility, it has the advantage of making it possible to separate the income effect of a price change from the substitution effect. A conventional demand curve would show only that more will be taken at a lower price, but there is no way of knowing to what extent the increase is associated with the substitution of one good for other higher priced goods and to what extent it is due to the increase in real income which occurs when the price of a good is reduced.

Hicks has demonstrated that the income effect of a price change can be separated from the substitution effect by introducing a compensating variation in income which will enable a consumer to reach the same indifference curve made possible by an assumed change in the price of the good.[5] Thus, in Figure 17–3 a new price line is drawn parallel to the origi-

FIGURE 17–3

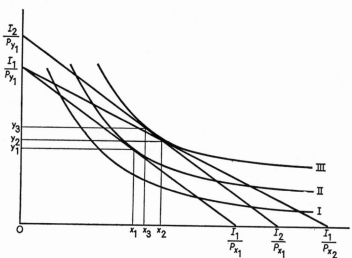

nal one drawn from $\dfrac{I_1}{P_{y_1}}$ to $\dfrac{I_1}{P_{x_1}}$. It connects point $\dfrac{I_2}{P_{y_1}}$ on the vertical axis, which represents the ratio between an assumed new income, I_2, and the price of Y, to point $\dfrac{I_2}{P_{x_1}}$ on the horizontal axis, which represents the ratio between the new income and the price of X. The assumed increase in income enables the consumer to reach indifference curve III and buy quantity O_{x_3} of X and O_{y_3} of Y. The initial move to indifference curve III was accomplished via the reduction in the price of X and the optimum purchase at the lower price was O_{x_2}. It is evident, therefore, that the increase in consumption from O_{x_1} to O_{x_3} is the result of the income effect, while the difference between O_{x_2} and O_{x_3} resulted from substitution effect. By way of contrast, the older marginal utility approach obscures the difference between these two effects because it does not lend itself to separating the income effect of a price change from the substitution effect.

---

[5] Hicks, *op. cit.*, chap. ii, pp. 29–33.

MODERN WELFARE ECONOMICS

Optimum in the Consumer Sector

Taken in its broadest sense of maximum social well-being, the problem of welfare intrudes into the field of ethics and is usually considered beyond the scope of the inquiries of the economist. While economists have usually attempted to separate positive economics from normative economics, they have been at special pains to do so since the appearance of Lionel Robbins' *Essay on the Nature and Significance of Economic Science* (1932). Robbins maintained that only propositions involving the word "is," as distinct from those involving the word "ought," are appropriate to positive economics. Hence, all welfare propositions have, in his opinion, ethical content, and he considered that welfare is not a proper area for study by economists.

While Robbins' dictum that value judgments have no place in economics has generally been accepted, such leading exponents of modern welfare theory as Hicks and Lerner have maintained that welfare economics can be made ethically neutral by inquiring only into the conditions under which the resources of the community are best used to satisfy given wants within the framework of a given distribution of income. This is maximum welfare in the Paretian sense. It requires the simultaneous achievement of the subjective optimum and the physical optimum. That is, it requires that goods be distributed among consumers in such a manner that no one can better his position except at the expense of someone else and that products as well as factors are allocated in such a way that no greater product can be produced with the same factor input.[6]

Expressed in terms of indifference curves, the attainment of the subjective optimum, i.e., optimum conditions of exchange, requires that the marginal rate of substitution between all pairs of consumer goods must be equal to the ratio of their prices for all buyers. This can be demonstrated with the aid of a "box" diagram, such as is shown in Figure 17–4, which combines two sets of indifference curves by rotating the second set of curves so that they are convex to the origin O' (concave to O). Curves I, II, III, and IV represent succesively better combinations of the two goods, A and B, from the vantage point of one consumer, while curves I', II', III', and IV' show the same thing for a second consumer. There are, of course, numerous other indifference curves which are not shown in the diagram.

Figure 17–4 is drawn on the assumption that the total quantity of goods which are available for exchange between two consumers is OQ_0 of A and OQ_1 of B. Given their incomes and their indifference curves, there are various possible quantities of both goods which each could acquire by

---

[6] Myint, *op. cit.*, chap. vii; John R. Hicks, "Foundations of Welfare Economics," *Economic Journal*, Vol. XLIX (December, 1939), pp. 696–712.

FIGURE 17–4

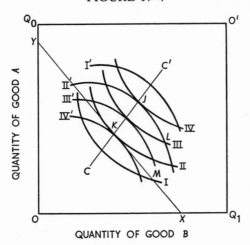

QUANTITY OF GOOD B

trade. Any point in the box, indeed, represents a possible division of A and B between the two consumers. It can be shown, however, that the consumers will tend, through trade, to move toward some point on the line *CC'*, that is, a point of tangency between two indifference curves. For example, if point *L* represents the distribution of goods A and B between the two, the first consumer is on his indifference curve III, and the second is on his indifference curve II'. If point *J* is established by trade, the second consumer remains on indifference curve II', but the first moves up to his curve IV. In fact, every point on the line *CC'*, drawn through the points of tangncy between the two sets of indifference curves represents a greater total utility for the two individuals than any point not on the curve. *CC'* is therefore known as a "contract curve," and any exchange which results in a movement toward the contract curve may be construed as an increase in welfare.

In order to demonstrate which point on the contract curve will obtain by trade, it is necessary to make some assumption concerning the rate of exchange between commodities A and B. If the rate of exchange is assumed to be OY of A for OX of B, a price line or line of attainable combinations can be drawn, shown by *XY*. As we have seen previously, each consumer will do best by seeking the point at which the price line is tangent to the highest indifference curve he can reach. In this case the preferred point for both will be *K*, at which the price line is tangent simultaneously to indifference curve II for the first consumer and to curve III' for the second. *K* represents an optimum for the consuming sector in the sense that neither individual could move to a higher indifference surface by trading without pushing the other party to a lower one. Figure 17–4 therefore demonstrates that consumers will maximize their gains from exchange by moving to a point on the contract curve which equates the marginal rate of substitution between goods A and B for consumer 1 to that for consumer 2, and which equates both to the prevailing price ratio.

Pareto generalized this conclusion by defining the optimum as a situation in which it is impossible to improve anyone's position by either exchange or production without diminishing that of someone else. The necessity for achieving the optimum in the producing sector as well as the consuming sector is therefore implicit in Pareto's formulation, although complete exposition of the requirements of the general optimum did not appear until the 1930's, when they were spelled out by Lerner, Lange, Bergson, and Hicks.

Optimum in the Producing Sector

The indifference curve technique for analyzing consumer behavior led Hicks to develop substitution curves and transformation curves to study the behavior of firms in the rational utilization of factor inputs and the production of outputs. Just as an indifference curve indicates the various combinations of two commodities which yield equal satisfaction to a consumer, so a substitution curve, or isoquant, shows various combinations of two factor inputs which yield the same total quantity of a given product. Like an indifference curve, an isoquant curve will be convex to the origin. Because different resources are not perfect substitutes for one another, it will take increasing quantities of resource B to substitute for resource A in order to produce the same quantity of a product. This is the same thing as saying that the marginal rate of technical substitution of factor A for factor B is diminishing. The slope of an isoquant at any point measures the marginal rate of technical substitution of A for B at that point. In theory, the marginal rate of substitution of A for B to produce some output, X, may be either positive or negative. But rational producer behavior rules out a positive substitution ratio because it implies that the application of more of A *and* B results in the *same* output. Clearly, it would be unprofitable for a firm to use more than the minimum factor input required to produce a particular volume of output. This is shown in Figure 17–5, in which ridge lines X and Y are drawn to mark off the limits of rational factor employment. Those portions of the isoquants which lie outside of the ridge lines X and Y, as shown by the broken lines in Figure 17–5, are uneconomic factor combinations and are therefore not relevant to production decisions.

---

[7] Abba P. Lerner, "The Concept of Monopoly and the Measurement of Monopoly Power," *Review of Economic Studies,* Vol. I (June, 1934), pp. 157–75; "Economic Theory and Socialist Economy," *ibid.,* Vol. II (October, 1934), pp. 51–61; "A Note on Socialist Economics," *ibid.,* Vol. IV (October, 1936), pp. 72–76; Hicks, "Foundations of Welfare Economics"; Abram Bergson, "A Reformulation of Certain Aspects of Welfare Economics," *Quarterly Journal of Economics,* Vol. LII (February, 1938), pp. 310–34; also Oscar Lange, "Foundations of Welfare Economics," *Econometrica,* Vol. X (July–October, 1942), pp. 215–28.

FIGURE 17–5

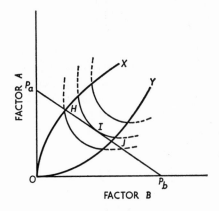

In order to determine the optimum output which can be produced with a given factor expenditure, it is necessary to know the prices at which the factors can be purchased. Assume that their prices are P_a and P_b, respectively. Thus the firm can purchase any combination of the two factors which lies on the outlay or isocost curve. This curve connects that point on the vertical axis which represents the use of a given budget to purchase factor A only to that point on the vertical axis which represents the purchase of factor B only. It is therefore analogous to the price line in indifference curve analysis. The position of the budget or isocost line in Figure 17–5 indicates that the firm could purchase any factor combination lying on it, such as *H, I,* and *J.* But the best combination is *I,* for this combination enables the firm to achieve a bigger output, i.e., to produce on a higher isoquant, with a given factor input. This is the combination at which the ratio of the marginal rates of substitution between A and B is equal to the ratio of their prices. It is therefore the optimum factor combination. Generalizing this conclusion for all firms using A and B implies that the marginal rate of technical substitution must be the same for all firms using both factors. If this condition is not satisfied, it is possible to increase the total product by substituting one factor for another until a further shift will no longer add anything to the total product.

Maximum efficiency of resource use also requires that each firm produce an optimum amount of each product it turns out. The various combinations of two products, say A and B, which can be produced with a given input of factor X can be represented by a transformation curve. Unless the two products are jointly produced in fixed proportions, e.g., hides and meat, outputs of A must be sacrificed to obtain outputs of B, given the input of X. Thus a product transformation curve will be *concave* to the origin. Its slope at any point measures the marginal rate of transformation between the two products or, what amounts to the same thing, the ratio of the marginal costs of the two products. The individual firm produces the optimum combination of two products, say A and B, with a given factor input when the marginal rate of transformation between them is equal to the ratio of their prices. If this condition is not satisfied, the firm could produce more of A and less of B (or vice versa) and add to its profits. Generalizing this conclusion to all firms producing A and B and paying the same price for their factor inputs implies that the ratio of their marginal rates of transformation to the marginal cost of producing the two goods must be equal. If this condition is not satisfied, a reallocation of production could increase the output of either or both products without any change in factor input or the output of other commodities.

Achievement of the economic optimum requires the simultaneous satisfaction of the marginal conditions in the consuming sector and in the producing sector. That is, the marginal rate of substitution between two commodities must not only be equal to the ratio of their prices, but must also be equal to the marginal rate of transformation and the ratio of factor prices. Demonstration of the simultaneous achievement of the marginal conditions in the economy as a whole requires simultaneous consideration of all sectors of the economy; that is, it requires a general equilibrium approach. The more limited partial equilibrium analysis also utilizes the equimarginal principle to define the position of maximum advantage for the individual consumer, factor, or firm. But while a consumer will maximize his own position by following the marginal rule, it does not follow that his position coincides with the optimum unless firms are also producing the products he consumes in their optimum proportions and with the optimum combination of factors. The possibility of treating all these variables simultaneously is the advantage of the general equilibrium approach to the welfare problem as opposed to the more limited partial equilibrium analysis.

Perfect Competition and the Satisfaction of Marginal Conditions

Simultaneous satisfaction of the marginal conditions in the consuming sector and in the producing sector requires that the prices to which consumers equate the ratios of their marginal rates of substitution are the same as those to which producers equate the ratios of their marginal rates of transformation. This can take place only if commodity prices are everywhere equal to marginal costs and factor prices are everywhere equal to the value of their marginal products.

We have already seen that when products are produced under monopoly, oligopoly or monopolistic competition, the negative slope of a firm's average and marginal revenue curves will result in a price which is consistently above marginal cost, and a smaller than optimum output even in an equilibrium situation. Similarly, when there is imperfection in a factor market, factor prices will be less than the value of their marginal products, and factor inputs will be smaller than they would be if the firm were faced with an infinitely elastic factor supply curve. Thus the marginal conditions cannot be satisfied if there is imperfect competition in either the factor markets or the product markets.

It does not follow, however, that they will be satisfied under pure competition either. The presence of pure competition implies simply that there are so many buyers in the market that no one buyer or seller can influence the price. These requirements are necessary but not sufficient to satisfy the marginal conditions of the optimum. The absence of complete knowledge and freedom of entry and exit into or out of a market can also result in a violation of the marginal conditions. Lack of information among buyers may prevent the establishment of a uniform price among sellers even if the product is homogeneous and there are a large number of participants in the market. Pure competition would not guarantee that a consumer who behaves rationally but is ignorant of the market might not pay a higher price than is necessary for his purchase. Lack of perfect knowledge may also occur on the producer side of the market. Entrepreneurs may misjudge the future price at which output can be sold and hence produce too much or too little, even under pure competition. Similarly, they may incorrectly anticipate future factor prices, or changes in the state of the arts, and therefore fail to combine factors in their optimum proportions, even though competition in the factor markets is pure. Thus the more stringent conditions of perfect competition, which requires also that there be perfect knowledge and mobility on the part of all market participants, must prevail for the marginal conditions of the economic optimum to be satisfied.

The significance of this conclusion is that it verifies on an analytical level the classical doctrine that perfect competition maximizes welfare within the framework of given wants and a given pattern of income distribution. That is, the optimizing character of perfect competition in the realm of exchange and production has been logically deduced from the marginal conditions. It is therefore completely different from the idealization of perfect competition by classical and neoclassical thinkers, who made perfect competition an ethical norm inferred from the philosophy of the natural order or the principle of greatest happiness. It is also independent of the philosophical doctrine of the harmony of interests and the political doctrine of laissez-faire. Pareto and the welfare theorists have made a distinct contribution to economic analysis by demonstrating that the economic optimum is achieved if the marginal conditions are satisfied. They have thereby eliminated the ethical connotation of perfect competition and the implicit apology for laissez-faire contained in analyses that are premised on the assumption of perfect competition.

Once the nexus between perfect competition and laissez-faire was destroyed, it became apparent that private ownership of the means of production is not essential to the satisfaction of the marginal conditions. The substitution of state ownership of the means of production for private ownership does, of course, confront the planning board with the problem of establishing the values of the factors of production. But it is generally accepted that if the principle of consumer sovereignty is adopted, a planning board can rationally price the factors of production by simulating the behavior of the perfectly competitive market.[8] "Optimum output and optimum factor proportions can then be achieved by instructing plant managers to follow the marginal principle."[9]

The Proposal for Marginal Cost Pricing

Recognition that the profit-maximizing output of a monopolist or competitive decreasing-cost industry is smaller than that at which price equals marginal cost has led to the proposal that marginal cost pricing be introduced in such cases. The rationale of this proposal is that a consumer is deprived of the opportunity of choosing in a rational way between spending his money in alternative ways if he is unable to obtain additional units of a product at marginal cost because the price of the product does not reflect the value of the factors in another use. It has therefore been argued that the state should intervene to prevent sales at prices which diverge from marginal cost by firms which attain their maximum profit with a smaller output than that which would result if they operated at their maximum technical capacity.

Although the proposal for marginal cost pricing has received considerable attention in recent years, it is by no means new. Marshall was among the first to argue that in the case of commodities produced under conditions of increasing return, aggregate satisfaction can be increased by expanding output sufficiently to equate price and marginal cost, and by subsidizing the subsequent loss to the producer.[10] This suggestion was subsequently elaborated and given greater precision by his disciple, Arthur C. Pigou.[11] More recently, the possibility of using a system of taxes and

---

[8] Proof that rational pricing of the factors of production is possible in a socialist economy was first offered by Oscar Lange and Fred M. Taylor, in *On the Theory of Socialism*, Minneapolis, University of Minnesota Press, 1938. Their argument was a rebuttal to that of Ludwig von Mises that a socialist economy is necessarily chaotic because of the absence of a free price market. Von Mises' view is published in F. A. Hayek, ed., *Collectivist Economic Planning* (London, 1935). See also the view of Enrico Barone, *The Ministry of Production in a Collectivist State,*" republished in the same volume.

[9] See Lerner, "Economic Theory and Socialist Economy." Also see Bergson, *op. cit.*

[10] Alfred Marshall, *Principles of Economics* (8th ed.; London: Macmillan & Co., 1920), pp. 469–76.

[11] Arthur C. Pigou, *Economics of Welfare* (London: Macmillan & Co., 1920), p. 225.

subsidies to facilitate the achievement of minimum cost output has been presented with special vigor by Hotelling and Lerner.[12]

In principle, the manner in which the state would decide whether or not to intervene in a particular case to secure a larger output is quite simple. It would be guided by the rule that whenever the price of a product is greater than its marginal cost, the output of the product is less than the optimum and should be increased. Figure 17–6 shows the output and price

FIGURE 17–6

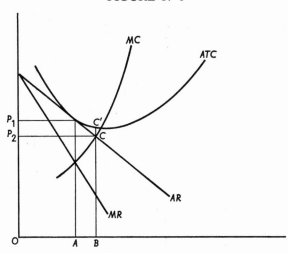

of a firm which is operating on the decreasing portion of its average cost curve. The firm will produce output OA, which will be sold at a price P_1. Intervention by the state to enforce marginal cost pricing would expand output to OB and reduce price to $P_2 = MC$. The amount consumers would pay for additional units of the product would then be equal to the value of the resources used in producing additional units of the product. Total output of the good is increased, and the welfare of consumers is increased, since the reduction of price enables them to move to a higher indifference curve. A glance at Figure 17–1 (page 315) will verify this conclusion. Before the introduction of marginal cost pricing a consumer might have bought combination B of goods X and Y. If the price of X is now reduced to its marginal cost, the consumer is able to buy a combination like that represented by point D, which puts him on a higher indifference curve.

However, if the state compels a firm to sell its output at a price equal

---

[12] Harold Hotelling, "The General Welfare in Relation to Problems of Taxation and Railway and Utility Rates," *Econometrica*, Vol. 6, No. 3 (July, 1938), pp. 242–69; Abba P. Lerner, *Economics of Control* (New York: Macmillan Co., 1944).

to marginal cost when the average cost of output is higher than marginal cost, it will sustain a loss. If average cost is BC', as in Figure 17–6, and marginal cost is BC, this loss will be equivalent to CC'. Proposals to introduce marginal cost pricing into decreasing-cost industries have therefore generally been combined with provisions for adequate compensation. The funds for compensation are gotten from taxes which fall wholly on consumers, who are taxed in proportion to the increase in consumer surplus they gain as a result of the policy. The rationale for the introduction of the compensation principle as a criterion for improvement in welfare is that any policy designed to improve welfare will necessarily involve a redistribution of income. Since there is no objective way of establishing the optimum distribution of income, the compensation principle seeks to offset the redistributional effects of any policy (e.g., marginal cost pricing) proposed to improve welfare.

While a considerable literature has evolved concerning the compensation principle, the basic test is that a policy can be regarded as improving welfare if it is possible to compensate those who are injured by the policy out of the gains of those who benefit and still leave someone better off (on a higher indifference surface than before). The compensation principle is therefore a device for avoiding the necessity for making a value judgment concerning the distribution of income. But it also contains an implicit bias in favor of the existing distribution of income because compensation is intended to restore the distribution which existed before the contemplated change was introduced. Unfortunately, however, the concept of consumer surplus is so nebulous and its measurement so difficult that it would seem almost impossible to avoid the income redistribution effects inherent in marginal cost pricing. Moreover, even if it were possible to avoid the redistribution of income, we cannot be certain that marginal cost pricing will increase welfare unless it is assumed that the original pattern of income distribution is the most desirable one. Indeed, this qualification is inherent in the theory that maximum welfare is achieved when the marginal conditions are satisfied in both the consumer and the producer sectors of the economy.

LIMITATIONS OF THE PARETIAN OPTIMUM

Second-Order and Total Conditions of Welfare

Satisfaction of the marginal or first-order conditions guarantees that either maximum or minimum positions have been achieved. First-order conditions do not, however, make it possible to distinguish between maxima and minima. To make this distinction, second-order conditions are needed. In the context of indifference curve analysis, second-order conditions require that all indifference curves be convex and that all transformation curves be concave to their origins.[13] When these conditions are satisfied, the most efficient use of resources to produce an output of a *given* composition to satisfy *given* wants within the framework of a *given* distribution of income is guaranteed. But even then, there are further conditions that must be met because it is possible to have several maxima. As Kenneth E. Boulding so aptly expressed it, the marginal conditions do not enable us to distinguish "the top of a molehill from Mount Everest."[14] It is also necessary that what Hicks has called the "total conditions" of welfare be met. This is analogous to finding the highest peak in a mountain range. The total conditions of welfare require that it be impossible to improve anyone's welfare either by altering the distribution of income or the composition of output. However, any attempt to spell out the total conditions of welfare involves value judgments, while the marginal conditions, which merely define the conditions under which an economic system functions at maximum efficiency to satisfy given ends with available resources, specifically rule out value judgments as to the ethical quality of these ends. While it is analytically possible to separate questions concerning the efficiency of resource use from questions concerning the justice or desirability of resource use in one alternative rather than another, value judgments must, in the final analysis, be made by someone. Policies to improve welfare will fall short of their goal unless the ends toward which society desires to move, either as a basically free enterprise economy or as a planned economy, are given expression in what Bergson has called the "social welfare function."

One of the ways of constructing a social welfare function which has recently been examined is to tabulate individual votes on selected alternatives in order to determine the majority vote. The difficulty with this method is that the expression of an order of choice by individuals presents problems of aggregation. No clear consensus can be arrived at by aggregating individual preferences.[15] It has been suggested that it may be fruitful to look to the other social sciences to provide the value judgments needed for welfare economics. Social psychologists, anthropologists, and sociologists are now seeking to establish by empirical means the "value consensus" of society. If their efforts eventually materialize with sufficient precision, they may provide the foundation for a social welfare function. Economics can

---

[13] If isoquants were concave, satisfaction of the marginal conditions would define an economic minimum. Similarly, if transformation curves were convex to their origin, satisfaction of the marginal conditions would define an economic minimum.

[14] Kenneth E. Boulding, "Welfare Economics," in B. F. Haley (ed.), *A Survey of Contemporary Economics,* Vol. II (Homewood, Ill.: Richard D. Irwin, Inc., 1952), pp. 1–38.

[15] Kenneth J. Arrow, *Social Choice and Individual Values,* Cowles Foundation for Research Economics at Yale University (New York: John Wiley & Sons, Inc., 1963).

then conceivably apply the maximization formulas to ends which have been established outside economics and which reflect the value consensus of society.

There is, of course, another point of view, namely, that limiting economists to the acceptance of social value judgments may simply perpetuate the status quo, and this itself involves a value judgment. Ideally, of course, the economist who is required in his capacity as a policy maker or adviser to introduce value judgments should do so explicitly, and then only on the basis of the best available data; he should also be ready to reevaluate his value judgments as experience with policy indicates that they were wrong. In any event, it is in the very nature of the case that the economist who ventures beyond pure analysis into policy, particularly as it touches upon questions of welfare in the broadest sense, necessarily is called upon to make value judgments, Robbins' assertion as to their impropriety not withstanding.

Social Costs and Social Benefits

Another limitation of the Paretian optimum is that it leaves out of consideration what Pigou called marginal social costs and marginal social benefits. According to his thinking, social costs and benefits as well as private costs and benefits must be taken into consideration when welfare is conceived of in an absolute sense rather than in a relative sense.

The marginal private benefit of producing a product is, quite simply, the marginal revenue product it yields to its producer. The marginal social benefit is the additional gain which its production confers on the community as a side effect but for which no payment can be exacted. The construction of parks or other undertakings to beautify the surroundings of a producer's location is a classic example of a social benefit. Conversely, the marginal social cost of production is the incidental loss imposed on society which is not fully compensated for by the prices consumers pay. Pollution of the air and water near factory sites, industrial noises, and dirt are typical examples of the kind of social costs Pigou had in mind.

The obvious difficulty of the concepts of the social product and the social cost is that they must have a recognized market price if they are to be taken into account. Any attempt to bring them into relation with the measuring rod of money is necessarily arbitrary. Pigou's technique was to sum up all the direct and indirect costs, valued at market price, to calculate social cost. But this method is vitiated by the fact that market prices reflect only private costs and not social costs. Thus, there is no objective way of knowing when the marginal social cost of resources is the same in all alternative uses and therefore no direct way of judging whether economic reorganization is required in order to improve welfare.

CONCLUDING REMARKS

The reformulation of the theory of optimal consumer and producer behavior by Hicks and others and the emergence of a body of welfare economics which defines the conditions of optimum exchange and production are a continuation of the work of the utility and general equilibrium theorists of the nineteenth century. Both aspects of this continued development of microeconomic analysis have relied heavily on the use of the indifference curve technique and Pareto's concept of the economic optimum. With respect to demand analysis, this technique has the obvious advantage of making it possible to separate the income effects of price change from the substitution effects, though its chief advocates also claim that it avoids the concept of cardinally measurable utility.

The use of indifference curves and transformation curves has also facilitated demonstration that simultaneous satisfaction of the marginal conditions in both the consuming and the producing sectors is the first-order requirement for the achievement of an economic optimum in the Paretian sense. It makes it possible to demonstrate, within the framework of given ends and the distribution of income, whether a reallocation of products or resources through the process of trading can place at least one individual on a higher indifference curve without worsening the position of anyone else. As long as marginal rates of substitution or transformation exceed the ratios of the prices of products or factors, it is always possible for a reorganization to effect an improvement.

When perfect competition prevails, the marginal conditions are automatically satisfied. This is because the ratio of the price to which consumers equate the marginal rate of substitution between each pair of products will be the same as the ratio of the marginal costs to which producers equate the marginal rate of substitution between each pair of factors and the marginal rate of transformation between each pair of products. It follows that if there are firms whose profit-maximizing output is smaller than that at which price equals marginal cost, welfare in the Paretian sense can be increased by the introduction of marginal cost pricing, provided that producers are compensated through a system of subsidies for the losses they would incur. The objective of paying subsidies in this case is to preserve the original distribution of income.

The most vulnerable aspect of modern welfare economics, apart from its inability to treat what Pigou termed "social costs" and "social benefits," is that it limits itself to defining the economic optimum when consumer wants and the distribution of income are assumed given. While it thereby avoids the necessity of making value judgments, the fact remains that in the real world, programs for social improvement necessarily involve value judgments. Conceivably, the day will come when research in other social sciences will have progressed sufficiently to provide the economist with social welfare functions which can guide reorganizations of a sort which will improve welfare in the aggregate but will benefit some parties at the expense of others. This, of course, transcends the Paretian concept of the optimum; the marginal conditions are a guide only to changes of a sort which involve mutual benefit to all parties or, at least, benefits which do not worsen the position of any party while improving that of another.

SUGGESTIONS FOR FURTHER READING

BOULDING, KENNETH E. "Welfare Economics," in B. F. HALEY (ed.), *A Survey of Contemporary Economics*, Vol. II. Homewood, Ill.: Richard D. Irwin, Inc., 1952.

HICKS, JOHN R. *A Revision of Demand Theory*. Oxford: Clarendon Press, 1956.

———. *Value and Capital*, Parts I–II. 2d ed. Oxford: Clarendon Press, 1946.

MYINT, HLA. *Theories of Welfare Economics*. Cambridge: Harvard University Press, 1948.

REDER, MELVIN W. *Studies in the Theory of Welfare Economics*. New York: Columbia University Press, 1947.

ROBERTSON, DENNIS. "Utility and All What?" *Economic Journal*, Vol. LXIV (Dec. 1954).

RUGGLES, N. "The Welfare Basis of the Marginal Cost Pricing Principle," *Review of Economic Studies*, Vol. XVII (1) (1949), pp. 29–46. See also "Recent Developments in the Theory of Marginal Cost Pricing," *Review of Economic Studies*, Vol. XVII (2) (1950), pp. 107–26.

SAMUELSON, PAUL A. "Consumption Theory in Terms of Revealed Preference," *Economica*, N.S., Vol. XV No. 60 (November, 1948), pp. 243–53.

THE CONTRIBUTION OF
JOHN MAYNARD KEYNES
AND SOME LEADING
FOLLOWERS

Chapter

18

INTRODUCTION

Life and Times (1883–1946)

The impact of *The General Theory of Employment, Interest and Money* in the profession as well as in the realm of public policy has exceeded that which could reasonably have been expected from even such distinguished and influential thinker as John Maynard Keynes. The reason for its sweeping success, in the face of the long-standing entrenchment of "received doctrine" and a generally negative reception in nonacademic circles at the time of its publication in 1936, is that it had something for everyone. One would have to go back to Adam Smith to find a comparable degree of persuasiveness with respect to public policy; to David Ricardo for the kind of rigorous analysis which inspires the deductive thinker; and to Karl Marx for someone who attracted sufficiently zealous and able followers to carry his message to the world.

Heredity appears to have destined Keynes to make a distinguished contribution to the world.[1] His father was John Neville Keynes, Registrar of the University of Cambridge, whose *Scope and Method of Political Economy* (1891) is not only a classic in its field but remains an eminently useful treatise on the subject of methodology to this very day. His mother served as Mayor of Cambridge as recently as 1932. They educated their son at Eton and King's College, where he excelled in mathematics, besides studying the classics, philosophy, and economics, the latter under such leading lights as Henry Sidgewick and Alfred Marshall.

In 1906, having passed the civil service examination, he went into the India Office for two years before returning once more to King's College, where he specialized in teaching Marshall's *Principles of Economics*. The academic life, broadened to include cultural as well as business interests which provided a handsome additional income, suited him well.

---

[1] Biographical details are readily available in the *London Times*, "Obituary," April 22, 1946; and in the volume by Roy F. Harrod entitled *The Life of John Maynard Keynes* (New York: Harcourt, Brace & Co., 1952). A bibliography of Keynes's extensive writings is appended to Seymour Harris (ed.), *The New Economics* (New York: Alfred Knopf, 1947).

But he was always involved in public affairs in one capacity or another, particularly with respect to matters of trade and finance. This aspect of his career was in perfect keeping with his predominantly pragmatic approach; economics as a pure science interested him far less than economics in the service of policy. Indeed, Keynes's contribution to the theory and practice of political economy must be seen in perspective against the war and interwar years in order to be fully understood and appreciated. These years were marked by the breakdown of trade relations and the gold standard during World War I, followed first by inflation, exchange rate instability, and balance-of-payments disequilibria and later by deflation and mass unemployment on an international scale. Theoretical examination of these catastrophic phenomena and, more important from Keynes's point of view, practical solutions to the problems they created were therefore the order of the day.

With the outbreak of World War II, Keynes devoted himself to questions concerning war finance and the ultimate reestablishment of international trade and stable currencies. His ideas on these matters were offered in a pamphlet, *How to Pay for the War,* published in 1940, and in the "Keynes plan" for the establishment of an international monetary authority which he proposed in 1943. Although Keynes's plan was rejected, the proposal which was adopted at the 1944 Bretton Woods Conference, which Keynes attended as the leading British delegate, clearly reflected the influence of his thinking.

At the time of his death, early in 1946, shortly after working out the American loan agreement, he was the leading economist not only of England, but of the world. He was a brilliant theorist but valued theory primarily as a guide to policy. Thus, Keynes, perhaps more than any other single individual, is responsible for the return to what in the old days was known as "political economy."

The Evolution of "The General Theory"

Though reference is often made to the "Keynesian revolution," the fact is that, from the standpoint of Keynes's own intellectual development, *The General Theory* is more in the nature of an evolutionary maturation of concepts which began to emerge in the years following World War I.[2] Though he was schooled in traditional theory, his examination of the relationship between depression and monetary deflation after World War I led him to ponder the question of the ability of a free system to operate automatically at full-employment levels. The train of thought which ulti-

---

[2] Joseph A. Schumpeter has given a most lucid account of the gradual unfolding of the Keynesian "message." See "John Maynard Keynes, 1883–1946," *American Economic Review,* Vol. XXXVI, No. 4 (Sept. 1946), reprinted in his *Ten Great Economists* (London: Oxford University Press, 1951).

mately developed out of this question later became the essence of the Keynesian message. Even his first publication, *Indian Currency and Finance* (1913), which is regarded as an outstanding examination of the functioning of the gold exchange standard, foreshadows his later view on the need for wise monetary policy in order to have economic stability. But this message first emerged clearly in *The Economic Consequences of the Peace* (1919), which won him international fame. In it, he presented, in addition to his vigorous polemic against reparations payments, a vivid examination of the breakdown of what he called "that extraordinary episode of laissez faire capitalism." The picture he sketched was of a system made economically moribund by the passing of the conditions necessary to entrepreneurial success: a rapidly growing population and plentiful investment opportunities born of innovation and scientific progress. Thus, Keynes's Weltanschauung in the period after World War I was one of economic stagnation. Nothing was yet in sight of the theoretical schema of *The General Theory,* which was to be published more than a decade later during the worldwide depression of the 1930's. But there are few better examples in the history of economic thought of the relationship between the germination of an economic analysis and its crystallization into theoretical propositions than we find in *The Economic Consequences of the Peace* and *The General Theory of Employment, Interest and Money.*

His *Tract on Monetary Reform* (1923) was another stepping-stone to *The General Theory.* In it, he advocated that the volume of note issue be controlled by the central bank independently of the gold reserve as a means of achieving economic stabilization via price level stabilization. Two aspects of this work are significant as regards the ultimate development of Keynes's thinking: The first is its unmistakably prescriptive nature; the second is its conception of money as an active agent in the economic process. Both are important signposts along the way to *The General Theory.*

The "economics as a guide for policy" character of Keynes's work is somewhat obscured in his *Treatise on Money* (1930). But that work contributed at least one other important principle which ultimately became embodied in *The General Theory.* This is the principle that decisions to save and decisions to invest are unrelated to one another. Their separateness was, however, glossed over—or better still, lost sight of—by those who conceived of the interest rate as a device to equilibrate savings and investment. It was in order to emphasize the separateness of these decisions and the idea that private thrift is not a virtue when investment opportunities are lacking that Keynes adopted definitions of saving and investment in the *Treatise* which recognized the possibility of their diverging from each other. Thus, if $S > I$, there will be a cumulative contraction, while $I > S$ will bring about a cumulative expansion. This formulation was intended not only as a tool for monetary theory but also as a guide for monetary policy, whose obvious goal is to keep $S = I$.[3] It proved to be one of the more successful of Keynes's many terminological innovations, though the *Treatise* as a whole was received with less applause than any previous work. While the definitions of savings and investment introduced in the *Treatise* were abandoned in *The General Theory,* the idea of savings and investment as separate phenomena and as magnitudes which are not equated by the interest rate is another of the foundation stones of *The General Theory.*

The completion of *The General Theory* only five years after the *Treatise* represents Keynes's crowning achievement. It is his magnum opus not only as a cumulation of his previous efforts, but also as his last major publication. It brought him so enthusiastic a following that there emerged a whole school which adopted and proliferated his ideas. Among those who carried the Keynesian message to the world are a remarkable number who are notable and possibly even outstanding thinkers in their own right. Roy F. Harrod, Joan Robinson, and Richard F. Kahn were among the leading English economists whose thinking appeared to be progressing in the same general direction as Keynes's when *The General Theory* appeared. Alvin Hansen, Abba P. Lerner, and Paul A. Samuelson are among the leading Keynesians on this side of the Atlantic. All have the distinction of having added in an original way to the body of theory which Keynes presented in *The General Theory of Employment, Interest and Money.*

The Revival of Macroeconomic Analysis

With the publication of *The General Theory,* macroeconomic analysis once more claimed the center of the stage. Not the allocation of resources among alternative uses, but rather whether resources would be employed at all, became the primary question economic theory sought to answer. This is the question to which Keynes addressed himself and which he made the basis for his fight with the "classics." Keynes thoughtfully provided us with a footnote explaining his use of the term to include "the followers of Ricardo, those, that is to say, who adopted and perfected the theory of the Ricardian economics, including (for example) J. S. Mill, Marshall, Edgeworth and Prof. Pigou."[4]

Two things are worth noting before proceeding with the precise nature of Keynes's criticism of the classics. The first is that no single individual associated with the classical or neoclassical tradition ever held all

---

[3] A most useful examination of the nature and usefulness of the savings and investment terminology of the *Treatise on Money* is Friederick A. Lutz, "The Outcome of the Savings-Investment Discussion," *Quarterly Journal of Economics,* Vol. LII (August, 1938), pp. 588–614, reprinted in *Readings in Business Cycle Theory,* Philadelphia, The Blakiston Company (1944).

[4] John Maynard Keynes, *The General Theory of Employment, Interest and Money* (New York: Harcourt, Brace & Co., 1936), n. 3. This work is cited hereafter in the footnotes as *The General Theory.*

the ideas that Keynes attributes collectively to all of them. What he did, in effect, was to create a convenient and more clearly defined target at which he could aim the shots he was about to fire. The second point is that the problem to which Keynes addressed himself, namely, the problem of the level of economic activity, is fundamentally different from that with which his classical and neoclassical predecessors concerned themselves. On a macroeconomic level the classicists (i.e., the orthodox writers who preceded Marshall) were more concerned with the problem of long-run secular development than with the problem of cyclical disturbance. The latter problem was conceived of primarily as a problem of gluts and overproduction, and was considered to be self-correcting. Though the nature of the self-corrective mechanism was not explored in more than a cursory fashion, it was Say's law, with its dictum that supply creates its own demand, which provided the basis for their conclusion. Neoclassical theorists, that is, those in the Marshallian tradition, were mainly concerned with the problem of optimizing and relating the price-determining process to the maximizing activities of individuals and firms. Thus, when Keynes focused his attention on the problem of an underemployment equilibrium, he was dealing with a problem that his predecessors scarcely touched on. One would, for example, search Marshall's *Principles of Economics* in vain for any discussion of the problem of underemployment or its relationship to income determination. Yet, this is the essence of the Keynesian problem and the basic difference between it and all that went before. It is its analysis of the problem of aggregate demand and the implications of this analysis for policy making which separate Keynesian theory from the traditional. Yet, Keynes himself was, by training, a strict neoclassicist. This is perhaps one reason why he was able to exert so much influence over his similarly trained contemporaries.

KEYNES'S CRITICISM OF NEOCLASSICAL POSTULATES

Wage Theory

The General Theory of Employment, Interest and Money is premised on Keynes's criticism of the neoclassical theory that an economy with flexible wages and prices tends automatically to generate full employment. This theory was implicit rather than explicit in neoclassical thinking, for the latter was concerned primarily with the problem of value and distribution and the allocation of resources among alternative uses. It therefore has a distinct microeconomic bias which is very much in evidence in the postulates on which its wage theory is based.[5] These postulates are (1) that the marginal product of labor tends to fall as employment increases, (2) that the real wage of labor tends to equal its marginal product and to reflect the

---

[5] *Ibid.,* chap. ii.

psychic disutility of employment at the margin, and (3) that the money wage bargains which are made between workers and their employers also determine the level of real wages. Neoclassical thinkers concluded, on the basis of these postulates, that if there is unemployment, it must be due to the unwillingness of workers to accept a reward which corresponds to their marginal productivity. It follows that an increase in employment can be brought about only by reducing wages until they are equal to labor's marginal product.

Keynes, however, rejected this conclusion and maintained that unemployment resulted from what he termed "insufficient aggregate demand."[6] Given the state of the arts, it is the level of employment which determines the marginal product of labor and, therefore, the real wage. Thus, he argued, the level of real wages is not determined independently of the level of employment. Moreover, the level of real wages cannot be reduced simply by reducing the level of money wages. Money wage cuts are not an effective way to reduce real wage rates because the total demand for consumer goods is dependent mainly on labor income. The wage bargain determines only money wage rates and not real wage rates. "There may exist no expedient by which labor as a whole can reduce its real wage to a given figure by making revised money bargains with the entrepreneurs."[7] Real wages can be reduced only as a result of an increase in employment which results from a prior increase in aggregate demand.

This brings to the foreground the postulate concerning the reaction of workers to wage reductions. Neoclassical theorists maintained that money wages tend to equal real wages and that the latter reflect the psychic disutility of employment at the margin. Workers will therefore reject offers of additional employment at lower money wages. Neoclassical thinkers consequently regard their unemployment as *voluntary,* on the presumption that it could be alleviated by a reduction of money wages.

The mechanism by which real wage levels were thought to be adjusted so as to make them compatible with full employment is therefore important. Clearly, what is necessary from the standpoint of employer incentive to expand employment is a reduction in the level of *real* wages. Competition among workers for jobs will obviously depress money wages rates if the labor market is purely competitive. But whether the level of real wages will also fall along with money wages depends on the behavior of prices. If prices fall just as rapidly as money wages, real wages will remain constant, or if prices actually fall faster than money wages, real wages will rise. In either case, there is no incentive to give more employment. Prices must fall by less than money wages, so that real wages are reduced, for employment to expand.

---

[6] *Ibid.*, p. 16.
[7] *Ibid.*, p. 13.

A reduction in real wages in consequence of declining money wages is virtually a certainty in a single industry or sector of the economy, since there is no reason to expect that the prices of goods on which wage earners spend their income will fall proportionately. For an industry or a sector of the economy a reduction in money wages will therefore provide a basis for increased employment. Whether money wage rate reductions can be equally effective in alleviating widespread unemployment such as is encountered during a period of depression depends upon a number of considerations. Specifically, a reduction in money wages reduces labor income as well as employer costs and may therefore reduce the aggregate demand for goods. If prices fall as rapidly as money wages, real wages cannot fall, so that there is no stimulus to employment.

Keynes rejected the idea that workers should be considered as voluntarily unemployed because they are unwilling to accept reduced money wages. He agreed that workers generally are reluctant to accept money wage rate reductions but argued that they will accept additional employment at the current money wage even if it is associated with price increases and, consequently, a reduction in the level of real wages. Keynes therefore considered workers to be voluntarily unemployed only if they refused a cut in *real* wages, i.e., refused to work in consequence of a rise in consumer prices. He did not regard worker unwillingness and institutional barriers, such as minimum-wage laws to a downward revision of wages, as major impediments to increasing employment because it is generally not possible to decrease the real wages of workers via a money wage rate reduction. Thus, he rejected not only the neoclassical conception of voluntary unemployment but also its prescription of a downward reduction in the money wage rate as the best means of alleviating this condition.

The Theory of the Interest Rate

The real impediment to stimulating employment during a depression is the difficulty of maintaining the aggregate demand for goods at a level associated with full employment. Classical and neoclassical thinkers recognized that an economy can experience gluts and lapses from full employment as a result of cyclical fluctuation. But they argued that in the long run, flexible commodity prices and wage rates would prevent overproduction and unemployment, and that the interest rate could be relied on to channel all savings into investment. In terms of this logic, aggregate demand could not be deficient in the long run because any income that is saved automatically becomes invested. Many of the business cycle theorists who wrote between 1900 and 1936 were of course skeptical that the interest rate reliably performed this function. But it was Keynes's emphasis on the monetary aspects of interest rate determination which brought to light the reasons why the interest rate could not be relied on automatically to equilibrate savings and investment.

Neoclassical thinkers conceived of the interest rate as being determined by the intersection of a positively sloped schedule of the supply of loanable funds and a negatively sloped schedule of the demand for funds, as shown in Figure 18–1. Elasticity may be deduced on the supply side of the market if a preference for spending versus saving is assumed and if the only motive for saving is the interest income it yields. The elasticity of the demand schedule may similarly be deduced from the schedule of the marginal productivity of capital. If, now, competition is assumed on both sides of the market, so that the interest rate is free to fluctuate, it will settle at that level which equilibrates savings and investment.

Keynes, however, maintained that the interest rate does not automatically channel savings into investment in the manner conceived by neoclassical thinkers. The main reason for its inability to function in this way is that

FIGURE 18–1

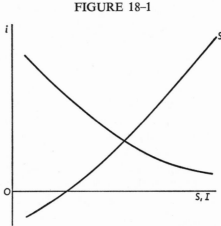

there is an asset demand for money as well as a transactions demand. Keynes regarded a demand for money per se not only as being perfectly rational but as satisfying such a basic psychological need that he conceived of interest as the price for parting with liquidity rather than as a reward for abstinence. Interest can reward abstinence only in a full-employment economy, for this is the only circumstance in which additional investment necessarily curtails consumption. Thus, he regarded the neoclassical conception of interest as inappropriate in any but a full-employment economy.

Keynes further attacked the neoclassical theory of interest as being indeterminate. According to this theory, the interest rate is determined by the intersection of a savings schedule and an investment demand schedule, as in Figure 18–1. However, Keynes maintained, it is impossible to determine the position of the savings schedule until the level of income is known. There is a different level of savings for every level of income. Yet, we cannot know the income level without first knowing the volume of investment, and the latter depends not only on the productivity of new capital at the margin but also on the rate of interest. Changes in the investment demand schedule and the savings supply schedule are therefore interdependent and render the interest rate indeterminate within the neoclassical framework. What was needed, therefore, Keynes thought, was a new approach which would not only explain interest as a monetary phenomenon, but which would also integrate monetary theory into the general theory of income, output, and employment. His theory of aggregate effective demand was intended to provide such an approach.

KEYNES'S THEORY OF EMPLOYMENT, OUTPUT, AND INCOME

The Principle of Aggregate Effective Demand

Keynes relates that one of the main problems he encountered in presenting an aggregate analysis was the choice of units.[8] His analysis obviously required some way of expressing both physical magnitudes (e.g., output and employment) and monetary magnitudes (e.g., income). He simplified his analysis by restricting it to the short run, in which organization, technique, and equipment can be assumed as given. Changes in output and employment will then closely parallel each other, and wage rates and prices can be expected to move together. But a short-run analysis does not eliminate the effects of a change in the value of the monetary unit. If the monetary unit is changing, the money value of output is not a true indication of its real value, nor are the money costs of producing output a measure of real cost. The usual approach to this problem is to correct income (or output) data for price changes. But Keynes chose to correct for wage rate changes instead, so that corrected national income figures reflect changes in employment. In the short-run situation with which he was dealing, the choice between correcting for price changes and wage rate changes is, of course, less important than it is in the long run, when changes in technique are likely to cause changes in output which are unrelated to changes in employment. But Keynes appeared to distrust the whole technique of correcting for price changes. Accordingly, he chose to express the physical aspect of changes in the level of economic activity in terms of labor units of employment and the monetary aspect in terms of a constant wage unit associated with a standard unit of employment of "ordinary labor."

These units are used in constructing the aggregate demand and aggregate supply schedules which Keynes devised to demonstrate the determination of the economy's level of activity. The aggregate demand schedule relates sales proceeds (converted into real terms of means of an index of wage rates) to the output produced by varying amounts of employment. It

---

[8] *Ibid.,* chap. iv.

is shown in Figure 18–2 as consisting of $C + I$, where C is the demand for consumer goods and I is the demand for investment goods. The aggregate supply schedule, which Keynes called the Z function, is also shown in Figure 18–2. It is a schedule of the proceeds required to cover the factor costs, including normal profit, of the output produced by the employment of varying quantities of labor. Thus, Z is a function of N, the level of employment, and is given in the short run. The intersection of the two schedules determines the equilibrium level of employment, ON_1. But, Keynes insists, this level is not necessarily a full-employment equilibrium for reasons which will become clear when the determinants of consumption and investment are examined.

FIGURE 18–2

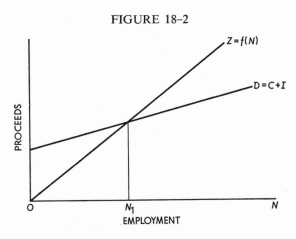

The introduction of the principle of aggregate effective demand in *The General Theory* marks a milestone in the history of economic analysis because it is the culmination of a number of earlier efforts to develop the income-expenditure approach as opposed to the quantity theory approach to aggregate demand. The difference between the quantity theory approach and the income-expenditure approach is that the latter conceives of aggregate demand as the sum of consumption and investment expenditures rather than as the money stock times its velocity of circulation. The expenditure stream is separated in order to take account of the factors affecting these two independently determined magnitudes. The quantity theory approach, by way of contrast, makes no analytical distinction between consumer demand and investment demand but simply assumes that income which is not used for consumer goods purchases will, because of a flexible interest rate, be used for capital goods purchases. The proportions in which consumer goods and capital goods are bought may become altered as their relative prices and utilities change, but all will find a market at some price. In short, the theory of aggregate demand implicit in the quantity theory is precisely the same as that which is implicit in Say's law. Thus, Keynes, by adopting the income-expenditure approach, avoids the invalid neoclassical conclusion that sales proceeds will necessarily cover the cost of producing the full-employment output because the money value of that output is associated with the creation of an equivalent money income. The sales proceeds which businessmen can expect to realize depend on the level of consumption and investment expenditures. Keynes therefore proceeds to examine the determination of these separate expenditure streams.

The Determination of Consumption Expenditures

Although Marshall recognized that saving is related to income, and J. M. Clark presented the idea of a "tendency toward saving a progressively larger proportion of our income as our income itself gets larger,"[9] the hypothesis that consumption is a stable function of real income was given its clearest and most explicit statement by Keynes.[10]

Keynes formulated his hypothesis concerning the relationship between consumption and income in terms of real income, the implication being that people are not subject to "money illusion"; they can and do see through the "veil of money." While he makes some reference to statistical evidence, his hypothesis that "other things being equal" consumption expenditures depend primarily on real income is an a priori rather than an empirical proposition. The consumption function, $C = f(Y)$, which is shown in Figure 18–3 as CC', indicates the changes in consumption expenditures associated with changes in real income where the "other factors" which might affect consumption expenditures remain unchanged. These other factors are exogenous and, if they change, will produce *shifts* in the consumption function. Windfall gains or losses such as might occur in a stock market boom or crash, major changes in expectations with respect to the availability of goods such as would be experienced in wartime, changes in fiscal policy, and major interest rate changes are objective factors which Keynes mentioned as being capable of producing shifts in the propensity to consume out of given income if they occur. However, in the absence of unusual events, Keynes maintained that the propensity to consume out of a given income is a highly stable function of income because the subjective, or endogenous, factors which determine consumer behavior change only very slowly.

These subjective factors are the psychological characteristics of human behavior and the social institutions and practices affecting the distribution of income and its disbursement. They are unlikely to change rapidly. People accustom themselves to certain living standards, and certain practices emerge with respect to the frequency of wage, dividend, and other payments and the size of retained earnings. These factors change so gradually that the slope and position of the consumption function are likely to be quite stable. This is the basis for Keynes's formulation of what he

---

[9] J. M. Clark, *Economic Reconstruction* (New York: Columbia University Press, 1934), p. 109.

[10] *The General Theory,* chaps. viii–x.

FIGURE 18-3

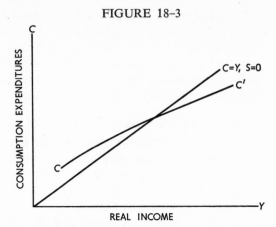

considered to be a "fundamental psychological law" with respect to determining the normal slope of the consumption function. This law is that "as a rule, and on the average, consumption will increase as income increases but not by as much as the increase in income."[11] Thus the value of the marginal propensity to consume, $\dfrac{\Delta C}{\Delta Y}$, which constitutes the slope of the consumption curve, is less than unity. It will therefore cut through a curve such as the one drawn at a 45-degree angle in Figure 18–3, which shows how the consumption function would look if all income were spent. It follows that for a given dollar increase in real income the *absolute* increase in consumption will be less than the absolute increase in income. The implication is clear that as the income level of an economy rises, consumption expenditures become a smaller component of aggregate demand.

This far-reaching hypothesis has, naturally enough, invited all manner of empirical testing. When properly interpreted, the proposition has stood up remarkably well. United States Department of Commerce data show that for the economy as a whole, excluding abnormal periods such as the war and early postwar years, the marginal propensity to consume is less than one, just as Keynes maintained. But there eventually developed a considerable controversy about the nature of the long-run consumption function. This controversy led to an important refinement in the original Keynesian theory which will be discussed below.

The Marginal Propensity to Consume and the Multiplier

Not Keynes, but R. F. Kahn has the distinction of having fathered the concept of the multiplier.[12] But while Kahn was the first to formulate the

---

[11] *Ibid.*, p. 96.

[12] R. F. Kahn, "The Relation of Home Investment to Unemployment," *Economic Journal*, Vol. XLI (June, 1931).

idea that an increase in investment has an expansionary effect which is greater than the increase in investment itself, it was Keynes who recast the principle from its original form as a tool for analyzing the employment effects of public investment into a tool for analyzing the income effect of investment.

The importance of increments of new investment for increments of income had of course already been stressed by business cycle theorists such as Knut Wicksell, Michael Tugan-Baranowsky, and Arthur Spietoff. But it was the formulation of the multiplier principle which revealed two fundamentals concerning the relationship between investment and income which were not clearly understood before. The first is that the expenditure of new money can have an expansionary effect on an economy with unemployed resources which is larger than the size of the expenditure itself. The second is that any expansionary process is necessarily limited and loses vitality because of leakages from the expenditure stream. Both of these questions had become intensely practical issues during the Great Depression of the thirties, when there was considerable interest in proposals to stimulate economic activity by the introduction of "scrip" money. Thus the theory of the multiplier made a very timely appearance.

Keynes reasoned that an increment of investment can initiate an expansionary process because it increases income and, unless the marginal propensity to consume is zero, also consumption expenditures. This, in turn, eventually increases the demands for the factors of production and their incomes. Since a zero marginal propensity to consume is most unlikely, Keynes thought that an increment of investment would be certain to raise the income level by more than its own amount. Precisely how great the leverage will be depends on marginal propensity to save. Any portion of an increment of new investment which leaks away from the current expenditure stream cannot generate additional new income. If for example, one third of a new investment of $100,000 is saved rather than spent to finance new consumption, only $66,666.66 generates new income in the next period. If the propensity to save is such that one third of this amount is also drained into cash balances in the next period, national income will increase by an additional $22,222.22. Each successive round of expenditures will add an additional amount to national income. Given a marginal propensity to save of .33, a new investment of $100,000 will eventually, other things being equal, raise national income by three times this amount, or $300,000. Thus the multiplier, which is the ratio between an increase in income and an increase in investment, is the reciprocal of the marginal propensity to save. Since the magnitude of the marginal propensity to consume is somewhere in the range of zero to 100 percent, the value of the multiplier will be between 1 and infinity. The operational significance of the multiplier is that, other things being equal, it indicates the expansion in national income which may be expected from any income creating expenditure in consequence of its affect on consumption.[13]

The increase in income associated with the operation of the multiplier principle obviously can only take place with a time lag. Yet, Keynes chose not to emphasize the dynamic aspects of the multiplier when he presented what he termed "the logical theory of the multiplier which holds good continuously without time lag, at all moments of time." Within the framework of this static conception of the multiplier, the new equilibrium income level is conceived as being determined by the increment of new investment times a multiplier derived from some "normal" marginal propensity to consume.

Considerable criticism has been directed against Keynes's use of the timeless multiplier. It has been maintained that there is a difference between the conception of the marginal propensity to consume as an algebraic expression and the marginal propensity to consume as a psychological factor determining behavior with respect to additional increments of income.[14] It may, for example, be possible to say a good bit with respect to the way in which consumers will react to an additional increment of income, e.g., a tax cut. Yet, it does not follow that a quantitative estimate of its effect on consumption will enable us to predict what the aggregate increase in income will be or how quickly it will take place.[15] The direct and

---

[13] The multiplier may be derived as follows:

$$M = \frac{\Delta Y}{\Delta I} = \frac{\Delta Y}{\Delta S} = \frac{1}{\frac{\Delta S}{\Delta Y}} \tag{1}$$

$$\Delta Y = \Delta C + \Delta S \tag{2}$$

$$\frac{\Delta Y}{\Delta Y} = \frac{\Delta C}{\Delta Y} + \frac{\Delta S}{\Delta Y} = 1 \tag{3a}$$

$$\frac{\Delta S}{\Delta Y} = 1 - \frac{\Delta C}{\Delta Y} \tag{3b}$$

$$\therefore M = \frac{1}{1 - \frac{\Delta C}{\Delta Y}} \tag{4}$$

[14] See Alvin Hansen, *A Guide to Keynes* (New York: McGraw-Hill Book Co., Inc., 1953), chap. iv, for a discussion of the several senses in which the concept of the multiplier has been employed. Gottfried Haberler has argued that the relationship between the multiplier and the marginal propensity to consume is tautological. See his article, "Mr. Keynes' Theory of the Multiplier: A Methodological Criticism," *Zeitschrift für Nationalökonomie*, Vol. VII (1936), pp. 299–305. Reprinted in *Readings in Business Cycle Theory, op. cit.*, pp. 193–202.

[15] Inquiry into the sources of leakages raises an even more important question, namely, whether a multiplier effect will take place at all. Robinson and Harrod have extended the *General Theory* to include foreign trade and noted the importance of leakages associated with the marginal propensity to import. See J. Robinson, *Essays in the Theory of Employment* (Oxford: Basil Blackwell, 1937), R. F. Harrod, *International Economics* (Chicago: University of Chicago Press, 1939), Chap. VI. More recently the effect of price increases which may alter the distribution of income and thereby reduce the multiplier effect of exogenous spending has been examined. See

indirect effects of additional investment cannot be reduced to a formula as simple as the timeless multiplier. During the transition period there may be a series of $\frac{C}{Y}$ ratios whose values will differ from what they would have been if the expansion had been foreseen and from what they eventually will be when the community has settled down to a new steady level of investment. Thus the relationship between new investment, consumption, and income expressed by the timeless multiplier which abstracts the transition period is at best only an approximation which holds true over periods of time which are sufficiently long that complete adjustment to new conditions is possible.

The Determination of Investment Expenditures

Since increases in consumption expenditures are, in general, dependent on prior increases in income, Keynes emphasized the volume of investment as the crucial economic magnitude. In so doing he followed in the tradition of business cycle theorists such as Wicksell, Tugan-Baranowsky, and Spietoff who pointed to investment as the key variable in the economy. Keynes was not however, primarily concerned with explaining fluctuations in the level of investment and income, but in explaining their equilibrium level. The central question of the Keynesian theory of income, output, and employment is, therefore: What determines the willingness of entrepreneurs to purchase new capital goods? The answer to this question depends, obviously, on the relationship among three elements: the cost of the capital goods, the expected dollar yield, and the market rate of interest.

The inducement to invest in a capital asset will be strong if the prospective yield a purchaser expects it to produce compares favorably with its supply price. The prospective yield of a capital good is a series of annuities, $Q_1, Q_2, \ldots Q_n$, which are expected to be obtained as proceeds from the sale of its output during its life after deducting running expenses. Its supply price is its replacement cost, "the price which would just induce a manufacturer newly to produce an additional unit of such assets." Thus the marginal efficiency of a particular type of capital is the relationship between the prospective yield of one more unit of that type of capital and the cost of producing it. More specifically, Keynes defines the marginal efficiency of capital as "the rate of discount which will make the present value of the series of annuities given by the returns expected from the capital asset during its life just equal to its supply price."[16] Thus, if C_r represents the replacement cost of a particular type of asset which is expected to yield

---

Paul Davidson and Eugene Smolensky, *Aggregate Supply and Demand Analyses* (New York: Harper and Row, 1964), chapter X. Increased tax revenues out of rising incomes and increased interest rates in the absence of an expanded money supply are other sources of leakage that may offset the multiplier effect that Keynes assumed an increase in exogenous spending would necessarily have.

[16] *The General Theory,* p. 135.

returns over n years, the marginal efficiency of capital can be calculated by solving for r in the equation

$$C_r = \frac{Q_1}{(1+r)} + \frac{Q_2}{(1+r)^2} + \cdots \frac{Q_n}{(1+r)^n}$$

Each successive return in the series will come to the prospective purchaser only after the time between the beginning of the production process and the final sale of the product elapses. It must, therefore, obviously be discounted over a period of time, and the marginal efficiency of capital is the rate of discount which equalizes the expected series of yields and the supply price of the asset.[17]

It is important to note that while the marginal efficiency of capital is a rate, it is not the same thing as the rate of interest on money. It is the relationship between r, the marginal efficiency of capital, and i, the rate of interest at which money can be borrowed, which determines whether a particular investment will be made or not. An investment will be made if $r > i$; the inducement to invest comes to an end when $r = i$, as it eventually will, because of the tendency for the marginal efficiency of capital to fall.

Keynes lays much stress on the role of expectations in governing the investment demand schedule. Expectations concerning the ability of a particular asset to continue yielding the same net return are revised downward as the physical quantity of a particular capital asset increases because the sale price of its output will diminish. Then, too, a capital good which has a long service life may eventually have to compete with equipment which cost less per unit of product, or which can be satisfied with a lower rate of return because the money rate of interest may then be lower.[18] Thus, anticipations play a major role in determining the inducement to invest. It is not only the expected current yield of an asset which a prospective purchaser of new capital will take into account, but also the future yield, which is surrounded by an even greater degree of uncertainty and risk. The effect these factors have on the state of long-term expectations is vividly described in chapter xii of *The General Theory*, which observes that the ability of entrepreneurs to estimate prospective yields is especially precarious because they are usually influenced by the expectations of those who deal in the stock market no less than they are guided by the expectations of entrepreneurs themselves. This Keynes regarded as one of the least desirable features of laissez-faire capitalism. "When the capital development of a country becomes a by-product of the activities of a casino, the job is likely to be ill-done."[19]

---

[17] Keynes himself pointed out that his marginal efficiency of capital is the same concept as Irving Fisher's "rate of return over cost" (*ibid.*, p. 140).

[18] *Ibid.*, chap. xi, Sec. III.

[19] *Ibid.*, p. 159.

The Liquidity Preference Theory of Interest

Uncertainty regarding the future affects not only the marginal efficiency of capital, but also our willingness to part with our cash resources. To hold cash, says Keynes, "lulls our disquietude," and the rate of interest we demand for parting with liquid assets in exchange for earning assets measures the "degree of our disquietude." He therefore regarded interest as compensation for illiquidity and the determination of its rate as a monetary phenomenon arising out of the store-of-value function of money.[20]

Keynes's emphasis on the desire to hold money as a store of wealth represents a sharp break with his predecessors, who assumed that the only demand for money is for transactions purposes. Keynes maintains that money is demanded to satisfy three motives: the transactions motive, the precautionary motive, and the speculative motive. The amount of cash needed to carry on personal and business transactions and the additional amount desired to meet possible future contingencies vary directly with the economy's level of output. Since expenditures normally increase as business activity expands, the transactions demand for money increases with national output and income. The precautionary demand for money also increases as the volume of business activity expands and is therefore functionally related to output. The amount of cash wanted for transactions and precautionary reasons is generally interest-inelastic, though conceivably there may be some motivation for economizing the cash balances held for these purposes if interest rates become very high. However, the aggregate demand for money to satisfy the speculative motive usually shows a continuous response to gradual changes in the rate of interest; i.e., there is a continuous curve relating changes in the demand for money to satisfy the speculative motive and changes in the rate of interest reflected in changes in the prices of bonds and debts of different maturities.[21]

The reason for the unique behavior of the speculative demand for money is easily understood in terms of the behavior of bond yields. Fixed income bonds are not greatly inferior to money itself as highly liquid assets where there is an organized market, even though they are not exchange mediums. However, their disadvantage is the risk of price changes, which correspondingly alter their yields. If the market price of a bond rises, the ratio of its fixed dollar income to the bond price falls. Its yield, which is the income to be earned by illiquidity, is therefore falling. Low interest rates and bond yields may be less attractive to a wealth holder than cash itself, even though the latter earns no income at all, because when bonds are bought at a relatively high price (low yield), a subsequent small drop in price may be sufficient to wipe out the income earned from illiquidity. Cash

---

[20] John Maynard Keynes, "The General Theory," *Quarterly Journal of Economics*, Vol. LI (Feb., 1937); also reprinted in Harris, *op. cit.*

[21] *The General Theory*, p. 197.

is then a relatively more attractive asset than a bond. Thus the preference for liquidity for speculative purposes is virtually unlimited if the market is convinced that bond prices cannot rise further.

The relationship between interest rates and the demand for money is shown graphically by the L curve in Part A of Figure 18–4. Since some cash balances will be required almost irrespective of the interest rate, the segment of the curve representing the sum of the transactions and precautionary demands is shown as interest-inelastic at rates above i_4. The speculative demand for cash, however, is sensitive to small changes in the interest rate and approaches perfect elasticity when the rate is very low, e.g., at a

FIGURE 18–4

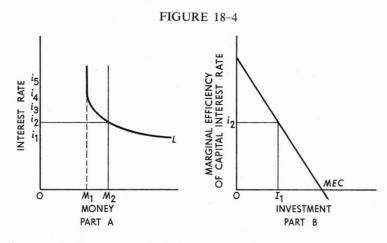

level corresponding to i_1 in Part A of Figure 18–4. Thus the total demand for money, as represented by the L curve, is the sum of the transactions, precautionary, and speculative demands. According to Keynes's liquidity preference theory, the interest rate is a monetary phenomenon which results from the interaction of the total demand for money and its supply. The supply of money depends primarily on the actions of the monetary authority and the commercial banks. Thus, if the money supply is given at OM_2, as in Part A of Figure 18–4, the interest rate is established at i_2; OM_1 is the proportion of the money supply held for transactions and precautionary purposes, while M_1M_2 satisfies the speculative motive.

Part A of Figure 18–4 makes it apparent that in the Keynesian analysis the interest rate equates the demand for and the supply of money. It does not, as in the neoclassical analysis, equate savings and investment.[22]

---

[22] Savings and investment are nevertheless equal in the Keynesian system. There are two aspects to this equality. The first is definitional: Savings and investment are both defined as being equal to the unconsumed portion of current output. The second is an equilibrium relationship. Any change in investment causes a change in the income level and, given the propensity to consume, on the level of savings, so that when the adjustment process is complete, savings equal investment at the equilibrium

Rather, it is the interest rate which, together with the marginal efficiency of capital, determines the level of investment, as shown in Part B of Figure 18–4. The schedule of the marginal efficiency of capital is the schedule relating the demand for new capital goods to the expected rate of return. For simplicity, the curve has been assumed to be linear (although it is not possible, a priori, to know what its shape is). Its slope is necessarily negative because the net income stream which can be expected from additional units of a given capital good is certain to fall and its supply price is likely to increase. As long as the expected return from investment is higher than the rate of interest, it will be profitable to invest. Thus, when the interest rate is at i_2 and the investment demand curve is as given in Part B of Figure 18–B, the volume of investment will be OI_1.

It is evident that in the Keynesian analysis, money is far from being the passive medium of exchange and unit of account that classical and neoclassical thinkers assumed it to be. It is, rather, an active determinant of the level of income, output, and employment because its relationship to the marginal efficiency of capital determines the worthwhileness of investment. Given the schedule of the marginal efficiency of capital, it is the rate of interest which determines the volume of real investment. Given the quantity of money as decided by the monetary authority, and given the level of output, wealth owners determine whether they will profit most from holding money or from holding other types of assets. The relative advantage of each alternative will be equal at the margin because wealth holders will shift from one alternative to another whenever one appears to offer a superior opportunity for gain. Thus the state of expectations, the preference for liquidity, the rate of interest, and the prospective yield on capital assets are all interrelated.[23]

IMPEDIMENTS TO FULL-EMPLOYMENT EQUILIBRIUM

The Liquidity Trap

The primary objective of the Keynesian system is to demonstrate that a full-employment equilibrium is only one possibility among many and that there are numerous obstacles to its achievement. The level of output, employment, and income is determined by the intersection of the aggregate demand function with the supply function; and even with flexible wages and

---

income level. Since the equality of savings and investment is an ex post phenomenon, many people prefer to define savings and investment in terms which recognize specifically ex ante (i.e., planned as opposed to realized) inequalities between them. The lengthy and not particularly fruitful controversy which developed concerning the relative merits of various savings-investment formulations is admirably reviewed by Lutz, *op. cit.*

[23] These interrelationships are examined by Keynes much more precisely in the article on "The General Theory," *Quarterly Journal of Economics,* Vol. LI (Feb. 1937), than in *The General Theory* itself.

commodity prices, the intersection may result in an unemployment equilibrium. While full employment is not precluded from the Keynesian model, the liquidity trap which may develop during a depression, when the lack of profitable investment opportunities is already a problem, presents an added deterrent to its achievement.

A liquidity trap consists of an accumulation of idle balances at very low rates of interest. It may develop during a period of depression as a result of a decrease in the transactions and precautionary demands for money. Some portion of the monetary stock generally used for satisfying these requirements is no longer needed when wages, prices, and incomes move to a lower level. If these amounts were shifted to the purchase of securities, the circular flow would be maintained. But if security prices rise to a level at which yields are so low that further monetary investment is unattractive, the speculative demand for cash balances will have become interest-elastic. Efforts of the monetary authority to reduce interest rates by increasing the money supply will then be ineffective. The central bank is generally capable of exerting pressure on interest rates because under most circumstances it is possible to buy or sell bonds, thereby inducing the public to hold either more or less cash by bidding their prices (and therefore interest rates) up or down. There is, however, a floor below which the interest rate is not likely to fall even when the monetary authority is seeking a policy of extreme monetary ease. Liquidity preference may become "virtually absolute in the sense that almost everybody prefers cash to holding a debt which yields so low a rate of interest" that the earnings from illiquidity do not offset the risk of loss on capital account.[24] It is evident from Part A of Figure 18–4 that an enlarged money supply could not reduce the rate of interest below i_1. The additional stock would be absorbed into hoards. This "liquidity trap" presents the main impediment to the effective use of monetary policy as an antidepression device.

The Ineffectiveness of Wage Reductions

The neoclassical argument that full employment can be automatic was largely premised on the assumption of flexible money wages and prices, which would make possible the real wage adjustments needed to achieve full employment. Keynes, however, maintained that workers will refuse money wage rate reductions even though they will not refuse reductions in real wages, and that even if labor as a whole is willing to accept money wage reductions, prices will be reduced all around by an equal amount because short-run marginal costs are largely wage costs. Real wages will therefore not fall, and there will be no incentive to increase employment. In short, there is no automatic mechanism which will insure a full-employment equilibrium.

---

[24] *The General Theory*, p. 207.

The only circumstances under which Keynes agreed that falling money wages and prices might have favorable effects on employment would be if they exerted a monetary influence which revised interest rates downward. He thought the probable mechanism of this favorable effect would be that the transactions demand for money would fall along with money wages and prices. If the total money stock is unchanged, the smaller cash requirement for transactions needs will free cash balances for the purchase of securities. This will raise security prices and reduce interest rates. Given the schedule of the marginal efficiency of capital, additional investments will then be profitable, so that the level of aggregate demand may increase until full employment is reached. However, while this is a theoretical possibility, Keynes hardly regarded it as a likely occurrence because in a severe depression the interest rate may fall to the level of the liquidity trap before investment has risen sufficiently to restore full employment.

Another possible avenue to full employment via a flexible wage policy was suggested by Arthur C. Pigou and has been dubbed the real balance effect or "Pigou effect."[25] Pigou reasoned that the price reductions associated with wage rate reductions would increase the real value of the cash balances of individuals. This, he thought, might increase the volume of real spending, i.e., shift the consumption function upward. If, in fact, an increasing (real) value of wealth stimulates consumption, then conceivably there is always some reduction in wages and prices which will be sufficient to increase consumption sufficiently to eliminate any deficiency in aggregate demand.

It is generally conceded that the Pigou effect would be realized were it not for the several institutional and dynamic factors which militate against it. First, neither wages nor prices are, in fact, sufficiently flexible in a downward direction. Nor is there any a priori reason to assume that an increase in real balances will be associated with an increased propensity to consume. This would be the case only if the propensity for the accumulation of wealth can be assumed as constant.[26] But if peoples' taste for wealth increases over time, or if the distribution of wealth is altered in favor of those whose propensity to accumulate is greater, the wealth effect argument is unconvincing. Keynes himself, though he appears not to have recognized the relationship between the wealth position of consumers and consumption expenditures, seemed to think that wage reductions would in all probability shift the consumption function downward because wage reductions have the effect of shifting income from workers to the rentier class, which has a lower propensity to consume.

---

[25] Arthur C. Pigou, *Employment and Equilibrium* (London: Macmillan and Co., Ltd., 1941), pp. 96–130.

[26] George Katona has suggested that the "taste for wealth cannot be assumed to be constant." See *Psychological Aspects of Economic Behavior* (New York: McGraw-Hill Book Co., Inc., 1951), pp. 91–93.

Secular Stagnation

Even if the interest rate has some degree of downward flexibility, Keynes thought that the level of the investment demand curve is too low to stimulate investment adequately during a depression. He observed that: "Today and presumably for the future the schedule of the marginal efficiency of capital is, for a variety of reasons, much lower than it was in the 19th century."[27] He suggested that population growth, invention, wars, and territorial expansion, which once served to stimulate the opportunities for profitable investment, are now less reliable sources of new capital demand. But he did not develop this argument with any degree of thoroughness. Indeed, there are only very general references to it in *The General Theory,* and the secular stagnation thesis is more specifically associated with Alvin Hansen than with Keynes.[28]

Yet the idea that the potency of the long-run factors influencing investment demand was becoming weakened is evident in Keynes's treatment of the problem of income and employment. It was largely because of his skepticism concerning the long-run adequacy of investment demand that the concern of *The General Theory* is the level of income and employment instead of an examination of cyclical fluctuations in these magnitudes. By way of contrast, traditional business cycle theories assumed that the normal equilibrium of the economy is full employment and that the business cycle is an oscillation around a full-employment norm. *The General Theory* implies that there is no such norm and that the economy can equilibrate at various possible levels of employment. The rejection of the full-employment norm is partly a rejection of the idea that wage rate and interest rate flexibility can correct lapses from full employment and partly a rejection of the idea that the investment demand schedule is sufficiently high to insure adequate aggregate demand as a normal condition.

There is, of course, a great deal in Keynesian theory which business cycle theorists anticipated. Beginning with Wicksell, many theorists focused attention on the relationship between the savings-investment process and the equilibrium of the economic system. Though they were concerned primarily with the impact of disturbing forces on the price level rather than on fluctuations in output and employment, the key factors in these analyses, as in Keynes's, were those affecting savings, investment, hoarding, and the money supply. A number of these theorists even advocated positive action by the monetary authority as opposed to reliance on the self-corrective power of the system as the proper means of dealing with these disturbances. But all of these theories conceived of the business cycle as a disturbance to a full-employment equilibrium. What they concentrated on, therefore, was

---

[27] *The General Theory,* pp. 307–8.

[28] Alvin Hansen, "Economic Progress and Declining Population Growth," *American Economic Review.* Vol. XXIX, No. 1 (March, 1939).

explaining the business cycle as the product of forces capable of generating a cumulative expansion (or contraction) which eventually is, for one reason or another, brought to a halt. But they did not attempt to explain what determines the level of income, output, and employment, nor did they have the conception of an underemployment equilibrium. This is precisely what the Keynesian theory provided. *The General Theory* is, of course, not a contribution to business cycle theory. But it did stimulate the development of a model which, by demonstrating the interaction between the multiplier and the acceleration effect, made it possible to understand the turning points of the cycle without the need to rely on outside limiting factors.[29]

SOME REFINEMENTS OF KEYNESIAN ECONOMICS

The preceding section has presented the concepts and propositions presented by Keynes himself. That body of theory has, however, been considerably embellished since the publication of *The General Theory*. For example, Alvin Hansen and John R. Hicks have advanced an eclectic theory of interest, which integrates the liquidity preference theory with the older loanable funds theory.[30] While this theory is important, it is a conceptually simple refinement of the Keynesian system. But there have been other developments which have reached out to new horizons beyond Keynes's essentially static, short-run theory of income determination. Theories concerning the behavior of the consumption function in the long run are an important example of this sort of development. So, too, is Samuelson's construction of a model demonstrating the interaction of the multiplier and the accelerator. And finally, there are the growth theories which are the most recent addition of Keynesian inspiration. These have made a prodigious appearance during the last fifteen years, and already there is a vast body of literature devoted to this latest and perhaps most significant aspect of modern macroeconomics.

Growth theories go considerably beyond the Keynesian theory of employment and income. They ask not what determines the current level of income and employment, but rather at what rate income, output, and employment must grow in order to insure that the growing stock of labor and capital will continue to be employed. Keynesian theory, being a short-run theory, assumed a constant capital stock and therefore concentrated only on the income-creating effects of investment (and consumption). But the investment process not only creates income; it also enlarges

---

[29] See Chap. 19 below for a discussion of the interaction of the multiplier and the accelerator.

[30] Alvin Hansen, *Monetary Theory and Fiscal Policy* (New York: McGraw-Hill Book Co., Inc., 1949), chap. v; John R. Hicks, "Mr. Keynes and the Classics," *Econometrica,* Vol. V (April, 1937), pp. 147–59.

the stock capital. The question of the growth rate required to insure full-capacity use of a growing capital stock, therefore, poses a new—and until recently, neglected—problem in economic theory. Growth theory is thus more than a refinement or addition to the original theory. It changes the parameters of the Keynesian model and will therefore be treated in the following chapter.

The Hicks-Hansen Explanation of Interest Rates

Keynes maintained that neoclassical theory did not provide a determinate solution of the interest rate because the savings supply schedule, which, together with the investment demand schedule, is supposed to determine the rate, is itself dependent on the income level. Yet the income level is not known until the volume of investment is known, and the latter itself depends on the interest rate. In other words, the interest rate is indeterminate because the savings schedule and the investment demand schedule are interdependent.

It has been argued that the Keynesian criticism of indeterminacy is equally applicable to his own theory. The liquidity preference theory, according to which interest is determined by the intersection of the liquidity preference schedule and the supply schedule of money, also does not yield a determinate rate of interest because there is a different liquidity preference schedule for every level of income. Even though the schedule of liquidity preference for speculative purposes is independent of the level of income, it is necessary to know the income level in order to know what the transactions and precautionary demands for money will be. With a given money stock, the amount of money which will be available to be held as a speculative asset will then be known. Thus the Keynesian theory of interest rate determination, like the neoclassical theory, does not yield a determinate solution.

It has, however, been demonstrated that the Keynesian theory and the neoclassical theory can together provide a determinate solution because they include all of the variables of the interest rate problem.[31] These variables are (1) the savings function, (2) the investment demand function, (3) the liquidity preference function, and (4) the quantity of money. They have been combined to construct two new curves, the *IS* curve and *LM* curve.

The *IS* curve is derived from the relationship between the investment demand schedule and a family of savings functions. Each of these conceives of saving as a function of both income and the interest rate. Figure 18–5 shows a different savings schedule for every possible combination of interest rate and income level. Thus, when income is Y_1, the savings schedule is S_1Y_1, and, given the investment demand curve, savings will equal invest-

---

[31] See Hansen, *A Guide to Keynes,* chap. vii.

FIGURE 18–5

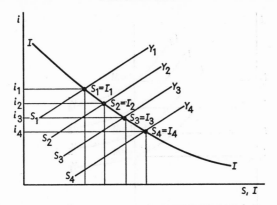

ment at interest rate i_1. Similarly, when income is Y_2, the savings schedule will be S_2Y_2, and savings will equal investment at i_2. The locus of all the points at which savings and investment are equal provides what Hansen and Hicks have called the *IS* schedule, as shown in Figure 18–6. The *IS* function expresses interest as a function of three variables: savings, investment, and the income level. It is the *IS* function which, together with a curve which has become known as the *LM* function, determines the rate of interest.

FIGURE 18–6

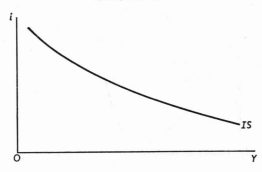

The *LM* curve is derived from the relationship between a family of liquidity preference curves and the schedule of the money supply. There is a different liquidity preference schedule at every income level; hence the family of curves L_1Y_1, L_2Y_2, L_3Y_3, L_4Y_4, as shown in Figure 18–7. These curves, together with the money supply, *M*, made available by the monetary authority, show the various combinations of income levels and interest rates which are consistent with the willingness of the public to hold the fixed supply. Thus, if the income level is Y_1, the demand for money will be equal to the supply at interest rate i_1. But the same money supply will be

FIGURE 18–7

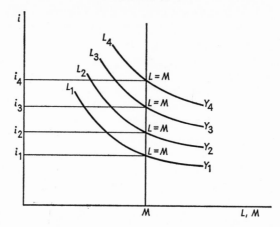

held at a higher rate of interest if the income level is higher. Thus, it is impossible to determine what the interest rate will be solely from the relationship between the family of liquidity preference curves and the schedule of the money supply. It is possible to establish that at each level of income the given quantity of money will be held at a different rate of interest. That is, there is a different rate of interest which is compatible at every income level with the condition $L = M$. Thus, in Figure 18–7, $L = M$ at an interest rate of i_1 when income is Y_1; $L = M$ at an interest

FIGURE 18–8

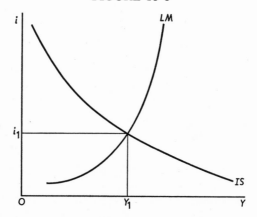

rate of i_2 when income is Y_2; and so forth. Together with the money supply, these combinations provide the data for the LM curve in Figure 18–8. The upward slope and increasing inelasticity of this curve shows that a greater preference for liquidity will, with a given quantity of money, manifest itself in a higher interest rate rather than a greater volume of hoards.

It should also be observed that higher income levels will be associated with higher interest rates because at higher income levels the transactions and precautionary demands for money increase, so that there is less left out of a given money stock to satisfy the speculative motive. This puts an upward pressure on the interest rate and accounts for the increasing inelasticity of the *LM* curve.

Figure 18–8 also shows the *IS* curve from Figure 18–6 which relates interest rates, income levels, and various possible savings and investment equilibria. Since two of these variables are also required for the construction of the *LM* curve, the two curves can be shown on the same graph. The interest rate may then be conceived of as being determined by the intersection of the *LM* and *IS* curves, which bring together the supply of savings, the demand for investment funds, the demand for cash, and the supply of money as the four variables of the problem. The intersection point of the two curves represents a stable monetary equilibrium if realized savings and investment are equal to planned savings and investment, and if the amount of money people wish to hold is equal to the actual money stock.

Even though Keynes incorrectly maintained that the determination of the interest rate is a strictly monetary phenomenon, with the schedule of liquidity preference and the quantity of money being the two determinants, he did appreciate the possibility of constructing the *IS* curve on the basis of the neoclassical formulation.[32] He even said specifically that the level of income and the interest rate must be "uniquely correlated." He thus led the way to the recognition that, given the consumption (savings) schedule, the investment demand schedule, the liquidity preference schedule, and the quantity of money, both the interest rate and the level of income are mutually determined, even though it was left for later writers to give these interrelationships specific formulation.

The Long-Run Consumption Function

Although Keynes pointed out the influence of many variables other than income which affect consumption, he maintained that consumption is a "fairly stable function" of income. But the question as to whether the relationship between consumption and income is one of proportionality or one in which the proportion of consumption to income can be expected to decline as income rises became a much-debated issue after his work was published.

While Keynes thought it a reasonable proposition that consumption will, as a general rule, increase less than in proportion to an increase in income, Hicks, in *A Contribution to the Theory of the Trade Cycle,* asserted that "there is no convincing theoretical reason why the proportion in which income is divided between consumption and saving should change

---

[32] *The General Theory,* pp. 178–81.

in one way or the other with a change in income."[33] Present empirical data support Keynes's position for the short run, for they show that cyclical variations in consumption expenditures are proportionately smaller than variations in real income. However, this evidence does not necessarily mean that the long-run relationship between consumption and income may not be a proportional one. If this is the case, the marginal propensity to consume is constant over every range of income; but if consumption increases proportionately less than income, the consumption function flattens out. If this is the case, consumption expenditures would become increasingly less reliable sources of aggregate demand and would therefore throw a relatively greater burden on investment outlets.

A number of people, among them Arthur Smithies and James Duesenberry, have advanced the hypothesis that the true long-run relationship between consumption and income is a proportional one. The data published by Simon Kuznets, showing that decade by decade, from 1869 to 1958, there has been a long-run constant ratio between consumption and income of about 88 percent, appear to lend some empirical support to the proportionality hypothesis.[34] It should, however, be recognized that while a consumption function shows what consumption would be if income were at a particular level, the Kuznets data, which are in the form of aggregate amounts over a decade, show what percentage of the national income actually was spent on capital formation. However, Smithies feels that the Kuznets data support his hypothesis that there has been an upward secular drift of the consumption function and that the long-run relationship between consumption and income is a proportional one.

Smithies has suggested several reasons why such an upward secular shift of the consumption function, that is, an increase in consumption relative to income and essentially independent of its growth, has taken place in the United States. One is that population has become increasingly urbanized. Since a rural population typically saves more and spends less than an urban one, the shift of population to cities is probably a factor which has contributed to the upward drift of the consumption function. The constant stream of new consumer goods which have become available, along with the emergence of various financial institutions catering to satisfying demands for consumer credit, is probably another factor. The change in the age composition of the population is still another factor which has probably served to increase consumption expenditures independently of the income level. The retired population has also increased, so that a larger percentage of people are consumers without being current income earners.

Smithies tested his hypothesis that there has been an upward shift in

---

[33] John R. Hicks, *A Contribution to the Theory of the Trade Cycle* (London: Oxford University Press, 1950), p. 36.

[34] S. Kuznets, *National Product Since 1869* (New York: National Bureau of Economic Research, Inc., 1946).

the consumption function by taking annual data, corrected for changes in price and population, for the period 1923–40 and fitting them to an equation which assumes that an annual increase of $1.15 in per capita consumption takes place independently of any change in disposable income. By using his equation and the income levels Kuznets estimated for earlier periods, he obtained hypothetical values for consumption expenditures which were not far off from the Kuznets estimates.[35]

Smithies' efforts to explain the inherent or true long-run relationship between consumption and income does not exhaust the recent work in this area. There have been numerous additions to the literature since his study was published, though the final word has probably not yet been said with respect to the nature of the long-run consumption function.[36] It should be recognized, however, that even if consumption does increase proportionately with long-run increases in income, the *absolute* amount of savings will increase, even though the *ratio* of savings to income is constant. This implies that in order to maintain full employment, a growing economy will have to generate a sufficient volume of investment outlets to absorb the increasing volume of savings forthcoming at higher levels of income. This is entirely in accord with Keynes's own conclusion concerning the constant and increasing burden to find investment outlets. At present, we are of course increasingly concerned with the relevance of this fact to the prospects for long-term growth. If, in the next few decades, consumer demand can be expected to expand in the same proportion as our productive powers, and therefore real income, the other components of aggregate demand (private investment, government, and net foreign demands) also need only to increase in the same proportion. Since the hypotheses which have been advanced concerning the probable nature of the long-run consumption function suggest that this can reasonably be expected, the threat of stagnation implicit in *The General Theory* appears to have been softened. The importance of this conclusion in terms of policy leaves no doubt concerning the significance of the concept of the long-run consumption function and its behavior.

CONCLUDING REMARKS AND COMMENTS

In 1935, John Maynard Keynes wrote to George Bernard Shaw that the book he was writing on economic theory would revolutionize the way the world thinks about economic problems. His prophecy has been amply

---

[35] Arthur Smithies, "Forecasting Postwar Demand," *Econometrica,* Vol. XIII (January, 1945).

[36] See, in particular, James Duesenberry, *Income, Saving and the Theory of Consumer Behavior* (Cambridge: Harvard University Press, 1949); and Milton Friedman, *A Theory of the Consumption Function* (Princeton: Princeton University Press, 1957).

fulfilled, for *The General Theory* has changed our conception of the essential nature of the economic problem. From the time of the classics the economic problem had been thought of in terms of the unending struggle between scarcity and unlimited human wants. In the era of Malthus and Ricardo, this struggle was given expression in the controversy over the Corn Laws. When John Stuart Mill wrote, the Corn Laws were no longer at issue, but his vision of the stationary state was nevertheless premised on the solution of the scarcity problem via the intercession of human wisdom, especially as it relates to population growth. Marshall and the marginalists changed the focus of the problem to the level of the individual economic entity, e.g., the consumer, the employer, and the industry; but they did not change the conception of the problem as being inherently one of scarcity. Their concern was with the allocation of resources among alternative uses, and they therefore continued the classical conception of the economic problem as having its origin in the scarcity of resources.

The awareness that the economic problem had another aspect, namely, "poverty in the midst of plenty," came to Keynes after World War I. But the general view that the economic problem is one of scarcity persisted into the depression. Only prolonged unemployment on a mass scale eventually made it apparent that scarcity is not the only dimension of the economic problem. The rational allocation of resources is the sole problem only when all resources seeking employment can be absorbed into the production process. Keynes argued that the level of employment depends on the level of aggregate demand and showed that even an economy with flexible wages, prices, and interest rates may not be restored automatically to full employment. A full-employment equilibrium is only one of many possible equilibria and the classical and neoclassical analysis is therefore a special rather than the general case.

Keynes's emphasis on the inability of the system to make automatic adjustments because of imbalances between consumption and production reminds us immediately of the Marxian analysis. Marx, too, emphasized the inherent instability of the capitalistic system and, like Keynes, found investment to be the crucial factor. Marx attributed the declining rate of profit to the inability of capitalists to realize surplus value from investment. This, in turn, meant that the ability to accumulate capital inhibited investment and therefore delayed revival. Keynes, on the other hand, saw the problem as being rooted not in impediments to accumulation, but in impediments to investment, which caused an insufficiency of aggregate demand.

But while both Marx and Keynes stressed factors affecting investment as the cause of breakdown, there are important differences between the two systems. One of these is that Marx's system is inseparable from his conception of the social relationships underlying commodity exchange and, consequently, the labor theory of value. The increasing exploitation of labor, coupled with the decreasing rate of profit and of surplus value, leads to increasingly severe breakdowns, which are the prelude to the destruction of the capitalistic system. For Keynes, the main factors causing breakdowns are derived from basic human propensities. He thus saw a basis for government intervention when aggregate demand is inadequate to create full employment. But he regarded the destruction of capitalism as being neither desirable nor inevitable. On the contrary, he felt that the essentials of the capitalistic system could be preserved without sacrificing full employment if government exercises the proper controls. Precisely what the nature of this intervention should be was not given detailed examination by Keynes. But the social philosophy which underlies the concluding chapter of *The General Theory* is that there are certain areas which should not be left to individual initiative. Keynes suggests that:

The state will have to exercise a guiding influence on the propensity to consume, partly through its scheme of taxation, partly by fixing the rate of interest and partly, perhaps, in other ways. Furthermore, it seems unlikely that the influence of banking policy on the rate of interest will be sufficient by itself to determine the optimum rate of investment. . . . [But it] is not the ownership of the instruments of production which it is important for the state to assume. If the state is able to determine the aggregate amount of resources devoted to augmenting the instruments and the basic rate of reward to those who own them, it will have accomplished all that is necessary.[37]

Thus, what Keynes proposed is essentially a mixed economy in which investment is socialized but in which private self-interest will continue to function in all areas in which it is compatible with full employment. He regarded this as "the only practicable means of avoiding the destruction of existing economic forms in their entirety and as the condition of the successful functioning of individual initiative."

It is apparent that to Keynes himself, the theory of aggregate effective demand was presented as an anchor for his policy recommendations to England during the thirties. There is no question that *The General Theory* contributed in a significant way to the acceptance by government of the responsibility for maintaining the level of employment at satisfactory levels. Fiscal policy has come into its own since the time of *The General Theory*.[38] There is also no doubt that the popularity of *The General Theory* in the prewar period derived in no small measure from the fact that it took a positive approach to the problems of its day. This is not to say, however, that *The General Theory* cannot be divorced from the specific problems of

---

[37] *The General Theory,* p. 378.

[38] What does, however, seem strange is that *The General Theory* has so frequently been interpreted as being a polemic against monetary policy. To anyone familiar with Keynes as a monetary theorist, the importance of monetary policy is implicit in *The General Theory.*

the 1930's. The principle of aggregate effective demand, which is the core of the Keynesian theory, is independent of this particular institutional setting and is neutral as far as policy is concerned. So are the concepts of the consumption function, the liquidity preference function, and the marginal efficiency of capital. These concepts have become the essential tools with which the determination of income and employment is to be analyzed. *The General Theory* is a contribution to economic analysis precisely because its concepts and analytical apparatus have a validity which transcends the stagnationist outlook which nurtured it. The fact that the economic experiences of the postwar era have not borne out the stagnationist forebodings of *The General Theory* indicates not that Keynes's theory is "wrong," but that the assumptions he made about the future position of the consumption and investment functions were wrong. Continuous study is needed in order to know what values to attach to the variables in the aggregate model Keynes created.

One of the remarkable aspects of Keynes's work is that it has stimulated work in other related areas. Econometricians are constructing and testing aggregate models, and a whole new field for statistical research has been opened up which is devoted to the collection and analysis of national income and product data. Apart from their obvious use in measuring the performance of the economic system, these data appear to be offering an increasingly acceptable basis for making value judgments about its functioning. Indeed, we may speculate whether the greatest long-term effect of Keynes's work may not prove to be the attitudinal changes which appear to be associated with a system of national income accounting. The fact that economic decisions are increasingly being made in terms of their impact on gross national product and employment, rather than in terms of private profits and losses, suggests that such changes are in the making. Of course, our value standards in the economic sphere have long since moved away from those associated with a system of unrestricted free enterprise. But the development of the concept of gross national product and its related aggregates, and the collection of data to give these concepts quantitative expression, has provided an objective criterion for judging the effectiveness of productive activity for the economy as a whole. Before the development of national income accounting, the effectiveness of productive activity was measureable only in terms of private profits and losses. Now that rational accounting measures have been applied to the economy as a whole, one may at least wonder whether the use of a system of national income accounts may not produce attitudinal changes which will eventually alter the functioning of the economic system itself to conform with changing value standards. If this proves to be the case, it would be a more far-reaching long-run effect of Keynesian theory than any we have yet observed, because it would almost certainly alter in some way the institutional framework within which economic forces work themselves out.

SUGGESTIONS FOR FURTHER READING

DILLARD, DUDLEY. *The Economics of John Maynard Keynes*. New York: Prentice-Hall, Inc., 1948.

HANSEN, ALVIN. *A Guide to Keynes*. New York: McGraw-Hill Book Co., Inc., 1953.

KAHN, RICHARD F. "The Relation of Home Investment to Unemployment," *Economic Journal,* Vol. XLI (June, 1931).

KEYNES, JOHN MAYNARD. *The General Theory of Employment, Interest and Money*. New York: Harcourt, Brace & Co., 1936. NOTE: Chapters iv, vi, xiv, xvi, and xxii–xxiii do not advance the main theme of the book.

KLEIN, LAWRENCE R. *The Keynesian Revolution*. New York: Macmillan Co., Paperback edition, 1961.

LEKACHMAN, ROBERT (ed.). *Keynes' General Theory: Reports of Three Decades*. New York: St. Martin's Press; London: Macmillan & Co., 1964.

McCRACKEN, H. L. *Keynesian Economics in the Stream of Economic Thought*. Baton Rouge: Louisiana State University Press, 1961.

Chapter 19

CONTEMPORARY CONTRIBUTIONS TO THE THEORY OF ECONOMIC GROWTH AND FLUCTUATION

INTRODUCTION

The Place of Cycle and Growth Theory in Economic Analysis

Theoretical and empirical interest in aggregate economics has continued unabated since the publication of *The General Theory*. The main effort on a theoretical level during the last two decades has been directed at making the Keynesian theory dynamic so that it will explain not merely the determination of income and output at any given time but also their behavior over time. Since the end of World War II, there has been a special interest in the problem of secular growth, that is, in the ability of an economy to generate sustained increases in the level of per capita income. Starting with the elementary proposition that the economy's output and income at any moment of time are determined by the supply of resources, the state of the arts, the institutional setting, and the psychological propensities which govern consumption and investment, the behavior of output over time can be explained in terms of hypotheses constructed on several different levels.[1] The simplest assumes that only one of the determinants of output is an endogenous variable subject to secular variation and that the others are either exogenous or endogenous constants which may be treated as parameters in a growth model. A more complex hypothesis would examine the effect on output of two or more variables which are assumed to have a particular secular pattern of behavior. In principle, all of the determinants could be assumed subject to secular variations of a sort which will affect the long-term trend of output. Still more complex is a model which not only treats all of the determinants of output as variables, but explains rather than assumes the behavior of each.

The construction of a growth model on this level would necessarily

---

[1] The article on "Economics of Growth," by Moses Abramovitz, examining the various levels on which the phenomenon of growth may be studied and suggesting the reasons why growth theory is still an underdeveloped area in economics, continues to be most useful in placing the problem in perspective. See Bernard F. Haley (ed.), *A Survey of Contemporary Economics*, Vol. II (1952), pp. 132–82.

draw upon disciplines other than economics. This is the case whenever the behavior of a variable cannot be explained, at least to a significant degree, in pecuniary terms. Secular changes in population and the labor force, and changes in the state of the arts and in social and political institutions, are among the more obvious factors which affect output in the long run whose behavior cannot be explained wholly or even largely in terms of economic principles. Present-day economists, as will be seen, have therefore dealt with these variables by excluding them from their analyses. That is, they have reduced the growth problem to more manageable proportions by assuming that factors such as population growth and the state of the arts are exogenously determined data which lie outside the mechanism of the model.

There is a striking difference between recent contributions to the subject of growth and those of the classical school. In the classical model, growth was seen as depending on the response of the population, and therefore the labor force, to a market rate of wages which depended on the size of the labor force and the willingness of capitalists to provide the wage fund and other forms of capital. The inducement to accumulate capital was, in turn, thought to depend on profit. That is, capital accumulation was thought to require a total product which is large enough so that there is a residual for profit after the rent of the landlords and the wage requirements of the laboring population are met. Accumulation would, they thought, increase production in addition to stimulating population growth and therefore would be conducive to further progress. Growth would cease when the tendency toward diminishing returns raises the cost of labor's subsistence to a level which leaves an insufficient margin for profits after wages and rent to stimulate further accumulation. The stationary state will then have become a reality.

After John Stuart Mill, there was little interest in the growth problem. Except for Marx's inquiry into the "law of motion" of the capitalistic system, discussions of the growth problem were conspicuous by their absence after 1850. It was simply taken for granted during the nineteenth century that though there would be frictions, the growth process would continue. Economic theory therefore became largely concerned with other questions, the most important of which was the problem of value and distribution. Neoclassical theorists were not concerned with reconstructing the classical growth model, even though they had discarded most of the notions on which that model was predicated. Nor were they particularly concerned with explaining economic fluctuations. In fact, until the Great Depression, orthodox thinkers regarded the business cycle as a phenomenon which temporarily interfered with the orderly functioning of a self-equilibrating economic system. Business cycle theory, therefore, existed only on the very periphery of economic theory, and no one speculated about the relationship between fluctuation and economic growth.

The first really fresh approach to the problem of economic growth was that of Joseph A. Schumpeter, who was, prior to the recent past, virtually alone in his concern with this problem. He devoted a great part of his life to the development of the hypothesis that economic development and fluctuation are related phenomena in dynamic economies.[2] According to Schumpeter, economic growth has its origin in innovational changes which are spearheaded by the unique few, who, by virtue of their vision and daring, assume a position of economic leadership. Such changes alter not merely the technical aspects of production but, because of their inconsistency with existing economic relationships, induce reorganizations in the sociological superstructure. The process of innovation interrupts the circular flow because it is facilitated by bank credit, which enables innovators to bid resources away from other sectors of the economy. As long as the banking system is able to provide credit, the system expands on a wave of innovation to a new level of prosperity because the profits of successful innovators are great and attract imitators. But the imitators are less able than the original innovators, and they arrive at a less propitious time. Their miscalculations, coupled with tightened credit, tend to force marginal firms into bankruptcy. These failures are the harbingers of depression, for they reflect the necessity of correcting the errors which have been made in the process of expansion. Error correction is the painful process of weeding out inefficiencies. This process is, to Schumpeter, the essence of depression. But the process is, for all its destructiveness, also creative, for the gains of innovation are truly assimilated by the economy only in a depression. Morover, the struggle for survival which typifies depression also stimulates and encourages the next surge of innovation which will propel the economy to its next level of economic achievement. Thus, Schumpeter views the process of capitalist development as being inherently unstable, because it is always accompanied by the turbulence of cyclical expansion and contraction.

There is still another aspect of Schumpeter's theory of capitalist development which must be noted. This is his view that the process of capitalist development will not continue indefinitely.[3] The lifeblood of capitalist development is entrepreneurship. As long as the rugged individualism of early capitalism predominated, the system maintained its vitality. But with the growth of the corporation to a position of dominance, the control of industry has passed into the hands of hired managers. As a result, the position of the bourgeoisie has degenerated to that of a stockholder, so that instead of leading the capitalist process, it merely participates indirectly. Thus, Schumpeter, like Marx, believed that capitalism will eventually destroy itself, but for fundamentally different reasons. He

---

[2] Joseph A. Schumpeter, *The Theory of Economic Development,* translated by Redvers Opie (Cambridge, Mass.: Harvard University Press, 1934).

[3] Joseph A. Schumpeter, *Capitalism, Socialism and Democracy* (New York: Harper & Bros., 1942).

thought capitalism was destined to lose its vitality not as a result of the increasing misery of an exploited proletariat, but rather because the bourgeoisie loses control of the enterpreneurial process. The productive system becomes not less efficient as capitalist development advances, but rather more so; but in spite of its technical superiority, the system will cease to command popular support because so few persons have the opportunity for individual action in a bureaucratic society. Capitalism, Schumpeter believed, would tend to become sociologically untenable. This is one reason why he rejected so violently Keynes's political economy with its prescriptions for reforming the capitalistic system. Quite apart from his belief that prescription has no place in scientific economics, Schumpeter was of the opinion that the measures proposed by Keynes would, if anything, hasten the process of capitalism's decline because most of them were inherently anticapitalistic in nature. Nor could he accept the idea that oversaving and underinvestment could become chronic and therefore result in secular stagnation in the Keynes-Hansen sense of the term. Capitalist evolution does indeed tend to "peter out" or stagnate; but this, in Schumpeter's view, is "because the modern state may crush or paralyze its motive forces."

Contemporary theories of economic growth are quite different from those of Schumpeter. Schumpeter conceived of economic development as an evolutionary process which unfolds in historic time. Contemporary growth theory, at least as it applies to industrially advanced economies, is much narrower in scope than Schumpeter's theory, in that it abstracts from changes in the sociopolitical milieu. It also conceives of time in a different sense than did Schumpeter. It is concerned with the relationship between functionally related macroeconomic variables at different points of theoretic time. Much of this theorizing is Keynesian in inspiration. While Keynes's examination of the behavior of the macroeconomic variables that determine income and employment was static and short run, he implicitly recognized the eventual need to also examine the long-run changes in these magnitudes and their effect on income and employment. It is necessary to go beyond the income-creating role of investment in order to inquire at what rate income and investment must grow to bring about the full employment of the incremental addition to the economy's productive capacity. Keynes was concerned only with the income-creating aspect of investment and excluded the effect which capital enlargement has on productive capacity. This approach was a reflection of the institutional setting which nurtured his theory. During the depression the employment of existing resources was the primary concern, and it is therefore at least understandable that the problems created by new additions to the capital stock were overlooked. A moment of reflection will, however, reveal that if additions to the stock of capital simply accumulate as excess capacity, the rate of investment will most assuredly be reduced, and so, therefore, will the equilibrium level of income. It is thus plain that if the equilibrium level of income does not increase sufficiently to absorb the additions to the capital stock resulting from new investment, it will decrease, and the level of employment with it. In the long run, employment is a function of the rate of growth of both investment and income. This, in turn, raises the further question as to whether growth in this limited sense of the term is self-perpetuating once a satisfactory rate is attained. Are divergences from the required growth rate self-correcting? Are these corrective forces related to the instability which appears to be characteristic of the capitalistic system?

These questions demonstrate that the theory of economic fluctuations—or, as it once was called, business cycle theory—is inextricably related to growth theory. Though business cycle theory has never occupied a prominent place in the history of economic analysis, contemporary interest in the problem of economic growth has put the problem of economic fluctuation into a new perspective. Much of this contemporary interest reflects its Keynesian inspiration. This is particularly true of the contributions which were made during the 1940's and early 1950's. More recently, however, there have also appeared a host of contributions which are more neoclassical than Keynesian in nature. The section which follows will serve to identify some leading contributors to the neo-Keynesian and neoclassical contemporary theories of growth and fluctuation.

Contributors to Contemporary Theories of Growth and Fluctuation

A list of those who have contributed to the staggering volume of literature generated by contemporary interest in the theory of economic growth and fluctuation would be very long. There are, however, perhaps a half dozen persons who have truly broken new ground. Of these, two made noteworthy contributions prior to the publication of Keynes's *General Theory,* namely, the late Joseph A. Schumpeter (1883–1950) and Jan Tinbergen (1903–   ).

Schumpeter's work in the field of business cycles and economic development spans more than two decades. As has already been noted, his theory of innovation provided the central theme around which all his thinking in the area of growth and fluctuation revolved. The hypothesis that innovation is the prime mover of the economy was first presented in *The Theory of Economic Development,* which was translated from the German in 1934. It was further elaborated in *Business Cycles,* published in 1939, and *Capitalism, Socialism and Democracy,* which first appeared in 1942. In addition to his substantial contribution to business cycle literature, he also wrote numerous essays which have been included in *Essays of Joseph Schumpeter* (1951) and *Ten Great Economists* (1951). At the time of his death, his unpublished works included a treatise on money and his magnum opus, *History of Economic Analysis,* which was published posthumously in 1954. The quality and magnitude of his work have earned Schumpeter a major place among those who have made substantive contributions to economics. Indeed, there are some who would rank him as the greatest economist of his time, in spite of the fact that, unlike his contemporary Keynes, he founded no school that bears his name and there are only a few who carry on his work.

The work of Jan Tinbergen, who is Professor of Econometrics, Rotterdam School of Economics, The Netherlands, is known to English readers largely through a translation by J. J. Polak under the title *The Dynamics of Business Cycles* (1950). Tinbergen has pioneered in the construction of models demonstrating that such economic phenomena as self-perpetuating commodity cycles and cycles in the production of durable capital goods can be explained in terms of the time lag which takes place when stocks are adjusted to changes in demand.

Most other contributors to current theorizing about economic growth and fluctuation are followers of Keynes. Some, like Roy F. Harrod, John R. Hicks, and Joan Robinson, were already prominent scholars when they turned their attention to making the Keynesian analysis dynamic. Others, like Paul A. Samuelson, Evsey Domar and James Duesenberry, are younger men whose reputations have largely been earned on the basis of their contributions to macrodynamics. Since biographical information about Robinson and Hicks has already been included elsewhere, it will be omitted here.

Roy F. Harrod was one of England's leading economists. His most important books are *International Economics* (1933), *The Trade Cycle* (1936), and *Towards a Dynamic Economics* (1948). He was also a frequent journal contributor and joint editor of the *Economic Journal* in addition to being Keynes's biographer. His "Essay in Dynamic Theory," which appeared in the *Economic Journal* in 1939, marks the first attempt to make Keynes's static analysis dynamic.

James Duesenberry of Harvard University, along with Evsey Domar, Robert M. Solow, and Paul A. Samuelson, all of whom are presently at the Massachusetts Institute of Technology, are among the younger generation of contributors to the theory of economic growth and fluctuation. The work of Domar and Duesenberry in this area is largely of Keynesian inspiration, while that of Solow is more neoclassical. All are active participants in the current development of the theory of growth and fluctuation. Their most recent contributions, along with those of most of the older contributors previously identified, are to be found in the various professional journals published here and abroad.

GROWTH, FLUCTUATION, AND DYNAMIC PROCESS ANALYSIS

The Nature of Dynamic Process Analysis

While dynamic process analysis enjoys great prominence today as a method of studying economic problems, particularly in the field of income analysis, historically speaking the static approach has predominated. Even

Alfred Marshall, who was most impressed with the phenomenon of change, presented his analysis within the framework of a quasi-static method. This is largely because he was even more impressed with the regularities he thought to be inherent in the functioning of the economic system than he was with the changes which are continuously taking place through time. Since almost any problem in economics can be treated dynamically, the choice between the static and the dynamic method is largely a matter of the way in which change is perceived by the investigator. Present-day investigators of economic problems are greatly concerned with studying functional relationships between economic variables at different points of time. Whereas a static approach concerns itself with an instantaneous or timeless examination of economic variables, a dynamic analysis is concerned with their rate of change. The essential characteristic of a dynamic process (or system) is that it is self-generating over time, much like a servomechanism. Its motion through time is the result of its "built-in" response to an initial internal condition or its response to changing external conditions.[4]

The pattern which a particular process will generate over successive periods depends on the numerical value of its determining variables. If this value is a positive number greater than one, the process is one which increases at a geometric rate. The compound interest problem is a classic economic illustration of the operation of this type of process. The value of a principal invested at a certain rate of interest increases at a geometric rate. Its value at the end of t period is determined according to the formula

$$X_{(t)} = (1 + r)^t X_0$$

where X_0 is the principal initially invested and r is the interest rate. This formula may be rewritten in a simpler form as

$$X_{(t)} = X_0 a^t$$

where $a = (1 + r)$. Any dynamic process which is characterized by growth, whether or not it is in the realm of economics, will behave according to the same principle as a sum of money invested at compound interest. That is, $X_{(t)}$ will increase exponentially as t increases and will, when shown graphically, result in a curve which is sloping upward at an increasing rate.

If the product of an initial magnitude, a, and the exponential value of the variables which determine its value in time, t, is a positive number greater than one, the process is one of growth. If, for example, $X_0 = 3$ and $a = 2$ the numerical values of the process are 3, 6, 12, 24, 48, . . . for

---

[4] See Paul A. Samuelson, "Dynamic Process Analysis," in Howard Ellis (ed.), *A Survey of Contemporary Economics*, Vol. I (Philadelphia: Blakiston Co., 1949).

$t = 0, 1, 2, 3, 4, \ldots$ But if the value of a is equal to one, the process is self-sustaining without either growth or decay. If its value is a fraction less than one, e.g., $\frac{1}{2}$, $\frac{1}{3}$, $\frac{1}{4}$, the process is one of decay over time. That is, a magnitude whose value is determined by a fraction which is continuously raised to higher powers becomes progressively smaller and approaches zero.

A negative value will create still another pattern, namely, one of oscillation rather than steady exponential growth or decline. If, for example, $X_0 = 50$ and $a = -2$, an explosively oscillating pattern will be generated whose sequence is $+50 - 100 + 200 - 400 + 800. \ldots$ Or if a is a negative fraction which is less than one, the result is an oscillation which is dying out or becoming damped.

Any dynamic process, whether or not it is economic in nature, will have a pattern like that of one of the cases described above. Jan Tinbergen appears to have been the first to perceive that these principles have economic application. He constructed a cyclical model based on his observation that the present supply of hogs depends on their price one time period ago, while the demand depends on the present price.[5] This study led him to the examination of output cycles in the production of durable goods, such as cargo vessels, which do not depreciate completely from one production period to the next, and which are typically characterized by a considerable time lag between the beginning of a production period and its completion.[6] The significant variable in the process is, therefore, the rate of increase in the stock of the capital good in time t. According to Tinbergen's reasoning, new orders are placed whenever the actual stock of capital, k, differs from the desired stock. Obviously, therefore, the rate of increase depends partly on the size of the initial stock and partly on current needs. The latter reflect both the durability of the capital stock and changes in demand which alter the size of the desired stock. Production will thus behave in an oscillating pattern of alternate expansion and contraction.

While Tinbergen's model antedates Keynes's *General Theory* and subsequent attempts to make it dynamic, it is in a sense a prototype for a variety of post-Keynesian dynamic models, which are conveniently called "capital stock adjustment models." All of these models have certain assumptions in common. The first is that investment creates new income through the operation of the multiplier. Most models assume a long-run constant propensity to consume, so that the average and marginal propensities to consume are equal. The second assumption common to recently constructed dynamic models is a definitional distinction between autonomous and induced investment. Autonomous investment is conceived of as being an exogenous factor resulting from technological changes, increases

---

[5] A description of this contribution, written in English, is M. Ezekiel, "The Cobweb Theorem," *Quarterly Journal of Economics,* Vol. LII (1938).

[6] Jan Tinbergen, "Ein Schiffbauzyklus," *Wirtschaftliches Archiv,* 1931.

or major shifts in population, or public investment. Such investment is defined as independent of current demands and income levels. It is therefore outside the explanatory mechanism of the model. Induced investment, on the other hand, is directly dependent on past changes in the level of consumption or income. It is, in short, an endogenous factor which causes the stock of capital to adjust in such a manner as to maintain a desired relationship between output and the stock of capital. Most models assume a constant capital-output ratio which reflects technological requirements. The incremental value of this ratio, $\frac{\Delta K}{\Delta Y}$ is known as the acceleration coefficient or relation. It will become evident from the discussion which follows that post-Keynesian models depicting economic growth and/or fluctuation typically involve the interaction of the multiplier and accelerator, and therefore utilize these assumptions.

The Samuelson Multiplier-Accelerator Model

The first dynamic model constructed on the basis of Keynes's work was Samuelson's model of the interaction of the multiplier and the accelerator.[7] Unlike the Keynesian instantaneous multiplier, this model reveals the process by which investment increases income. It also brings to light a number of other effects which the process of investment has on income creation. The first is that the equilibrium income level which will result from a single injection of new investment is different from that which will result from sustained injections. The second is that there is an additional leverage to national income which derives from the operation of the acceleration principle. The third is that, depending on the value of the multiplier and the acceleration coefficient, national income will behave either in an oscillating or in an explosive fashion.

These various possibilities were demonstrated by Samuelson with the aid of model sequences which disaggregate the additions to national income associated with the injection of autonomous expenditure (assumed to consist of governmental deficit spendings) to show that they are comprised of three components: the injection itself, private consumption expenditures induced by the injection, and additional investment induced by the increase in consumption. Thus, national income in time t may be written $Y_t = G_t + C_t + I_t$. Governmental expenditures are, of course, autonomously determined. Present consumption, C_t, depends on a, the marginal propensity to consume, and the income of the preceding period. Present investment is assumed to be induced; its magnitude depends on the increase in consumption since the preceding period and b, the capital coefficient. Coefficients a and b are both assumed to have a constant value. Expressed in symbols, current consumption expenditures may be written as $C_t = aY_{t-1}$;

---

[7] Paul A. Samuelson, "Interactions between the Multiplier Analysis and the Principle of Acceleration," *Review of Economics and Statistics*, Vol. XXI, No. 2 (May, 1939).

current investment expenditures as $I_t = b(C_t - C_{t-1}) = abY_{t-1} - abY_{t-2}$, and governmental expenditures as $G_t = 1$. National income can therefore be expressed in terms of a difference equation of the second order:

$$Y_t = 1 + a(1 + b)Y_{t-1} - abY_{t-2}$$

According to this equation the behavior of national income over time depends on the frequency of the governmental injection and the values of coefficients a and b. The various possibilities can most easily be grasped by reproducing one of the tables Samuelson constructed for this purpose (see Table 19–1).

TABLE 19–1

THE TOTAL INCREASE IN NATIONAL INCOME RESULTING FROM A STEADY INJECTION OF $1.00 OF NEW INVESTMENT WHEN THE MARGINAL PROPENSITY TO CONSUME EQUALS ONE HALF AND THE RELATION EQUALS UNITY

(1) Period	(2) Current Governmental Expenditure	(3) Current Consumption Induced by Previous Period's Income	(4) Induced Current Investment Equal to Increment in Current Consumption $(C_2 - C_1)\beta$	(5) Total Rise in National Income (Sum of Columns 2, 3, and 4)
1.	$1.00	$0.00	$0.00	$1.00
2.	1.00	0.50	0.5000	2.00
3.	1.00	1.00	0.5000	2.50
4.	1.00	1.25	0.2500	2.50
5.	1.00	1.25	0.00	2.25
6.	1.00	1.125	− 0.1250*	2.00
7.	1.00	1.00	− 0.1250	1.875
8.	1.00	0.9375	− 0.625	1.875
9.	1.00	0.9375	0.00	1.9375
10.	1.00	0.96875	0.03125	2.00
11.	1.00	1.0000	0.03125	2.03125
12.	1.00	1.015625	0.015625	2.03125
13.	1.00	1.015625	0.00	2.015625
14.	1.00	1.0078125	− 0.0078125	2.00

* The negative value for induced investment should be construed to mean that there is less investment in this particular period for the economy as a whole than there otherwise would have been.

Table 19–1 shows the effect on national income of a hypothetical autonomous injection of $1.00 continuously over fourteen periods when a, the marginal propensity to consume, is one half and b, the acceleration coefficient, is one. The acceleration coefficient, or relation, is the ratio of new capital required to satisfy the net increase in consumption demand. This factor governs the volume of investment induced by the operation of the multiplier. It cannot, therefore, be immediately operative. Thus, in period 1, national income increases only by the amount of the injection itself; whereas in period 2, it increases by $2.00. The latter increase consists of three components: $0.50 is the increase in current consumption induced by the previous period's investment, $0.50 is the increase in investment induced by that increase in consumption, and $1.00 is the result of autonomous governmental expenditures.

It is apparent from Samuelson's model that when conditions are such that increases in consumption induce new investment, the increase in national income which results from an autonomous injection proceeds much more quickly than it could on the basis of the multiplier alone. If the only leverage to national income were that associated with the multiplier, it would require nine periods before the increase in national income approached $2.00, given the assumptions on which Table 19–1 was constructed. As shown in Table 19–1 this level is reached by the second period when there is also an acceleration coefficient of unity at work. Furthermore, national income will, under these assumptions, increase by more than that which could be achieved on the basis of the multiplier alone; i.e., it will reach a maximum of $2.50. Thereafter, it will decrease because current consumption induced by the previous period's income is decreasing, so that induced current investment is also reduced. This contraction process is of course limited, for while induced investment can fall to zero, it is never, in practice, a negative figure, for this would imply a physical destruction of capital. Eventually, if autonomous injections are continued, the previous period's income will increase, and induced investment will again be positive, so that national income rises again and then subsequently falls. The pattern is one of decreasing fluctuation around the multiplier level.

This is precisely what the preceding discussion of dynamic process analysis would lead us to expect. Samuelson's model makes the movement of national income from one period to the next depend on its level in the preceding period and two constant coefficients, a, the marginal propensity to consume, and b, the acceleration coefficient. When the values of a and b are one half and one, respectively, and both consumption and induced investment are dependent on the income of the preceding period, continuous autonomous investment will generate a process in which income fluctuates with decreasing amplitude around a level to which a constant continuous government expenditure would raise national income on the basis of the multiplier alone. If the values of the marginal propensity to consume and the acceleration coefficient are higher—for example, two thirds and two—the amplitude of the oscillations in national income will be greater. Still higher values of these coefficients—for example, four fifths and four —will result in a national income which is ever increasing at a rate which eventually approaches a compound interest rate of growth. Thus, there are three different patterns of behavior with respect to national income which can conceivably result from a given sustained government expenditure and various possible values of a and b.

There is, of course, nothing in Samuelson's model to indicate which of these patterns is likely to obtain, although experience indicates that the actual pattern has been and is likely to continue to be a cyclical one rather than one in which expansion levels out at the multiplier level or continues explosively. The model also demonstrates that, given an initial impulse, cycles can be self-perpetuating in an economy in which the marginal propensity to consume is less than one and there are variations in the level of induced investment. Expansions cannot continue indefinitely because the marginal propensity to consume is such that consumption increases by less than the value of output. Similarly, the model makes it apparent that a cumulative downward movement cannot continue indefinitely because, while induced investment may be zero, it will never be negative, so that once this floor is reached, there will be an upturn. Post-Keynesian contributors to business cycle theory have found this model particularly useful because it has made it unnecessary to introduce limiting factors into the analysis, as was done in traditional business cycle theory, in order to explain an upturn or downturn in the level of economic activity.

The various cyclical patterns that emerge from Samuelson's models are implicitly fluctuations around a static or stationary level. This is, of course, not the case. Any economy experiences change over time in the direction of either secular stagnation or growth. Obviously, a model can be constructed to portray either situation. What is therefore needed is a working hypothesis in terms of which a model can be constructed. The stagnation thesis provided such a hypothesis during the thirties. Since the war, the emphasis, as has already been observed, has been upon growth. The fundamental importance of the growth forces such as population movements, new markets and products, and other stimuli to autonomous investment have of course long been appreciated. But as has already been noted, the initial approach of post-Keynesian thinkers has been to view the process of sustained growth as requiring a continuous expansion in the level of induced investment. Such an expansion is necessary in order to achieve the full utilization of a growing capital stock. Roy F. Harrod was aware of this aspect of the growth problem as early as 1939.[8] But it remained for Evsey Domar to formulate the equation expressing the rate of growth of the national product which is required if excess capacity is not to develop. This contribution is examined next.

Domar's Growth Equation

What Domar presented is not a *theory* concerning growth but rather an expression of the problem of economic growth in terms which make apparent the dynamic aspects of the growth process. He effectively demonstrated that in order to determine the rate of growth of the national product which is required to maintain full employment, it is essential to take into

---

[8] Roy F. Harrod, "An Essay in Dynamic Theory," *Economic Journal,* Vol. XLIX (March, 1939), pp. 14–33.

account the dual character of the investment process. That is, it must specifically be taken into account that because investment both increases productive capacity and generates income, "it provides us with *both* sides of the equation the solution of which may yield the required rate of growth."[9]

Domar reasoned that the necessary growth rate of income required in order fully to employ a growing capital stock depends on the long-run savings function and the productivity of the additional increments of capital which result from net investment. The larger the volume of investment and the more each additional dollar of investment adds to productive capacity, the greater the rate at which income and investment will have to increase in order to give full employment to the growing capital stock. Specifically, the required rate of growth is the product of the marginal propensity to save, or the saving ratio, and the productivity ratio. Therefore, with a constant marginal propensity to save and a given productivity ratio, and full employment in year t, in order that full employment continue to obtain in year $t + 1$, investment and income will have to grow at an exponential or compound interest rate. That is, they will have to grow at a rate which is the product of the productivity ratio and the savings ratio. Domar's growth equation is, therefore, $\frac{\Delta I}{I} = os$, where o is the productivity ratio and s is the savings ratio.[10]

To use Domar's own simple numerical example: If income per year is $150 billion and the marginal propensity to save, s, is 12 percent, in

---

[9] Evsey Domar, "Capital Expansion, Rate of Growth and Employment," *Essays in the Theory of Economic Growth* (New York: Oxford University Press, 1957), p. 73.

[10] The productivity ratio is customarily designated by the symbol o. It is the reciprocal of the marginal value of the capital-output ratio $\frac{\Delta K}{\Delta Y}$, where K is the net increase in capital stock resulting from investment. Domar's formula can be derived in the following way:

$$o = \frac{\Delta Y}{\Delta K}$$

$$s = \frac{\Delta S}{\Delta Y}$$

$$M \text{ (the multiplier)} = \frac{1}{s}$$

Equate aggregate supply and aggregate demand by:

$$M\Delta I = I \cdot o$$
$$\frac{\Delta I}{s} = I \cdot o$$

Transposing:

$$\frac{\Delta I}{I} = s \cdot o$$

order that full employment be maintained, an amount of $150 $\left(\dfrac{12}{100}\right)$ billion must be invested.[11] This will increase productive capacity by the amount invested multiplied by the productivity ratio, *o*. If *o* is 25 percent, the productive capacity of the economy will rise by the amount invested, *s*, times *o*, i.e., by $150 $\left(\dfrac{12}{100}\right)\left(\dfrac{25}{100}\right)$ = $4.5 billion. National income will therefore have to rise by the same annual amount. That is, its relative rise will have to equal the absolute increase in investment divided by the income itself, or $\dfrac{150\left(\dfrac{12}{100}\right)\left(\dfrac{25}{100}\right)}{150}$ = 3 percent, which is the value of *os*.

The expression $\dfrac{\Delta I}{I} = os$ indicates that it is not sufficient, in Keynesian terms, that yesterday's savings be invested today. Investment today must always exceed the savings of yesterday; the economy must continuously expand at a constant annual percentage (or compound interest) rate equal to the product of the marginal propensity to save and the average (to put it briefly) productivity of investment.[12] If investment and income do not grow at the required rate, unused capacity will develop, and both capital and labor will be idle. It therefore becomes apparent that investment, by increasing productive capacity, can create unemployed labor. The productivity effect of investment implies that investment, or the lack of it, presents a twofold problem: If investment is insufficient today relative to savings, there will be unemployment; but if enough is invested today, still more will have to be invested tomorrow in order to maintain full employment. This is the essence of the growth problem.

It should be obvious that the very existence of the growth problem derives from the stability of the savings function and the capital coefficient. If a reduction in investment tended automatically to be offset by an increase in consumption, the problem of maintaining the necessary rate of growth to give full employment to a growing capital stock would not exist. Similarly, if investment were accompanied by technological changes associated with the deepening of capital, productive capacity would grow less rapidly than if the capital coefficient remained constant or reflected technological changes of a capital-saving variety. Steady growth requires that the relationship between the savings and capital ratios be such that there will be continuous full employment of an accumulating stock of capital. This condition is automatically assured when a constant proportion of income is

---

[11] Evsey Domar, "Expansion and Employment," *American Economic Review*, (March, 1947), pp. 34–55. Republished in his *Essays in the Theory of Economic Growth*, pp. 83–108. Example appears on p. 92.

[12] *Ibid.*

added to capital every year and capital bears a constant ratio to income, for income will then expand continuously at a constant proportional rate.[13] Domar has the distinction of having formulated this principle in specific terms and of recognizing productive capacity as a key element in the growth problem, even though he was anticipated in its perception by Harrod.

While Domar's growth equation identifies the rate of growth of income and investment which is necessary fully to utilize the growing capital stock of an economy in which the marginal propensity to consume is less than one, his formulation is not, of course, a *theory* of economic growth. It does not offer a hypothesis which purports to explain—as did, for example, Schumpeter's theory of innovation—what forces propel the economy along an upward path. Nor was he concerned with the ability of an equilibrium growth rate to perpetuate itself or the related question of divergences from the growth rate and their consequences. His treatment of the growth problem is simply a straightforward application of the principle that any magnitude which is increasing over time must continue to increase exponentially, or it will either level off or decline. But it nevertheless constitutes a major step forward as far as dynamic economic theory is concerned, for the growth equation is an analytical tool which is fundamental to all contemporary theorizing on the problem of economic growth and fluctuation.

HARROD'S DYNAMIC ECONOMICS

Roy F. Harrod's "Essay in Dynamic Theory" reveals that as early as 1939, he fully appreciated the importance of making Keynes's employment theory dynamic. Accordingly, he outlined a dynamic theory based upon the marriage of the acceleration principle and the multiplier. The coefficients are assumed to operate without a time lag, thus producing a model in which income will grow geometrically. By proceeding in this manner, he specifically rejected the approach initiated by Tinbergen, which seeks to construct a dynamic theory by the introduction of time lags between certain adjustments. Harrod proceeded as he did on the ground that while the introduction of a lag will produce a model whose pattern is one of oscillation, "there is some doubt as to the nature of the trend on which the oscillation is superimposed."[14] Moreover, he thought it possible that the trend of growth may *itself* generate forces making for oscillation. His

---

[13] Joan Robinson has spelled out the assumptions on which models of continuously expanding economies are generally based. See "The Model of an Expanding Economy," *Economic Journal*, Vol. LXII (March, 1952); reprinted in Joan Robinson, *Collected Economic Papers,* Vol. II (Oxford: Basil Blackwell, 1960), p. 74.

[14] Harrod, "An Essay in Dynamic Theory," *op. cit.,* p. 14.

objective was the formulation of a hypothesis to explain why this may be the case.

Quite apart from the merits of Harrod's approach, the case he presented in 1939 for a dynamic economics in the "Essay" was most eloquent. He observed that "once the mind is accustomed to thinking in terms of trends of increase, the old static formulation of problems seems stale, flat and unprofitable." As things turned out, however, it was not until the postwar period that interest in the problem of growth and fluctuation really gained momentum. Harrod himself revitalized matters by offering a volume of five readings entitled *Towards a Dynamic Economics* in 1948. Essentially, this volume fleshes out the theory presented in skeleton form ten years earlier. It attempts to explain not only the circumstances under which a steady rate of growth will be perpetuated, but also how an economy might fail to realize its potential and experience depression or be exploded into a too rapid expansion in which inflationary pressures are created. Harrod's theory is therefore a theory of short-run fluctuation quite as much as it is a theory of long-term growth.

Harrod's Warranted Rate of Growth and Its Perpetuation

The most important concept in Harrod's analysis is the "warranted rate of growth." It is defined as "that rate of growth which, if it occurs will leave all parties satisfied that they have produced neither more nor less than the right amount. Or, to state the matter otherwise, it will put them into a frame of mind which will cause them to give such orders as will maintain the same rate of growth."[15] The concept is also expressed symbolically as $G_w = \dfrac{s}{A_r}$, where G_w is the warranted growth rate, or $\dfrac{\Delta Y}{Y}$; s is the long-run constant average and marginal savings ratio; and A_r is the ratio of an increment of induced investment to new income. This formulation reveals that Harrod's theory of growth is essentially a capital stock adjustment theory, i.e., the growth process is viewed as one which manifests itself in additions to capital stock which in turn increase income. Its Keynesian origins are plainly in evidence; paralleling the equilibrium requirement that desired savings must equal desired investment in the static Keynesian model, so in Harrod's growth form of the model the equilibrium requirement is that the desired ratio be maintained between the capital stock and the rate of output. If, now, the propensity to save is given, and the relationship between capital and output is a technological constant, it follows that the capacity to produce output will grow at a constant percentage rate determined by the productivity of additions to capital stock and the proportion of the increase in output devoted to the creation of new capital. It is plain, therefore, that Harrod's G_w, like Domar's *os,* is an exponential

---

[15] *Ibid.,* p. 16.

growth rate. But what Harrod has given us, in addition, is a hypothesis concerning the origin of the forces which propel the economy along its steady upward path of growth and of the manner in which divergences may take place from the equilibrium path. This hypothesis is essentially a theory of entrepreneurial investment behavior in which the key role is played by the effect of expectations on induced investment.

Harrod, like many other business cycle theorists, is of the belief that the psychology of human behavior is such that in the absence of evidence to the contrary the business community expects that economic conditions in the foreseeable future will generally be similar to those of the immediate past. The behavior of businessmen is predicated on the assumption that they can safely project current economic events into the future. Thus, Harrod's conception of the warranted rate of growth implies that the rate of growth of income in period t will be followed by an equal rate of growth in period $t + 1$, i.e., $G_t = G_{t+1}$. This is the case because the anticipations of period G_t were in fact realized, so that business firms, projecting satisfactory output and investment decisions into the following period, expect a similar rate of growth in the following period which, in turn, tends to perpetuate itself precisely because businessmen behave in such a way that expectations are realized. It is worth noting that Harrod's theory envisions businessmen as repeating in period $t + 1$ not the *amount* of output and capital outlays of period t, but their *rate of growth*. This is essential to the whole concept of the warranted rate of growth, for the latter is the growth rate which insures the full utilization of the productive capacity represented by the new capital stock of the period.

Divergences from G_w and Cyclical Fluctuation

In addition to the warranted growth rate, there is another growth rate which Harrod identifies as "the natural growth rate," or G_n. Contrary to what one might expect, there is no inherent tendency for this rate to obtain. The natural growth rate is, rather, a "ceiling" or maximum growth rate consistent with the full employment of all resources (not just capital) and the rate of technological progress. While the warranted growth rate *may* coincide with the natural growth rate, this is not necessarily the case. The warranted growth rate may diverge from the natural growth rate; and these divergences are, according to Harrod's theory, the source of cyclical fluctuations.

If G_w exceeds G_n, the economy will experience a tendency toward stagnation because the growth rate of savings and investment, and therefore the capital stock, is greater than that which is associated with the full employment of labor resources. Excess capacity will therefore appear and put a damper on business expectations. Investment will decline further, so that the actual growth rate will be still further below the warranted growth rate. Only more investment could have avoided this decline. Thus, we are confronted with a seemingly paradoxical situation in which the only way the capacity resulting from some previous level of investment can be fully utilized is by investing even more. In similar fashion, if $G_n > G_w$, the economy will experience a state of secular exhilaration; realized investment will be less than acceleration-induced planned investment. Existing capital stocks will be utilized intensively and provide high rates of return, so that there is a continuous stimulus to new investment. Harrod's warranted rate of growth is thus seen as being inherently unstable. Divergences from G_w are not associated with the development of corrective counterbalancing forces. On the contrary, any divergence from G_w leads to an even greater divergence.

The unstable character of Harrod's warranted rate of growth derives from the assumption that there is no lag between the receipt and the spending of income. The absence of an investment lag is evident in its formulation as $G_w = \dfrac{S}{A_r}$. With respect to the volume of induced investment, this means that changes in income are instantaneously followed by investment outlays. Because the model does not assume an investment lag, induced investment is treated as a function of the current income of which it is itself a component. Thus, if income increases between period t and t_1 acceleration-induced investment will take place which increases income and induces still more investment, and thus income. The change thus perpetuates itself in the same period. Conversely, a reduction in income is instantaneously reflected in a self-perpetuating reduction of the income level. Harrod's system is, therefore, one which will either "explode" and experience an astronomically large income or else break down.

HICKS'S THEORY OF THE TRADE CYCLE

Criticism of Harrod's Dynamic Theory

The central theme of Hicks's *A Contribution to the Theory of the Trade Cycle* (1950) was presented in article form a year prior to its publication. Although his interest in the analysis of cyclical fluctuations was already apparent in various chapters of his *Value and Capital* and *The Theory of Wages,* the particular occasion for writing the article previously referred was to review Harrod's *Towards a Dynamic Economics.*[16] The observations made with respect to Harrod's thesis then became the basis for his own positive contribution to the theory of growth and fluctuation.

Hicks's immediate concern in reviewing Harrod's work was the inher-

---

[16] Hicks's review, and those by Joan Robinson and David McCord Wright, have been reprinted in Alvin Hansen and R. V. Clemence, *Readings in Business Cycles and National Income* (New York: W. W. Norton, 1953).

ent instability of his warranted rate of growth.[17] While he agreed with Harrod that the tendency of the economy to fluctuate does reflect the operation of the acceleration principle, he also felt that Harrod's model could be made more realistic and useful by the introduction of time lags. Such lags, he maintained, would give the model mathematical stability without sacrificing the economic instability on which the substance of the argument depends. A lag is necessary to make a system such as Harrod's determinate, i.e., to hold it to a given path, so that it will not "explode out of time dimension." Hicks also felt it necessary to produce a theory which would explain what he thought to be the predominately periodic character of the business cycle. Periodicity could not, in Hicks's view, be explained as the result of the summation of random causes, as was suggested by Eugen Slutsky.[18] Rather, he envisaged the economy as having a long-run growth trend from which there are periodic fluctuations which he believed can be explained in terms of a model premised on relatively few simple assumptions.

Hicks's Model

In constructing his model, Hicks assumed that the level of autonomous investment, which reflects the natural growth forces of the economy, grows at a constant percentage rate. It follows that in his model the equilibrium income level will also grow at a constant percentage rate. The system may move along this path of steady growth or oscillate around this equilibrium position. Its experience will depend both on the previous level of income and capital stock and on the values of the savings and acceleration coefficients which are the parameters of the equation.[19]

The model assumes a time lag with respect to both consumption and investment. Current consumption is therefore made to depend on the propensity to consume and the income level of the preceding period, while induced investment depends on previous consumption and the acceleration coefficient. Hicks believes that the acceleration coefficient has a sufficiently high value to produce a steady divergence away from equilibrium like that depicted in Harrod's model. But he maintains that there are constraints which set a definite limit to the extent of expansions and contractions, so that the level of economic activity fluctuates around an upward-moving equilibrium level. Given the level of autonomous investment, the limit to any expansion process is the full-employment ceiling. Once this has been

---

[17] John R. Hicks, "Mr. Harrod's Dynamic Theory," *Economica*, N.S., Vol. XVI, No. 62 (May, 1949), pp. 106–21.

[18] Eugen Slutsky, "The Summation of Random Causes as the Source of Cyclical Process, *Econometrica*, Vol. 5 (April, 1937).

[19] A useful nonmathematical explanation of the results which emerge from equations of the sort written by Hicks is included in Alvin Hansen, *Fiscal Policy and Business Cycles* (New York: W. W. Norton & Co., 1941), chap. xii.

reached, there can be no further rise in income. Net investment then falls to zero, which reduces income through the operation of the multiplier; and as a result, there is an inducement to reduce the stock of capital. The cumulative expansion thus turns into a cumulative contraction. In similar fashion, Hicks takes the position that a downward displacement from the equilibrium level cannot contract income and output indefinitely. When output decreases, induced investment ceases, but it does not become negative. Capital equipment is not destroyed but is simply absorbed into excess capacity. Since the reduction in investment is limited to zero, there is a lower limit to the reduction of income. Thus, according to Hicks's theory, as long as the fundamental data of the system remain unchanged, actual output and income must fluctuate between the limits set by the full-employment level and the level of zero net investment. These limits prevent the unlimited expansion and contractions which are inherent in Harrod's model.

Some Criticisms of Hicks's Theory

One aspect of Hicks's model which has been called into question is the implicit assumption that the acceleration coefficient has a high enough value to produce a strong recovery once the process of cumulative contraction has been brought to a halt.[20] Actually, such empirical evidence as is available suggests that the acceleration principle does not help very much in the explanation of fluctuations in real investment.[21] Alvin Hansen has therefore offered a theory of fluctuation which assumes a weak acceleration coefficient.[22] He conceives of upswings as petering out because they are generated by accelerators whose value is so low that even when they interact with fairly large multipliers, they are never strong enough to bring about expansions which will reach the growth ceiling. As was shown by our discussion of the nature of dynamic processes, the assumption of an acceleration coefficient which has a low value will produce deviations from equilibrium which become smaller and smaller; that is, a low acceleration coefficient would produce damped cycles even if the value of the multiplier is fairly high. But there is no evidence that cycles are becoming damped. Hansen is therefore of the opinion that fluctuations in autonomous investment cause cyclical movements which are merely intensified by the interaction of the multiplier and the accelerator. While autonomous investment is not so responsive to cyclically varying stimuli as induced investment, booms encourage and depressions retard the exploitation of innovations.

---

[20] James Duesenberry, "Hicks on the Trade Cycle," *Quarterly Journal of Economics,* Vol. LXIV (August, 1950).

[21] J. Tinbergen, "Statistical Evidence on the Acceleration Principle," *Economica,* N.S., Vol. V (May, 1938).

[22] Alvin Hansen, *Business Cycles and National Income* (New York: W. W. Norton & Co., Inc., 1951), p. 484.

Thus, Hansen believes that long-term movements of income are largely controlled by alterations in the equilibrium position of the economy which are associated with autonomous investment and that there is a ratchet effect which keeps the economy from slipping back to its previous low in a period of cyclical decline. This ratchet is the result of the tendency for consumption expenditures to rise in proportion to income when income is rising, and to fall proportionately less than income on the downswing. The tendency for certain business expenditures to freeze may also contribute to the ratchet.[23]

DUESENBERRY'S THEORY OF GROWTH AND FLUCTUATION

Criticism of Capital Stock Adjustment Models

Duesenberry's *Business Cycles and Economic Growth* (1958) examines the qualifications he feels must be made in the simple capital stock adjustment models in order to improve their usefulness as explanatory devices. He is critical of all models, including Hicks's, which explain fluctuations in terms of adjustments in capital stock which take place simply as a result of the interaction of the multiplier and the accelerator.[24] His examination of American business cycles leads him to conclude that

. . . cycle explanations based on the acceleration principle are not really consistent with the pattern of movement of income and investment which has been observed. In addition, the evidence that ceilings have played an important role in bringing on depressions is elusive at best. . . . the models used by the acceleration theorists are much too simple. More realistic models will prove to have substantially different dynamic properties. . . .[25]

The system might at one time have conformed to the weak acceleration model proposed by Hansen and at another time bounced off the ceiling in the manner described by Hicks. At other times it might have followed still other patterns.[26]

Capital stock adjustment models are inherently weak, in Duesenberry's view, because they are predicated on a distinction between induced and autonomous investment which is not too meaningful. While these two categories of investment can be conceptually distinguished, the fact is that the distinction is considerably less than clear-cut with respect to actual new investment. Apart from investments by new firms or to produce new

---

[23] W. Goodwin, "The Problem of the Trend and the Cycle," *Yorkshire Bulletin of Economic and Social Research,* Vol. V (September, 1953).

[24] James Duesenberry, *Business Cycles and Economic Growth* (New York: McGraw-Hill Book Co., Inc., 1958), p. 7.

[25] *Ibid.,* p. 4.

[26] *Ibid.,* p. 7.

products, decisions to purchase new equipment are based on cost comparisons between the old and the new. New equipment will offer a cost advantage when it is technically better able to produce or when the demand for output is so great that the intensity of operations raises the operating and/or maintenance costs of using existing equipment. In an actual engineering situation, all three considerations will influence the decision to buy new capital, so that there is no practical distinction between autonomous and induced investment. Duesenberry therefore believes that the acceleration principle operates in a more complicated way than a theory like Hicks's implies. Differences in investment behavior are not apparent in a model such as Hicks's, in which it is implicitly assumed that no investment takes place anywhere until excess capacity is eliminated. Only then does the multiplier-accelerator process come into play again. But the fact is that not all industries have the same degree of excess capacity, and not all are confronted with the same considerations with respect to new investment. Some may continue to invest even when the level of aggregate demand is low. The accelerator is not simply a technological constant but also reflects the market processes which affect the investment behavior of the firms in the economy.

Multiplier-accelerator models also, in Duesenberry's opinion, underestimate the role of autonomous investment and other exogenous factors in stimulating revival. The amount and distribution of the technical change which has taken place during the depression is, he believes, more important than the numerical value of the acceleration coefficient in explaining recovery. He also regards the thesis that booms are checked by bottlenecks as being unfounded. In his opinion, equipment shortages are unlikely to be a serious impediment to expansion because industries typically have standby capacity. The practice of investing in new equipment because of technological improvements rather than physical depreciation contributes to the development of a productive capacity adequate to most peacetime booms. A ceiling is, if anything, more likely to derive from labor rather than capital shortages. Even here, however, Duesenberry feels that the effect of a labor shortage is more likely to be on the rate at which output can increase rather than on the level of output.

Qualifications of the Acceleration Principle

Duesenberry's model, in common with other multiplier-accelerator models, is premised on the proposition that investment is related to income and the size of the existing capital stock. However, instead of treating the accelerator as a technological constant, Duesenberry argues that firms choose investments whose rate of return over cost exceeds the marginal cost of raising funds for investment. A firm will maximize its profits by investing an amount which will equate the marginal cost of raising capital to the marginal efficiency of investment. It follows that the marginal cost of raising capital is one of the crucial variables in determining the volume of investment.[27]

There are several recent studies which indicate that firms are greatly influenced in their investment decisions by the imputed costs of retaining earnings, borrowing, or selling equities. These support Duesenberry's contention that the marginal cost of raising capital is not identical with the market rate of interest.[28] Whenever a firm needs more capital than it has available from its internal sources, it is confronted with a cost-of-capital schedule which is increasing even if the market cost of borrowing has not changed. This fact explains why investment may not be responsive to reductions in the money rate of interest even if the marginal efficiency of investment schedule is elastic. It also supports the hypothesis that changes in investment are not simply to be explained in terms of the operation of the acceleration principle. The acceleration principle makes new investment depend only on the ratio of capital stock to demand. Actually, investment depends on the expected rate of return over cost and on the cost of funds to the firm. While an increase in demand relative to capital stock will stimulate investment, Duesenberry concluded that the operation of this principle is qualified by the effect which the level of profits, retained earnings, past dividend rates, and other financial factors has on the cost of capital to the firm. Unlike the simple accelerator models, Duesenberry sees the effect of changes in income on the rate of investment as being much smaller than is envisaged in other models. He believes that this factor operates to give the economy more stability in its actual functioning than is exhibited in models predicated on the operation of a simple accelerator.

Duesenberry also regards the multiplier aspect of the usual multiplier-accelerator models to be less than entirely satisfactory. Models based on the interaction of the mutiplier and the accelerator generally suppose that saving is a function of income and is independent of factors influencing investment. Duesenberry, however, maintains that the propensity to save is at least partly dependent on the variables influencing investment. Business savings constitute about one half of gross savings, and their volume depends on the proportion of income going into profits. Since the latter is highly correlated with the rate of investment, it follows that the propensity to save cannot be completely independent of the volume of investment. Savings and investment both depend on profits. They therefore tend to move in the same direction, which increases the stability of the system. The stability of the system is further enhanced by the tendency of consumption expenditures to lag behind changes in income. All of these considerations have the effect, in Duesenberry's opinion, of making the

---

[27] *Ibid.*, chap. v.

[28] J. Meyer and E. Kuh, "Acceleration and Related Theories of Investment," *Review of Economics and Statistics,* Vol. XXXVII (August, 1955); also Meyer and Kuh, *The Investment Decision* (Cambridge: Harvard University Press, 1957).

economic system more stable than is suggested by models predicated on an unqualified acceleration principle.[29]

Duesenberry's Growth Analysis

Although Duesenberry's analysis leads him to envisage an economy in which a variety of factors interact to give it more stability than is consistent with most multiplier-accelerator models, the experience of the economy also depends on its ability to maintain steady growth. At any point in time, there are exogenous variables, such as population, government expenditures and taxes, and the form and structure of business and financial institutions, which affect the parameters of the endogenous system. Over time, these exogenous variables will of course change and alter the parameters of the system, and consequently its behavior. Ideally, changes in exogenous variables, and therefore the parameters of the endogenous system, should be examined. Since this would require analytical tools and concepts outside economics, Duesenberry's approach is to assume that parameter changes do take place but so smoothly that he can confine his attention to the analysis of the effects of structural changes on the rate of growth of income and capital stock.[30] His model therefore conceives of movements in aggregate income as being determined by a capital adjustment process in which the income and capital stock of one moment of time determine the rate at which income and capital stock will change in the next moment of time. Subsequent magnitudes of income and capital stock are therefore determined by the behavior of the endogenous variables of the system which are inherited from the past. These, in turn, generate later values of income and capital stock in a continuous going-on process.

Like Harrod's model, Duesenberry's entails two growth rates. The one is the growth rate of capital, and the other is the growth rate of income.[31] Capital stock grows whenever gross investment exceeds depreciation. Income grows whenever planned investment exceeds planned savings. If capital stock and income are both growing at the same rate, the capital-income ratio, $\frac{k}{y}$, is constant. This ratio is a crucial magnitude in Duesenberry's hypothesis because it determines both the growth rate of capital and the growth rate of income. If the rate of growth of income and capital stock are equal, so that the capital-income ratio, $\frac{k}{y}$, remains constant, the income of the economy can grow steadily because it is generating a sustained growth in demand. Similarly, if the economic structure changes in

---

[29] Duesenberry, *Business Cycles and Economic Growth, op. cit.*, chap. iii.

[30] *Ibid.*, p. 203.

[31] *Ibid.*, pp. 204–6.

a way which raises the rate of growth of income and the rate of growth of capital by the same amount, the equilibrium rate of growth of income will be raised. Lapses from steady growth therefore derive, according to Duesenberry's analysis, from structural changes which cause the rate of growth of capital and income to be different. When the rate of capital accumulation exceeds the rate of growth of income, the increase in the ratio of capital to income will reduce investment, even though income may at first grow if the initial conditions are appropriate. The rate of growth of income will therefore decline until it becomes negative.

Two sets of factors are capable of generating declines in investment which can bring on depression. One type occurs when the structure of the system is such that capacity tends to rise faster than aggregate demand. This causes profits and investment to decline, so that income eventually falls. This type of depression is essentially like the one described by Hansen. A change in the structure of the system or other circumstances that bring the period of disinvestment to an end stimulates recovery in this case. The second type of depression which Duesenberry thinks possible is that which occurs as a result of shocks. Speculative booms, monetary crises, labor shortages, etc., which affect investment and to a lesser extent consumption expenditures, can interrupt the growth process. But these shocks are not likely, in Duesenberry's opinion, to be capable of generating major depressions. It takes severe shocks, such as the collapse of a speculative boom in a particular sector, to precipitate a major depression. The depressions which occurred before 1929 were caused by a variety of shocks, but income never fell to a level from which it could not recover soon after the initial impact of the shock had worn off. In contrast, the depression which began in 1929 was so much worse than its predecessors because of changes in the structure of the economy which affected both its growth potential and its stability.

Growth is possible only if planned investment exceeds savings in each successive period, and this requires that someone be willing to borrow more than the savings made out of the disposable income of the preceding period. Since most businesses other than public utilities have historically shown themselves to be reluctant to borrow to any great extent, Duesenberry concludes that while sustained growth is possible, it is not likely to occur without outside driving forces such as population growth and the relatively rapid growth of capital-intensive industries. There is no built-in mechanism which makes growth a certainty in a capitalistic system. Indeed, Duesenberry regards it as a remarkable coincidence that with all of the savings functions and profit functions and other behavior variables which were possible, the ones which came into existence during the nineteenth century were so well adapted to the characteristics of that century. He concludes, therefore, that for a capitalistic economy, there is no inherent tendency either to grow or to be free from cyclical disturbance.

NEOCLASSICAL GROWTH MODELS

The Problem of Departure from Steady-State Growth

One of the questions to which Harrod's growth model gave rise concerns the question of stability. A model in which growth is conceived to proceed at a constant rate is one which has a steady-state path. Such a steady-state path is said to be stable if a divergence from the equilibrium path causes reactions which will tend to bring the system back to equilibrium. In Harrod's model, as has been seen, movement along the steady-state path is possible only if warranted growth, G_w, is equal to G_n, the natural rate of growth, the highest rate of growth that can be achieved, given the parameters of the system. Harrod concluded that equality between G_w and G_n is possible only as a special case. With a constant proportion of income devoted to savings and a given labor-to-capital ratio and capital-to-output ratio, and a labor force which grows at a constant rate fixed by noneconomic forces, there are several conditions which must be fulfilled if G_w is to equal G_n. First, the amount people plan to save must equal the amount they plan to invest. Second, producers must have precisely the amount of capital they need for current production. Third, capital stock must grow at the same rate as output. These conditions can be fulfilled only in the special case in which all business expectations are fulfilled. Any divergence between G_w and G_n, instead of resulting in self-correction, only serves to accentuate the departure from the steady-state path. Thus, Harrod concluded that full-employment steady-state growth is in general not possible.

One way, as has been seen, to construct a model which will not "explode," as Harrod's does, is to introduce lags in consumption and investment in the Hicksian manner. But there is another way, namely, to construct a model in which any tendency for the economy to grow more or less rapidly than is consistent with steady-state growth is avoided by the operation of price adjustments. These affect key parameters like the capital-output ratio and the savings ratio, and thereby cause changes in either the warranted rate of growth or the natural rate of growth to bring them to equality with each other. The characteristics of such a model are much more neoclassical than the Harrod, Hicks, and Duesenberry models, which are largely of Keynesian inspiration.

A Variable Capital-Output Model

Models in which the capital-output ratio is variable rather than fixed occupy an important place in the most recent literature on growth theory. Some of the individuals who are particularly associated with the construction of such neoclassical models are James E. Meade, Robert M. Solow, T. W. Swan, and Paul A. Samuelson. Solow has characterized the Harrod-

Domar-Hicks models as "balanced on the knife edge of equilibrium growth." This balance manifests itself in an opposition of the warranted and natural rates of growth which derives from the assumption that production takes place under conditions of fixed proportions. "If this assumption is abandoned, the knife-edge notion of unstable balance seems to go with it."[32] The Solow model is designed to demonstrate this proposition. It is predicated on the assumption that output consists of a single composite commodity produced by labor and capital. It assumes that the labor force increases as a result of population growth, which reflects the operation of noneconomic exogenous factors. It assumes technological change to be absent, so that the rate of increase in the labor force is in effect equivalent to Harrod's natural rate of growth. The problem, then, is to determine whether there is a rate of increase in the stock of capital which is consistent with the rate of growth of the labor force. If there is, the warranted rate is equal to the natural rate; i.e., the knife-edge conditions of the Harrod model are satisfied. But if these two rates are not initially equal, Solow demonstrates that the inherent instability of the Harrod model is not inevitable.

For example, if the savings associated with full employment are in excess of what is required to enable the capital stock to grow at the same rate as the labor force, the warranted rate of growth will be above the natural rate. The real rate of interest will tend to fall in this situation; and as a result, a deepening of capital, which increases the capital-labor ratio and therefore the capital-output ratio, takes place. This serves to reduce the warranted rate of growth. The deepening process will continue as long as the warranted rate continues above the natural rate. When the warranted rate has fallen to the level of the natural rate, growth will continue along the steady-state path. Conversely, if the size of the initial capital stock is such that the warranted rate is below the natural rate, capital and output will grow at a faster rate than the labor force until the warranted rate of growth is equal to the natural rate. In short, the model shows that the natural rate of growth and the warranted rate of growth are not inherently divergent from each other if a method of production is chosen in which the capital intensity is appropriate to the size of the capital stock.

The construction of models in which the capital-output ratio is variable is, of course, only a first step in the direction of exploring the long-run behavior of short-run parameters. It is also necessary to examine the long-run savings-income ratio, the rate of growth of population, the ratio of the labor force to total population, and the nature and impact of technological change, and to construct models which reflect their impact. The literature examining these magnitudes on a theoretical level has been accumulat-

---

[32] "A Contribution to the Theory of Economic Growth," *Quarterly Journal of Economics,* Vol. LXX (February, 1956).

ing over approximately the last twenty years.[33] There are not, however, very many definitive generalizations which we can make as yet about the long-run behavior of short-run parameters. Our inquiry will not, therefore, go further than it has, i.e., the statement of the problem and the tentative beginnings that have been made toward its solution.

CONCLUDING REMARKS

Contemporary macroeconomic theorists have addressed themselves in the main to the task of making Keynes's model dynamic by examining the behavior over time of variables which are short-run parameters in a static model. The parameter on which attention was immediately focused was the size of the capital stock. A new era in macroeconomic analysis began when Domar was prompted to ask at what rate income and investment must grow in order fully to utilize the capacity created by new investment. He demonstrated that, given the marginal propensity to save and the productivity ratio, investment and income will have to grow at an exponential or compound interest rate.

While Domar did not offer a theory of growth, his statement of the growth problem was soon followed by a number of other theoretical inquiries which examined not only what the conditions for growth are but also, quite naturally, what brings about lapses from growth. It is in this manner that the theory of economic fluctuations, which historically was only a peripheral question for the economic theorist, came to be elevated to its present position of importance.

Harrod's initial attempt to create a dynamic economics with his 1939 "Essay" turned out to be a rather abortive effort, but his second attempt provided the basic structure for numerous capital stock adjustment models which explain the generation of income through time on the basis of the interaction of the multiplier and the accelerator. His model was predicated on a given propensity to save and a technically determined capital-output ratio, and assumed that the response of investment to changes in consumption and of consumption to changes in investment take place without a time lag. The capacity to produce output and income, or what Harrod calls the "warranted growth rate," therefore increases at a constant percentage rate which is determined by the productivity of additions to the capital stock and the level of savings. Thus the warranted rate of growth is, like Domar's "necessary" rate of growth, one which exhibits an exponential increase. Harrod therefore offered the hypothesis that cyclical fluctuations are caused by divergences between the warranted rate of growth and the natural rate of growth.

---

[33] A convenient summary of these developments is to be found in *Surveys of Economic Theory*, Vol. II (London: Macmillan & Co.; New York: St. Martin's Press, 1965).

392 · *DEVELOPMENT OF ECONOMIC ANALYSIS*

Since the publication of Harrod's work, other models, also predicated on the interaction of the multiplier and the accelerator, have been created. Hicks constructed a model in which income oscillates around a growth trend predicated on autonomous investment. The upper turning point of the cycle is explained in terms of the full-employment ceiling. Hansen, on the other hand, relies on the presence of a weak accelerator to explain the upper turning point. There is general agreement that the lower limit to the downturn derives from the fact that new investment cannot be less than zero. More recently, Duesenberry has taken the position that cycles before 1929 and since 1929 are too different to lend themselves to any single explanation as simple as that contained in the usual multiplier-accelerator models. Accordingly, he presented a model in which divergences between the rate of growth of income and the rate of growth of capital stock bring about the alterations in investment which characterize cyclical swings, whereas steady growth is conceived of as taking place if the rate of growth of income and the rate of growth of capital stock are equal.

While Duesenberry's theory of fluctuation and growth is very sophisticated, it is nevertheless still a model which is very much in the Keynesian tradition. It is largely aggregative in nature and approaches the problem of growth and fluctuation exclusively in terms of changes in the economy's capacity to produce which are generated by changes in the capital stock resulting from new investment. Such a model, even when it is based on a greatly qualified acceleration principle, has its limitations. Even in our present stage of knowledge, there is much that we know about the growth process that has not yet been given formalized expression in a model. A number of writers have, for example, made the observation that when there is a period of sustained growth, not all industries and sectors participate equally.[34] Usually, only a few major industries dominate and lead the upward movement by their response to a unique factor, such as a major innovation which affects them to the exclusion of the rest of the economy. This certainly suggests the desirability of expanding the scope of our models to enable them to encompass also the behavior of the individual sectors of the economy and the role they play in the process of growth and fluctuation.

Another, although related, limitation of the Harrod-Hicks-Duesenberry models is their assumption of both a fixed capital-to-output ratio and a fixed labor-to-output ratio. This implies that the ratio of capital to labor is also fixed and that there is therefore no possibility of substitution between capital and labor. The assumption of constant capital coefficients in modern growth models is a carry-over from the static short-run Keynesian analysis. The ratio of capital to labor does not remain constant over the long run but

---

[34] The behavior of individual sectors in the growth process has been especially emphasized by Walt W. Rostow, *The Process of Economic Growth* (London: Oxford University Press, 1953).

reflects the growth of population, the labor force, the supply of entrepreneurial talent, and changes in the state of the arts as well as the growth of capital stock. Changes in these variables not only generate increases in the capacity of the economy to produce, but as they change, it is likely that they will also generate structural changes in the economy. That is, they are likely to alter such key determinants of the capacity-creating and income-generating process as the savings-income ratio and the capital-output ratio. The introduction of changes such as these into constant-coefficient models like Harrod's, Hicks's, and Duesenberry's would make them more neoclassical in nature than Keynesian.

But even this will not fully comprehend the growth problem. The process of growth is far more complex than any model which manipulates capital-output and savings-income ratios and population growth rates can possibly show. Growth is also conditioned by the entire cultural milieu within which the economy functions. It may, for example, be asked whether entrepreneurs exploit the profit opportunities that the economic system generates, or whether their actions generate the opportunities which put the growth process into motion. An economy may fail to grow not because profit opportunities are nonexistent but because the environment is not conducive to entrepreneurial activity. There is considerable awareness of the significance of such influence; however, the tools of the economist are still inadequate to deal with those aspects of the growth problem that are noneconomic. The present practice is to abstract all the noneconomic factors which comprise the sociocultural milieu. But noneconomic factors cannot be indefinitely laid to one side, for economic growth is only one aspect of the whole process of social development. Neither economics nor any other single social science is now able to provide concepts and analytical tools adequate for the complete study of the growth problem.

Indeed, the growth problem in all its ramifications serves perhaps more forcefully than any other single problem to make us aware of what economic analysis can and cannot do. The science of economics is essentially concerned with examining phenomena and interrelationships which can be reduced to or expressed in terms of pecuniary gains and losses. As long as growth is conceived of in terms of changes in the stock of capital and the employment of labor which are made in response to changing profit expectations, the growth problem is amenable to examination by economists with economists' tools. But as soon as it becomes necessary to introduce such things as population and labor force changes, or institutional changes or innovations, the principles of pecuniary gains and losses are considerably less useful, or perhaps not useful at all. At this point, other disciplines such as sociology, demography, social psychology, and cultural anthropology can contribute to a more thorough understanding of the noneconomic aspects of the growth process as it unfolds in different institutional settings. The growth process is so diverse among different countries and in different periods that it may defy all efforts to formulate reliable and universal generalizations about it. It is certain, however, that of all the areas the economist has sought to probe, the limitations of his analytical tools are nowhere more apparent than with respect to the theory of economic growth.

There is, of course, no question that all those who have participated in the construction of models in which the prime mover of economic activity is the adjustment of the capital stock have materially furthered the development of ecnomic science. More specifically, they have pioneered in the development of macrodynamics by their application of the principles of dynamic process analysis to studying the behavior of macroeconomic variables over time. This is a major contribution to a subject matter which, methodologically speaking, has historically been concerned primarily with examining the determination of static equilibria.

These pioneering efforts undoubtedly point to the direction and area in which much future effort will be concentrated. Dynamics rather than statics will increasingly command the attention of the economist of the future; and for this work, he will require not only the analytical tools now at his command but also tools borrowed from the mathematician, the statistician, the engineer, and others who are currently concerned with the analysis of dynamic processes.

SUGGESTIONS FOR FURTHER READING

BRUTON, HENRY J. "Contemporary Theorizing on Economic Growth," in BERT F. HOSELITZ and JOSEPH J. SPENGLER et al. (eds.), *Theories of Economic Growth* (New York: Free Press of Glencoe, Inc., 1960).

DOMAR, EVSEY. *Essays in the Theory of Economic Growth.* London: Oxford University Press, 1957.

DUESENBERRY, JAMES. *Business Cycles and Economic Growth.* New York: McGraw-Hill Book Co., Inc., 1958.

HAMBURG D. *Economy Growth and Instability.* New York: W. W. Norton & Co., Inc., 1956.

HARROD, ROY F. "An Essay in Dynamic Theory," *Economic Journal,* Vol. XLIX (March, 1939).

———. "Second Essay in Dynamic Theory," *Economic Journal,* Vol. LXX (June, 1960).

———. *Towards a Dynamic Economics.* London: Macmillan & Co., 1948.

HICKS, JOHN R. *A Contribution to the Theory of the Trade Cycle.* London: Oxford University Press, 1950.

———. "Mr. Harrod's Dynamic Theory," *Economica,* N.S., Vol. XVI No. 62, (May, 1949), pp. 106–21.

HOSELITZ, BERT F.; SPENGLER, JOSEPH J.; *et al.* (eds.). *Theories of Economic Growth.* New York: Free Press of Glencoe, Inc., 1960.

MATTHEWS, R. C. O. "Duesenberry on Growth and Fluctuations," *Economic Journal,* Vol. LXIX (December, 1959).

SOLOW, ROBERT M. "A Contribution to the Theory of Economic Growth," *Quarterly Journal of Economics,* Vol. LXX (February, 1956).

SOME REFLECTIONS ON ECONOMIC THEORY AND ITS METHODOLOGY

The study of history terminates when past developments merge into current events. Our examination of the historical development of economic theory is therefore at an end. Though the focus of this book has been on the development of economic analysis, we should be aware that the substance of this discipline also has methodological implications which have at times been as much a matter of controversy as its content. This was the case, for example, with respect to economics at the end of the nineteenth century, when the historical school and the classical and neoclassical schools were involved in the famous *Methodenstreit*. While methodological controversy has not been in the foreground to nearly the same extent during the twentieth century, it should not be concluded that there are no major methodological questions of concern today.

Three main areas of current controversy may be identified. The first is the vogue of using mathematical analysis and statistical inference in conjunction with deductive reasoning. For certain problems and in certain circles, the use of these tools has become routine. But there is by no means agreement that progress in economics is contingent on the use of mathematical analysis, and there is still a considerable lack of understanding and communication between economists who are mathematically trained and those who are not. This suggests the desirability of surveying briefly the kinds of problems which have been particularly amenable to mathematical solution and also the limitations of the mathematical method.

A second area of controversy concerns itself with the philosophical and psychological preconceptions of economic theory. The appropriateness of many of the assumptions of economics has been called into question, and many suggestions have been made concerning the ways in which these assumptions might be improved upon. The appropriateness of the deductive method as opposed to empiricism has also been an issue.

A third area of controversy concerns itself with the role of the economic theorist as a policy maker. Should the economist properly concern himself with determining the most efficient way of achieving objectives or ends in whose selection he does not participate in a professional capacity? Or is it in his province to inquire also into what should be? It goes beyond the scope of this book to explore these areas of controversy in the detail their complexity requires. But it would be remiss not to give the reader enough of an appreciation about them to stimulate his future reading and thinking.

On the Mathematization of Economics

The mathematization of economics is its most distinctively mid-twentieth-century characteristic. The new period of mathematical economics is largely associated with the names of Abram Wald and John von Neumann. Wald's proof for solutions of general economic equilibrium and von Neumann's dynamic equilibrium of an expanding economy were conceptually new to economics when first presented, beside being mathematically significant. Even more noteworthy is the extent to which mathematics has assisted the economist, especially since World War II, in using economic theory for a variety of practical problems. Broadly speaking, there are two categories of economic problems which have especially lent themselves to mathematical formulation and solution. The first consists of what might be termed resource allocation problems; the second consists of uncertainty problems. Both are encountered on the level of the individual firm and on the level of the economy as a whole.

On the level of the firm the problem of resource allocation typically appears as a problem of determining what is optimal behavior when there are one or more "constraints" or side conditions which must be observed in arriving at a solution. Some typical problems are the selection of an optimum product line, the scheduling of production, the selection of alternative transportation routes or advertising media, etc. Problems of this sort are especially amenable to solution with the aid of the technique known as mathematical programming. Programming, whether linear or nonlinear, is a technique for computing optimal decisions in situations which do not lend themselves to solution by means of marginal analysis.[1] For example, a firm which produces a single product can determine its optimal output by observing the familiar rule of equating marginal cost and marginal revenue. But what is the optimum output of a multiproduct firm which has a given overall productive and/or storage capacity? In a case such as this, a number of interdependent decisions need to be made within the framework of irrevocable constraints. Arithmetic computation of all the alternative solutions would obviously be impractical, if not impossible. But with the aid of mathematical programming techniques and modern computers, the optimal solution can be calculated in a matter of a few minutes.

Mathematical techniques have also been pressed into service to solve resource allocation problems from the standpoint of the economy as a whole. Input-output models have been constructed to examine the resource

---

[1] R. Dorfman, Paul A. Samuelson, and Robert M. Solow, *Linear Programming and Economic Analysis* (New York: McGraw-Hill Book Co., Inc., 1958).

allocation problem empirically.[2] Such models demonstrate the interdependence which derives from the fact that the outputs of some industries are the factor inputs of others. They seek to determine, given the coefficients of production, how much net output can be made physically available for consumption and/or capital accumulation after the requirements for the intermediate products needed to carry on production processes have been satisfied. Mathematically, such interdependence is expressed in terms of N simultaneous equations with N variables. The equations express the input requirements which are associated with the production of the desired outputs which the variables represent. Their solution indicates what patterns of resource use are compatible with the availability of resources and production functions.

The construction of input-output tables is not without its practical difficulties. For example, the typical model makes the unrealistic assumption that the coefficient of production is fixed in order to get the kind of data that will be compatible with single-number entries. There is also the difficulty presented by the need to write and solve the cumbersome number of equations needed when any but the broadest industrial classification is used. The use of computers has of course greatly reduced the latter problem, but the difficulties of constructing input-output models are still formidable. However, their potential usefulness in facilitating the solution of all manner of planning problems is equally great.

In addition to facilitating the solution of various resource allocation problems, mathematical techniques are also being used to solve problems which arise because of uncertainties of various kinds. Many of the uncertainties which characterize economic phenomena arise because the collective actions of individuals reflect the influence of random variables. When these are operative it is only possible to make probabilistic statements with respect to the behavior of the variables they influence. While the laws of probability date back to the work of Pierre Simon de Laplace in the late eighteenth and early nineteenth centuries, social scientists have been slow to use them for formulating and verifying their hypotheses. Economists of that era virtually limited themselves to the formulation of verbal hypotheses. A few, like, Alfred Marshall, Leon Walrás and Augustin Cournot, expressed themselves in mathematical terms, but the empirical data and the techniques of statistical inference needed for verification were lacking. It is only during the last few decades that techniques based on probability theory have been developed to solve problems in economics that arise because of the influence of random variables. The development and use of these techniques are the special province of the econometrician.

---

[2] W. M. Leontief, *et al., Studies in the Structure of the American Economy* (New York, Oxford University Press, 1953).

Econometricians begin with mathematical formulations of economic hypotheses and then use statistical procedures to test the relationship among variables in order to make predictions which cannot be made on the basis of economic theory alone. Economic theory can tell us what variables are relevant for the explanation of the behavior of some related variable, but it cannot tell us the precise value it will assume in a given situation. Theoretical reasoning can, for example, tell us that a demand curve is in general negatively sloped and that a supply curve is positively sloped. But no amount of theorizing can tell us what value the price coefficient will assume. Empirical observations can, however, be used in order to establish price parameters. Then, given the values of the exogenous variables, it is possible to predict quantitatively the values of the price coefficient or some other endogenous variable in which we are interested. Econometric techniques have therefore made it possible to go beyond the generalization that price will rise or fall as a result of a particular change.

Knowledge of the principles of probability theory and the technique of statistical inference also promises to be a useful tool for guiding management decision making in situations of uncertainty, e.g., in the formulation of strategy when the strategy of a business rival is uncertain. It also seems a promising aid to the formulation of appropriate monetary and fiscal policy when used to ascertain the relationship among such key macroeconomic variables as consumption, savings, and investment. Numerous static as well as dynamic national income models have been constructed in recent years for the purpose of forecasting aggregate economic magnitudes.[3] Deductive logic alone is incapable of penetrating problems of this nature.

While mathematical formulations and statistical techniques are serving the economic theorist well, these tools are not without their limitations. Their primary advantage is that the use of symbols necessitates a rigor of formulation that is sometimes lacking in verbal hypotheses. The exercise of expressing the relationship among variables in terms of a set of equations and verifying the completeness of the theory by ascertaining that there are a sufficient number of equations to solve for the unknowns being sought provides a certain assurance that nothing important has been overlooked. Mathematics has made it possible to evolve conclusions from hypotheses which may not be readily apparent from the use of nonmathematical reasoning. However, a mathematical formulation is in no sense a guarantee that sound theory will result. The mathematical economist has the same need for care in selecting his premises and making logical deductions from them as does the literary economist. No degree of mathematical skill will make a poor hypothesis result in a sound conclusion. But a good theorist

---

[3] Laurence R. Klein, "The Uses of Econometric Models as a Guide to Economic Policy," *Econometrica*, Vol. 15, No. 2 (April, 1947); also by the same author, *Economic Fluctuations in the United States, 1921–1941* (New York: John Wiley & Sons, Inc., 1950).

who also has some mastery of mathematical techniques is in a far better position today than is the purely literary economist to stay abreast of new developments in his field and make contributions of his own.

Econometric techniques also have inherent difficulties. For example, it is usually not possible in dealing with economic phenomena to do more than include the variables which appear quantitatively most important. Nor are econometric techniques well suited for dealing with those factors which cannot be given quantitative expression. There is also the difficulty that derives from the fact that many of the hypotheses of economics concern individual households and firms, whereas many of the statistical data are available in terms of aggregates. The behavior equations which are valid for microvariables may not be at all valid for macrovariables.[4] Finally, it must be noted that even the most sophisticated empirical techniques do not diminish the necessity for sound theory. Theory is required to give direction to the selection, organization, and interpretation of data, just as statistical inference is essential to the testing of theoretical hypotheses.

On the Premises and Methodology of Economics

The twin issues of the premises and method of economics have been sources of continued and long-standing controversy. Critics of economic theory have protested against both the philosophical and the psychological premises from which economic laws have been derived and the use of the deductive method for establishing them. The issues are of course related, but it is well to recognize that one could question the appropriateness of certain premises as a foundation for economic theory and yet be sympathetic to the use of the deductive method.

The issue of induction versus deduction has been a recurrent one. The members of the Historical School and the Institutionalists of the early twentieth century were critical of the premises used by classical and neoclassical theorists, and also their efforts to establish propositions of universal validity by means of the deductive method. They maintained that induction rather than deduction is the proper methodological approach for studying economics. Though a large quantity of descriptive information resulted from their efforts, they were not successful in establishing any economic laws on the basis of their studies. This is equally the case with the efforts of today's institutionalists. While they are statistically rather than

---

[4] Paul H. Douglas' work on production functions, which was one of the pioneering efforts in the area of econometric research, was criticized because he attempted to apply the marginal productivity theory to industry as a whole to derive production functions. See articles by M. W. Reder, M. Bronfenbrenner, J. Marshak, and W. H. Andrews appearing in *Econometrica* during 1943 and 1944, Vols. 11 and 12. Douglas' studies, with Grace Gunn, are "The Production Function for Australian Manufacturing," *The Quarterly Journal of Economics,* Vol. 56, Nov. 1941 and "The Production Function for American Manufacturing in 1919," *The American Economic Review,* Vol. 31, March, 1941.

historically oriented, they have not been more successful in establishing reliable generalizations or solutions to problems than earlier champions of induction.[5] But their work has demonstrated how essential theory is as a guide to empirical study.

With respect to its premises, modern economics still reflects, in some degree, its origin in the protest against theology and metaphysics to which the Reformation and Enlightenment gave expression. It still reflects, in its preoccupation with the achievement of equilibrium, the belief of those like David Hartley, Thomas Hobbes, John Locke and David Hume that the laws of physics and astronomy have a counterpart in the behavior of men and the social universe. These early students of psychics maintained not only that human behavior originates in sense experience, but also that this behavior is sufficiently uniform to be expressed in terms of general laws analogous to those of physics. The principles they discovered about the functioning of individual consciousness were subsequently transferred to the social whole in order to try to explain social phenomena. This is evident in *The Wealth of Nations* and in the work of those who followed Adam Smith in deducing principles of economic behavior from premises drawn from sensationalist psychology. Sensationalist psychology continued to dominate in the thinking of the Utilitarians, though the Benthamites were characterized by an agnosticism that was totally absent from the writings of Smith. Hedonistic premises were similarly fundamental to the thinking of the marginalists, though the kind of economic laws they produced were deduced also from premises concerning the institutional framework of the economy. Even though Marshall tried to exorcize the spirit of hedonism from neoclassical economics, his efforts were not particularly successful. As a result, there is still an unmistakable aura of eighteenth-century pleasure-pain psychology evident in much of contemporary economic theory. Its critics regard this latent hedonism as one of its least satisfactory characteristics. They maintain that hedonism is an unsatisfactory theory of human behavior because it overemphasizes rationalism and egoism and does not adequately recognize that postnatal experiences and social institutions generate altruistic as well as competitive and acquisitive instincts. Most of these misgivings are supported by the findings of modern psychologists which confirm that human behavior is far more complex than the theory of sense experience implies.

Though modern economic analysis has not yet firmly divorced itself from the hedonistic approach to behavior, there is nevertheless, an increasing awareness that there is more to rational behavior than the maximization of a known utility or profit function. Thus the theory of the firm has been

---

[5] See, for example, the criticism of some of the work of the National Bureau of Economic Research in the area of business cycles by Tjalling C. Koopmans, "Measurement Without Theory", *Review of Economics, and Statistics,* Vol. XXIX (August, 1947).

extended to include not only a consideration of present profits but also such considerations as future profits, shares of the market, composition of assets, public image, and many others. There is also a sophisticated and fascinating approach to the problem of rational behavior in situations of uncertainty which derives from the application of game theory. But there is still a lamentable lack of collaboration between economists and psychologists. This is, for example, quite evident in the present emphasis on the role of expectation in governing behavior in the marketplace. Expectations are the result of learning experience rather than instinctive forms of behavior.[6] Yet the economist is generally not conversant with the principles with which psychologists explain learning. He therefore has little understanding about when and how expectations change and consequently is likely to have only a tenuous basis for explaining and predicting many aspects of consumer, investor, and business behavior. Nor will he be able to serve as an effective guide to the formulation of public policy in controlling those variables whose behavior is particularly sensitive to changes in expectations. Ideally, public policy should aim at counteracting the effects of cumulative expectations which are likely to produce undesirable changes in income, profits, and prices. Policies which give promise of accomplishing this are more likely to be forthcoming if those who help to frame them have some knowledge of psychology. The observation made so long ago by J. M. Clark that the economist cannot avoid psychology by ignoring it, and that he will "force himself to make his own and it will be bad psychology," is still true.[7]

Much the same observation may be made with respect to the importance to today's economist of being at least somewhat knowledgeable in other social sciences. Progress in economics in days gone by may have required the careful delineation of its subject matter from related disciplines like philosophy and politics. But today, an approach which also draws upon other social sciences seems a far more promising technique for formulating realistic hypotheses.

On Political Economy versus Economic Science

The point of view that economists need not only to be specialists in economic science but also general scholars who include in the province of their learning many related disciplines brings to the fore another issue of controversy with which economists have long been confronted. What is the proper role of the economist with respect to the formulation of policy? Should his province be only economic theory, or should it be political economy? Economic theory is concerned only with the generation of technical knowledge. Normative knowledge, on the other hand, consists of the

---

[6] George Katona, "Psychological Analysis of Business Decisions and Expectations," *American Economic Review*, Vol. XXXVI No. 1 (March, 1946).

[7] J. M. Clark, "Economics and Modern Psychology," *Journal of Political Economy*, Vol. XXVI No. 1, (Jan., 1918), p. 4.

use of technical knowledge to alter or redirect economic relationships. It lies not in the realm of economic science but in the realm of political economy.

Scientific examination in any field demands that its technical aspects be firmly separated from whatever purposive aspects it might involve. Thus the economist must be able during the course of his analysis to hold in a state of suspension all judgments concerning that which ought to be while he examines that which is. This separation was first accomplished with respect to economic phenomena in the seventeenth century, when economics was, formally at least, isolated from its parent discipline, philosophy. The later classicists were heroic in their efforts to preserve this distinction, especially after Nassau Senior's stricture that the economist qua economist must not concern himself with matters of policy. The formulation of policy, so the argument went, necessarily involves judgment and therefore individual biases, which are avoidable only by eliminating all concern with that which ought to be in order to stick rigorously to the analysis of that which is.

Yet the objective of practical application has been associated with economics from the very beginning. The mercantilists, of course, had little hesitancy about making policy recommendations without analysis. But the Physiocrats and Smith engaged in analysis in order to formulate and support policies they recommended. Theirs was an era of political economy in which analysis was quite frankly the handmaiden of policy. Thus, economics has actually been concerned with the generation of normative as well as technical knowledge from its earliest days.

While it is unquestionably necessary to preserve the distinction between technical knowledge and normative knowledge, most economists have instinctively rebelled against demands for the kind of schizophrenia which requires that they be "pure" theorists who never venture into the area of policy in their role of professional economists. Most economists hope that their science is "useful" in the sense that it enables them to make appropriate recommendations. Since such recommendations involve value judgments, decisions on "ends" may well come from outside economics. But once such decisions have been made, the economist's training qualifies him to choose the policies which are most likely to lead toward the achievement of predetermined goals. Economic theory, precisely because it clarifies what is possible under various circumstances, provides a basis for formulating alternative policies and selecting those which are most likely to satisfy previously established goals. Before we can seriously engage in discussions of policy, we must first know what is possible. The history of economic theory verifies that those who are skilled in the science of that which is possible in the economic sphere have also been skilled in the art of formulating policy. Adam Smith, David Ricardo, John Stuart Mill, and John Maynard Keynes were leading contributors to political economy in addition to being able theorists.

The economist is of course confronted with limitations on his capacity to advise. For example, a policy which is economically sound is not necessarily politically acceptable or administratively practical. Advice, moreover, must be based on prediction, and economic theory has historically been seriously deficient in this respect for numerous reasons. For one thing, the economist, in common with all social scientists, is unable to perform controlled experiments such as have become typical in the natural sciences. This limits the opportunity for empirical verification, not only of deductively established conclusions, but also of the premises which stand at the head of propositions of pure theory. There is also the possibility that socially significant forecasts are not neutral in their effects but alter human behavior in a variety of ways, the end result of which may possibly be to nullify the prediction. They may, of course, also have the opposite effect and work to reinforce rather than counteract a prediction. The pessimistic forecast which "comes true" because people have been forewarned to behave cautiously is not an uncommon phenomenon. But the most important impediment to precise prediction in economics derives from the fact that economists deal not with the behavior of matter which acts according to certain ascertainable laws of nature, but with human beings whose individual behavior is the product of free will and whose collective response can frequently be predicted only in probabilistic terms. As long as he lacked the tools of statistical inference, the economist was therefore often in a position of double jeopardy because he was ill-equipped to come forward either with empirically verifiable predictions or with a tenable basis for selecting among alternative policies. It is for this reason that the techniques developed by modern econometricians are such a valuable adjunct to economic theory. The alliance of economics with mathematics and statistics has made it possible for the economic theorist to test his verbal hypothesis. He is therefore also better able, as befits a theorist in this era of pragmatism, to determine the effect alternative policies are likely to have. The gap between economic theory and political economy has thus become narrower.

But though new techniques enhance his powers of prediction, the economist must continue to guard against inappropriate interpretation of his data. He must remember that the truths he is seeking are never absolute but stand always in relation to people's attitudes and beliefs and to the course of events. The history of economic analysis verifies that all doctrines contain a modicum of truth. But it is only under specific circumstances that this modicum of truth becomes the only truth. Whether we take the doctrines of the scholastics, the mercantilists, the classicists, or more modern thinkers, we shall find that the truth they profess to have discovered is indeed the truth if we think within their frame of reference. But each age has its own frame of reference, which includes not only that which is but also that toward which the society is striving. The Weltanschauung of the age remains an integral part of its functioning and is perhaps the most important factor conditioning and giving direction to economic and social trends. The most influential thinkers in the realm of economic and social affairs have always been those who understood the Weltanschauung of their age clearly enough to perceive the nature and the direction of the trends to come. The ideas of Smith and Ricardo were woven into the fabric of the late eighteenth and the nineteenth centuries precisely because they were compatible with the interests of the most influential members of society and anticipated the stream of events. It is for the same reason that ideas associated with Marx are today a force of great magnitude in many parts of the world outside of western Europe and the United States, while Keynesian ideas are a force of first order in the western world. If their ideas were inherently out of tune with the requirements of the milieu, they would have been shunted aside; they survive and are influential because the environment is hospitable to them. It follows that the more the economist can learn about the relationship between ideas and their ecology the better are his prospects for discovering the valid economic truths of his era.

SUGGESTIONS FOR FURTHER READING

DORFMAN, R.; SAMUELSON, PAUL A.; and SOLOW, ROBERT M. *Linear Programming and Economic Analysis.* New York: McGraw-Hill Book Co., Inc., 1958.

FRIEDMAN, MILTON. *The Methodology of Positive Economics.* Chicago: University of Chicago Press, 1953.

HAAVELMO, I. "The Probability Approach to Econometrics," *Econometrica,* Supplement, Vol. 12 (1944).

HUTCHISON, T. W. *The Significance and Basic Postulates of Economic Theory.* London: Macmillan & Co., 1938.

KRUPP, SHERMAN R. (ed.). *The Structure of Economic Science.* Englewood Cliffs, N.J.: Prentice-Hall, Inc., 1966.

MACHLUP, FRITZ. *Economic Semantics.* Englewood Cliffs, N.J.: Prentice-Hall, Inc., 1963.

MORGENSTERN, OSKAR. "Limits to the Uses of Mathematics in Economics," from a Symposium on Mathematics and the Social Sciences, American Academy of Political and Social Science, June, 1943.

MYRDAL, GUNNAR. *The Political Element in the Development of Economic Theory.* London: Routledge and Paul, 1953.

NABERS, LAWRENCE. "Veblen's Critique of the Orthodox Economic Tradition" in *Thorstein Veblen: A Critical Reappraisal.* (ed. DOUGLAS DOWD). Ithaca, N.Y.: Cornell University Press, 1958.

ROBBINS, LIONEL. *An Essay on the Nature and Significance of Economic Science.* London: Macmillan & Co., second revised edition 1935.

STIGLER, GEORGE. "The Mathematical Method in Economics," *Five Lectures on Economic Problems.* New York: Macmillan Co., 1950.

TINTNER, G. "The Definition of Econometrics," *Econometrica,* Vol. 21, No. 1, January, 1953.

INDEX OF NAMES

INDEX OF SUBJECTS

This book has been set in 10 and 9 point Times Roman, leaded 2 points. Chapter numbers and titles are set in 18 point Spartan Medium. The size of the type page is 27 by 45½ picas.